Practicing Kinship

Practicing Kinship

LINEAGE AND DESCENT IN
LATE IMPERIAL CHINA

Michael Szonyi

STANFORD UNIVERSITY PRESS
STANFORD, CALIFORNIA
2002

Stanford University Press
Stanford, California
© 2002 by the Board of Trustees of the
Leland Stanford Junior University

Printed in the United States of America on acid-free,
archival-quality paper.

Chapter 6 originally appeared as "Local cult, *Lijia,* and
Lineage: Religious and Social Organization in Ming and Qing
Fujian," *Journal of Chinese Religions,* 28 (2000), 93–125.

Library of Congress Cataloging-in-Publication Data
Szonyi, Michael.
    Practicing kinship : lineage and descent in late imperial
China / Michael Szonyi.
       p.   cm.
    Includes bibliographical references.
    ISBN 0-8047-4261-8 (alk. paper)
       1. Kinship -- China -- History.   2. Patrilineal kinship --
China -- History.   3. China -- Genealogy.   4. China --
History -- Ming dynasty, 1368–1644.   5. China -- History --
Qing dynasty, 1644–1912.   I. Title.
    GN635.C6 S96   2002
    929.7'0951 -- dc21   2001049747

Original printing 2002

Last figure below indicates year of this printing:
09   08   07   06   05   04   03   02

Typeset by TechBooks in 11 /14 Adobe Garamond and Expert

To Francine

Acknowledgments

It is a great though belated pleasure to thank those who have helped me to understand the richness of local materials and the challenges of using them to write history. Tim Brook, who first introduced me to Chinese history; Maybo Ching; Ken Dean; David Faure; and Paul Katz have read parts or all the manuscript, and I am grateful for their comments. David Ownby, a model of collegiality, deserves to be singled out for his reading and rereading of multiple versions and the detailed and sensitive critiques he offered. I am also indebted to many colleagues in China for their assistance. Yang Guozhen and Chen Zhiping were gracious hosts during my visits to Xiamen University. Li Ting of the Fujian Provincial Library generously provided me with access to the collections as well as other assistance. Ye Xiang of the Social Science Research Institute of Fuzhou and Lin Weigong of the Fuzhou Gazetteer Compilation Office have helped me in many ways over the years, and their local knowledge and enthusiasm has proved invaluable time and again. I am especially grateful to Zheng Zhenman, who accompanied me in many rambles both through the historical sources and the Fuzhou countryside and who helped me formulate many of the ideas presented here.

Professor Leo Chen of San Francisco provided my first introductions in Fuzhou. Chen Yizhi, Chen Zhuxi, and Chen Tianpei welcomed me to the region and into their homes and offered constant encouragement and assistance. Zheng Xiulin and his family offered me both practical assistance and, more important, their friendship, for which I am profoundly grateful. I am also indebted to all of the villagers of the Fuzhou region who allowed me to conduct interviews, attend rituals, and collect genealogies and other written materials. They are too numerous to mention by name, but without their help and interest this book would not be. I also thank research assistants, Dong Bo, who helped me with the translations, and Tim Sedo, who helped me with the editing. Richard Bachand prepared the maps. My thanks also go to Muriel Bell and Matt Stevens at Stanford University Press and Stephanie Lentz at TechBooks. Research for this project was supported while I was a student by the Rhodes Trust, the Social Sciences and Humanities Research Council, and the Canada–China Scholarly Exchange Program and later by the Fonds pour la Formation de Chercheurs et l'Aide à la Recherche of Québec.

These brief acknowledgments can barely begin to express my feelings and are a most inadequate recompense for the gifts they record. This applies to all the friends and colleagues listed above but especially to my family. I close with thanks to my parents, who first took me to China, and to Francine McKenzie, whose contribution to my work is beyond both measure and my powers of description.

Contents

Illustrations

Practicing Kinship

ONE

Kinship Ideas and Institutions in Fuzhou History

In 1874, Guo Bocang, a noted scientist and poet, celebrated the completion of a genealogy for the Guo lineage of Fuzhou, the capital of the southeastern coastal province of Fujian. For Bocang and his equally distinguished brother Boyin, who regularly performed the solemn rituals of ancestral sacrifice and had already constructed a grand ancestral hall and repaired their ancestral tombs, it must have been the high point of a lifetime of involvement in the institutions of patrilineal kinship. These activities, and the brothers' written reflections on them, have a great deal to tell us about the meanings of descent and lineage in Fuzhou society at the end of the late imperial era. During the late imperial period, ideas about lineages and the institutions and practices connected with them were intricately connected to the larger social context in which they were embedded. They were not stable or fixed, but flexible, multiple, and negotiated.

The genealogy compiled by Guo Bocang traced the ancestry of his lineage back one thousand years, to a Tang noble named Guo Ziyi, the prince of Fenyang.[1] According to the genealogy, the prince's descendants had migrated to the region from Henan province in the Five Dynasties period (907–60).

In the Yuan, a descendant named Guo Yao had settled in Fuqing county. Then in the sixteenth century, in response to repeated pirate attacks on their village, the descendants of Ziyi and Yao, Bocang's ancestors, had moved to the relative safety of Fuzhou city, where they had remained ever since. In 1842, thirty years before Bocang compiled the genealogy, he and Boyin had renewed contact with their ancestral home in Fuqing, from which the family had been cut off for the intervening centuries. In an account that may strike the modern reader as similar to recent descriptions of Overseas Chinese returning to their home villages, Guo Boyin describes the arduous journey down to the village, the warm welcome, and his joy at being reunited with people who must have been his distant relatives, even if their precise relationship was obscure. Ignoring what they considered to be minor discrepancies between their own genealogical records and those of the villagers, the brothers contributed money for the reconstruction of ancestral tombs and made offerings there. They also investigated the history of the officially authorized altar (*she*) of the village. Back in Fuzhou, the brothers participated in annual sacrificial rituals to their more recent ancestors, which were performed in a hillside hut near the ancestral graves. In 1850, they paid for the repair of this hut. Six years later, thirteen members of the family contributed funds for the acquisition of property at a prestigious site within the city and constructed there a splendid ancestral hall in which to sacrifice to their ancestors, recent and distant, through the generations. In 1868, Boyin purchased a salt warehouse and donated it to the hall to guarantee its finances. In the genealogy, Guo Bocang stresses that the rituals performed in the hall adhered to the chief canonical text for ancestral sacrifice, the *Family Rituals* written by the great neo-Confucian Zhu Xi (1132–1200).[2]

The numerous prefaces appended to the genealogy celebrate the lineage's adherence to canonical forms and universal values and the reliability of its claims of ancestry. But there is some diffidence about even the most basic claims. Bocang felt compelled to admit that he actually had no reliable evidence to support the reputed connection with the prince of Fenyang. When the Guo genealogy had been first compiled in the sixteenth century, the editor had lamented that the family's genealogical records had been destroyed by fire more than a century earlier. As a result, "the details of the early ancestors' laying the foundations cannot be known, and it is impossible to reconcile the branchings of the subdivisions into a unified descent line."[3] Bocang decided to limit his efforts to tracing his ancestry back to the settlement in Fuqing in the Yuan. But even then, he could not find convincing genealogical evidence to link himself and his brothers to the current residents of the village.[4] Nor was there unanimity of opinion concerning the performance of rituals of ancestor worship. Contracts and other documents in the genealogy indicate considerable debate within the lineage over how these rituals should properly be performed. This debate was ultimately resolved not by adopting the canonical prescriptions of the *Family Rituals*, but through a compromise between the prescriptions and their own family traditions. One key part of the debate had to do with the right to install ancestral tablets in the new ancestral hall. According to Zhu Xi's *Family Rituals*, this was an issue determined by genealogical seniority by generation and age. Among the Guo, this right became a commodity. Anyone could purchase by payment of a fixed fee the right to install an ancestral tablet in the Guo hall, and only those who paid the fee could have a tablet.

Guo Boyin and Bocang were leading figures in nineteenth-century Fuzhou society, but as I demonstrate in the following chapters, their genealogy is typical of late Qing genealogies from Fuzhou.[5] Such works explicitly describe a vision of agnatic kinship that accords with canonical prescriptions, in which men bear the same surnames as their fathers; practice virilocal marriage; trace descent from an ancestor who migrated from Henan to Fujian in the Five Dynasties period; and belong to a corporate lineage, whose members have built an ancestral hall in the official style, perform rituals in that hall according to the prescriptions of the *Family Rituals*, and worship the local tutelary deity at a temple derived from an official Ming altar to which their ancestors had been assigned. But many of the genealogies also contain subtle evidence suggestive of a different version of agnatic kinship, in which surnames are frequently changed, ancestry is fluid and unstable, and there is much variation in the performance of rituals in the ancestral hall. Still other versions of agnatic kinship appear in the oral tradition and in contemporary ritual practice. Elderly villagers in the Fuzhou region can point to many men who did not have the same surname as their father or who lived not with their own parents but with their wife's family. In the oral tradition, descent is often traced back not to a medieval aristocratic migrant from Henan, but to a rebel, a pirate, or a local bandit. The rituals performed by the villagers today, which they consider to be faithful reconstructions of rituals performed earlier in this century, differ markedly from those prescribed by the *Family Rituals* and official regulations issued by dynastic authorities. They include many elements that would have outraged Zhu Xi.

The villagers of the Fuzhou region do not find it difficult to deal with the multiple versions of kinship and its history that circulate in their society, but they are striking, indeed, seemingly contradictory, to the outside observer. This book is my attempt to arrive at a better understanding of them. It is a study of the history of patrilineal kinship organization in the Fuzhou region in the late imperial period, from the early Ming to the twentieth century.[6] It draws on, explores the interrelationship of, and integrates these different versions of kinship, presenting in turn yet another version. Kinship in Ming and Qing Fuzhou was reflected in practice. People made use of the concepts and social relations of kinship and its institutions in their lives. Some called on their kin to behave in certain ways, or wrote texts promoting certain behavior, and others responded to such calls. Their responses in turn affected the meaning of texts and behaviors, of how concepts and social relations were understood. By kinship practice, then, I mean the ways individuals confront, negotiate, and create meanings related to kinship and the ways these meanings become implicated in social relations and institutions, shaping and restricting the options open to individuals.[7] By emphasizing practice, I explore the relations between kinship as a conceptual system, as a set of institutional structures, and as social interaction. Kinship encompassed an arena of ongoing contest and negotiation between different conceptions of what kinship was and should be, and what it could and should do.

The focus of this study is kinship based on the principle of patrilineal descent, that is, common descent along the male line. This of course is not the only basis for kinship, but in Chinese history, and certainly for the people I write about, it is an important one. Following David Faure, I sidestep the debate in the anthropological literature about the correct definition of the term *lineage* by using it to refer to a self-professed patrilineal descent group.[8] This is a rather different usage than the one implied by Maurice Freedman in his influential paradigm of the Chinese lineage. By turning attention away from the rules governing the principles of descent and the classification of kin to the issue of control over resources, Freedman's work on the Chinese lineage in the 1950s and 1960s launched a new phase in the anthropological study of the lineage.[9] James Watson summarizes the essential criteria of the Chinese lineage in this paradigm: "a *corporate group* which celebrates *ritual unity* and is based on *demonstrated descent* from a common ancestor."[10] The first criterion is paramount, in that only a group that is incorporated through the joint possession of property can properly be called a lineage. Differentiation with regard to ownership of property is also essential to understanding the internal complexities of the lineage. In this formulation, material property, especially land, is thus the foundation of Chinese lineage organization. Other anthropologists, such as Myron Cohen and Arthur Wolf, have questioned the wisdom of isolating a lineage social formation based on Watson's three factors and relegating all other groups to a residual category, sometimes labeled the descent group.[11] As I show later in this work, the claim of membership in a patrilineal descent group can be of great social significance even without ritual unity or corporate property. Moreover, as Faure points out, ownership of corporate property is not a critical criterion for indigenous concepts connected to terms such as *zu* or *zongzu*. It is clear that whatever other relations may have existed between members of such groups, the focus of these Chinese terms is on the idea of groups related through common descent along the male line and that this was in itself considered an important bond.[12] For the historian, the important questions then become the following: What kinds of such groups existed in late imperial China? How did they arise? How did their members make claims of kinship connection? What meanings were attached to these connections, and how did they become so attached?

However the lineage is defined, no one would dispute that groups defined on the basis of common descent played an important role in late imperial Chinese society.[13] Some cultural historians have begun to explore the origins of this agnatic orientation, or ideology of familism, but most historical work has been devoted to the question of its institutionalization. In an early contribution to this field, Denis Twitchett argued that lineages organized in the way they did owing to the influence of neo-Confucian intellectuals who had a particular vision of how the social order should function, linking the ideology of familism to a larger project of cultural unification and moral improvement. The most extensive articulation of this approach has come from Patricia Ebrey, who has studied the lineage from both the perspective of its canonical texts and the efforts of local figures to put those texts into practice.[14] Kai-Wing Chow's work argues that lineage institutions became primarily disciplinary mechanisms by which the neo-Confucian educated elite attempted to reclaim moral leadership in their communities by imposing a strong social conservatism. Other historians have considered material factors rather than ideological ones as central to the institutionalization of the lineage, but they have also tended to focus on the role of elites. Thus Joseph Esherick and Mary Rankin see elites forming lineages as a means to protect resources from division. Hilary Beattie's study of an Anhui county suggests that lineage organization was part of a long-term strategy by which certain families sought to maintain elite status through a combination of investment in corporate land and lineage-based education.[15]

Watson's influential definition of the Chinese lineage, intended to facilitate the ordering of different types of kinship institutions, hints at important characteristics among the corporate lineages of the twentieth century in south China, but does less to address the historical development of these characteristics. Unless used with care, the definition also runs the risk of encouraging a teleological approach to the lineage that evaluates local specificities in terms of convergence or dissonance with an ideal type. Previous research has demonstrated that there was tremendous variation in the institutions and ideas of kinship across China as well as variation within the institutions of kinship as practiced in a specific time and place. Recent work has stressed the importance of attending to local contexts and the need to move beyond elite efforts to build lineage organization. For example, Faure's work on the New Territories stresses the importance of the penetration into local society of an official model of lineage but points out that it merged there with the tracing of settlement rights, which went on much more broadly in society. Zheng Zhenman identifies the popularization of descent-line ideology, rising local autonomy, and corporatization of property relations as central to the development of the lineage in different parts of Fujian. Chen Qi'nan and Zhuang Yingzhang have explored how the circumstances of Taiwanese development, in particular the gradual transition from an immigrant to a settled society, shaped the history of lineage organization there. Myron Cohen's work on north China suggests that even in the absence of corporate lineages as Watson defines the term, the familist ideology may still find expression in village social structure, symbolism, and arrangement of ritual.[16] The goal of such research is to make sense of lineage organization in specific contexts and to explore changes over time or space of institutions that are presumed in the local context to embody universal principles. Inspired by such research, this book does not focus on what the lineage is or is not, but rather works toward a more complete elaboration of the dimensions of organized agnatic kinship in a particular context, the Fuzhou region, with special reference to Nantai Island, which is situated in the Min River opposite the city of Fuzhou.

I do not attempt to trace in great detail, in thick description, the history of a single lineage or a single village on Nantai. This is not only because I lack anthropological training or because it was impossible to obtain official permission to live for an extended period of time in the countryside, though I did live unofficially in one of the villages in this study for several months.[17]

This approach is also driven by the source materials. It became evident early in the research for this project that although some aspects of the history of kinship practice were common, perhaps even universal, in the region, the available sources from no single village contain material touching on each of these different aspects. Indeed, there are some aspects that are hinted at in the sources, written and oral, for which it was impossible to find sufficient evidence from Nantai Island itself, forcing me to use material from farther afield, that is, from the city of Fuzhou or its surrounding counties. Nevertheless, I believe that the different dimensions of kinship discussed in this work were part of the common practice of kinship in the region, not only because most people in Ming and Qing Fuzhou probably practiced kinship in more or less the same way as their near neighbors, but also because kinship practices in different villages were strategic responses to a broadly similar social, ethnic, and intellectual context. To put it another way, all of the different forms of kinship practice that I discuss could potentially be found in any social group in the region and were actually practiced by many such groups, but they were recorded, in either a formal sense in genealogies and other written works or inscribed in ritual practice or oral tradition, only in some. Thus, the historian who wishes to investigate all of these different forms finds it necessary to cast a wide net.

From another perspective, even this wide net may strike some historians as too small, if not too fine. One might ask why local history is significant or useful to an understanding of Chinese kinship. My answer to this question would be twofold. First, the variation in the practice of kinship in Ming and Qing times is not necessarily illuminated by the study of a single genre of evidence from across China, be it gazetteers, genealogies, collected literary works, or ritual performance and oral history but only by considering multiple genres, and the multiple versions of kinship history they embody, together. Second, the full richness of these historical sources is only revealed when they can be placed in context, and this demands intensive research into the history of the local society in which the sources were generated. I believe local history is the best approach through which to consider multiple genres of sources together, to develop a detailed picture of the local economic and social context, and to explore the micropolitics of place, in other words, to turn the sources into a story. It is only by exploring and relating the manifestations of kinship in diverse, multiple local contexts that we can hope to fully understand the history of kinship representation and practice across China.

There are purely practical reasons for the geographic focus on a small region that does not correspond to any administrative unit. The rural areas of Nantai Island comprise between one and two hundred villages, depending on how the term *village* is defined. By foot and bicycle, during the years 1991–97, I was able to visit almost every one of them—though most of these visits were necessarily brief, to collect or take notes from over fifty genealogies, to observe rituals, and to interview villagers both formally and informally. I have made repeated and extended stays in all of the large villages of the island.

The basic argument, which I develop through a discussion of several dimensions of kinship, is that organized patrilineal kinship as it was experienced by the people of the Fuzhou region is best understood as the outcome of individual and collective strategizing in a field that was shaped by the widely shared agnatic orientation, an elite model of kinship, and a set of other factors that include ethnic differentiation; commercialization of the economy; transformations in the composition of local elites; and, in particular, responses to state policies for the registration of land and population since the Ming. Of course, these are not the only factors that shaped kinship practice, but they are factors that were particularly important in the Fuzhou region, and that have not yet received sufficient attention from historians. By considering these processes over a period of several centuries, I hope to introduce a stronger historical dimension to the study of organized kinship in China. The changing ideas and institutions of kinship can be related to the changing material and cultural world in which they operated, that is, to changing political and social structures and economic forces. By considering these processes in local society, from the bottom up, I move away from explanations of kinship in terms of the mechanistic implementation of an ideology of familism or the imposition of a unified orthodoxy by the state or social elites toward a more complex and multiple vision.[18] Organized patrilineal kinship in Fuzhou was neither static nor monolithic but rather was constituted in a network of changing representations.

THE SETTING

Because the argument that kinship practices have been historically constructed and influenced by aspects of local history is the crux of this work, we must begin with a brief introduction to the local setting.[19] The city of Fuzhou lies in one of the four major coastal plains of the mainly mountainous Fujian province in southeastern China. The history of the region is in large part a history of land reclamation. Virtually the whole Fuzhou basin, which now amounts to some four hundred square kilometers, has formed from deposits of sediment from the Min River. Ten thousand years ago, the region would have consisted of bracken swamp interspersed with rocky islands.[20] The development of the basin since then was initially a natural phenonemon, with alluvial sediments being deposited in what is now the southern channel of the Min, creating and enlarging the islands of Nantai and Langqi and leaving a more stable, deep-watered northern channel. But increasingly, land reclamation has been the result of human intervention. Irrigation works to store and distribute water were also introduced to the reclaimed land, and the opening up and deforestation of the upper reaches of the Min River made flooding a perennial concern.[21] Justus Doolittle, an American missionary who spent many years in Fuzhou in the mid-nineteenth century, described the appearance of the region from a surrounding peak at the time:

> The landscape of the valley of the Min, viewed on a clear summer's day from the top of the mountain or from its side, is very fine, consisting of numerous small streams and canals running in all directions, several scores of hamlets dotting the country, and rice-fields in a high state of cultivation (Figure 1.1).[22]

Figure 1.1. "Scenery of the Min, west of the southern suburbs of Fuhchau." Drawing of Fuzhou countryside by a nineteenth-century missionary.
SOURCE: Doolittle, 1865.

The economic history of Fuzhou in the late imperial period, as with other parts of south China, was profoundly shaped by the effects of a significant increase in commercial activity that many historians now believe occurred from the mid-Ming as part of a complex chain reaction of rising agricultural production, rising surplus, and rising trade.[23] Two important regional particularities of Fuzhou should also be mentioned. First, a strong foundation for the commercial development of the Ming had already been established in the Song. National and international trade had been an important part of the Fuzhou regional economy since the Song, when the region had a flourishing export trade, sending nails, tea, silk, and porcelain to Korea, Japan, Ryukyu, and even southeast Asia.[24] Already in the Song the cultivation of commercial crops, such as cane and fruits, was criticized for interfering with the cultivation of grain and thereby intensifying local food deficits.[25]

Thus, by the early Ming, the Fuzhou region was already highly commercialized, with significant production of commercial crops and handicrafts, circulation of which tied Fuzhou into wider domestic and international markets. The long-term effects on the Fuzhou region of increased maritime trade in the sixteenth century included increased agricultural specialization, commercialization, interregional trade, and the commutation of taxes and labor service levies that became known as the Single Whip reforms.[26] Agricultural specialization was encouraged by the introduction of new crops from abroad and by technical advances that improved yields from the major commercial fruit crops such as lychees, longans, and oranges. By the early seventeenth century, commercial fruit production was very widespread in the region. There were important developments in handicraft production as well. In the early sixteenth century, advances in loom technology pushed forward the sophistication of Fuzhou's textiles. Though silk was little produced in Fujian, it was brought from the interior to be dyed and woven. In the late sixteenth century, the Fuzhou economy continued to be involved in diverse and complicated trading networks, both domestic and international.[27]

A second regional particularity is the long-term disruption of the Ming economy by a series of events: first, the turmoil of sixteenth-century piracy and banditry; next, the Ming–Qing transition; and finally, the early Qing coastal evacuation and trade prohibitions, even as the basic processes of commercialization were not reversed. According to Zhu Weigan's tabulation of the available evidence on pirate violence, every county seat of Fuzhou prefecture with the exception of inland Minqing was besieged by pirates at least once between 1555 and 1561 (Map 1). Fuzhou city itself was surrounded

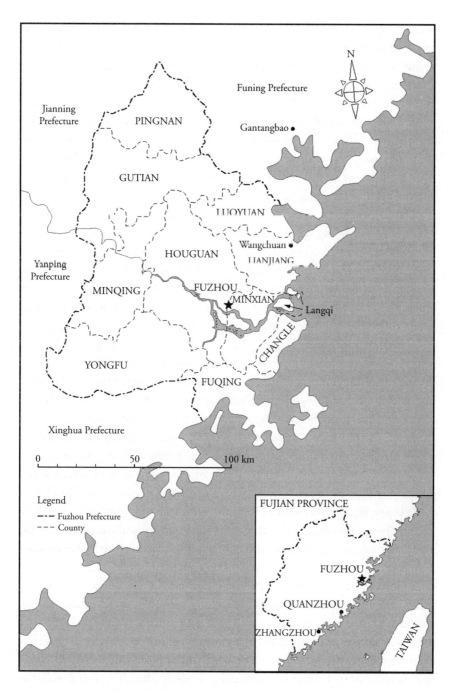

Map 1. Fuzhou Prefecture in the Qing.

and besieged by four separate groups of pirates. There were pirate attacks on the Fuzhou suburbs in 1557, 1558, and 1559, and the two major commercial suburbs of Nantai District and Hongtang were destroyed.[28] The largest pirate bands were eventually suppressed, but the coastal villages of Fuzhou were never really free of the danger of pirates.[29] Historical sources use the term *wokou*, meaning "Japanese," literally "dwarf," bandits to describe the pirates of the Ming. But So Kwan-wai and Lin Renchuan have shown that although some Japanese were involved in the pirate raids, most of the *wokou* were probably coastal-dwelling Chinese who turned to piracy in response to official prohibitions against trade.[30]

The displacement caused by piracy was followed a century later by the turmoil of the Ming–Qing transition. In 1645, when Qing forces had already taken control of most of north China, a Ming prince ascended the imperial throne and declared Fuzhou his capital. His need for revenue to maintain the regime drove up the tax burden on the local population considerably. The following year, the new emperor having fled, Qing armies entered the city unopposed and expropriated much of the remaining property. Scattered resistance in the suburbs of the city led to fierce retribution, and much of the starving citizenry ignored the strict prohibitions and fled. In 1647, not long after an outbreak of disease decimated the population of the area, a band of Ming loyalists laid waste to the Fuzhou area and besieged the city, causing further starvation until Qing relief forces arrived. Thereafter, the Fuzhou area suffered from the exactions of Qing forces that were garrisoned in and around the city as part of efforts to deal with the threat of Zheng Chenggong (Koxinga) and from the coastal evacuation that was ultimately ordered in the hope of starving Zheng's access to supplies.[31]

William Skinner has written that the economy of coastal Fujian did not recover from the combined effects of piracy and political turmoil until the opening of the treaty ports in the nineteenth century.[32] But Fuzhou's position as administrative and manufacturing center and trade entrepôt suggests that Skinner may have overstated the duration of the economic downturn. After order was restored, large numbers of government officials and Banner soldiers, by one account numbering over fourteen thousand, together with their entourages and families, were stationed in the city.[33] As an early twentieth-century source notes, "the chief products of Fujian are tea, wood and paper. None of these is produced in Fuzhou. But the great merchants and large traders who control the transport of these goods must assemble there and use it as their center."[34] Only one of these three major products, tea, was significantly dependent on international markets. Evidence collected by Wang Yeh-chien concerning food supply also gives strong support to the thesis of renewed prosperity. Wang estimates that the people of Fuzhou and vicinity imported half a million piculs per year of rice in the mid-eighteenth century. These imports must have been paid for through commercial agriculture, handicraft production, and trade. Nor did foreign trade languish until the arrival of Europeans. Direct trade between Fuzhou and Ryukyu was resumed in 1743, and the port continued to flourish into the nineteenth century, when the focus of trade was indeed redirected as a result of rising tea exports.[35]

NANTAI ISLAND

In the Qing, Fuzhou city and its surrounding countryside were under the jurisdiction of two counties, Minxian and Houguan.[36] The old walled city was situated a few kilometers to the north of the Min River, which is divided into two channels by a large island called Nantai. Between the city walls and the river lay a sprawling commercial district, confusingly also called Nantai.[37] Nantai Island is an irregular diamond-shaped island, some twenty kilometers along its length northwest to southeast, eight kilometers wide at its widest point. The island was formed over millennia by alluvial deposits washed down the Min, which accumulated around four former islets, now low hills. The names of many villages reflect the long process of land reclamation, and suggest that the island's current topography emerged only after the earliest human settlement.[38] Nantai Island has long been divided administratively and in terms of marketing arrangements into three subdivisions. Immediately south of Fuzhou city and joined to it since the Song by the stone Wanshou bridge was an urbanized area known as Cangshan (Storehouse Hill).[39] The rest of the island was naturally divided in past times by the relationship of its residents to the Fuzhou market. Residents of the southeastern half of the island traveled to Fuzhou and its Nantai commercial district via Cangshan and the Wanshou bridge. The villagers of the northwestern half of the island had easiest access to Fuzhou via a second bridge, the Hongshan bridge, first built in the mid-fifteenth century, in the north of the island. Their economic relationships were thus oriented toward Fuzhou's west gate and the market that stretched between this gate and Hongshan (see Map 2 and Table 1.1).[40]

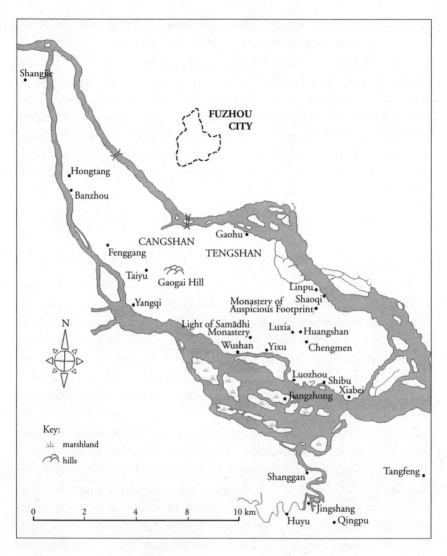

Map 2. Nantai Island and Vicinity.

In the first decade of the twentieth century, members of the local educated elite, with the encouragement of prefectural and county officials, compiled gazetteers for Minxian and Houguan counties. The two gazetteers list 140 different settlements for the whole of Nantai excluding the urbanized area of Cangshan.[41] For many settlements, population figures are also provided. In a section entitled "Great Surnames" (*daxing*), the gazetteers list the large lineages (*zu*) of the island and link these to the settlements they inhabit.[42] Together this data make it possible to develop a rough picture of settlement patterns on Nantai. Broadly speaking, there were three types of villages on Nantai. Some were single-lineage villages, inhabited by men of a single surname, together with their wives and children. The population of others was dominated by one to three large lineages, with small numbers of households headed by men of other surnames. Last, there were villages inhabited by people of many different surnames, none of which predominated. The largest settlements on Nantai, namely Yixu, Luozhou, Chengmen, Linpu, and Xiayang, all lay in the eastern part of the island and all belonged either to the first or second type. That is, they were populated by one, two, or three large groups all belonging to a single lineage. Xiayang and Luozhou were the two largest towns. They had formed through the coalescence of separate single-lineage settlements that had expanded into one another, two in the case of Xiayang and three in Luozhou, and thus had residents of two and three surnames, respectively. The smaller villages of eastern Nantai mostly belonged to the third group, that is, they were populated by people of different surnames and, at least in the eyes of the compilers of the gazetteer,

TABLE I.I

Main Settlements
and Lineages Discussed

Settlement	Lineage
Banzhou	Zhang
Fenggang	Liu
Fuzhou city	Guo, Ye
Gaohu	Zheng
Huangshan	Zheng
Huyu	Yang
Jiangzhong	Liu
Jingshang	Chen
Langqi	Chen, Dong
Linpu	Lin
Luozhou	Chen, Wu, Lin
Shanggan	Lin
Taiyu	Chen
Tangfeng	Huang, Li
Wangchuan	Lan
Yangqi	Yan
Yixu	Huang

were less likely to have formed noteworthy lineages. Such villages are located mainly in marginal land, either in the high rocky hills that first gave rise to Nantai Island or in the marshy lowlands that have most recently been reclaimed.[43] Almost all of the villages of western Nantai were small, numbering only a few dozen households. The most likely explanation for this is the frequent flooding that continues to submerge parts of the island each spring.[44] The discrepancy between the names of some settlements and the surnames of their current populations suggests that these villages may have been abandoned and resettled, perhaps repeatedly, probably as a result of flooding.[45]

The gazetteers also tell us something about the economy of Nantai Island, which by the late nineteenth century was highly commercialized, specialized, and professionalized. Besides rice, villagers in low-lying areas grew sugar cane and other fruit, and on higher ground wheat and vegetables for the Fuzhou market. A shellfish broker had set up shop in Linpu, whose residents "mostly make their living from shellfish." Many villages specialized in handicraft production for the nearby city, others for long-distance trade. The most notable local products in one part of the island were the bamboo implements produced in Guozhai. "The bamboo is brought from Yongfu. In the village, men and women mostly make their living from bamboo." The villagers of Panye and Chaibadun worked on boats that "transported stones to sell to all the provinces," whereas those of Yixu, Luxia, and Linpu worked on "firewood boats" that shipped lumber. On the south shore of the Min River opposite Nantai, "the villagers mostly work at ceramics and stone-cutting. The three hundred families of Tangyu village are all stoneworkers; the six hundred families of Huangshi village all work making porcelain."[46] Obviously things had changed over the course of the Qing dynasty, but the basis for this diversified, specialized, and highly commercialized village economy had been laid in the late Ming.

On one of the few sections of high ground in the west of the island lie the market of Hongtang and nearby the village of Fenggang, one of several Nantai villages that is studied in greater detail in the chapters that follow. In the Song and Yuan, this would have been the most prosperous part of Nantai, for at the time Fuzhou's main port lay just across the Hongshan bridge, and the road into the city's west gate passed through the main commercial district of the region. Beginning in the Song, Fenggang was the home of a number of important neo-Confucian scholars whose descendants today still live in Ming reconstructions of their mansions.

As the port at Hongtang silted up in the Ming, the town's berths and warehouses shifted to the east, and with them went the commercial heart of Fuzhou, which since the early Ming has been located due south of the city walls, in Nantai District.[47] Down the north shore of Nantai Island lies the town of Linpu, long linked to Nantai District by a ferry. Linpu was one of the earliest sites of continuous settlement in Nantai; a village by that name is recorded in the twelfth-century gazetteer, and its settlement history goes back at least four centuries earlier.[48] During the Ming the village produced the remarkable family of Lin Han, celebrated for producing "Five Ministers in Three Generations." The population of Linpu is overwhelmingly surnamed Lin, though, because it is an important market town, merchants of other surnames have settled there as well. Some physical relics of the town's past glory survive, including two memorial arches and several grand Ming homes. In the late nineteenth and early twentieth centuries, Linpu natives were active in the lumber industry upriver, and some of their enormous residences can also be seen today.

While Fenggang would have been the center of learning on Nantai in the Song, and Linpu in the Ming, in the Qing that honor was claimed by the town of Luozhou, an island on the south shore of Nantai. The town boasted its own academy, a Confucian temple, and almost twenty metropolitan graduates (*jinshi*) over the course of the Qing. We have little direct evidence on the economic history of the island, but there is no doubt that by the Ming at the latest Luozhou was already enmeshed in a dense network of roads, bridges, and ferries. Alluvial land was actively reclaimed from the river in front of the town; a poem describes the cultivation of citrus on such land, suggesting that this was already a major crop for the villagers. Construction projects during the sixteenth century give some sense of the wealth that was accumulating in the hands of at least some residents of the island in this period. Wooden bridges were replaced by stone bridges. Existing religious structures were rebuilt, and new ones established. An early seventeenth-century gazetteer describes Luozhou as having a populace of several thousand households, among which that of Wu Fu was the most prominent.[49] The town, which stretched out along the bank of the river, is divided into three settlements, each inhabited predominantly by members of a single surname: Zhouwei (End of the Island) is the home of the Lin of Luozhou, Wucuo (Wu Dwelling) is the home of the Wu, and Dianqian (Shopfront) is the Chen settlement. The Chen and Lin have a history of cordial relations with one another and of violent feuding (*xiedou*) with the Wu of Wucuo. Earlier in the

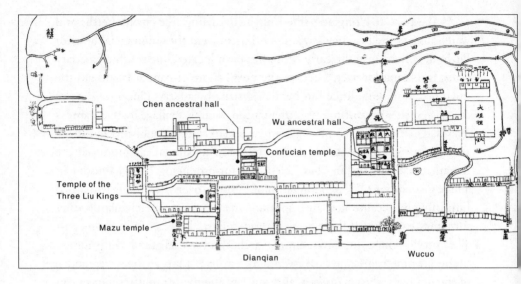

Map 3.   Luozhou. SOURCE: Luojiang Chenshi jiapu, 1933.

twentieth century, a long brick wall separated the settlements of Dianqian and Wucuo.[50]

In the mid-nineteenth century, a Luozhou man, Chen Jingliang, was one of the greatest landlords on Nantai. The document of division of his household estate lists 350 separate plots of land totaling several hundred *mu*; Chen also owned pawnshops in Fuzhou and Luozhou, granaries, and a paper warehouse.[51] Jingliang's grandson was Chen Baochen, who served as chief tutor to the last Qing emperor. His home in Luozhou was a luxurious wood mansion on stone foundations, extending to five courtyards and including a two-storied library. Beyond lay orchards and gardens from which the gardeners selected seasonal plants to decorate the house. Outside the main door, large wooden placards proclaimed the most recent family successes in the state examinations.[52] Chen's family also maintained a grand home in Fuzhou city, to which they traveled either by boat or by sedan chair, along a path that wound through orchards of lychee and orange trees irrigated by an intricate network of narrow waterways (see Map 3).

Not far from Luozhou is Yixu, the largest village on Nantai, with a population of over two thousand households of which all but a few belong to the Huang surname. In the past, the Huang of Yixu have had violent feuds

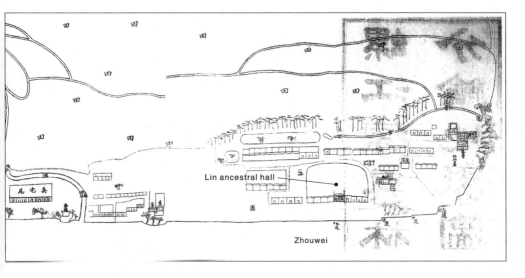

Map 3. (Continued)

with both the Lin of Linpu and the Chen of Luozhou. A number of Yixu men passed the military examinations, contributing to the village's fearsome reputation. Despite Luozhou's prominent sons, it is Yixu that is perhaps best known outside of Fuzhou. Lin Yaohua (Lin Yueh-hwa), one of the founding fathers of social anthropology in China, selected it as the site of fieldwork for his 1935 M.A. thesis at Yanjing University (see Map 4). Yixu and Luozhou both look out over the southern channel of the Min at Five Tigers Mountains, a row of peaks on the south shore. At the foot of these mountains lies the large town of Shanggan, whose most famous son is either the Republican premier Lin Sen or the railway union organizer and revolutionary martyr Lin Xianglian, depending on one's point of view. It is from these five communities that much of the material discussed in this work has come.

SOURCES AND SUMMARY

Whereas twenty years ago investigation of the lineages of Fuzhou could only have begun in the libraries of genealogies found outside of China, or perhaps among communities of Fuzhou people abroad, today it makes more sense to start in the villages of the region themselves. In many villages, lineage

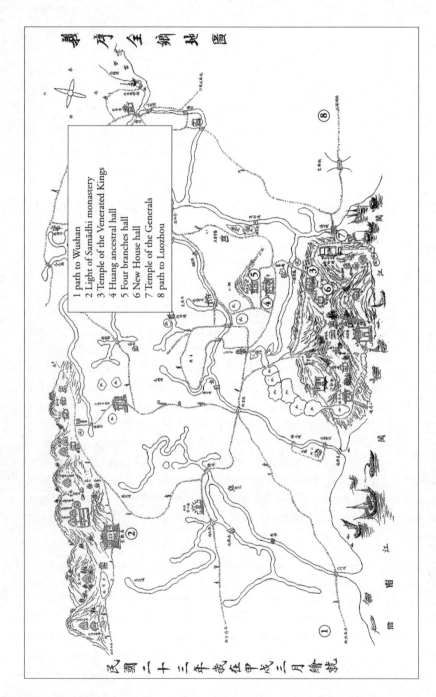

1 path to Wushan
2 Light of Samādhi monastery
3 Temple of the Venerated Kings
4 Huang ancestral hall
5 Four branches hall
6 New House hall
7 Temple of the Generals
8 path to Luozhou

Map 4. Yixu and Vicinity. SOURCE: Huqiu Yishan Huangshi shipu, 1932

ancestral halls have been built or rebuilt on a grand scale. New associational forms have emerged around the ancestral halls. Committees of management for the halls are made up of elderly villagers; lineage research associations, whose main project is to plan the recompilation of lineage genealogies, link the management committees to intellectuals and others who have left the village for the city. There are also quasi-official associations, such as the Fujian Surname Origins Research Association, formed by cadres working in cultural fields. This revival offers the historian new and exciting resources with which to explore the history and meaning of Chinese kinship.

The main sources for this study of the history of kinship practices in the Fuzhou region with special reference to Nantai Island are genealogies, oral history, and observation of contemporary ritual performance from the island. Previous studies of the lineage have not always taken the written genealogy as a point of departure, and where they have, it has often been to carry out the study of one particular lineage. Genealogies may be found in private hands, in ancestral halls, in government offices, or, as in one case discussed here, on a rubbish pile. Between 1992 and 1997, I collected or read *in situ* over three hundred genealogies from the former Fuzhou prefecture.[53] The study also makes use of a wide range of other sources. As capital of province and prefecture, there is detailed discussion of Fuzhou in each of the six surviving editions of the provincial gazetteer, beginning with the fifteenth-century *Bamin tongzhi* and continuing to Chen Yan's mammoth nineteenth-century compilation, and five prefectural gazetteers, including the *Sanshan zhi* of 1182, one of the best surviving Song gazetteers.[54] The region is also well served by other literary sources, both by authors native to the region and by officials posted there. Finally, I have consulted unpublished sources such as stone inscriptions, land deeds, and documents of household division.

I begin each chapter with a brief account of some aspect of contemporary observance, oral history, or ritual practice relevant to the subject of the chapter. There are several reasons for this. First, it is precisely in such contemporary observances and oral accounts that the disparities and tensions between the multiple version of kinship are revealed most clearly. Second, these accounts illustrate how people today conceive of kinship and how they express their conceptions through their voices, practices, and institutions, highlighting both the possibilities and the challenges of providing such an illustration for the people of times past. Lineage institutions are clearly being adapted to meet contemporary needs; the historical documents show that similar processes of adaptation and change have always been part of kinship practice. Finally, these contemporary accounts provide crucial evidence for the historical studies that follow. The popular memory illuminated by these sources may take us back only one hundred years or so, but this is enough to provide links to the world described in the written sources. It offers what is in some cases our only evidence on topics ignored by the documents. It can also provide important insights into how to read those written documents such as ritual liturgies and land deeds that survive but that are virtually impossible to contextualize without other support. Of course, the relationship between present and past must be considered critically. Although informants may say that they are simply recuperating past practices, the historian must be sensitive to the way practices have been reshaped to suit present circumstances and present needs, and memory too has been reshaped by the passage of time and the concerns of the present. Oral history and ritual practice are problematic genres of source material, but, given the uneven documentary record, we ignore them at the risk of closing off huge areas of historical inquiry about the Chinese past.

Each of the chapters considers a single dimension of organized agnatic kinship. These were hardly unique to the Fuzhou region, with the genealogy, ancestral hall, and so forth, being familiar to anyone who has read the anthropological literature on China, but I hope the overall argument is novel. The different dimensions may be imagined in terms of a sequence of widening concentric rings, each successive ring dealing with practices and institutions of a successively larger group. Chapter 2 discusses genealogy, which is a way to link the individual to his ancestors. The next three chapters consider various ways in which the descendants of a common ancestor might organize themselves and institutionalize their connection. Chapter 6 explores how these groups related to other groups in local society and to the state.

Chapter 2 offers a close analysis of several local genealogies in order to consider the tracing of descent through the writing of genealogy. Although most genealogies do more or less precisely what they set out to do, that is, to record agnatic descent with reference to the compiler, we also find clues that direct us toward the larger setting in which claims to kinship took on specific local meanings. Ancestors of many of the most prominent lineages of Qing Fuzhou were identified with the despised indigenous peoples of the region. The compiling of genealogies could serve as a way to make strategic claims about ethnicity, denying or obscuring earlier labels.

It is one thing for a group of people to make claims of common ancestry; it is something else to attach practical significance to those ties, to make them socially meaningful. Chapter 3 considers some of the new ways in which kinship became socially meaningful during the Ming. The basic argument is that the Ming state's military and taxation systems drove groups of kin to organize themselves. This chapter thus directs questions to both of the dominant paradigms in the existing literature on the history of kinship organization. Although much anthropological literature links the rise of lineages to the lawless frontier, I argue that it was the presence of the state, not its absence, that encouraged the formation of kinship groups. Although much social history stresses the role of the educated elite in kinship organization, this chapter presents evidence that groups of kin organized themselves at the bottom of society as well as at the top.

Complex political, social, and economic forces drove groups of kin to organize themselves. But these factors do not in themselves explain the particular institutional arrangements that developed around agnatic kinship. Chapter 4 explores the development of the most visible symbol of kinship organization, the free-standing ancestral hall. The proliferation of halls in the official style has been treated by historians as evidence for a process of cultural integration under gentry leadership. By comparing ancestral halls built in the Fuzhou countryside at different stages, I identify three distinct types of hall and link these to different historical periods. Prior to the fifteenth century, high officials built free-standing ancestral halls in accordance with state prescriptions and in the style advocated by Zhu Xi, in part to demonstrate their distinctiveness and exclusivity from the rest of local society. During the mid-Ming, commercialization seemed to many members of the educated elite to be destroying the rural social order, demanding that they respond as the natural leaders of society. In the late Ming, pirate incursions further stimulated literati involvement in local society, as they took charge of local defense efforts. The result was that the ancestral hall became a tool to construct a more cohesive local community under elite leadership, a sign of inclusiveness rather than exclusiveness. But other segments of the rural elite who had emerged as a result of commercialization also made use of ancestral halls as part of their own strategies to build local authority. The ancestral hall came to be shaped not only by neo-Confucian values, but also by the world of commerce, that is, by the input and interests of local merchants and moneylenders. Chapter 5 continues the investigation of the ancestral hall through a study of the rituals performed in it. Literati writings about these rituals present them as the simple reenactment of a script provided by the authoritative twelfth-century text of Zhu Xi. But it proved impossible to put Zhu Xi's prescriptions into practice. Careful analysis shows that the rituals of ancestral worship actually incorporated two older traditions, the Lantern Festival and the festival of Chen Jinggu—a goddess of women and childbirth—into a new tradition centered on ancestral sacrifice in the ancestral hall, which elites promoted in pursuit of their own strategies. Earlier popular practices were thus transformed, masculinized, and Confucianized.

Having considered the institutions and practices that developed among groups of kin, Chapter 6 then returns to the effects of the state on kinship organization, exploring the intersection of state policy, lineage, and local cult. The early Ming state implemented an official religious system that extended down to the rural community. In response, existing local cults were reshaped, manipulated, and represented so as to bring them in line with the official system. The close connection between registration for taxation and kinship, introduced in Chapter 3, thus extended also to local religious life. As ancestral halls spread through the Fuzhou countryside, it became common practice to parade the deities associated with a lineage to their ancestral hall, as manifest expression of the lineage's claim to the special protection of the deity. Issues of affiliation or disaffiliation with a given temple, of temple financing, and of ritual organization became matters determined not by individual preference, or by place of residence, but by the registered household to which one belonged, which over the course of the Ming had become virtually synonymous with the lineage.

Taken together, Chapters 2–6 illustrate that the meanings of kinship and descent in late imperial China were not stable or primordial, but negotiated and contested. To understand this requires looking at kinship ideas and institutions not just in terms of canonical rules that can be followed to a lesser or greater degree, but in terms of how ideas and institutions developed historically and were practiced in the lives of Fuzhou people. The institutionalization of kinship must be seen strategically, in the practices and representations of individuals and groups at all levels of society. To accommodate these various strategies, lineage institutions and practices had to be highly flexible, able to incorporate not only the neo-Confucian ideology of the educated elite but also popular practices and representations. Organized patrilineal kinship in Fuzhou was neither static nor monolithic, but rather was constituted in a network of changing representations. The practice of kinship in late imperial Fuzhou involved ongoing contest and negotiation between different conceptions of what kinship was and should be and of what it could and should do.

In the past century, the ideas and institutions of Chinese kinship have frequently been invoked in narratives of Chinese modernization. Kinship is generally discussed in one of two ways. Among revolutionary modernizers, institutionalized patrilineal kinship has been seen as an impediment to social and economic transformation, a feudal remnant that either must be actively eliminated or can be expected to dissolve as a result of other anticipated changes to society. More recently, kinship among the Overseas Chinese has been heralded as the basis of a distinct form of flexible capitalism, with the extended family firm being the praiseworthy response to pressures of globalization. In both these narratives, Chinese kinship is seen as a static and unchanging set of ideas, institutions, and practices. Does it matter to these narratives if kinship is seen as strategic, as something that is practiced? Individuals build their culture and community by adapting existing structures to serve new functions in new contexts, transforming inherited discourses as they are deployed. Institutional structures are transformed by the actions and choices of people working within them, reshaping the context in which subsequent generations make their own choices. Exploring the processes of cultural construction in late imperial China may thus ultimately illuminate similar processes at work in contemporary China and its diaspora and the choices open to the people who participate in its culture.

TWO

Genealogical Tracing
and Ethnic Labeling

Ask almost any older male resident of Nantai today about his origins and
he will tell you that his ancestors come from a place called Gushi county, in
Henan province in north China, and that they came to Fujian long ago as
followers of a man named Wang Shenzhi. Ask how he knows this, and he
will likely tell you that it is recorded in his genealogy, or at least was until
the genealogy was destroyed during the Cultural Revolution. In the early
1990s, a fever for genealogy spread through the villages of Nantai. Surviving
genealogies were brought out of concealment and copied, and new genealogies were compiled on the basis of surveys as well as whatever other evidence
was available. Newly established Provincial Surname Origins Research Associations, one for each of the major surnames in the population, began
to collect genealogies old and new, and held conferences on the challenges
of editing genealogies. The new genealogies that have been produced are
remarkable testimonies to the continuing importance of organized kinship
in the region. They may run to several large volumes, hardbound in bright
colors at considerable expense. They include lists of prominent historical
and contemporary people who share the same surname as the lineage and

photographs of lineage members, in China and abroad, who have donated funds to support the publication of the genealogy. The claim that the lineage descends from a founding ancestor who moved from north China is universal in these new genealogies, of which I have gathered several dozen. Some lineages have even dispatched members back to Henan to look for their roots (*xungen*).

The claim of north China origin is not new in Fuzhou. It appears repeatedly in the two early twentieth-century gazetteers of Minxian and Houguan, in the sections entitled "Great Surnames" (*daxing*), which appear to have been compiled on the basis of the written genealogies of local lineages. In both gazetteers, this section begins with the story of two semilegendary mass migrations to the Fuzhou region. In the early fourth century, "[the state] was weak and the Central Plains in turmoil. Eight surnames of noble lineages . . . the Lin, Chen, Huang, Zheng, Dan, Qiu, He and Hu, moved to central Fujian."[1] Then in the late Tang, the brothers Wang Chao and Shenzhi of Gushi led an army into Fujian, seized control, and established the short-lived kingdom of Min.[2] "Those who came with them were the thirty-six surnames."[3] The founding ancestors of many Nantai lineages are listed in the subsequent detailed surname-by-surname descriptions; most are said to have come to Fujian as part of one of these two great migrations. Guo Bocang's own family is listed under the Guo surname. Their ancestry is traced to Guo Ziyi, whose descendant followed Wang Shenzhi and settled in Fujian.[4]

The written genealogy is, among other things, a record of the tracing of transmission of descent, going back to the distant ancestors. Most genealogies tell histories of descent that are more or less straightforward. But as Freedman noted long ago, the genealogy is more than simply a family tree. "It is a set of claims to origins and relationships, a charter, a map of dispersion, a framework for wide-ranging social organization, a blueprint for action. It is a political statement." The genealogy is a strategic text, which is intended to produce and does produce certain social effects. It is part of the practice of kinship. Many previous studies have looked at clan rules and individual lineage genealogies. Rubie Watson, for example, has shown how one lineage in Guangdong used genealogy to construct a glorious history for themselves.[5] But less work has been done on reading genealogies in their larger context, exploring how genealogies and the compilation of genealogies are part of the broader strategies that shape the practice of kinship. In this chapter, I focus on how and why genealogy has been used to assert claims of descent from ancestors who have migrated from north China. The argument is divided into three sections. The first considers the genealogy as a genre of text, which follows the particular narrative conventions of the genre. Though most genealogies convey the impression that their contents have been added in strict chronological order, careful analysis shows that the most historically distant portions of the text are often the most recent additions. Although each successive edition of a single genealogy extends forward in time, including the generations of ancestors who have lived and died since the previous edition was compiled, it may also move backward in time, including generations of ancestors prior to that of the earliest ancestor recorded in the previous edition. Ultimately, this process of accretion can make it possible for the compilers of the current edition to make a convincing claim that their earliest ancestors migrated to Fujian from north China.

The second section explores the mechanics of this accretion. I argue that it is facilitated by the existence of two widely practiced variant forms of standard marriage practices—cross-surname adoption and uxorilocal marriage. Because cross-surname adoption was widely practiced in the Fuzhou region in the late imperial period, one could make a convincing argument for changing one's own surname, on grounds that it had already been changed at some time in the past, when an ancestor had been adopted by a family with a different surname. Changing it again was thus no more than reverting back to the original surname. Because uxorilocal marriage was widely practiced in the Fuzhou region in the late imperial period, one could make a convincing argument that one was related to people who lived in a distant place, on the grounds that one's male ancestor had been born there but had married uxorilocally into the village in which one now lived. I demonstrate that arguments such as these were frequently invoked in the genealogies of the Fuzhou region, and it is these arguments that are used to explain the accretion of earlier material in successive editions of particular genealogies, culminating in the accretion of evidence of north China origins.

The third section explores the motivations behind efforts to claim north China origins. I argue that ethnic labels were imposed on two groups living in the Fuzhou region in late imperial times, the Dan boat people and the She highlanders, both believed to descend from the aboriginal inhabitants of the Fuzhou region prior to Han immigration, and that these groups suffered various forms of discrimination. Claims of north China origin were part of a strategy to deny these labels, to demonstrate that one was not a member of a despised group, but descended from immigrants from the heartland of Chinese culture. This chapter is thus a study of how one aspect of the practice of kinship, the compilation of genealogy, was embedded in the broader context of Fuzhou society and how that broader context shaped the motivations and strategies that were part of the practice of kinship.

THE PROCESSES OF TRACING DESCENT

The written genealogy implies an understanding of descent in strictly chronological terms, from the earliest ancestors through generations of descendants to the living. But it is sometimes possible to recover traces of ruptures in the straightforward chronological logic of the descent line, to detect splices that have woven together the current segments of the lineage into the genealogy at some time in the past. The genealogy of the Huang of Yixu offers a rich case for analysis. The most recent compilation of this genealogy, published in 1932, contains twelve different prefaces to earlier editions, ranging in date almost one thousand years from 992 to 1932. The key to an informed interpretation of these prefaces and their relation to the history of Yixu is to ignore the chronological sequence of prefaces and consider instead the timing of the process by which each preface was added to the genealogy. The chronologically oldest materials in the genealogy are, I will show, in fact among the most recent additions to it, having been included only in the eighteenth century.[6]

The oldest prefaces describe a group of people surnamed Huang living in the vicinity of Tiger Mound (Huqiu), in Minqing county upriver from Fuzhou. Huang Dun, their founding ancestor, or first migrant ancestor (*shiqianzu*), was said to be a native of Gushi county, Henan, who had followed Wang Chao to Fujian. Reclusive by nature, Dun obtained a grant of land in Minqing where he had settled, opened up fields and gardens, married, and had six sons.[7] A great-grandson of Dun is said to have moved away from Minqing, and this man's son, Yuanzhi, compiled the first genealogy of Dun's descendants. A preface by Yuanzhi's acquaintance Zhang Jianmeng (*jinshi* 992) praises him for his honorable motives and his care in accurately tracing his descent line:

Yuanzhi worried about the genealogical records, fearing that over time it would become difficult to track down the branches. So he asked permission to compile a genealogical chart, for he wished to be able to distinguish close from distant relatives, and encourage the members of the lineage to do so as well. This can be called knowing one's roots and extending back to one's origins. . . . There are [now] few among the descendants of the gentry who consider genealogies important. Now Yuanzhi knows what is important. In this genealogy, he does not dare drag in and append that which is prior to the first generation or is unreliable, which would confuse all of the descendants. Beginning with Dun of the Tiger Mound, there was Bo. Bo had Jun. Jun had Teng and Zhen. Teng was [Yuanzhi's] father. Now the gradations of kinship across the generations, the distinctions of status and the relationship between the different branches of descent have all been clarified, in order to transmit this to later generations.[8]

In the thirteenth century, Yuanzhi's descendant Xingjian compiled a new genealogy, for which he solicited prefaces from two relatives. These prefaces suggest that Xingjian tried to include all of the descendants of Dun, now numbering over three thousand known individuals dispersed in a number of different communities, in a single genealogy.[9]

The next complete preface dates from the Jiajing period of the mid-Ming. The author, a member of the twenty-fourth generation and a county magistrate, indicates that there had been several attempts at compilation in the intervening three hundred years. Some of these had been limited in depth; others had been more complete, but all were now lost or decayed. "The ancestors who over time have served as officials have been posted to distant places. Devoted to the public good they neglected their personal interest; dedicated to the state they neglected their family, to the point that the genealogy is scattered and spoilt." This is the first genealogy for which we can get some sense of the content, which is substantial. According to the preface, the genealogy includes genealogical charts, ancestral injunctions, miscellaneous records, ritual descriptions, and accounts of the repair of tombs. The summary of lineage activities is both prescriptive and descriptive. "Cautiously and attentively they worship at the shrine and tombs. The lineage members assemble, in order not to forget the sentiments with which the early ancestors ordered the generations. When a genealogy is compiled, above the venerated can be respected and below the kin can be loved. Sentiments are warm and the agnates feel close."[10]

The Tiger Mound genealogy was compiled next in 1581, when two prefaces were solicited, one from a lineage member and *jinshi* named Huang Yinglin and the other from a Hanlin academician named Wang Yingzhong. Wang compares genealogy to the writing of history, tracing the origins of both to the *Spring and Autumn Annals*. Genealogy compilation began in the Han, he explains. It collapsed in the Five Dynasties period and was revived by the likes of Ouyang Xiu and Su Dongpo. "It flourishes especially in our current Ming dynasty." Both prefaces indicate that this is a genealogy linking descendants living in widely scattered villages, including Yongfu, Lianjiang, Luoyuan, and Gutian counties; Fuzhou city; and the Nantai village of Yixu. This is the first mention of Yixu in any preface. Huang Yinglin explains that since the Song, many of the descendants of Huang Dun have moved to Minxian and Houguan counties to be close to the provincial capital.[11]

There is a significant disjuncture between the seventh and eighth prefaces, apparent from their positioning in the genealogy. The first seven prefaces are printed in strict chronological order, with the last two dating from 1581. But the eighth preface records the compilation of a genealogy in 1491. The eighth preface is also the first to have been written by a resident of Yixu village, a man named Huang Xi. Xi's genealogy was a very humble effort, consisting only of genealogical information that Xi has been able to verify personally. His preface provides a different account of the settlement history of the Huang, beginning with the stock phrase: "In the late Yongjia period of the Jin (307–12), fleeing turmoil the nobles of eight surnames entered Fujian. The Huang was one of them." His account thus links his ancestors to the first of the two great migrations from north China, in the fourth century, unlike the versions we have just discussed, which invoke the second great migration, in the ninth. Xi has the Huang's earliest ancestors settling first in Fuzhou city and mentions Dun settling in Minqing centuries earlier than in the other accounts. In the mid-Song, Xi's direct ancestor Zhifu had married a woman of the Lin surname of Yixu. "His frequent contacts made him aware of the beauty of the landscape/geomantic virtues (*shanshui zhi sheng*) of [Yixu], so he decided to settle there."[12] In other words, he contracted a uxorilocal marriage that led to his settlement in Yixu. Zhifu was the founding ancestor of the Huang of Yixu. The preface then runs through the generations of descent to the four great-great-grandsons of Zhifu, each of whom is identified with the name of a settlement in the vicinity of Yixu.

Now, Huang Xi continues, after three hundred years, the Huang of Yixu have become a prominent lineage that ought to have a genealogy. The first member of the lineage to hold office had wished to compile one but had devoted himself to public affairs and so lacked the time. Xi wished to fulfill this early Ming ancestor's intention but did not know where to begin. He obtained a genealogy from a collateral branch, but it had many inconsistencies and contradictions, and he worried that if he based his own genealogy on this alone, there would be unavoidable errors. So he compiled his genealogy using a descent-line chart (*zongtu*) that his father had made, together with his own personal observations. This genealogy was never printed, but "preserved in the family, to await a later time, when an earlier genealogy can be obtained and compared for consistency."[13]

What can Huang Xi's remarks tell us about the contents of the genealogy he compiled? Xi was obviously unfamiliar with the way the Huang of Minqing traced their ancestry. The discrepancies in the story of the initial migration to Fujian suggest that Huang was simply recording various legends about famous people surnamed Huang in Fujian. His genealogy was narrow in scope and shallow in depth, recording only those relatives on the descent-line chart, all of whom were residents of Yixu. This chart must have been based on an oral genealogy that was probably related to ancestral sacrifice and the maintenance of the sites of sacrifice, such as graves and domestic shrines, and perhaps also rights of settlement.[14] Thus, at one level, Xi's genealogy marks the beginning of a shift from oral to written in the tracing of descent. The claims that are made about ancestors prior to settlement in Yixu are tentative and contradictory. The genealogy also operates at another level. Huang Xi's remarks suggest an attempt to use the language of agnatic kinship to link the inhabitants of several settlements in the Yixu vicinity. The identification of different settlements with the four great-great-grandsons of Zhifu is probably the description of an arrangement that different groups of people in the area who shared the Huang surname had come up with to reconcile their genealogical traditions. Finally, having a genealogy was seen as appropriate to a community like Yixu, and it was a source of consternation that the Huang did not yet have one. The theme of the official who is too public spirited and honest to look after his own interests is a familiar trope; here it is being deployed to illustrate why the Huang have none of the evidence of status that they should rightfully have.

As I will show in the next chapter, the Huang of Yixu were already becoming organized as a corporate lineage with joint property and ritual unity by the time their genealogy was next compiled, in 1629. Keying, the author of this edition, regrets the fact that the previous edition does not go any further back than ancestor Zhifu. He notes the problems with Huang Xi's version.[15] Keying explains that it took several years of work, traveling to Minqing and other places where his kin dwelt, before he learned the true history of the lineage. The implication, of course, is that he did not know this history prior to these efforts. The early history of the lineage that he provides corresponds exactly with that of the earlier Tiger Mound prefaces. Keying has clearly been in touch with the Huang there. He has also come to a definitive conclusion about the genealogical link between his family in Yixu and the descent line in Minqing. The crucial node was Yuanzhi, Dun's great-great-grandson and compiler of the first Tiger Mound genealogy. Yuanzhi is said to have six sons, each of whom moved to a different part of the Fuzhou region. Zhifu, the founding ancestor of the Huang of Yixu, was descended from the fourth son.

Keying also admits that his version is still tentative. "I did not dare to ask a member of the gentry to compile it, nor to solicit money from the relatives to have it distributed. Those who share the same heart as me preserve the handwritten copies, and await someone to do the task properly in the future."[16] As with his predecessor's, Keying's genealogy was not printed, not widely distributed, and not yet an effectively public marker of status. But Keying was well aware that a comprehensive genealogy could confer certain social benefits. "If we do not make a genealogy for [the ancestors] in order to link the blood lines, then our lineage will become nothing more than farmers and old men, who know what they give birth to, but not what has given birth to them." The problem was remedied twenty-three years later, when an itinerant scholar from Shaowu named Huang Guorui recompiled the genealogy. While Guorui was visiting the Light of Samādhi Monastery (Dingguangsi) near Yixu, he was shown Keying's genealogy. Guorui observed similarities between the Yixu genealogy and his own and offered to make another copy of the decaying work as a way of earning some money. Perhaps the holder of the genealogy was not sufficiently educated to do the job himself. The copying turned out to involve considerable editing. Huang Guorui reports that he "eliminated the troublesome; got rid of complications; added evidence as far as the facts were concerned, and ensured that there were no incorrect characters."[17] In other words, he turned the tangled and contradictory stories of ancestry into a coherent narrative of lineage history.

The final preface of interest comes from the recompilation of genealogy by Fuji in 1734. Fuji (*jinshi* 1733) is an important figure in the history of the Yixu Huang, who played a prominent role in the establishment and elaboration of its lineage institutions; we will meet him again in later chapters. Fuji wrote his own preface to the genealogy, which is extremely important if we wish to understand the evolution of the genealogy to its current form. He begins by outlining the earlier editions of which he is aware. He admits that the longest interval between successive compilations has been "as much as several hundred years, and even the shortest was eighty or ninety years. Although some households have kept their own records, these have been scattered or lost and are incomplete. So style and literary names, birth order, [details of] death and burial, and wives' surnames are not detailed in the genealogy." His kin had neglected more than just these details. While a child, Fuji had asked a relative to explain the relationship between the different branches of the Yixu Huang. The relative replied, "This is difficult to discuss, and I don't know the details. If you read the genealogy you will understand." But the various versions of the genealogy were mutually contradictory. So Fuji conceived the idea of attempting a recompilation. His first efforts in 1724 were stymied because he could not get his kin to update the fragmentary material he had collected. "The branch heads and elders were generally not interested." Fuji made a second attempt nine years later. "When the lineage and branch heads assembled in the hall on the first day of the year to worship, I humbly requested this of them, and they all agreed." After the work of editing the existing genealogies and interviewing informants as to the life events of the last several dozen years, Fuji was lucky to "receive the assistance of the ancestral spirits." A certain Puyu, from the nearby village of Shaoqi, happened to have an old genealogy that was very clear about the history of the early ancestors of the lineage. "I did not wish to ignore this, but nor did I wish to collate [this version with the others] confusedly." The solution was to organize his genealogy in two fascicles. The first fascicle contained accounts of the origins of the Huang surname, the description of the lineage branches, a "Stone Record of the Ancestor of the Tiger Mound," lists of office holders and virtuous lineage members, and various details about Yixu. The second fascicle contained the genealogical charts of the Yixu Huang, to which were appended the previous versions consulted. The guiding principle was that "the old genealogical records must be preserved; errors rectified; that which was not recorded included; the confused clarified; the superfluous excised, and that which is in doubt confirmed."[18] The various materials from Minqing, provided by Puyu, were now attached to the front of the genealogy, and the inconsistencies with any Yixu material were smoothed over. These materials included all the prefaces from Zhang Jianmeng's tenth-century version to the late Ming versions of Wang Yingzhong and Huang Yinglin, which were now attached to an Yixu genealogy for the first time (see Table 2.1.).

This detailed reading of successive prefaces of the Yixu Huang genealogy demonstrates a number of points. First, the prefaces written by residents of

TABLE 2.1
Prefaces in the Genealogy of the Huang of Yixu

Author	Date	Probable date of first inclusion in Yixu genealogy
Zhang Jianmeng	late tenth–early eleventh centuries	1734
Huang Jingshuo	early thirteenth century	1734
Huang Tai	early thirteenth century	1734
Huang Yong	mid sixteenth century	1734
Huang Zong	1581	1734
Huang Yinglin	1581	1734
Wang Yingzhong	1581	1734
Huang Xi	1491	1491
Huang Keying	1629	1629
Huang Guorui	1652	1652
Huang Fuji	1734	1734

Yixu suggest that the making of a written genealogy was understood as a strategic act that could serve various purposes. These included the marking of social distinctiveness and the solidification of ties between different local groups. The intervention of Guorui suggests that even ordinary villagers, illiterate or barely literate, and not just powerful educated elites, saw the value of compiling a written genealogy. The central point is that reading the genealogy in the order in which it is printed gives the misleading impression that successive compilers simply added new material to old. The sedimentation of material is actually much more complicated. The chronologically oldest materials in the genealogy, the series of Song prefaces from the Tiger Mound Huang, are in fact among the most recent additions to the genealogy, having been first included only in the eighteenth-century compilation by Fuji. While the period covered by a genealogy obviously expands in the direction of the future, as each compiler adds details of the most recent generation, it also expands in the direction of the past, as the compiler links his own lineage with others whose history of compilation is longer. Though the Huang of Yixu were among the greatest of the Great Surnames identified in the late Qing gazetteers, their conclusive descent-line history was not established until the mid-eighteenth century.[19] This descent-line history traced their ancestry back to a migrant from north China, whose other descendants lived in a distant county. The explanation for how and why their own founding ancestor, that is, their first ancestor to settle in Yixu, had left the original residence in Minqing was uxorilocal marriage, a topic to which we now turn our attention.

UXORILOCAL MARRIAGE AND
CROSS-SURNAME ADOPTION

Few of the foundation legends of Nantai and Fuzhou lineages include detailed explanations for why the founding ancestor chose to settle where he did, in the village that would come to be the lineage's home. The brief explanation found in the Yixu genealogy, that the founding ancestor settled where he did because of the geomantic virtues or beauty of the landscape (*shanshui zhi sheng*), is an extremely common one. In the oral tradition of the lineage, the explanation is often that the founding ancestor married a local woman and settled with her family, that is, the history of settlement is a history of uxorilocal marriage. This tradition is usually supported by the details found in the genealogical charts, which record the founding ancestor as having married a woman from a lineage acknowledged to have already been living in the village of settlement. The term *shanshui zhi sheng*, and the similar term *fengshui zhi mei*, may thus be interpreted as a euphemism for uxorilocal marriage.[20]

In this section, I discuss briefly the history of uxorilocal marriage and the related practice of cross-surname adoption in the Fuzhou region. I then show that in the genealogies, these practices are often invoked retroactively, as explanations for why the authors of the genealogy live in a place distant from their kin or have a different surname from their kin. Such arguments made it possible to link one's own genealogy to the genealogy of those distant kin, to add their descent-line history to one's own, and ultimately to link one's own genealogy to the genealogy of kin who could make a persuasive claim to descend from north China immigrants. In the final section of the chapter, I suggest one reason why people in Fuzhou wished to make this link. Many, perhaps most, of the foundation legends of Fuzhou genealogies begin with stories of cross-surname adoption and uxorilocal marriage.[21]

Cross-surname adoption and uxorilocal marriage created situations where a son might have a different surname from his father. They can thus both be seen as manifestations of a single problematic issue, violations of the principle of surname fidelity. Surname fidelity in China was a most serious matter, for as Ann Waltner has written, "kinship represented . . . an ultimate category, a category that humans had not the power to alter. Surnames represented the efforts of the sage kings to fix that category in terms useful to ordinary people."[22] But the principle was frequently overridden, for a variety of reasons. As in many other parts of China, the evidence from Fuzhou suggests that uxorilocal marriage and cross-surname adoption, though not the culturally preferred modes of marriage and descent, were common throughout the period from the Song to the early twentieth century. There were accepted procedures for both practices, indicating that they were fully entrenched in local culture as alternatives to the faithful transmission of the surname through the male line.

This can be demonstrated by a few examples, drawn from different sources spanning the millennium. An early case of cross-surname adoption is mentioned in a story about Fuzhou in the Song work the *Yijianzhi*.[23] In the fourteenth century, Wu Hai of Fuzhou claimed that more than half of all descent-lines had been violated by non-agnatic adoption.[24] In the early twentieth century, a local official surveyed for a study of Chinese customary law reported that "in Minqing, it is extremely common for an adopted son of a different surname to be established as heir. Once the relatives and the lineage have agreed, [the adopted son] may change his surname to that of the adoptive father, carry on his descent line and inherit his property."[25] Agnatic relatives could be expected to oppose cross-surname adoption and to insist on adoption of an agnate (*guoji*), because cross-surname adoption threatened their secondary inheritance rights.[26] Because of the importance of the principle of surname fidelity, and because of agnatic opposition, many lineages prohibited cross-surname adoption, which is therefore rarely mentioned in genealogies except in the context of foundation legends. Interestingly, the only explicit reference to cross-surname adoption in a generation subsequent to that of the founding ancestor that I have found in a genealogy comes from the genealogy of a non-Han group, the Lan of Wangchuan village, Lianjiang county, which records several such cases. Wangchuan village is on the shore of an isolated peninsula in the north of Lianjiang county. The Lan call themselves Miao people but have long intermarried with Han people in their area.[27] Lan Lucai, who lived from 1805 to 1854, had four sons. The second son was adopted by a cousin within the lineage, and the fourth "while young was sent out to be raised by Lin Tingzhong of Xialian, and to serve as his son." Some cross-surname adoptions involved transactions between affinal relatives. Lan Shiwu, whose son was born in 1836, "served as heir to his maternal uncle, of the Lin of Meiban."[28]

Uxorilocal marriage, like cross-surname adoption, was a strategy that could serve various purposes, including ensuring the continuity of the descent line in the absence of a male heir and contributing to the availability of labor within a household.[29] A family with a daughter but no son could contract a uxorilocal marriage, whereby a son-in-law was brought into the natal family. At least one of the sons produced by this marriage would bear the surname of the wife's father and have rights to his estate. As with cross-surname adoption, there is evidence of uxorilocal marriage being practiced in Fuzhou as far back as the Song. Again the earliest source is a story from the *Yijianzhi*, in which a certain man is "married uxorilocally to a family of sea dwellers, and made his living fishing."[30] In the fourteenth century, Wu Hai mentions uxorilocal marriage in an essay on the compilation of his own family genealogy and is highly critical of it:

> Descendants who have no sons, and who do not establish a member of the descent-line [to serve as their posterity], but rather establish a son-in-law or a daughter's son [to serve as their posterity] are not to be recorded [in the genealogy]. Under the vertical line should be written "cut off" because they have themselves abandoned the ancestral descent-line.[31]

There is genealogical evidence of the practice from the Song onward. The genealogy of the Liu of Fenggang mentions a certain Gui who lived in the early Song and married uxorilocally into a Chen household, taking on that surname. Doolittle describes the practice in the nineteenth century. "It not unfrequently occurs that a rich family, having only one daughter and no boys, desires to obtain a son-in-law who shall be willing to marry the girl and live in the family as son. . . . He who agrees to go and live with his father-in-law, sometimes agrees also, at the time of marriage, to take the ancestral name of his father-in-law, and regard himself as his son."[32]

Both cross-surname adoption and uxorilocal marriage resulted in violations of the principle of surname fidelity. That is, they led to sons having different surnames from their fathers. This situation could sometimes also result from wholesale conversions of surname by adult males. In his investigations into his ancestry in the nineteenth century, Guo Bocang was at pains to distinguish his own family from another group with the same surname that had an ugly secret:

> In the past, the Ma, the Yang and the Guo were travelling together by boat. They ran into strong winds and were blown ashore at Shanqian. Having

undergone the same turmoil, the descendants of the three surnames were particularly close. They took tallies with the three surnames into a temple and asked [the gods] for a response. The response came back Guo, so the Ma and the Yang adopted that same surname.[33]

Because of such practices, the very straightforward principle of surname fidelity is revealed to have been anything but straightforward in late imperial Fuzhou. It was not at all unusual for a son to have a different surname from his father and for adult men to live far away from their kin.

Zhang Jing / Cai Jing and Restoring the Surname (Fuxing)

Uxorilocal marriage and cross-surname adoption were not the preferred forms of marriage and transmission of descent, but they were nonetheless widespread and common in Fuzhou in the late imperial period. Because the descendant of a cross-surname adoptee or of a man who had married uxorilocally would not share the surname of his ancestors, these practices also gave rise to frequent discussions of the issue of restoring the surname (*fuxing*). The mid-Ming era case of Cai Jing, known to posterity as Zhang Jing, is a particularly well-documented example of what restoring one's surname might mean. Cai Jing was born on the small island of Banzhou, near Hongtang, which at the time was the main port for Fuzhou. In 1517, he passed the *jinshi* exams and was appointed to the magistracy of a county in Zhejiang. In 1525, he was transferred to Beijing and held a series of offices there before his 1537 appointment as junior vice-minister in the Ministry of War and concurrently governor-general of Guangdong and Guangxi.[34] At some time prior to 1543, Cai Jing began efforts to restore his surname to Zhang. The main evidence for these efforts are a memorial he wrote requesting the change, a genealogical preface he wrote in 1550 to celebrate the successful restoration of the surname, and correspondence on the matter between Jing and his father Cai Hai. According to these accounts, Jing claimed that his sixth-generation ancestor had been a man named Zhang Zongben, who served as assistant magistrate in nearby Lianjiang county. Zongben's only son Masi married a woman of the Cai surname, whose family lived in Fuzhou city.[35] Jing offered contradictory versions of Masi's story. The 1550 preface records that Masi died while his son Rong was only a child. Because there were no paternal kin in Fuzhou who could raise the boy, Rong was brought up by his maternal relatives, the Cai, and came to have their surname. In other words, he was adopted. But Jing's memorial claims

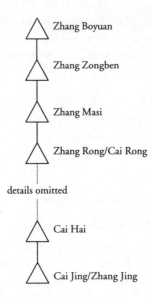

Zhang Boyuan

Zhang Zongben

Zhang Masi

Zhang Rong/Cai Rong

details omitted

Cai Hai

Cai Jing/Zhang Jing

Figure 2.1. Descent Line of Zhang Jing.

that Masi married uxorilocally into the Cai family. Because his father-in-law had no heir, Masi's son Rong took the surname Cai and inherited his estate.[36] The differences are superficial. In both versions, the end result is that Zhang Masi's son Rong is surnamed Cai. Thereafter, Rong's descendants for four generations up to Jing himself had borne the Cai surname. (Figure 2.1.)

Jing's motivations for restoring the surname are discussed in the correspondence with his father. Having searched unsuccessfully for genealogical records that would provide details about his ancestry, "troubled night and day, searching but to no avail," he wrote his father requesting permission to pursue the matter. "The waters come from the sky but all return to the sea; this refers to origins. The leaves cover the twig but fall around the trunk; this refers to roots. Looking at it this way, we ought not to falsely bear the Cai surname forever." Hai ordered him to abandon the scheme, which he considered unfilial to the point of disloyalty, invoking the famous name of Qu Yuan in support of his feelings. "A man of *ren* does not turn his back on virtue and erase his name; a gentleman does not serve the new and so abandon the old." Jing was unmoved and responded with the argument from the *Zuo Zhuan* that ancestral sacrifices could not be maintained by someone who did not in fact descend from the ancestor through the male line, for the ancestor simply would not accept them. "I have heard it said," he wrote, "that if the offering comes from someone not of the line, the spirits will refuse it."[37] Jing was willing to admit that the Cai were owed a debt for sheltering young Rong, but this was really a debt for their having enabled the Zhang line not to be extinguished and was not infinite. Now that the mourning grades of Zhang Zongben's father-in-law had been exhausted, the ledger had been cleared.

After much negotiation, Hai suggested as a compromise that Jing do as he wished but only after Hai's death. Then, according to his biography in the genealogy, on his deathbed Hai changed his mind. Too weak to write, Hai asked a relative to inform Jing, who was away holding office, that he now accepted the argument about the efficacy of sacrifice to the Zhang and not the Cai. "The descendants are not flourishing. Can it be that because we have not restored our surname, we do not obtain the assistance of ancestors?" Hai urged Jing to find further genealogical records to transmit to posterity.[38] Despite Hai's apparent change of heart, it was only while Jing was mourning his death that he was able to fulfill the wish they now shared.

At this point Cai Jing could not trace his ancestry back more than a few generations, to Zongben's father Boyuan, who was said to have moved to Fujian from Jiangxi. But then he met a man named Zhang Yintao who was visiting Fuzhou. Yintao was from the upriver town of Nanping and belonged to a family of some distinction. His granduncle was a *jinshi* of 1460. Yintao's cousin, the grandson of this uncle, was also a *jinshi*, who had held the office of Minister. Yintao himself was a county magistrate. His family traced their ancestry to Nanchang, whence they had moved to Fujian in the Yuan period. Yintao must have brought his written genealogy with him to Fuzhou, for while he and Cai Jing were discussing their ancestry, Yintao pulled out the genealogy, and they discovered records of an ancestor six generations back whose details corresponded to those of Boyuan. Cai Jing was overjoyed. He had found his ancestors.[39] Shortly thereafter he petitioned for the imperial favor of allowing him to restore his surname, and the request was granted. Cai Jing became Zhang Jing. In celebration, he compiled his own genealogy, beginning over sixty generations earlier with an ancestor in north China and copying the details directly from Zhang Yintao's genealogy.[40]

Zhang Jing presents his decision to undertake the formal process of restoring his surname as a simple moral imperative. We might also interpret it as a strategic effort by an upwardly mobile elite individual to create a pool of potential allies or to establish links with a more illustrious family, converting personal success in examinations and office holding into a share in the enduring success of a distinguished descent line. But ultimately we do not know why he chose to take these steps. My purpose in telling his story has been to illustrate that it was precisely the institutions of cross-surname adoption and uxorilocal marriage that made it plausible to claim that one's surname ought to be changed, that is, that one was related to kin who had a different surname or who lived far away. In other words, it was precisely because cross-surname adoption and uxorilocal marriage were widespread in practice that it was possible to deploy them rhetorically in narratives of descent tracing. In many genealogies from Fuzhou lineages, these claims were invoked to explain why the compiler had linked his own genealogy to that of another group of people who lived in a distant place and sometimes did not even share the same surname.[41] Successive linkages of this type could ultimately be used to enable a plausible claim to a lineage that could identify an ancestor who had migrated from north China. In the next section, I discuss one reason why compilers of genealogies should be anxious to make such a claim.

ETHNIC LABELS, DIFFERENTIATION, AND DISCRIMINATION

Sources from the late imperial period often divide the residents of the Fuzhou region into three types of people, the descendants of migrants from north China, who would today be called Han Chinese, and two indigenous groups known as the Dan and the She. The distinction is made on the basis of both historical origins and contemporary cultural practices, such as language, modes of production, family relations, and dress. These types cannot be described as ethnic groups; it is not at all clear that the markers of distinction were sources of identification or solidarity for those to whom they were ascribed. But they are ethnic labels: the members of each type are presumed in our sources to share certain characteristics that are considered to be rooted in primordial origins and that serve to differentiate them from the members of the other types. But the distinctions were never as straightforward as the labels suggest. As we shall see, large numbers of people in Fuzhou, as in other parts of south China, have made the transition from non-Han to Han over the centuries.[42]

The historical sources of the region present the indigenous people, Dan and She, as descendants of the tribal Min Yue peoples who had lived in

the area before large-scale immigration from north and central China. The
Chinese term for these peoples itself reflects a sense of primordial differentiation. The *Shuowen jiezi* glosses the term "Min," the ancient name for
what is now Fujian, as referring to a group "which belongs to the snake class
(*shezhong*)."[43] In the reign of the Han emperor Wudi (140–87 B.C.), who
exercised a vague suzerainty over the region, the indigenous people were ordered evacuated and resettled in central China, whereupon the region "was
left vacant." Immigrants from what is now central China began to move into
the Fuzhou region in the first century A.D., and several counties that correspond to those present in late imperial times were founded at that time.[44]
But the original inhabitants of the region had not disappeared. According to
the *Taiping huanyuji*, "after [the Han evacuation], there were those who fled
and hid in the mountains and valleys." A ninth-century author wrote that
"Fujian enjoys the abundance of being by the sea. The people are fierce and
esteem ghosts. Those who live in the mountain fastnesses and those who
make their homes afloat on rafts do not speak the language of China."[45]
From the Tang, if not earlier, Chinese authors distinguished the Chinese
from two other groups, those living in the hills and those living afloat. Several of the surnames that would by Ming–Qing times be the largest in Fujian
were associated with these indigenous peoples. The *Taiping huanyuji*, citing
a Tang source, reports that the local people in ancient times "belonged to the
snake class. There were five surnames. Those called Lin and Huang are their
descendants." In what would become an enduring pattern of state efforts to
manage the boat dwellers, in 625 a Tang official sent subordinates to pacify
(*zhaofu*) them, that is, to persuade them to give up piracy and to bestow
titles on their leaders. Later they were asked to pay taxes at half the standard
rate. But they did not renounce their unique lifestyle. "They generally live
aboard boats, linking up at sea, and their locations are not fixed."[46]

As we have seen, a second major influx of population occurred at the
end of the Tang, associated with Wang Shenzhi and his brothers. But this
did not mean the disappearance or assimilation of the boat people or the
highlanders, and there are numerous references to them from the Song. The
most detailed description is by Cai Xiang (1012–67), a native of Xinghua,
south of Fuzhou:

> In Futang [modern Changle county] there are boats on the water, with whole
> families living aboard. In winter cold and summer heat, eating and drinking,
> while sick, when marrying, they do not leave [their boats]. How strange is
> their way of life! Looking at their tastes, they take everything they need from

the water. Day and night they eat their meals from a tray; they are ignorant
of the flavors of cooking. Their clothes are simple; they are ignorant of the
beauty of silks. Their women pin up their hair with thorns; they are ignorant
of cosmetics. They protect themselves with mats and sheds from the wind and
rain; they are ignorant of the benefits of construction. Back and forth they
go through the year, from young to old, passing from life to death. There is
nothing they do in accord with norms. Compared to [the land-dweller who]
conceals the heart of a bandit, seeks profit and searches for good fortune, is
happy in times of good fortune, and exterminated in defeat, who is to say
which is better?

In another text, Cai uses the term Dan to describe these unusual people.[47]

Another distinct group in the Tang sources were the highlanders, the
people who lived "in the mountains and caves." Later sources portray the
establishment of Han administrative control over the highlands in terms of
the pacification of these groups. Thus, the foundation of Gutian county,
which would be placed under the administration of Fuzhou prefecture, is
explained by the submission of people previously outside the control of
the state. The county "originally comprised the mountains and caves [i.e.,
wasteland] of Houguan [county]. In 741, while supervisor-in-chief Li Yaqiu
was serving in the prefecture, the powerful surnames of the caves [led by] Liu
Qiang, Lin Yi and Lin Xibei submitted in succession. So the establishment
of Gutian county was memorialized."[48] But these "powerful surnames of
the caves" remained distinct from the Chinese populace and troublesome,
as revealed by a proclamation issued by Liu Kezhuang (1187–1269):

> Those who [live] on the streams and in the caves belong to more than one
> type. There are the Man, the Yao, the Li, and the Dan. Those in Zhangzhou
> are called the She. . . . The She excel at using poison . . . and practice shifting
> cultivation in the deep mountains, creeping about like rats. The She do not
> fulfill the service levy. She lands are not taxed; the origins of this are long ago.
> Wealthy and powerful families began to enter their territory . . . and take over
> their livelihood. Officials also demanded local products such as honey, tiger
> and monkey skins. The She could not bear it, and petitioned the prefecture
> without relief, so they . . . raided and plundered.[49]

Liu's reference to the service levy and agricultural taxation point to another
aspect of differentiation between Han Chinese and the indigenous peoples
of the region, that is, different liability for tax. This differentiation was
linked to the extension of state power. According to a Ming gazetteer, the
Dan boat-dwellers, unlike the She highlanders, had been liable for regular

taxation after the Tang. But this liability was eliminated in the tenth century, and localities imposed instead a special tax on fishermen and other boats. The Ming established the Fishing Tax Office (*Hebo suo*) to collect a fish tax (*yuke*) from coastal fishermen, according to assessments determined early in the dynasty. But many fishing families evaded the tax, increasing the obligations on those who remained. As a result, the tax collections were first reduced and then commuted.[50] As late as 1629, Minxian is reported to have had a Fishing Tax Office.[51] Thus, another factor shaping differentiation between Han, Dan, and She was the evolving policies of the state and its officials, who, throughout the late imperial period, continued a long-term effort to bring the Dan and the She into civilization, to pacify them, and to subject them to administrative, disciplinary, and fiscal structures.[52]

Although the Dan and She were held in many sources to be descendants of the original inhabitants of the region, stories also circulated that they were descended from the followers of various military and political leaders, forced to disperse to marginal places, such as the waters and highlands, when their ruler was defeated.[53] Thus, in some tenth-century sources, the boat dwellers were associated with the remnants of a defeated Jin warlord.[54] In others, the Dan and She were implicated in the legends of Wang Shenzhi, the founder of the recently fallen Min kingdom.[55] In the Yuan, the Dan were said to be Song loyalists, and in the Ming, remnants of the Mongols. In the Ming and Qing, many Dan considered themselves to descend from the followers of Chen Youliang (1320–63), a military strongman in the declining years of the Yuan. Chen had been defeated and killed by Zhu Yuanzhang at the battle of Lake Boyang in 1363, and his followers dispersed. The legend that Fuzhou's Dan were descended from his followers is recorded in the *Record of the Autumn Waves of the South Bank*, a late Qing description of prostitution in Fuzhou. "For generations it has been said that when Chen Youliang was defeated at Lake Boyang, nine of his followers fled to the land between Lu[zhou] and Hang[zhou], and made their living as boatmen. Their descendants sank into prostitution."[56]

Simple stereotyping might be at the root of the association of the Dan with prostitution and the term by which they have been commonly known, Crooked-Foot (*quti*); the latter because their leg muscles were presumed to be deformed as a result of living their lives on board their boats. But any elderly native of Fuzhou can elaborate on the various types of real discrimination suffered by the Dan. Many Dan informants told me that they were indeed unaccustomed to walking on land because land dwellers would not allow them on shore and would beat them if they were so discovered. Another name for them was "Old Ninety-Five Cents" because when they did come ashore, their money would only be accepted at a substantial discount. The Dan were unable to improve their lot by the most preferred route because they were not allowed to sit for the examinations. In 1729, the Yongzheng emperor had issued an edict forbidding these and other forms of discrimination against the boat people of Guangdong, who were also called Dan. But clearly discrimination and stereotyping persisted, at least informally.[57]

Though Chinese sources typically describe the differences between the Dan and She, and the Chinese against which they were contrasted, as primordial—rooted in different origins and descent and expressed in different language, practices, and political economy—there was considerable fluidity across the divisions that separated them. In the early twentieth century, both She and Dan continued to be perceived as distinct groups, living at the margins of local society, but some were believed to be assimilating to the majority population:

> The origins of the She are unknown. . . . They build dwellings in the deep mountains, living together with their kin. . . . They find matches amongst themselves, and do not intermarry with ordinary people. . . . It is hard for them to make a living; many bind twigs into brooms and carry these to the various markets to sell. Or they endure hard labor doing miscellaneous work, serving the merchants. Their customs are not the same; their language is not the same. For a long time they have been seen as outsiders. In the last few decades, they have gradually assimilated to the locals. Among the Lei and the Lan there are some who sojourn in the provincial capital, and there have been some who participate in the examinations.[58]

The same process of partial assimilation was ascribed to the Dan in another early twentieth-century gazetteer:

> The county has a type of people who live aboard boats and are able to remain deep under water for a long time. They are commonly called Crooked-Foot, a variant of which is pronounced like "beggar." These are in fact the Dan. They live on boats and rafts on the rivers and seas, and are found all over the place. Their floating homes move about with them, so they have no fixed address, but divide up the harbours and bays. Their surnames are mainly Weng, Ou, Chi, Pu, Jiang and Hai. There are some who come ashore and build homes, but they are not accustomed to work as laborers or merchants. They continue to pay the service levy tax. They are the descendants of the

snake.... They have no connection to the people of all the rest of Fujian, who migrated here from the central plains.[59]

There is also evidence of Dan groups settling ashore, usually on marginal lands. In the early twentieth century, the population of the village of Jingpu in northern Nantai was described as follows: "They are all fishing households; only twenty or thirty families of which live ashore."[60]

In one striking example of the fluidity of the divisions between Han and She, in 1898 a man named Zhong Dakun who was compiling his genealogy traveled to Funing, north of Fuzhou. There he learned of the existence of "a type of mountain people" who were enrolled in the tax registers and whose customs differed from those of ordinary people only in their dress. They were known as She and ran into constant difficulties at the hands of the non-She who lived all around. Zhong suggested they alter their style of clothing "to be the same as the majority," and the She enthusiastically responded. There must have been some resistance to their efforts to eliminate their distinctiveness, because the matter came to the attention of a local official who turned to the famous edict of the Yongzheng emperor to support the argument that they should not suffer discrimination.[61]

Despite flexibility in practice, one essential criterion distinguishing Han from Dan and She was the claim of migration from north China. In the next section, I illustrate how the tracing of descent back to a migrant ancestor from north China was used strategically by individuals and groups in the Fuzhou region in the Ming–Qing period to distinguish themselves from Dan and She.

GENEALOGY AND SOCIAL TRANSFORMATION:
THE LUOZHOU CHEN

A variety of reasons might explain the impulse to create a genealogical connection with people who had not previously been considered one's ancestors. The reworking of ancestry was commonly a kind of Confucian social engineering, creating a particular vision of the past to serve as a model for the present and future.[62] It might, as in the case of Zhang Jing, be a matter of building a pool of potential allies among the elite. In Fuzhou, it was very often also a way to make claims about ethnic differentiation. We saw earlier how the devices of uxorilocal marriage and cross-surname adoption could be used in lineage foundation legends to link oneself with another lineage, living elsewhere, perhaps with a different surname. Ultimately, these devices could be used to claim a connection to migrants from north China and thus to distinguish oneself and one's ancestors from the despised indigenous peoples of the Fuzhou region, the Dan and the She. The foundation legends in many Fuzhou area genealogies make use of such devices, but it is rarely clear whether the claim to north China origin is being used to reinforce an existing identification with Han culture or is an attempt to deny a Dan or She identity. In some cases, though, it is possible to deduce which process is at work. The Chen of Luozhou, among the most prominent of Nantai lineages in the late Qing, provide an example. The Luozhou Chen first compiled a printed genealogy in 1763. Chen Ruolin and Chen Baochen, both high officials, wrote prefaces for two subsequent compilations, in 1820 and 1933. As with the Huang genealogy, the successive prefaces show that the foundation legend of the lineage was initially quite tentative and vague, but was elaborated and put on more solid ground with research by successive editors. The Chen foundation legend is simple. Prefaces to all three editions identify the founding ancestor as a certain Juyuan, who settled in Luozhou in the Hongwu period of the early Ming. It was claimed that he had been later awarded an honorific title, by virtue of the official success of one of his descendants, so he is also referred to in the genealogy as [Gentleman for] Summoning (Zhengshi Lang). "Our lineage's settlement in [Luozhou] originated in the previous Ming dynasty with [Gentleman for] Summoning Juyuan. But from where he moved, and to what people he belonged cannot be detailed."[63] All that could be said was that he had moved to Luozhou because he admired the "beauty of its landscape/geomantic virtues" (*fengshui zhi mei*), which as we have seen, is a common euphemism in the genealogies for uxorilocal marriage.[64]

As early as the first edition of the genealogy, a theory about Juyuan's origins was developed. The Chen settlement in Luozhou is called Dianqian (Shopfront). The compilers of the first edition mention a legend that the Luozhou Chen are descended from the Chen of a village called Chendian (Chen Shop), in Changle county. While compiling their genealogy, they visited a number of Chen settlements in surrounding counties. In the genealogy of the Chen of Chendian, they had found a record of a member of the eighteenth generation who also had the honorary title of Gentleman for Summoning. There were discrepancies in the names of his wife and descendants, but these were ignored. The Gentleman for Summoning from Chendian must have been their own founding ancestor Juyuan. This legend could not be verified, so the compilers simply noted that Juyuan had originated in Chendian. They decided that their genealogy should "only begin with the first ancestor who migrated [to Luozhou], and not dare pursue where he comes from."[65] The Chendian legend is not mentioned in Chen Ruolin's nineteenth-century preface, but it reappears in Chen Baochen's twentieth-century version, now transformed from legend into confirmed truth. The old genealogy "mentions Yuxi, Jingmen, and Chendian villages. I visited these ancestral halls to consult their genealogies and verify the truth. The origins of founding ancestor [Gentleman for] Summoning will never be forgotten—this is the work of the genealogy."[66]

Chendian is now a very poor and isolated village. When I visited, I was told that their genealogy was destroyed in the Cultural Revolution, and that only a fragmentary account of one family, compiled by a lineage member living in Taiwan, now survives. This work offers two explanations of their descent line. The first traces them back to the Chen of Yingchuan, Henan province, a choronym widely shared by Chen lineages throughout southeast China.[67] Their ancestors were part of the great southward flight of noble families in the fourth century. A later descendant, Chen Baxian, was the founder of the Chen dynasty. His great-grandson Chen Yuanguang served as an official in Xinghua, from whence his descendants moved to their current home in the Fuzhou region. The second version, which simply states that the founding ancestor of the lineage moved from Gushi to Changle, links the Chen to that great, late Tang migration to Fujian associated with Wang Shenzhi.[68] The oral tradition of the lineage, which elderly villagers are adamant was verified by the old genealogy, also holds that their ancestors migrated from Gushi county to Fujian in the train of Wang Shenzhi.

But the oral traditions of the Chen of Luozhou provide a very different perspective on their origins, one that ties them to the Dan boat people. Recall that Chen Youliang was widely considered to be the progenitor of the Dan people in Ming and Qing times. In 1994, while traveling to a ritual celebration in which the Chen of Chendian would also be represented, one of my informants from Luozhou explained that I should not put much stock in the connection between his lineage and the Chendian Chen:

> The relationship between us and them is false. We do not really belong to the same line. To tell the truth, our founding ancestor was Chen Youliang. Doesn't it say in the genealogy that our founding ancestor moved to Luozhou

in the time of Zhu Yuanzhang? After Chen Youliang was defeated by Zhu Yuanzhang, he fled here, to Luozhou, to hide out. If anyone had known that he was Chen Youliang, Zhu Yuanzhang would have had him killed. So he pretended to be from Changle. It's not really true.

This story is widely known among the men of the older generation of the Luozhou Chen. Local historians have also recorded that when the Luozhou Chen ancestral hall was desecrated in the Anti-Four Olds campaign in the 1960s, a document was discovered in one of the ancestral altars that confirmed the Chen were the descendants of Chen Youliang.[69] The oral version of the Luozhou Chen foundation myth is thus a claim to Dan origins.

A passage in the Luozhou village gazetteer supports this argument that the Chen were once Dan boat dwellers. The text suggests that the Chen had once sought to free themselves from the obligation to pay the fish tax that was levied on the Dan. It was through the efforts of Chen Changlie, who lived in the sixteenth or seventeenth century, that they were relieved of this obligation.

> Chen Changlie was the headman (*baozheng*) of the island.[70] There were previously no households on the island [Luozhou] registered as fishermen households [for the purpose of allocation of tax responsibility]. Profit-seekers appropriated the boat licenses, distributed them through the ward (*tu*), and took responsibility for tax payment.[71] When the fish tax was imposed, there were no tax rolls. The headman served as nominal taxpayer. He allocated the tax due among the [people of] the ward. The tax was called the fish tax, so the gentry, the old and the weak were not given allocations. [Responsibility] was allocated to the descendants of boat people. The farmers of the southern fields and the rest of the population bore the burden. Moreover, the situation of the gentry, the old and the weak was not fixed, and there were frequently calls to adjust [the allocations]. There were even troubling remarks that the tax payments had been muddied, which made difficulties for the headman. When Changlie took on the position of headman, he was troubled and said, "There are not even any fishermen, and the tax is not fixed on specific fishermen. These allocations and adjustments vex every household. I cannot bear to accept this." So he got together with the other headmen and hurried to report this. The official magnanimously permitted [their exemption from the tax]. So they carved a stone record so that the [runners of the] county *yamen* should forever respect [this decision].[72]

Chen's biography suggests that he tried successfully to relieve the local people from an obligation to pay the fish tax, a levy on Dan households, collected by the Fishing Tax Office. Evidently, the unit of account for the tax was the fishing boat, or rather, the fishing boat license. That the villagers were not at that time enrolled in the regular land tax system but rather were responsible for payment of this fish tax indicates that they were or had been boat-dwelling Dan. As they had settled ashore and taken up agriculture, the allocation of tax responsibility to individual fishing boats clearly no longer bore any relationship to the real situation, hence the opportunity for profit-seekers to enrich themselves by allocating the individual boat licenses. Moreover, many of the islanders were now farming. They had struggled with the survival of the fish tax allocations until Chen Changlie decided to renegotiate their status with the local magistrate. Chen might have requested that the population be allowed to register for the regular land tax in exchange for exemption from the fish tax. However, he did not, which suggests that the islanders were already paying the land tax, and his efforts were actually directed at simply sloughing off the remnants of their former status. The implication of Chen's biography is that he and the other residents of Luozhou were in the process of transforming their relationship with the state and of denying their status as Dan. This was but one aspect of the larger transition from Dan to non-Dan. Another aspect was the tracing of their descent, via uxorilocal marriage, back to the Chen of Chendian and thence back to a distant migrant from north China. It was a way of rewriting their own history as part of the larger strategy, eliminating their debased Dan status in the domain of ancestry just as Chen Changlie had eliminated it in the domain of taxation. Since the narrative of descent from Chen Youliang persists in the oral tradition, it is not really correct to say that they eliminated this ancestry. Rather, they have two, or at least two, narratives of descent, only one of which appears in writing.

The Liu of Jiangzhong, an island of alluvial sands in the Min River just off Luozhou, present another example of the tracing of descent as an instrument in the denial of status associated with the Dan and the assertion of Han identity. The Liu ancestors are said to have lived in boats moored off the town of Luozhou since the late Ming. In 1834, a Liu household built the first dwelling on the sands, reclaimed the land, and began farming. Together with the residents of nearby Menkou, another settlement in the sands, they constructed a temple and a dragon boat to compete in the annual races.[73] Informants in Luozhou and other nearby villages insist, and indeed members of the Jiangzhong Liu themselves admit, that their origins are as Dan fishermen. But their genealogy traces a founding ancestor who was a land-dwelling member of the prominent Liu of Fenggang, a lineage of impeccable pedigree that in turn traces its ancestry back to the ninth-century migration from central China. The Liu of Jiangzhong are thus undergoing the same transformation from Dan to non-Dan. They have constructed a plausible narrative of descent that explains their migration to the region; they have not yet forgotten, nor have their neighbors allowed them to forget, their origins as despised Dan.

CONCLUSION

When we see evidence for uxorilocal marriage and non-agnatic adoption in household registers or in contemporary ethnography, we can be reasonably sure that what is being recorded involves the physical movement of individuals and the transfer of different kinds of rights between people and households. But when we read of these phenomena in the genealogies, I suspect we are often actually reading arguments about the tracing of descent after the fact. The genealogies show that throughout the late imperial period uxorilocal marriage and cross-surname adoption were widespread not only as practice, that is, involving the actual physical transfer of individuals and the transfers of rights over individuals, but also in the form of rhetorical strategies, that is, involving claims about the physical transfer of individuals and the transfers of rights over individuals rather than actual transfers. Specifically, uxorilocal marriage and non-agnatic adoption provided the basis for legends of settlement and for explaining how and why certain groups came to live in certain settlements and to have certain surnames. Uxorilocal marriage and cross-surname adoption provided plausible explanations for creating agnatic kinship in a context which attached great social importance to it. The inclusion of uxorilocal marriage and cross-surname adoption in the repertoire of socially accepted practice created potential for tracing descent in strategic ways. The case of Zhang Jing shows that even within a single family, not everyone necessarily agreed that such a claim was good strategy. It was hard to know how best to serve one's ancestors and one's own life chances. Scholars have written much on the Great Rites Controversy that paralyzed the Ming court in the early sixteenth century, but minor rites controversies seem to have been a common occurrence in late imperial China.[74]

Understanding how and why descent tracing was important to Nantai lineages requires a careful reading of the genealogical material and also consideration of the local oral traditions. The thrust of this chapter has been to argue that ethnic labeling and discrimination underlay the tracing of descent by Fuzhou people in the Ming and Qing periods. The descendants of migrants from north China to Fuzhou made claims about their ancestor's migrations as a way of distinguishing themselves from and asserting their higher status than people indigenous to the area. Dan boat people, and perhaps people identified as belonging to other discriminated-against groups, either made similar claims or negotiated with people who had already made such claims, to piggyback themselves onto those claims as part of strategies to avoid the real and symbolic discrimination they suffered. The compilers of genealogies did their utmost to cover their tracks, to present seamless narratives of descent that were not even open to doubt. It would have been literati well versed in the neo-Confucian culture of kinship who were most successful at doing so, and because it was the genealogies that they compiled that were most likely to be printed, and hence most likely to survive, the sources available are particularly difficult to decode.[75]

Claims to truth and falsehood were embedded in the written genealogies themselves. These claims thus form part of a larger picture of the interconnections between agnatic culture and other aspects of the local social environment. A good example comes from the Yang of Huyu. The Yang genealogy was compiled around 1830 and contains the following account:

> Nanshan had previously compiled the genealogy. It is said that in the Ming–Qing transition, mountain bandits rose up everywhere. The Yang surname of Minghang and the bandit leader called Big Hand were of the same mold. They came together to Huyu and plundered. The genealogy was seized and carried away by the Yang of Minghang [and adopted as their own]. For this reason, the generational order of their genealogy is the same as ours [for those generations] prior to the early Qing, while after the early Qing they are very different. We have no contact with them. Fengxi wanted to inspect the old genealogy and went to Minghang to enquire after it. They refused to let him see it. In 1783, I went to Minghang to inspect the genealogy. They told me theirs had been burned up. Furthermore, they falsely claimed that the Huyu [lineage] had moved here from the Minghang. This is truly outrageous talk. Our lineage records from the Ming and Qing as well as oral legends do not mention this. In future, we should not go to Minghang to inspect the genealogy again.[76]

The identification in the Huyu genealogy of the Minghang Yang as mountain bandits raises the intriguing possibility that they were identified at the time as She people. According to this version, what was going on here was not the manipulation of the content of a genealogy but its actual physical seizure and its use in tracing a certain descent narrative.

Since the Song, commentators in Fujian had been skeptical of the widely circulating claims to originate in Henan. How could so many of the local residents really be descended from migrants from Gushi? One frequently given answer was that Wang Shenzhi was from Gushi, and he had favored men from his native place when appointing officers to the Min Kingdom, and so many people had tried to pass themselves off as Gushi natives.[77] An eighteenth-century provincial gazetteer reprints a testament, copied from a Putian genealogy, which dismisses the claim of Gushi origins. Rehearsing the story of Wang Shenzhi's conquest of Fujian with troops from Gushi, the account continues, "Special treatment was thus given to these people of Gushi for reasons of native-place solidarity. For this reason, up to the present day, all the lineages claim they come from Gushi. This is actually indiscriminate and spurious."[78] In the face of widespread falsification, it was important to stress the reliability of one's own tracing of descent. The autobiography of Guo Tang, dated 1469, which appears in the genealogy compiled by Guo Bocang, records,

> When people of Fujian talk of their ancestors, they all say they come from Gushi and Guangzhou. The reason for this is that Wang Xu surrendered Guangzhou and Shouzhou prefectures to Qin Zongquan. Wang Chao and his brothers led the people of Gushi in following him. Then Xu quarreled with Zongquan, so he uprooted the people of these two prefectures and moved south with them. Belonging to this group, Wang Shenzhi came to Fujian. Out of native-place solidarity, he particularly esteemed people from Gushi. In central Fujian, when they talk of surname and lineage, they falsely claim [to come from] Gushi. Only we Guo really do come from [Gushi]. Of that there is no doubt.[79]

Other people's genealogies might be falsified; Guo's own was genuine.

The authors of our sources were well aware that many genealogies, though never their own, fictionalized the tracing of descent back to a migrant from north China. They misunderstood the real reason for this, which lay not in the Tang but in their own time. A north China ancestor was a way to make and support claims about self-differentiation, distinguishing oneself from the indigenous peoples of the Fuzhou region and associating oneself with the Chinese culture that was presumed to have been imported from outside the region. The authors of genealogies that were traced back to Gushi were thus grappling onto particular markers of identity, appropriating language of inclusion and exclusion.[80] Tracing descent back to north China was an assertion of connection to Chinese culture and a denial of the low status of those outside that culture, those presumed to descend from the indigenous peoples of the region, the Dan and the She. As with other invented traditions, genealogy represents "an attempt to establish continuity with a suitable historical past."[81] But tracing descent through the compilation of genealogy was only part of the broader practice of kinship. In the next chapter, I begin to explore other ways in which kinship was practiced, ways which were shaped by other elements of the larger history in which meanings and institutions became attached to kinship.

THREE

Organizing Kin: The *Lijia* and the Lineage

Local understandings of the geography and settlement of Nantai illustrate the important role played by the practices of patrilineal kinship in structuring economic activity before 1949. Old men from Nantai villages can still recall the owners of the alluvial islands in the Min River surrounding Nantai. Many islands were owned collectively by, and named for, local lineages or by specific branches within lineages. The villagers also recall associations, many of them linked to the worship of a particular deity, that were formed by groups of male cousins and that served as vehicles for the pooling of funds for investment purposes.[1]

In the previous chapter, I showed how genealogical tracing was used by the people of Fuzhou in late imperial times to create ties to other people on the basis of claims of common ancestry. It is one thing to know or to claim that one is related to someone; it is quite another to attach practical significance to the connection. In this chapter, I explore some of the ways that ties based on kinship principles became socially significant and were institutionalized as part of strategies for dealing with changes in local society. In the early Ming, agnatic kinship took on new significance in the lives of the people of the Fuzhou region—as a mode for the assessment and distribution of various rights and responsibilities. Agnatic kinship emerged as the basis on which groups in local society organized themselves to deal with the responsibilities imposed by the Ming household registration and tax and labor service systems.

Maurice Freedman suggested that because institutionalized kinship served to promote mutual assistance and unified action, lineages flourished in south China, where the weakness of government power encouraged the formation of social structures for mutual protection and defense.[2] Historians responded to Freedman's explanation with the counterargument that lineage organization should be understood as the product of elite efforts either to protect their resources or to impose on the populace, with the support of the state, the cultural hegemony of their own neo-Confucian model of social organization.[3] In this chapter, I argue that in the Fuzhou region it was not the absence of the state but rather its presence that drove the construction of kinship organization in the Ming and Qing. Moreover, there were powerful forces driving the articulation of kinship organization that came not from the top of the social order but from the bottom. In the Fuzhou region, groups of agnatic kin organized themselves to deal with the implications of state policies of the early Ming. Individuals and groups in local society who could not claim exemption from taxation devised a complex of strategies to respond effectively to the system of taxation and population registration established in the Ming. These strategies persisted into the Qing and beyond. This chapter also considers two other economic factors that generated strategies of kinship organization. The fundamental principle governing the transmission of property, partible inheritance, might have suited an economy based on stable landholding, but it was inadequate to deal with the effects of commercialization and reclamation of alluvial land. Where household estates included not just land but also commercial enterprises, it was inefficient and sometimes even impossible simply to divide the estate between the sons of the household head. Similarly, where a household estate consisted of the rights to a stretch of foreshore or an alluvial island that was constantly altering in size and value because of flooding and reclamation efforts, trying to divide the estate into equal shares was a recipe for conflict. In both cases, more complex kinship organizations arose out of efforts to respond effectively to these challenges. But there was nothing inevitable about the creation or formalization of organizations of kin. It was a strategy generated by particular social and economic circumstances. As I show in the last part of this chapter, where kinship organizations did not make sense to their members, such organizations disappeared or could even be deliberately dissolved. Thus the patterns that by the mid-Qing had given rise to what has been labeled lineage society should not obscure the real picture of competition, and even conflict, over how groups in society should be organized and how kinship should be practiced.

MING POLICIES OF REGISTRATION AND TAXATION

Historians have long been struck by the activism and interventionism of the early Ming. Hoping to create a secure and stable rural order, the Hongwu emperor implemented policies that can even be compared fruitfully to twentieth-century efforts at state building through the deeper penetration of the state into local society. At the heart of these policies were the division of the populace into hereditary occupational registrations—the most important being commoner, military, and artisan—and the creation of a tax system founded on two principles: that agriculture should serve as the chief source of state revenue and that all adult males should be liable for government service.[4] These two sets of policies had profound effects on Fuzhou society, whose members devised complex strategies to best respond to them. In both cases, successful strategies involved the organization and cooperation of groups of kin.

Military Registration (Junhu)

In the early Ming, large numbers of families in Fujian were registered as soldier-households, responsible for providing troops for coastal security. According to He Qiaoyuan, writing in the late Ming:

> Of the seven types of household registration, commoner and military are the most important. There are about one-third as many military households as commoner households, and the number of individual members is about half the number of those in [households] with commoner registration. Why is it that there are half as many [people registered in] military households as in commoner households? It is because in the early period of the dynasty, when there was concern that the number of military registrations was insufficient, from every family with three adult males (ding), one was conscripted. Those who committed crimes were also often registered [as military households],

such that fathers could not avoid being separated from their sons, and brothers from their brothers.[5]

Gazetteers and genealogies nationwide are rich in cases of conscription in the early Ming. In Fuzhou, Zheng Tianrui, who lived near Chengmen, "substituted for his brother when men were conscripted for military service" in the early Ming. Chen Dongzhu of the Nanyang Chen was "drafted into the Yongning garrison because of the policy of conscription." Conscription is sometimes invoked as an explanation for migration to Fujian. For example, the ancestors of the Pingyang Chen lived in Zhejiang. In the early Ming, one ancestor refused a call to serve in government, preferring to live as a recluse. "The Hongwu emperor was angered that he would not serve, and so conscripted his third son Fuyi to serve in the military in Fujian. After some time, he returned to [Zhejiang]. Then fourth son Yaji was conscripted and sent to Fujian."[6]

Detailed population registers for Fuzhou do not survive from the Ming, but He Qiaoyuan's estimate that as many as one-quarter of all registered households and one-third of the total population were registered in the military seems remarkably high. One possible explanation is that military registration was intended not just to build the strength of the army and navy but also as a means to control segments of the population, such as the Dan, that were believed to be potentially unruly. State officials had sought ways to keep track of the Dan and the She since the seventh century.[7] Local authorities elsewhere in China in the early Ming dealt with the potential threat of the unregulated Dan by drafting them into the military. Thus, in 1383, an official in Guangdong was ordered "to register ten thousand Dan in Guangzhou in the navy. At that time, the Dan moored by the islands and in the bays and had no fixed abode. Some became bandits. It therefore [was decreed] that they should be registered and put into the service [of the state]."[8] Similar policies may also have been implemented in Fujian in the Ming; such efforts were certainly made in the Qing. In the early Kangxi period, for example, the provincial governor authorized a plan to "unite the fishing boats" and recruit some three thousand "village braves and people of the harbors" to serve in the naval forces.[9]

Registration as a military household did not imply that all members of that household were soldiers. Rather, it signified the responsibility of the household as a whole to furnish one soldier and to fulfill various obligations such as provisioning the military unit to which this soldier was assigned with equipment and agricultural produce. If a military-registered household failed to provide an able-bodied soldier, a Troop Purifying Censor would be dispatched to investigate. The activities of these investigators were discussed in a fifteenth-century letter sent by a man from Xianyou to the Fujian vice-commissioner of administration:

> Last year an order was given to the army to replace 30 percent of all deserters. . . . Guo of the Imperial Bodyguard had just been appointed in Fujian. He hoped to make an outstanding contribution in order to raise his status. In carrying out this order, he beat anyone who had held the position of village elder (*lilao*) in the last ten years nearly to death. He beat them incessantly from morning to night, insisting that the 30 percent quota be met. Some households of old men and women had no adult males able to serve in the army. Their sons-in-law were made to report [for service]. These were called "soldiers by virtue of being a son-in-law" (*nüxu jun*). There were cases of [someone being chosen from among] the descendants of those who had previously been registered in the military on the basis of their genealogical records. These were called "soldiers by virtue of having the same surname" (*tongxing jun*). There were cases of people who had purchased the land of soldiers who had left no posterity, and other people who wanted to acquire their land reported them. These were called "soldiers by virtue of having acquired property" (*deye jun*). People were beaten from morning till night, until the quota was met. . . . The village elders' families had no more adult males in their household and all their property was gone before they heard the end of it.[10]

Registration as a military household was hereditary, and such households were forbidden to divide their registration. This made sense in the context of the system. If the multiple sons of the head of a military-registered household, responsible for furnishing a single soldier, divided the household and registered individually, it would be unthinkable that each son should now be expected to furnish a single soldier, effectively multiplying the obligation. But if the original obligation remained, this made the task of the responsible authorities hopelessly complicated. How would the Troop Purifying Censors determine which son's household was required to produce a soldier? From the perspective of the authorities, it was far easier simply to forbid the division of the original household. Regardless of the actual living arrangements of the descendants of that household, whether they lived as a single household or maintained a number of separate domestic and economic units, it was up to them collectively to make sure that there was always a soldier at his post.

The commutation of personal service obligations, which was an important aspect of the monetization of the economy in the Ming, also took place in the military realm, with a hereditary army increasingly giving way to a professional one. Formally, state officials accepted the substitution of monetary payment for military service and used the income to hire mercenaries. Informally, military-registered households hired mercenaries themselves to fulfill their obligations.[11] Tu Zhiyao, a provincial graduate (*juren*) of 1654, described as follows the situation in the Wan'an battalion in Fuqing in the late Ming:

> When the Wan'an battalion was established [in the late fourteenth century], the Tu, Hou and Ke surnames were the largest. They all speak Quanzhou dialect, while a few *li* beyond the walls [of the fort the people speak the local] Fuqing dialect. Every military household at first [provided] only one person to serve in the military. Afterwards the descendants became numerous. Some were wealthy, so they had a bondservant fulfill the military obligation, while the other descendants performed one of the four occupations and did not serve in the military. Within the jurisdiction of the garrison, they were called surplus military (*junyu*). The surplus military intermarried with the common people.[12]

Guo Bocang's own family history provides an illustration of how a particular group of kin developed strategies of organization in response to these various aspects of the military registration system. Guo's early ancestor Yao was said to have settled in the village of Zelang in Fuqing county in the Yuan. The document of household division of Yao's grandson, Yuanxian, dated 1374 and discovered centuries later by a descendant, tells us that Yuanxian registered with the local authorities as a tax-paying household in the early Ming and had three sons and one daughter. After his death, his estate was divided among the three sons[13] (Figure 3.1).

Though the document of division indicates that Yuanxian's three sons now each maintained a separate household, they did not report the division of the original household to the authorities but rather remained under the single registration established by Yuanxian. Some twenty years later, the whole family became implicated in a serious criminal matter. In 1395, a police officer stationed at Zelang fort murdered the county magistrate of Fuqing. Yuanxian's son Jianlang was involved. As punishment, his family's registration was converted to that of a hereditary military household. Initially, Jianlang personally fulfilled the obligation to provide an able-bodied soldier. He was conscripted into a local garrison and later transferred to a post in

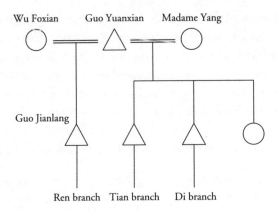

Figure 3.1. Descent Line of Guo Yuanxian.

far-off Xi'an. Jianlang had by this time married and had a son, who remained behind in Fuqing. In 1405, Jianlang died at his post, and the family was called upon to provide a replacement.

At the time, Jianlang's son was either dead or unwell, the evidence is contradictory, and his grandson was still an infant. We can imagine the consequences for Jianlang's relatives, who expected the imminent arrival of a Troop Purifying Censor to conscript a replacement. Jianlang's brothers scrambled to resolve the situation by providing a replacement for Jianlang, thereby foreclosing the possibility that they might collectively be called to account for "desertion." All of the adult male descendants of Yuanxian gathered and drew lots to see who should enter military service. A certain Wei was the unlucky one, and he was sent off to fill Jianlang's post in Xi'an. He probably did not go willingly, for an account of the incident records that "the whole lineage appreciated his righteous actions, so they gave him a reward to encourage him." It appears that he may also have tried to disguise his origins to relieve the family of the responsibility to furnish a replacement when in time Wei himself grew old. "After he entered the army, on his own authority Wei altered the name on the registration from Guo Jian[lang] to [Guo?] Guiqing."

In addition to the responsibility of providing a soldier, registration as a military household involved the responsibility of providing funds for his expenses. In 1416, Guo Wei returned from the north to collect those funds. But, having accepted the duty ten years earlier of serving in the military, he now seems to have used this visit as an opportunity to engage in extortion against the kinfolk who had decided his fate. He was given fifty taels, but "he was required to personally write a receipt, guaranteeing that he would not come back to the ancestral home to try and get more money." When Wei returned to Shaanxi, he took with him his younger brother. At this point, the relatives in Fuqing seem to have lost track of both men. They had numerous descendants, but the genealogy provides few details.

Over a century later, in 1522, Wei's great-grandson Biao together with two other soldiers came back from Shaanxi to Fujian. In the intervening years, his relatives in Fuqing had fallen victim to extortion from another direction. A neighbor who was responsible for keeping the local population records used the pretext that the Guo had been remiss in fulfilling their obligations as a military-registered household to extort money from them. "Biao reported that our family had members in Shaanxi who fulfilled the responsibility, so it was unnecessary to conscript someone in the place of original registration. He reported this to the county [magistrate] and brought back a certificate of proof." This service further increased the debt of obligation that Yuanxian's descendants collectively owed to the descendants of Wei. Just as not all of Yuanxian's descendants were soldiers, not all of Wei's were either. Biao's great-grandson was a merchant. In 1575, he came to Jianyang on business and took advantage of the opportunity to visit the ancestral home. Either in response to demands for repayment of that debt, or perhaps to forestall such demands, the relatives in Fuqing raised eleven taels that they handed over to him. He returned four years later and may have been given more money at that time.[14]

The aftershocks of the initial registration as a military household lingered into the seventeenth century. By this time, fleeing pirate attacks along the coast, all of the descendants of Yuanxian had moved away from their ancestral home—many of them to the comparative safety of Fuzhou city. In 1603, soldiers from the north tracked them down in Fuzhou and demanded further payments. Zhike, a member of the eleventh generation, gathered all the relevant evidence to forestall their demands. "I showed them the family contract, so that they would understand that their military service is due to their inherited obligations. It is not a matter of [our] being unfair. They should not come and demand money from us."[15]

The consequences of Jianlang's criminal involvement, and his family's subsequent registration as a military household, thus extended over a period of more than two hundred years. All of the descendants of Jianlang's father, Yuanxian, were affected by the transfer of registration and were forced to devise strategies in response. In short, they were forced to organize. In the first phase of this organization, Yuanxian's descendants had to come up with an acceptable method to find a replacement conscript for the recently deceased Jianlang. The solution involved a lottery and also the pooling of funds to ensure that the person selected in the lottery would actually fulfill the responsibility. This was not the end of the matter, though, for the conscripted soldier continued to make repeated financial demands on his kin back in Fuqing. Because it would have been potentially disastrous had the soldier deserted, these kin had no choice but to maintain some kind of organization to ensure that these demands be met. Moreover, as the incident of 1522 shows, Yuanxian's descendants in Fuqing were also forced to organize in response to blackmail from powerful local people who claimed that they were not fulfilling their hereditary military responsibilities. Even after most of Yuanxian's descendants had actually fled Fuqing for Fuzhou, the consequences of their hereditary registration continued to haunt them and to shape strategies that required them to organize and stay organized.

Another case of a group of kin organizing themselves to respond to the system of hereditary military registration is the Lin of Zhuti, in Changle county. This case is particularly interesting, since the strategies that were devised included uxorilocal marriage, surname changes, and a subsequent application to "restore the surname." The details are found in the genealogy of the Lin of Zhuti. Unfortunately, the surviving handwritten copy of this work is badly decayed, having been damaged by water and insects. The most recent preface of the genealogy that can be deciphered is dated 1535 and is by Nanjing Minister of Works Lin Tingxuan (*jinshi* 1482), but the current edition of the genealogy probably dates from the late sixteenth or early seventeenth century.[16]

Lin Tingxuan knew little of his early ancestry and admitted as much. He traced his ancestry back to the first legendary north Chinese migration into Fujian, claiming descent from a Jin general who had settled in Quanzhou. The general's descendants attained considerable prominence, and one of them later moved to Changle. Unfortunately, because of "military turmoil," all genealogical records had been lost, and so Tingxuan's genealogy was based entirely on the data contained on spirit tablets in his ancestral shrine. The first ancestor about whom Tingxuan could provide details was his great-great-great-grandfather, who lived from 1302 to 1344. According to Tingxuan's account, this man had three sons, the youngest of whom, Haosheng, was Tingxuan's great-great-grandfather. In a 1492 petition to "restore his surname" back to Lin, Tingxuan claimed that Haosheng had married the daughter of Huang Xiuqing of Zhuti. They had two sons, Yiliang and

Guangrong, before Haosheng's premature death. Because his father-in-law Huang Xiuqing had no male heir, he forced the boys to change their surname from Lin to Huang and recorded them in the household registers as his heirs.[17] Some time later, Huang Xiuqing finally produced his own heir, Huang Shenliang.

Yiliang and Guangrong must have lived in the late Yuan. According to the "Collective Agreement on Military Matters," a document dated 1570 and reprinted in the genealogy, the family's status was converted to military registration in the early Ming:

> Because of the matter of pirate defence, in 1392 Huang Zhulang was conscripted to serve as a soldier of the Meihua battalion of the Zhendong Guard. In 1394, he was transferred to the Gaopu battalion of the Yongning Guard, under the command of the Wang'an company commander, which had hitherto been stationed at sea. The original household registration was divided into eight branches, which provided a subsidy of 2.4 taels in annual rotation. In 1501, Huang Zhong took over the service obligation. Lineage uncle Tingxuan went on his behalf to the Dinghai Circuit [office] to request that he be relieved of the duty at sea. This boon was granted, and [Zhong] was allowed to remain in the barracks fulfilling the duty of head of the flag [-bearers?] (*qijia*). In 1506, Tingxuan reflected on his observation that the descendants in the original registration were impoverished and in difficult straits. He personally used his surplus funds to purchase fourteen *mu* of military fields, located at Xiting in sector (*du*) 5. Out of the income of the fields, once the annual tax payment was made, there remained 4.1 taels, which was to be used by the whole lineage to meet the costs of the subsidy for military expenses. In 1516 Huang Zhong fell ill and died. Huang Tong replaced him in fulfilling the military service obligation, and undertook the management of the rental property.[18]

This document sheds new light on Tingxuan's desire to "restore the surname." The genealogical charts of Lin Haosheng's descendants no longer survive, but the simplified picture in Figure 3.2 can be reconstructed from other texts in the genealogy. Important questions remain unanswered but the gist of the situation is clear. At the time when Zhulang was conscripted, and his family was registered as a hereditary military household, he was still under the registration of his maternal great-grandfather Huang Xiuqing, and it was the household registered under the name of Huang Xiuqing that was assigned the military registration. As a result, the descendants of Huang Xiuqing, including Tingxuan and his immediate relatives, inherited the responsibility of supplying one full-time soldier to the military. Xiuqing's descendants were

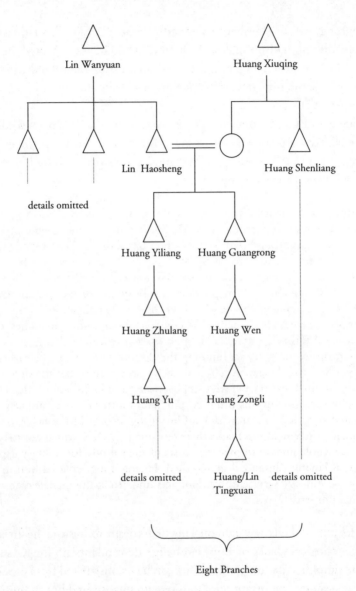

Figure 3.2. Descent Line of Huang Tingxuan.

divided into eight branches. In practice, a single member of the descent group personally fulfilled the military responsibility, and his relatives paid him for this service. The annual rotation through the eight branches was an organization to administer the responsibility for this payment. The arrangement was not a completely stable one. The danger always existed that someone would shirk his responsibility by not making the appropriate payment when it was his turn in the rotation. This would have been of particular concern to the wealthier members of the group, who would probably be expected to make up for the shortfall. Moreover, there was also the possibility that the soldier might flee his post and that a Troop Purifying Censor would descend on his relatives to demand a replacement.

As Tingxuan rose to prominence, he found the situation problematic for another reason. The soldier who was personally fulfilling the service obligation put pressure on Tingxuan to intervene on his behalf and have him reassigned to less onerous duties. Tingxuan's strategy for dealing with these problems was twofold. First, he established a permanent estate to support the payment of the stipend and handed the management of this estate over to the recipient, the soldier himself. Second, he tried to "restore his surname" in hopes of obscuring or denying his connection with the hereditary military obligation. Tingxuan's petition is probably not entirely truthful. Obviously, his ancestor Haosheng had married uxorilocally into the family of Huang Xiuqing. His claim that Xiuqing had forced Haosheng's two sons to change their surname to Huang obscures the fact that this uxorilocal marriage had been undertaken voluntarily, that is, Haosheng had agreed by the uxorilocal marriage that his sons would bear the Huang surname. Since it was Xiuqing's household that had been transferred to military registration, it was his son Huang Shenliang who should inherit the registration. Yiliang and Guangrong really belonged to a separate registration and, after all, were not patrilineal descendants of Xiuqing's household. The descendants of Yiliang and Guangrong had been good enough to fulfill a share of the hereditary responsibility, but now that Tingxuan had set up a permanent fund to meet that responsibility, it was no longer necessary for these descendants to have any involvement. "Restoring the surname" was thus a denial of the obligation to provide military service by denying a kinship connection with the descent group whose registration as a military household was what had brought about this obligation.

Tingxuan's petition was accepted, and his surname was changed from Huang to Lin. But his efforts to shake off hereditary responsibility were not entirely successful, as the conclusion of the "Collective Agreement on Military Matters" indicates:

In 1532, Commander Yu ordered that all those who were formerly liable for duty at sea must return to their original post. [Huang Tong] came to the family complaining of the difficulties of being stationed at sea. So the lineage members agreed that 3.75 *mu* of the sacrificial estate . . . with an income totalling 15 piculs, and on which the rent was 47 catties per picul, should be given over to the person who was fulfilling the military service obligation, in order to meet the expenses of being stationed at sea. The soldier himself was to have the management of these properties that had been set aside, and was responsible for the annual tax payment. The ancestral family was not liable. As for the Soldier's Eight-tenth Rice (*fubing miba*) [another tax to pay military expenses], this was the responsibility of the ancestral family, and the soldier is not liable. When Huang Tong grew old, his grandnephew Huang Kun took over the obligation. He is not to shirk it, nor is he to add to the worries of the ancestral family. In all, the fields total 17.75 *mu*, which are given over to the soldiers fulfilling the military obligation to manage in rotation. They may not sell it off for their own private benefit.[19]

Clearly, despite Lin Tingxuan's efforts to cut off his connection with the military obligation associated with the household originally registered under the name of Huang Xiuqing, the persons fulfilling that obligation continued to trouble him and his relatives for subsidies. Their demands could not be ignored, and a further attempt to institutionalize and fix the family's commitments was made. It appears that with this second transfer of property rights, the claim to kinship connections was satisfied. The Lin family had finally freed themselves of the inconvenience of a connection to the Huang. Tingxuan's edition of the genealogy was obviously intended to explain and to justify the severing of this connection.

In the Fuzhou region, over the whole of the Ming dynasty, the descendants of those conscripted into hereditary military registration were forced to organize into corporate patrilineal groups in response to the exigencies of the state's population registration system. From their initial registration as a military household, the Guo of Zelang and the Lin of Zhuti had to develop strategies to ensure the fulfillment of their collective obligations to provide military service. The pattern of organization that resulted was but one variant of a broader trend whereby hereditary military households came to hire substitutes to fulfill their obligations. In the cases of the Guo and the Lin, both groups in effect hired the mercenary from within their own family. The system of hereditary military registration in the Ming thus affected the meaning and practice of kinship in the Fuzhou region in two ways. On the one hand, laws associated with military registration required that, regardless of their actual living arrangements, individuals and families patrilineally descended from an ancestor who had been given a military registration remain under a single common household registration. On the other hand, again regardless of actual living arrangements, these individuals and families were forced to organize themselves to ensure that the military obligations were being fulfilled, thereby avoiding trouble with the authorities. For the descendants of Yuanxian, this meant, in the first instance, organizing for the selection of the household member who would actually serve in the military and, in the long term, organizing to raise the funds necessary to keep that household member, or his descendant or other delegate, in place. It also required the maintenance of clear genealogical and other records to ensure that, in the event of future complications, the household members who remained in Fujian could prove that the household as a whole was not defaulting on its obligations. For the descendants of Lin Haosheng, this meant establishing capital in the form of land, the income from which could be used to meet the expenses of the soldier. Later, there were complex machinations and manipulations of kinship to conceal the collective responsibility that underlay the establishment of this capital. In both cases, the organization was formed not at the behest of members of the educated elite, and not to emulate some model of neo-Confucian kinship organization, but rather by ordinary folk searching for ways to respond to the powerful but malleable demands of the state. The organization that resulted was not a gentry-style lineage oriented around an ancestral hall in the official style, but it was nonetheless certainly a corporate kinship group tracing common descent, that is, a lineage.

Commoner Registration (Minhu)

Military registration was a special case in the Ming population registration system, but the pressures that it generated on families and the organizational responses they devised could be similar throughout the general population. The basic philosophy of the Ming taxation system was that the rural populace provided most essential services to the state. Households under different registrations simply provided different services. The *lijia* was the institution that coordinated the fulfillment of services for ordinary households. The effects of the *lijia*, and the strategies devised by the populace to deal with those effects, were comparable to those that have been demonstrated for military registration.

The *lijia* system as implemented in the reign of the Hongwu emperor divided the population into units called *li*, each consisting of 110 households. Each *li* was further subdivided into ten units called *jia*, each consisting of ten households. Each of the ten *jia* was responsible in a decennial rotation for providing both labor service and material requisitions for state needs for one year. The ten wealthiest households in the *li*, measured in terms of land ownership and number of tax-bearing males (*ding*), were the *jia* heads. Each *jia* head served as *li* head (*lizhang*) in a separate decennial rotation, responsible for overseeing the fulfillment of labor service and other responsibilities. The system was an immensely cumbersome one, which Ray Huang has likened to raising water from a deep well drop by drop, but it fulfilled the state's ideological objective of participatory administration and, by shifting the administrative burden onto the populace, it saved the government considerable overhead.[20]

Liu Zhiwei's recent work on Guangdong makes the important point that the *lijia* system was one of tax allocation and collection and not, as many later historians have mistaken it, one intended to maintain an accurate census of the population. Indeed, the system never encompassed the whole rural population:

> The Ming dynasty used the *lijia* system to organize a portion of society, so that they paid tax to the state and fulfilled labor service duties. In this way, these organized households could obtain the status of good people (*liangmin*), and enjoy many kinds of legal rights. Those who were not registered or who left their registration were not under the control of the dynasty, did not pay tax or provide labor service, but also did not enjoy such rights as legal occupation of land or participation in the examinations.[21]

The system in practice turned out to be vastly more complicated than the principles behind it. In the early Ming, the *lijia* system of population registration was superimposed onto a complex preexisting sub-county administrative system. The terminology of the system is made even more confusing by the use of the term *li*, with the identical character, to refer both to the units of the *lijia* tax and service levy administration, and to a preexisting unit of the sub-county territorial administration, the *li*, or subcanton.[22] Variation in the administrative practices of the three counties that comprised the Fuzhou suburbs created further complications.[23] For the magistrates of all three counties, the most basic geographic subdivision of the county was the ward (*tu*). There were 127 wards in Minxian, sixty-eight in Houguan, and forty-seven in Huai'an in mid-Ming. Although the ward was in principle a territorial unit, it was essentially a unit for registration for taxation. So the demands of rational administration meant that the system of wards functioned best when wards were roughly equalized not in terms of geography but in terms of cultivated acreage and population.[24] Although we have no records of the *lijia* registration figures for the Fuzhou region in the Ming, it appears that when the system was first established, each *lijia* hundred was virtually coterminous with a ward. This made perfect sense because the ward was intended to serve as a unit of territory describing the area farmed by about one thousand people, and the *lijia* hundred was a unit of population that included 110 households.

After the establishment of the *lijia* system in the late fourteenth century, the exactions demanded of *lijia* households grew continually over the early to mid-Ming, reaching a high point in the sixteenth century.

> The service levy obligations of the *lijia* households consisted originally only of pressing for tax payment and assembling labor for public works. Later, they became responsible for meeting various government expenses. They had to take care of the [official] sacrificial expenses, the Village Drinking ritual and the ceremony of Welcoming the Spring, for example. Gradually this extended to paying all kinds of miscellaneous personal expenses of the officials. All kinds of expenses appeared for which there was no basis. As soon as a single document was issued, there was no way to avoid it. Moreover, the secretaries and *yamen* runners also demanded bribes and money in this manner. The *lijia* [households] were pushed into bankruptcy.[25]

Official efforts to deal with these and other problems in the labor service allocation system would eventually culminate in the Single Whip reforms. In the meantime, the heavy pressures led to evasion and efforts to escape from the *lijia* system. As a result, the number of registered households and population actually decreased in Fuzhou in the Ming, something local officials struggled to rationalize:

> From 1391 to 1483, in a period of 92 years, the number of households in our locality declined by 8,896 and that of mouths by 48,250. This means a loss of between 60 and 70 percent. Why is it that after a long period of peace and recuperation there should be such a decline? It is probably because [local officials] were afraid that [reporting] an increase would put a greater burden on the people and they therefore connived at the evasions and omissions without bothering to check.[26]

Though the heavy exactions pressured people to find ways to get around the *lijia* system, there were other factors that encouraged households to maintain their *lijia* registered status. As He Qiaoyuan explained:

At present, those households of the common people which are registered are called officially registered fiscal males (*guanding*) and those which are not registered are called unregistered fiscal males (*siding*). Each officially registered fiscal male must pay approximately three [copper] cash to the authorities. As for the private fiscal males, the local runners determine the numbers of members in the family, the extent of their property, and exact funds [accordingly], in order to meet the expenses of the *yamen*, and other circumstances.[27]

It could be useful to belong to a registered household because the formal tax and labor service responsibilities that registration implied paradoxically served to some degree to insulate one from extortion by *yamen* runners and *lijia* heads. Similarly, despite the higher obligations due from the *lijia* head households, these households had the legal right to pass on their obligations to the households under their jurisdiction. Liu Zhiwei and Katayama Tsuyoshi have shown for the Pearl River Delta that *lijia* registration was also important as a guarantee of legal land ownership rights because it implied obligations to pay tax on specific properties.[28]

Because the *lijia* was an exclusive system, it came to have a social meaning beyond the fiscal realm, as is suggested by a Qing source from Zhangzhou in southern Fujian:

All the *li* heads are households with many members and much property, so they always bully the weaker households. Within the *li* head's household, even the old and the children all refer to themselves as *li* head, treating the heads of the *jia* households as if they were the households of their own children, as if they were people under their control. Even the old and white-haired members of the *jia* households, when they come across the children of the *li* head household, have to use the [respectful] terms of address [appropriate] to a man of a senior generation (*shuhang*). It even comes to the point that when members of the *jia* households die leaving behind sons and daughters, the *li* head household can simply arrange their marriage, or even sell them off.[29]

In principle, the distribution of households was to be reevaluated every ten years, and the assignment of *lizhang* was to be adjusted according to the changing circumstances of the households of the *li*. In practice, household registration in the *lijia* system and the responsibility to serve as *li* head tended to become fixed and even hereditary. The reasons are not difficult to fathom. Since the real interest of the state in compiling the registers was to stabilize the tax base, officials were less concerned about accuracy than continuity in the units liable for tax, the *hu*. This term is usually translated as *household*, a convention that I follow here, but it is important to keep in mind that the *hu* need not have been a group of individuals sharing kinship ties, common residence, and a joint economy. Rather, in late imperial China, *hu* was also an administrative term describing a unit of tax collection. Since the *hu* was the unit by which labor service was assessed, it was not in the interest of the different descendants of a single family to register as separate *hu*, since this would mean an increase in both the total and the individual liabilities.[30] Many scholars have already noted that after the initial compilation of *hu* registers, *hu* as well as the *li* and *jia* that they comprised became "in official discourse... units of fiscal account bearing little relation to actual population." Thus by the late Ming, He Qiaoyuan could write, "When the official registers are compiled, the population is estimated on the basis of the [tax] rice amounts. The figures are not actually accurate measures."[31]

Once the actual situation of the population and the *lijia* registrations had diverged, and in the absence of accurate reassessment, the only way to assure delivery of tax and labor services was to continue to assign them according to the existing registrations and leave it up to local society to find ways to meet the exactions. For example, when early sixteenth-century officials in Fujian implemented a series of surtaxes on the existing land and head taxes, local communities simply devised their own methods to meet the exactions. These efforts are described in Zheng Ji's (1440–1516) "Preface to the New *Lijia* Registers" of Xianyou, south of Fuzhou:

> This year it was my younger brother's turn to serve as *li* head (*lizheng*). He assembled all the other men who were involved in the same matter, so they could devote themselves wholeheartedly to thinking things over. They agreed that to meet the exactions on schedule, they should prepare this register. [For all the obligations from the ceremonies on] the Emperor's Birthday and the Village Drinking ceremony down to the most trivial of labor services, and the various troublesome exactions, the obligations have been assessed and classified by type.... Altogether, the total annual expenses are just under 500 taels. So the annual obligations of each *jia* come to between twenty and thirty taels, only one-seventh or one-eighth of the amount that used to have to be paid [when the obligations were distributed according to a decennial rotation]. After the register was compiled, it was presented to the *yamen*. The one hundred and forty households of this *li* have collectively vowed to uphold it, so it will become the principle by which the annual exactions are met.[32]

Clearly this was a locally inspired attempt to respond to higher taxes. The existing *lijia* heads simply contracted to pay the taxes due, in other words to provide tax collection services, without even pretending to allocate these according to the *lijia* system.

As with the hereditary military obligations discussed earlier, *lijia* status and obligations generated pressure to organize on the patrilineal descendants of ancestors who had registered in the system. The Li of Tangfeng, to the southeast of Nantai, provide a good example.[33] Their genealogy traces descent back to one Huang Youcai, who had married uxorilocally into the Li family in the Yuan dynasty. His first and second sons bore the surname Huang, but his third son was surnamed Li, and the relations between the descendants of the sons remained ambiguous for centuries. A mid-Ming document entitled "Record of Matters Related to the Household Registration," by Li Hengchu, outlines the tax status of those of Youcai's descendants who were surnamed Li. Recall that in the Ming, each ward was roughly coterminous with a *lijia* hundred, and the terms were sometimes used interchangeably. The Li were registered in the seventh *jia* of the second ward of Zhide subcanton of Minxian.[34] The Li served as the *jia* head for the ten households of the seventh *jia*. Eight of the nine remaining *jia* headships in the ward were held by households of a single family, the Lin of Tangfeng.

When the *lijia* system was first implemented in the early Ming, the system worked well. "Local customs were virtuous and the people encouraged honesty and humility." When it was their turn in the decennial rotation to serve as *li* head and take charge of tax collection and transmission, the *jia* heads "anxiously worked for the common good." Because the distribution of obligations across the ten households of the *jia* was fixed by custom, the expenses associated with headship were not excessive, at least not initially:

> When it was the turn of our lineage members to fulfill the current year's labour service obligations, it was not especially difficult. It was not necessary to do a personal inspection of the persons and dwellings [in order to assess them]. Nor did we bear the exceptional burden of paying land taxes on behalf of people who had died. Instead, the money was made up by their surviving relatives, or [the sale of] dwellings and implements, and from wastage fees and capitation charges. . . . In this way, the costs of holding the rotation in a given year could be limited to seventy or eighty taels.[35]

But over time, the allocation of taxes became more difficult. First, there was the general increase, mentioned earlier, in the exactions demanded of *lijia* heads throughout Fujian. A far more serious, purely local problem also arose. In 1583, Lin Cai, of the Lin of Tangfeng, passed the *jinshi* exam.[36] Lin Cai's status gave him a personal exemption from labor service obligations. But many of his relatives who remained in Tangfeng also claimed exemption from *lijia* obligations on the basis of Cai's new status. Not only did this limit their labor service obligations directly, but it also reduced their tax obligations as a whole, and on this basis, they claimed, they were no longer liable to serve as *li* heads in the decennial rotation. Obviously there was no one willing to take on the responsibility in their place, which is hardly surprising given that households of the Lin were required to serve as *li* head in eight of every ten years. The annual burden now fell entirely on the Li, or perhaps partly on the other previous *jia* head in the ward, although no more is heard of them. This meant a huge increase in their tax obligations:

> In addition to the 800 or more cash [formerly due annually], the obligations of our kin for each year for the labor service [now] also include the burden of repeated exactions for the following or successive years. For each period, the expenses come to several taels. What a farmer is able to accumulate over nine years is insufficient to meet the labour service obligations for the single year when it is his turn. Many of the lineage members have been bankrupted or impoverished. This is the painful burden that has resulted from our lineage members having entered the tax registration together with the Lin.

The Li's response to the considerable increase in their tax obligations went through two stages. Initially, the lineage members were divided into ten groups. Ten individuals were named as "Nominal Named [Household Head]" (*zhengming*) and registered as having personal responsibility for taxes due in one year of every ten.[37] When it was his turn in the decennial rotation, the Nominal Named Household Head had to pay all of the *lijia* exactions.[38] The Head then allocated the total amount due for the year to a subgroup of lineage families who were linked to his turn in the rotation. So long as every family paid the amount due when it was their turn in the rotation, they could be confident that they would face no further exactions until the time of their next turn in the cycle. Later in the sixteenth century, local officials would try to implement a similar payment method in parts of Fujian under the name "ten-sectioned tapestry" reform.[39] But the Li were not following official instructions; rather, they devised their own organizational structure to ensure that state exactions were met.

When Hengchu's great-great-grandfather held the position of Head, he tried to adapt the decimal system of Nominal Named Household Heads to better suit local conditions. He met with representatives of each of the three branches of the Li and agreed that each should appoint its own Nominal Named Household Head, who would then be responsible for tax collection from within his own branch. The genealogy does not make the point explicitly, but it is safe to guess that each branch in turn set up an organizational rotation among its member households to ensure that the obligations were even each year. "This was truly a case," wrote Hengchu, "where although the burden could not be shared equally, at least the benefits and suffering were."[40] Just as hereditary military registration had forced patrilineally related kin of the Guo surname to cooperate and set up mechanisms to ensure that the obligations associated with that registration were fulfilled, *lijia* registration led the Li of Tangfeng to organize themselves for the fulfillment of those responsibilities. It was the Ming taxation system that drove this organization.

The *lijia* system would be greatly transformed during the late Ming and Qing. In theory, the Single Whip reforms of the late Ming narrowed and eventually eliminated its functions by attaching the service levies to the land tax. But this did not happen immediately, and there is much evidence that, in the early Qing, at least the costs of tax collection were still being borne by remnants of the original *lijia* registrations in Fujian.[41] The state's methods to register the population for the purposes of tax assessment thus continued to influence the ways in which groups of kin organized themselves. In about 1690, Xing Yongchao, the governor-general of Fujian–Zhejiang, implemented a tax reform known as "allocating tax households to the descent-line" (*lianghu guizong*) or "unifying household registration within the descent-lines" (*guizong hehu*). The reform, which was also put into place elsewhere in south China in the mid-Kangxi period, was another attempt at resolving the old problem of uneven distribution of wealth among the households of each *jia*. This uneven distribution meant that labor service taxation was either unfair, if all *jia* were levied the same amount regardless of their situation, or uneven, if each *jia* was taxed according to its wealth and receipts rose and fell according to the situation of the *jia* liable for each year. Governor-General Xing's solution was to reorganize the *jia* in terms of cultivated acreage. This involved shifting around and clarifying the registration status of each registered household. In Fujian, all households were ordered to affiliate themselves with the household registration established by their Ming ancestor for the purpose of creating the new equalized *jia*. In practice, the reform was played out very differently than its official promulgators had intended. Once all the household registrations had been clarified,

the wealthiest households were assigned *lijia* headships and became responsible for local tax assessment and collection, serving, in effect, as taxation
subcontractors for the magistrate.[42] The effects on local social organization
are illustrated by documents from the genealogy of the Lan of Wangchuan,
Lianjiang county. This is an interesting case that draws together several issues
previously discussed: ethnicity, descent tracing, and registration for taxation.

According to the handwritten genealogy of the Lan of Wangchuan, first
compiled in the early nineteenth century and then recompiled in the 1870s,
their earliest ancestors migrated from Guangdong to Zhangzhou in the Sui,
a claim that is common to many She groups throughout Fujian.[43] In the
Ming, their ancestor Yaoye together with three brothers moved to Cailing
in Lianjiang. Yaoye's family had never registered in the *lijia* system. This
became a cause of some concern, as was expressed by Yaoye's great-grandson
Chaocan:

> We have not yet drawn up a plan for the generations of descendants to
> come. First we must make arrangements for the marriages of the sons and
> daughters in front of us. People think we are temporary sojourners in this
> place, having come from Zhangzhou or Quanzhou. When we are arranging
> marriages, we encounter suspicion because of the dialect difference. . . . It has
> been this way for several generations. Since we have not been entered into the
> official registration, how can we establish property, and how can we arrange
> marriages?[44]

Chaocan's remarks indicate clearly that household registration, although intended for tax purposes, had come to have legal and social implications. The
legal implication was that a member of a registered household could appeal
to the *yamen* if his rightful ownership of registered property was contested,
whereas someone without registration did not enjoy this protection. Thus
household registration served as a mechanism whereby the state guaranteed
the land tenure of registered households in return for their ensuring tax
collection. As a result of this implicit contract, registration became also a
marker of social status, and lack of registration was a corresponding cause
for suspicion, affecting marriage possibilities and strategies. Thus, just as we
saw in Chapter 2 that there might be powerful reasons to attempt to shed
identification as Dan or She, there could also be strong reasons to acquire
lijia registration.

The Lan seem to have first taken steps to become registered in the mid-
seventeenth century, when it was reported that a certain Wu Qianzhang

had sent to the county magistrate a request to be relieved of his household registration, on the grounds that because his family had "few fiscal males and little tax bearing property, it is exceedingly difficult for him to fulfill the labor service levies." The Lan hoped to take over Wu's registration, but nothing came of this initial attempt. What ultimately led to the acquisition of registration was Xing Yongchao's tax reform in the early Qing. The Ming population registers of the county had been lost in the Ming–Qing transition. In 1692 the county magistrate introduced the policy of allocating tax households to the descent line. The Lan were unable to comply with the order to identify the *lijia* registered household from which they were descended, for their ancestors had never been registered in the system.[45] According to a contract preserved in the Lan genealogy, the situation remained unstable, and potentially dangerous, until 1708. In that year, a *lijia* head named Zeng Mingsheng organized a group comprising people of thirteen surnames, including the Lan, to purchase the registration of one of the households in his *jia*, possibly the same Wu household whose registration the Lan had tried to purchase earlier. The implication of the text is that the sale had become necessary because the original holder of the registration could no longer meet his *lijia* obligations.[46] The thirteen names in the contract refer to the founding ancestors of thirteen local lineages. These thirteen lineages paid a small sum of money to the previous holder of the registration and a much larger sum to have the transfer confirmed at the *yamen*. They drew up a contract specifying the distribution of ownership of the registration according to the initial investments of the thirteen participating groups.[47] The share in ownership is expressed in terms of "official fiscal males" (*guanding*). The contract lists the ownership of 114 *guanding*, and the total expenditures came to eighty-seven taels, suggesting that each share represented an initial investment of about three-quarters of a tael. The Lan took responsibility for fifteen shares, each of which was endowed in the name of a particular individual descended from the founding ancestor, Yaoye, and his brothers.[48] The tax obligations associated with the registration were doubtless allocated according to the number of shares held by each group, a point so obvious that the contract does not even mention it.[49]

This official registration thus resembles a corporation, in which investors acquire ownership by investing their money, and their share of ownership depends on the size of their investment relative to the whole. Corporate landowning groups, many of which were dedicated to ancestral sacrifice, were extremely common in late imperial China and Taiwan.[50] Whereas we think of a corporation as a way of owning economic capital such as land, this corporation owned an official household registration; that is, capital of a different kind. Unfortunately, neither the genealogy nor my informants in Wangchuan could provide further information on how the Lan were able to use their registration to their advantage. But as I show in Chapter 6, soon after they acquired the registration, the thirteen surnames constructed an altar to the god of the soil (*shetan*), a privilege restricted to registered households.

The Lianjiang contract provides an interesting example of the convertibility of different types of capital—economic, legal, and symbolic. Though investment in the registration was acceptance of a liability, that is, a portion of the service levy due from the household, its legal and social benefits must have made registration a commodity with value. There was evidently a market for household registration in the Fuzhou region in the late Qing that mediated the supply and demand for this commodity. The actors in this market for household registration were groups that traced descent to a common ancestor and that organized themselves as investors in shareholding corporations when they participated in this market. Such organization was driven not by Confucian ideals and principles nor by frontier conditions but rather by the strategies that the people of the region had evolved for dealing with the imperial state. The policy of allocating tax households to the descent line thus has implications for our understanding of the nature of state control in local society in the Qing. The early Ming *lijia* system was based on place of residence, that is, on territorial principles. But the pressures of that system led local groups to organize themselves on different lines, and they did so through kinship and descent principles. With the policy of allocating the tax households to the descent line, early Qing officials were really adopting the very principles by which society had organized itself and trying to reimpose those principles in ways more satisfactory to state interests. This in turn gave rise to new popular strategies.

The policy of allocating tax burdens to the descent lines also encouraged individuals and groups in one area to reactivate or create ties with other individuals or groups who were already registered for tax payment, sometimes in distant places. In 1697, the magistrate of Zhangpu county in southern Fujian complained that he was rarely able to collect the full amount of a tax nominally allocated to adult males (*ding*). The reason for this was as follows:

Many of the registered *ding* in Zhangpu live in nearby counties. There are also males with Zhangpu registration living as far away as Minxian and Yongfu counties in Fuzhou, and Nan'an in Quanzhou. Their household head goes annually to collect their tax. If they are not able to fulfill his demands then he frequently reports them and asks to have them arrested. When they are asked when they moved away, it may be a hundred years, or two hundred years ago, and the more recent ones [are too numerous] to mention.[51]

The magistrate was unwilling to challenge these claims explicitly, but his implication is that these people had not really migrated from Zhangpu, but simply used the tracing of patrilineal descent as a means of avoiding taxation in their county of residence. Of course, they tried to avoid paying any taxes in Zhangpu as well. Since no ties were maintained between the person responsible for the payment of tax in Zhangpu, the household head, and the putative descendants in Fuzhou prefecture, this organization would not meet any of Watson's criteria for the existence of a lineage, "a *corporate group* which celebrates *ritual unity* and is based on *demonstrated descent* from a common ancestor." But this should not lead us to dismiss the importance of the phenomenon. In response to the demands of the tax and registration system, people in Fuzhou during the Ming and Qing made use of organized patrilineal kinship in different ways. Regardless of the degree of organization or lack of organization that resulted, all of these strategies were forms of kinship practice.

OTHER REASONS TO ORGANIZE: LAND RECLAMATION AND COMMERCIAL ENTERPRISES

Previous scholars have noted that the endowment of corporate estates to support ancestral sacrifice could play an important role in the development of lineage organization. The high level of commercialization and the importance of reclaimed alluvial land in the local economy in the Ming and Qing generated other reasons for formal organizations to be attached to agnatic kinship. Ownership of reclaimed alluvial land, of rights to the coastal and riverine foreshore where further reclamation could be planned, and of commercial enterprises, was an important part of the patrilineal inheritance system. When a household divided its estate, it was relatively straightforward to divide rights to ordinary land.[52] Rights of ownership in alluvial land and commercial enterprises, by contrast, were not at all easy to divide. As a result, these rights often became corporate property owned in common by all the descendants of the ancestor who had first reclaimed the land or established the enterprise.[53] Those who claimed descent from that ancestor had to organize themselves to allocate their rights in and responsibilities arising from this collective inheritance.

The people of the coasts and rivers of the Fuzhou region had long engaged in the reclamation of islands and shoreline.[54] The basic techniques of land reclamation and irrigation have changed little over the centuries.[55] The ultimate goal of this reclamation was not always to create fields for agricultural production. Where it was not possible to raise the level of the riverbed or seabed above the waterline, it could still be profitable to use sand- and mudbanks for the commercial harvest of shellfish.[56] Because of the potential income that could be earned from sandbanks cultivated with shellfish, control of the shoreline and alluvial islands was a valuable asset. The genealogies of lineages living in coastal villages contain many examples of lineage members claiming ownership of shoreline and islands and sometimes registering their claims with the authorities. In return for the payment of taxes, registration offered some guarantees of one's landholding. Thus the genealogy of the Qiu of Xiaojiang in Lianjiang records, "in the Hongwu period [of the early Ming], our first generation ancestor Ruliu personally served as tax captain (keliangzhang). He [registered] the shallow and deep sandbanks before his gates, extending south to Beikanhou and north to Niumen Sanya as the boundaries. [This area] carries tax obligations totalling 7.5 piculs."[57]

In the early Qing, in an attempt to cut off support for the Ming loyalist Zheng Chenggong, the population of much of the southeastern coast of China was ordered evacuated in what William Skinner has called a "scorched-earth policy." Though modern scholars doubt that the order was fully implemented, there is no doubt that the policy caused great turmoil and suffering throughout the region.[58] The evacuation was applied to the whole coast of Fujian in 1662 and repealed incrementally at different times and in different places. It was not until 1680 that the last evacuees were allowed to return to their home. As people returned to the coastal areas, they once again laid claim to ownership of the valuable stretches of the foreshore. Thus when the order was revoked in Funing prefecture in 1665, "refugees were given permits to return to their livelihood of fishing and netting in the inner harbours within the boundaries. At that time, one after another [people from] Zhujiang, Shahe, Hongjiang . . . reported and received permits for land reclamation." Genealogies from Lianjiang contain contracts that describe a process in the early Qing that is similar to that of the early Ming, with individuals and lineages returning from evacuation and registering with the authorities for the payment of tax on a stretch of shoreline.[59]

In late imperial China, the usual practice was for households to divide with each passing generation. Sometimes, the younger generation divided the estate they inherited from their father upon his death; it was also not uncommon for sons to divide their father's estate while he was still alive. Where the estate consisted of land or money the division of property could be straightforward. Each son received an equal share, with the eldest son sometimes getting an extra share.[60] But where the property consisted of alluvial islands or claims to a stretch of foreshore, it was virtually impossible to devise an equitable settlement. Islands and sandbanks were constantly shifting shape, sometimes being washed away in spring flooding only to reappear downstream.[61] Even where sandbanks and islands were relatively stable, if the property was used to cultivate or gather small shellfish, dividing the rights to harvest into specific portions was difficult or impossible. Instead, the property was usually vested in a common estate, in which all the descendants of the individual who had first registered ownership of the property received a share. Rights to the alluvial land were then assigned in terms of a percentage of the shellfish harvest. In Fuzhou, the right to harvest the property was usually auctioned off and proceeds distributed to the shareowners once any corporate expenses had been met. The Qiu of Xiaojiang, for example, after the death of early ancestor Ruliu who had first established ownership of the foreshore, established the following rules to manage this stretch of shore. "Kinfolk or villagers who [wish to] plant stakes, punt in boats, set traps, or hang nets in order to catch fish must pay the auction fees in the middle of the seventh month. The auction fees are to be used to pay the tax and to meet the costs of sacrifice. If there is any surplus, it should go to a public account. The origins of this are long ago."[62]

Because alluvial land and sandbanks could be highly profitable, and their ownership status ambiguous, there were frequent disputes and even violent feuds over control of such property. In the late Qing and Republican period, the Lin of Shanggan and the Huang of Yixu had a reputation for seizing alluvial land belonging to others.[63] The powerful Lin of Shanggan often seized control of alluvial lands on the pretext that they had originally been islands owned by people of Shanggan, which had been washed away by flooding and then reformed in their current location. After 1949, Fuzhou residents joked with land-reform teams that the Shanggan Lin had "flying islands."[64] There was therefore a certain advantage to having alluvial islands under corporate ownership, for this facilitated defense of the land if it came under attack. On the other hand, alluvial land that had been seized by force would also tend to be corporately owned. This could create very complex organizational arrangements, sometimes encompassing multiple lineages and multiple surnames.[65] Alliances might also be formed to generate investment for the reclamation of new alluvial lands. For example, the island of Sanhexing was reclaimed by three lineages of Wushan, who shared ownership.[66] Organizations based on principles of patrilineal kinship were not the only way to organize ownership of alluvial land. In one Changle village, sandbanks that were cultivated with razor clams were collectively owned by all the residents of the village. Every household resident in the village was entitled to a share in the estate.[67] But most of the alluvial land and sandbanks in the Fuzhou region were held by self-professed patrilineal descent groups, that is, by lineages. The basic explanation for this was not the need to accumulate investment capital nor the problem of defending against seizure but the difficulty of dividing individually owned alluvial land when the household of the ancestor of the lineage was divided.

Another type of property that was not easily divided when households divided their estate was capital invested in a business. Groups of kin were forced to develop ways of dealing with the division of ownership in such cases. The Wenshan Huang of Fuzhou city provide a good example.[68] In the second half of the nineteenth century, a number of lineage members were extremely successful in business. Huang Yongdong (1813–71) worked as the manager of a native bank and then established his own firm, which handled the trading of paper. His son, Shujing, established another paper trading firm and served as the manager of a paper conglomerate. Shujing died in 1899, and, in 1906, his widow, Madame Lu, supervised the disposition of his estate. The will survives:

> My husband was one of three brothers. My husband was the eldest, followed by Shuzhao, and Shuyan. . . . They either studied for the exams, or engaged in trade, each according to his own abilities. Thus younger brother Shuzhao engaged in commerce, but he died early. Younger brother Shuyan had a will to study, so he happily did so. I had four sons. . . . Because younger brother Shuzhao died without any descendants, our fourth son Kun was made his heir. . . . My late husband left a legacy solemnly commanding his sons to maintain their enterprise [together] in order to expand their property. The sons received this legacy and respected it well. So for many years they were very successful in business. . . . Now, all the property and business, aside from some to be set aside as a sacrificial estate and some to be set aside as a retirement fund, will be divided into five even shares. My husband's younger brother Shuyan gets one share, and our son Kun who has been designated heir of

another branch also obtains one share. We have collectively decided to evenly divide the property and businesses, and to use the shares to establish the Corporation of the Hall of Shared Accumulation (*gongji tang gongsi*). The profit earned each year is to be distributed as living expenses according to the number of people in each household, and the remainder reinvested in the company.[69]

Although the will uses the language of an ordinary document of household division, in fact the division of ownership did not affect the operation of the family business, which continued as before. But this resolution proved unsatisfactory, probably because the brothers and cousins who had a share in ownership were dissatisfied with the way the business was being managed or the living stipends being distributed. So in 1920 the group drew up a new contract:

We have together discussed and come to this agreement. The total income earned from the collective property of the Hall of Shared Accumulation will be managed in rotation by the five branches. . . . Each branch will take a turn in the rotation for one year, and when the rotation has run its course, it will start again anew. The rota holder each year receives two hundred *yuan* from the income of the collective property. The remainder is to be used to meet the expenses of the spring and autumn sacrifice and for the purpose of expanding the property.[70]

Now the management of the family business really was divided, with each branch of Shujing's descendants taking charge for one year in rotation. This type of organization is different from any of those discussed previously, because here the issue was not creating a new organization but instead adapting an existing organization, a family business, to suit the new context created by household division. The Huang were well organized as a single household; the initial contract was intended to maintain that organization after their division into several households.

What all of these examples illustrate is that there were a wide variety of forces in local society that compelled groups of kin to organize themselves in different ways. Involvement in commerce and land reclamation would have affected some but not all of the residents of the Fuzhou region; in one way or another, the demands of the tax system affected all. In none of the cases discussed above was there a member of the educated elite involved in the process of organization, at least not in the initial stages. Nor did the organization that resulted resemble a lineage organized by members of the degree-holding elite and focused on the ancestral hall and Confucian rituals of ancestor worship. But these organizations, which used kinship ties to manage resources and obligations, were self-professed patrilineal descent groups of real social significance. They were lineages just the same.

COUNTERTRENDS

The preceding section has shown that groups of patrilineally related kin could organize themselves in the absence of corporate property and of the leadership of educated elites, and for purposes other than the emulation of a neo-Confucian model of kinship organization. But such groups were organized in the pursuit of the individual and collective strategies of their members, strategies that were shaped by ideas about kinship as well as other factors in local society. The strategies described in the genealogies could often work against the institutionalization of the lineage, interfering with the establishment of corporate property and the performance of ancestral worship. The case of the Chen of Langqi, a large island at the mouth of the Min River, just downriver from Nantai, provides an example. The Chen's founding migrant ancestor, Adjutant Xun, is said to have settled in Fuzhou in 902.[71] His descendants opened up lands on Nantai Island at Tengshan, and the genealogy claims that the proper name for Tengshan (Teng hill) is really Chenshan (Chen hill).[72] Xun's later descendant, Ximan, first settled on Langqi in 1469 and registered his household with the authorities. Ximan was buried on New Year's Day, so his tomb was known as the New Year's Day (*Zhengyi*) tomb. A plot of land was purchased to support sacrifice on the anniversary of Ximan's death; this plot was called the New Year's Day plot. The genealogy suggests that the sacrificial estate was small, but it was sufficient to pay the cost of "several taels of tax surcharge, which had been attached to the household registration," in addition to the expenses of the annual sacrifice. At first, other state exactions were also met from the income of the land, but when these grew too heavy, it was necessary to collect funds from the individual households made up of Ximan's descendants, all of whom were still officially registered under his single household registration. Ximan's descendants were successful farmers and grew numerous. "By the eighth or ninth generation, the lineage increasingly flourished." As a result, they were forced to assume the position of *li* head and to pay the periodic expenses of recompiling the tax registers.[73] The first time this charge had to be paid, the income from the sacrificial estate was used, leaving almost nothing for the sacrifice. "Several men gathered to ascend to the tomb, burn [incense], bow, and that was all. This was because the rice [i.e., the rental income] was used to [pay] the recompilation [fees]."[74] To prevent this situation from recurring, in subsequent years a portion of the income from the sacrificial estate was set aside for the next recompilation, and the remainder was used for the sacrifice. The estate continued to be managed in this way into the early eighteenth century, when a lineage member wrote:

> All those who live in the tenth *jia* consider this estate to be the property of the tenth *jia*. Those who have not been called on to pay for the costs of recompilation are envious of the profit [from the estate] and desirous of obtaining it. For several generations [the registers] have not been recompiled, so several generations [of our own family] have not obtained any benefit from this, and so they also wish to obtain it. Is not their greed extreme?

Here, the two characters of a name have been cut carefully out of the genealogy. There is no way of knowing why, or when, this was done:

> Recently,   and others, in order to assess liability for tax surcharges, investigated the [records of] annual exactions. One or two fiscal males had been added to [the obligations of each] ward, but those already assessed with many fiscal males refused to accept [the new liabilities]. They claimed that these should be paid out of the [estate associated with] the ancestral registration. Although this income was specified as being for the costs of recompilation, even the venerated elders could not correct this. It had become the custom.[75]

This account is confusing because it does not distinguish between the exactions imposed by the state onto the group registered under the single household registration of Ximan and the exactions imposed by the group's leaders onto the actual membership of the group. But if this distinction is kept in mind, it becomes possible to understand the significance of the document. The members of the lineage were liable for tax payments as a group by virtue of their common household registration. How these tax payments were distributed was an internal matter for the lineage. When the group's taxes were raised, the lineage member whose name has been so mysteriously excised from the genealogy was charged with allocating the increase. To do so, he attempted to update the lineage's own records of "annual exactions." But the largest households within the lineage, on whom the surcharge would have weighed most heavily, refused to accept this, arguing that the funds should come from the corporate property endowed in the name of the founding ancestor, for this is how tax supplements had been financed in the past. Ultimately, lineage leadership was unable to respond to this challenge, and the income from the sacrificial estate of the group came to be devoted solely to meeting tax obligations. Thus organizational structures initially set up to ensure the maintenance of sacrifice lost that function and came to serve instead simply as a means to meet tax obligations. This is not the only example of this process in the genealogy of the Chen of Langqi. A document dated 1570 records the collapse of sacrifices at the tomb of ancestor Xuanyi. Though the tomb was large and impressive, the sacrificial estate associated with it was sold off in the late fifteenth century to meet commuted labor service expenses. As a result, there were no more funds to sustain sacrifice, and the tomb fell into disrepair.[76] The organization of the Langqi Chen and other lineages in late imperial Fuzhou was thus articulated through the interaction of ancestral sacrifice, corporate property, and the demands of the Ming and later the Qing taxation systems, and it was by no means certain which factor would dominate and, hence, what outcome would result.

CONCLUSIONS

The nature of the Ming taxation system forced groups of patrilineally related kin in the Fuzhou area to organize themselves to ensure that their obligations as descendents of an ancestor whose household was registered with the authorities were fulfilled. People came to be registered as military households mostly for reasons beyond their control, but once registered, members of military households were forced to organize to ensure that their obligations to provide a soldier and the funds to support him were met. Military-registered households might have established a system whereby members of the household served as soldiers in rotation. But for most households, it made more sense to raise funds and pay a single member to serve continuously. When that individual died, it was necessary to find a replacement. If he were transferred, then his support had to be enlisted to ensure that the group was not open to accusations that it was not fulfilling its obligations. All of these measures required both organization and money. To ensure that lack of money never became a problem, members of some military-registered households donated property, the income from which could be used to guarantee that the costs of providing military service were always met. The result was that the descendants of an ancestor whose household was registered as a military household became a lineage, a self-professed patrilineal descent group for whom the claim of a patrilineal connection was socially meaningful.

Registration as a military household was often imposed; the decision to register as a commoner household usually involved more complex decisions. Registration was obviously essential to upward mobility, since only a member of a registered household was eligible to sit for the examinations. But household registration was of value even for a household without scholars. Registration was a contract with the state to provide tax and labor services. Failure to have such a contract did not mean exemption from taxes. Rather, it opened up one's household to informal taxation by *yamen* runners and by *lijia* heads, that is, members of those households who were not only registered but were charged with tax collection. As the *lijia* system collapsed over the course of the Ming, the services it provided were replaced by salaried labor, and the obligations associated with it were gradually commuted to cash and then attached to the land and head tax. But the registration of fiscal males, which the *lijia* system had required, remained the basis of the tax records into the Qing, and thus the mechanisms that groups of kin had set up in the Ming to limit their exactions continued to operate. Groups of kin who shared a single household registration by virtue of their common descent set up organizations and endowed property to ensure that the obligations associated with that registration were fulfilled.

Historians have often associated the development of lineage organization with the activism of the educated elite, which was undoubtedly the case in many instances. But the evidence presented in this chapter shows that the attachment of particular social meanings to kinship connections was not necessarily linked to degree holders and scholars. Indeed, because degree holders were exempt from the very obligations that led ordinary groups of people to organize, it was groups whose members were not at the top but at the bottom tiers of society who were most likely to organize themselves. But in the Fuzhou region it was not that the people at the bottom tiers of society lived in some anarchic frontier situation that forced them to organize. Rather, they did so precisely because it was impossible for them not to interact with the imperial state and its local representatives in Ming and

Qing Fuzhou. As Faure has pointed out, if the lineage is analyzed purely from the writings of elite authors who sought to promote a particular vision of kinship organization,[77] or for that matter from the perspective of anthropological fieldwork in modern conditions where the relationship between state and society is vastly different than it was in late imperial times, then it is all too easy to miss the broad bases for lineage formation in its historical context and to oversimplify the complexities and flexibilities of Chinese kinship.

FOUR

The Ancestral Hall

There has been no more striking expression of the revival of traditional practices on Nantai than the restoration of the great ancestral halls. Since the early 1990s, villagers have reclaimed these halls from their former uses as schools, storage facilities, factories, and, in the case of Shangjie village, a nightclub and rebuilt them in the grand style remembered by the older men from their youth. Funds from relatives overseas play an important role in reconstruction efforts; the commemorative inscriptions recording donations to such projects often list contributions in the currencies of many places, including Hong Kong, the United States, and Taiwan. But it is not only the wealthy and Overseas Chinese who contribute. The inscriptions list dozens, sometimes hundreds, of individual donors and donations, the smallest donation being only a few *yuan*. Other ancestral halls and lineage organizations donate commemorative mirrors and artwork that are hung in positions of honor, suggesting the revitalization of wider networks of territorial connections and relationships.[1]

The reopening of an ancestral hall is a spectacular event. Relatives living in Fuzhou return to the village to participate. Officials from the township government attend to make congratulatory remarks, linking the prosperity of the community with the success of national reform policies and hinting that the villagers should take care to impose their own limits on the revival of traditional practices, lest limits be imposed for them. Bands and operatic troupes are hired and village school children put on dances and other cultural performances. The whole event is videotaped by relatives from Taiwan and Hong Kong who have returned for the day and also by a hired professional cameraman—a somewhat grand title for a petty entrepreneur who has invested in a cheap video camera. The high point of the day is the installation of the ancestral tablets—some newly carved, others bravely concealed during the turmoil of the past fifty years. A considerable fee is charged for the right to install a tablet, and there is much discussion and gossip about who has endowed a tablet for which ancestor and who has preemptively installed a tablet to await his own death.[2] Or hers, for tablets may now be installed for women. At the end of the day the eldest men of the lineage, still in their green and blue padded Mao suits, raise their glasses with young businessmen, in Western suits and carrying cell phones, at a great feast.

In the previous chapter, I discussed a number of the factors that led groups of kin to organize themselves in the Ming and Qing. There was nothing internal to these factors themselves that drove the use of specific cultural forms in the institutionalization of kinship practice. Yet over the course of the late imperial period, one particular form, the ancestral hall, known to the people of Fuzhou today as the descent-line shrine (*zongci*) or the offering hall (*citang*), became the most visible symbol of organized patrilineal kinship throughout rural Fuzhou. In the fourteenth century, there were very few ancestral halls in the area; by the eighteenth century they were ubiquitous, with most villages of Nantai boasting at least one. This chapter explores the spread of ancestral halls in the Fuzhou region through a detailed discussion of the history of the ancestral halls in four Nantai villages: Fenggang, Linpu, Yixu, and Luozhou. This chapter asks how people in Fuzhou answered certain questions at different times. Why build an ancestral hall? Who was entitled to build one? Who was entitled to perform sacrifice in a hall? Who was entitled to receive sacrifice in one? Chapter 5 then looks more specifically at the performance of rituals in the hall, addressing the questions of how such rituals should be conducted and who should have the right to participate.

Historians have often treated the spread of ancestral halls as a process of cultural integration. Faure sees the ancestral hall in the official style as a cultural form introduced from outside south China to Guangdong society and then imitated by the people of the region to signify their participation in Chinese culture. Ebrey too has stressed the attention to the issue of cultural integration in the intellectual discourse about ritual performance in ancestral halls.[3] This emulation and integration is usually seen as serving a deliberate strategy by local elites who aimed to cement their authority over local society. Moving beyond official and elite discourses and into the practice of kinship in the village suggests that the spread of the ancestral hall was a highly complex process that should not be oversimplified. Halls were built for different reasons at different times. Their spread was the outcome of a host of sometimes mutually contradictory strategies and involved competition and negotiation between different representations and meanings.

The argument in this chapter builds on Ebrey's discussion of the spread of neo-Confucian ideas about the correct way to perform rituals of ancestral sacrifice from the Song. While there was, and would continue to be, considerable variation and eclecticism in the performance of these rituals, elite authors increasingly insisted that there was a common, correct standard, even as they sanctioned some of the variation as unavoidable. From the late Song to the early Ming, a small number of elite men from Fuzhou constructed ancestral halls, in which they performed sacrifice to their immediate lineal ancestors, in the style advocated by Zhu Xi in the *Family Rituals*. But through the early Ming, the builders of such halls were restricted to men who held high official position. Such halls were few in number and were considered in part to be markers of social status, as a physical demonstration of their exclusiveness.

The meanings and significances of ancestral hall construction in the Fuzhou region changed from the mid-Ming onward. A number of factors lay behind this development. First, there was a shift in the orientation of the educated elite toward local society. Intensifying competition and declining opportunities for government service led many members of the educated elite to assert informal leadership roles in local society as an expression of their moral preoccupations and sense of obligation. To these elites, commercialization seemed to be breaking down the social order. The outbreak of urban riot, rural rent-resistance, and widespread piracy only heightened this perception and intensified their localist orientation. This, coupled with their ideological engagement with what Chow has labeled Confucian ritualism, generated major shifts in ideas about ancestral halls.[4] By the mid-Ming, ancestral halls began to be used to reflect inclusiveness rather than exclusiveness, as part of efforts to create and strengthen community sentiment as well as to signify differentiation within communities. Second, as the halls became

THE ANCESTRAL HALL 93

more widespread, they became part of the accepted repertoire of local elite practices. Members of different types of elites, merchants and moneylenders, who were unable to claim leadership authority in local society on the basis of education or official position claimed authority on the basis of meritorious deeds supported by their wealth. They began to initiate the construction of ancestral halls themselves, to demand positions of leadership in the halls, and to reshape practices associated with the halls to better serve their interests.

What was the role of the state in these developments? With the confirmation of Zhu Xi's *Family Rituals* as the official orthodoxy, the imperial state took steps to promote adherence to its prescriptions. But rather than simply accepting imperial prescriptions, at every stage, groups in local society appropriated officially sanctioned principles and adapted them, turning them to their own purposes. This in turn generated new strategies of appropriation and subversion by other groups in an endless chain of transformations. State officials tried to channel these negotiations and transformations, but I suggest that they were always at least one step behind the strategies at work in the Fuzhou countryside.

In the final section of the chapter, I argue that these broad shifts do not tell the whole story. The development of ancestral halls in the Fuzhou region was not a straightforward or inevitable process. Within a given lineage, ancestral hall building went on in fits and starts, being shaped by changes in the social, economic, and political context of the locale and by the strategies of individual actors who, though committed to varying degrees to the moral and social value of ancestral worship, still sought to turn ancestral halls to personal advantage, conceiving of kinship and its institutions and practices as resources to be exploited. The specific interests of activist members of the lineage could delay or even prevent the construction of an ancestral hall. The meanings and significances of the ancestral hall, as with other aspects of kinship practice, have been constructed historically, shaped by factors both ideological and material and expressed in terms of strategies devised by countless individuals and groups.

ANCESTRAL SACRIFICE FROM SOUTHERN SONG TO EARLY MING

Before we can fully appreciate the changes of the Ming and Qing, it is important to have some sense of the ways rituals of ancestral sacrifice were performed in earlier periods. Descriptions of ancestral sacrifice from Fuzhou in the Song indicate considerable variation and eclecticism in practice. Ancestors received sacrifice at their graves; in Buddhist shrines either in monasteries or at gravesites; and in different types of dedicated halls, located at gravesites, in the ancestor's former residence, or elsewhere. The ancestors were represented by both images and tablets.

In the twelfth century, some people of Fuzhou performed large-scale collective sacrifices at the tombs of their ancestors. According to the *Sanshan zhi*, residents of Fuzhou city visited the tombs of their ancestors three times a year. The second of these three annual events took place in the third month:

> The people of the prefecture perform obeisances below the graves at the spring sacrifice at the time of the Cold Food Festival. The rich households and great surnames own land property to support the graveyards. When the sacrifice is over, the agnates assemble. They may number as many as several hundred people or as few as several dozen. Afterwards they hold a feast, arranging themselves in order and treating one another with familiarity. This is the way to honour the ancestors and encourage warm feelings among the agnates.[5]

In the Song, ancestral graves of some wealthy families were attached to Buddhist shrines. For example, the ancestors of Zhu Xi's son-in-law Huang Gan (1152–1221) had constructed a monastery near the family home outside Fuzhou's east gate, beside a family graveyard where "in spring and autumn, the kin assemble to sacrifice." Based on the number of generations of ancestors buried in the graveyard, Huang estimated that these sacrifices had been going on "without interruption" for over three hundred years. He complained that under the current arrangements, "at present, in spring and autumn when we bow and sweep below the graves, there is not enough room for anyone outside the area big enough to lay a mat."[6] This source, as with the gazetteer account, suggests that large groups of kin, extending well beyond the immediate family, sacrificed together.

Huang was a man of wealth and influence in Fuzhou, but his family did not have an endowment to support ancestral sacrifice along the lines described in the gazetteer. This was a cause of concern. "Although my kin donate money for the sacrifices each spring and autumn, among them are some who are poor and find this very difficult. With the passage of generations, people's sentiments easily become remiss. Aside from at the sacrifices, there are few visitors to the graves." In 1221, Huang decided to establish an endowment to ensure that the sacrifice would not be neglected. He purchased over four *mu* of property that he established as a sacrificial estate. Portions of the rental income were to be used for meeting the costs of sacrifice and for paying taxes and unexpected expenses; any surplus was to be reinvested in land. "After ten years, if the increase is substantial, it can be used to supply the agnates in need by rotation."[7] Thus at least in some families, kin were buried together in shared graveyards, which might be located in or otherwise associated with Buddhist monastic institutions. Descendants of the ancestors buried in these graveyards performed annual sacrifice at the graves. Since these rituals were performed generation after generation, the participants would include kin whose relationship with one another could be quite distant. To ensure the continuity of the sacrifice and to the benefit of their own prestige, wealthy individuals sometimes endowed corporate property, the income from which could be used to meet the expenses of the ritual. The gazetteer suggests that sacrificing at the graves was general practice but singles out "the rich households and great surnames" as having endowed property. It is reasonable to conclude that the marker of differentiation in practice was not that some kinship groups performed grave sacrifice and others did not, but that some kinship groups had wealthy members who had endowed property whereas others had neither such members nor such property. But the existence of a corporate estate probably did promote more regular performance of collective sacrifices.[8]

The people of late Song and Yuan Fujian also sacrificed to their ancestors in dedicated shrines located at or near their ancestors' residence. In the thirteenth century the Huang of Dongli, in Putian, sacrificed twice annually to thirteen generations of distant ancestors and gathered as a group at New Year's and other seasonal festivals at a shrine converted from the former residence of their ancestor. This structure is referred to as a shrine (*ci*), a family temple (*jiamiao*), and an image hall (*yingtang*), which suggests that the ancestors were represented in the form of painted portraits.[9] Other Song sources mention sacrifice in offering halls (*citang*), but this term often meant something quite different from the lineage ancestral hall that it would describe in later times. Usually the term refers to shrines established in honor of local notables, that were not necessarily connected in any way with kinship organization and were often maintained by state authorities.[10]

The variation and eclecticism of ancestral sacrifice in Fuzhou in the Song would not disappear in later centuries.[11] What did change were elite attitudes to these practices. From the Song onward, there was a growing commitment among the educated elite to the notion that there was a single correct way to conduct ancestral sacrifice, an orthodoxy, that the repertoire of kinship practices should be brought in line with this orthodoxy; and that the content of this orthodoxy had been spelled out in Zhu Xi's work, the *Family Rituals*. Zhu Xi restricted sacrifice to distant ancestors to the descent-line heir (*zongzi*) of the great descent line (*dazong*)—the firstborn of the main wife in successive generations back to a founding ancestor. Other descendants were entitled to form only a lesser descent line (*xiaozong*) and to offer sacrifice to four generations of ancestors. Though Zhu Xi prescribed offerings in a shrine located in the home, his writings were frequently interpreted as sanctioning the construction of the large, free-standing ancestral hall characteristic of Fuzhou villages in the Qing.[12] But the growing influence of the *Family Rituals* did not mean that the development of ancestral sacrifice in Ming–Qing Fuzhou was the triumph of a unitary state-sanctioned neo-Confucian vision of kinship. It was rather a contest between different representations of how kinship should be practiced, in other words, of what a lineage should be. The tension between neo-Confucian prescription and local strategy are well illustrated in the writings of two fourteenth-century thinkers. Wu Hai, a native of Fuzhou, constructed an offering hall, apparently dedicated solely to the sacrifice to his father. Wu endorsed Zhu Xi's prescription that only three or four generations of ancestors should receive sacrifice in ancestral halls.[13] He stressed that ancestral sacrifice was not simply instrumental for the development of kinship group cohesiveness, and he was highly critical of the practice of sacrificing to more distant ancestors, attempting to eliminate the practice among the Lin of Luotian, in Hubei.[14] Wu's contemporary Song Lian (1310–81), on the other hand, supported the idea of a dedicated shrine to distant ancestors in his commemorative record of the ancestral hall of the Lin of Lake Guoqing, in Putian, though in this case many generations of ancestors were represented by a single tablet.[15]

ANCESTRAL HALLS ON NANTAI ISLAND
IN THE MING AND QING

To demonstrate the shifts in kinship practice that are illustrated by changing ideas and practices around ancestral halls, in this section I trace the history of the ancestral halls of several Nantai lineages. The sixteenth century is when the earliest surviving ancestral halls on the island were built. The small number of members of the Fuzhou elite who built free-standing ancestral halls at that time used one or both of two arguments to justify them. Some claimed that they were entitled to build a hall because they had requested and received official permission to do so on the basis of the accomplishments of their ancestors. Others claimed the same right because they themselves had attained high office. On the basis of the arguments invoked to justify the construction of the hall, I describe such halls as official halls or gentry halls. These early halls stress exclusivity not commonality. They are a marker not of the shared identity of the educated elite or the descendants of prominent officials with the rest of local society but of their difference. Ancestral halls built on Nantai from the early to mid-Ming were an expensive demonstration of the commitment of their builders to Confucian orthodoxy and of their social distinctiveness. They were, at least in part, a type of status symbol. Over the course of the Ming, more and more individuals and families on Nantai began to construct free-standing ancestral halls in imitation of these earlier halls. In most cases, neither of the two justifications could plausibly be invoked. Rather, these halls were constructed as part of strategies to build local networks or to emulate patterns of conduct by the degree-holding elite and were justified in terms of the need to build stability and cohesion in local society. These halls were built in a spirit of inclusiveness, with the explicit goal of strengthening the bonds between groups of patrilineal kin. I label such halls popular halls. The history of ancestral halls on Nantai Island during the late imperial period followed a rough pattern of development from official to gentry to popular ancestral halls. This typology would have meant nothing to the people of Fuzhou at the time, and the boundaries between the different types should be seen as fluid rather than fixed. But as ideal types, they are still useful in articulating a pattern of development. Drawing attention to this pattern of development is important because it challenges overly simplistic approaches that consider the ancestral hall a static institution used instrumentally by local elites as part of a localist strategy to build a network of clients and allies and to indicate their adherence to national orthodox culture.

THE OFFICIAL HALL OF THE FENGGANG LIU

The oldest surviving ancestral hall on Nantai is the Shrine of the Eight Sages of the Liu Surname located at Fenggang on the northwestern arm of the island. While builders of many later ancestral halls sought official or gentry approval for their project by soliciting memorial writings and inscriptions, the Fenggang hall was maintained with official encouragement and was in part sustained with public funds disbursed by local officials. It is a classic example of what I have labeled the official type of ancestral hall.

The account of the Great Surnames of Houguan county in the 1906 gazetteer lists the Liu of Fenggang as one of three noteworthy families bearing the Liu surname. Their founding ancestor is one Liu Cun, who is said to have come from Gushi together with the armies of Wang Shenzhi.[16] For one thousand years, the Liu of Fenggang have enjoyed a prominent, and sometimes dominant, position in local society. One consequence of this is a very rich written record of the lineage.[17] Unlike many of the eminent lineages of late imperial Nantai, the history of the Fenggang Liu can be plausibly reconstructed on the basis of contemporary sources back to their first migrant ancestor, whose life is documented in a funerary record written in 933. This account explains how Liu Cun, and his three sons and three nephews, followed Wang Chao and Shenzhi into Fujian and eventually to Fuzhou, where they settled.[18]

Two of Cun's three sons died in battle serving Wang Shenzhi. The surviving son had three sons of his own, who came to dominate the northern arm of Nantai Island. They did so in part as military strongmen. Two of the sons commanded local militia. Only one, Gongshu, lived long enough to marry and have descendants. He was a physical giant with a swarthy complexion. At the time, Fenggang was troubled by bandits "swarming like bees, plundering the villages." Gongshu organized a local defense force, and the magistrate, "hearing of his ability and bravery, assigned him to administer the locality."[19] Military might remained important to the Liu of Fenggang for several generations, but descendants of the original migrants were also participating successfully in the examination system and holding higher and higher civil office. According to the genealogy, this began in the early to mid-tenth century, for Liu Cun himself, who was renowned for his longevity, "saw the descendants of the third and fourth generation attain the *jinshi* degree."[20]

The tombs of the early generations of the Fenggang Liu were not initially the focus of elaborate ritual activities. Gongshu's own tomb was built of large stones piled up with earth. The tomb was not "decorated with any embellishment, for the ancient ways esteemed simplicity." But this would change. According to a twelfth-century account, the tomb of Liu Cun's great-grandson Wenji, located near a temple to Guanyin, included a pavilion in which worshippers changed their clothes and an altar for sacrifices.[21] The Liu also built dedicated shrines for ancestral sacrifice. In the tenth century, Wenji built a shrine in Cun's honor in Fenggang. It was called an ancestral shrine (*zuci*) and was intended by Wenji to serve "as the site for the descendants to gather on New Year's Day to conduct the rituals."[22] A century later, a member of the seventh generation named Cheng (*jinshi* 1038) initiated the construction of a more impressive structure, which was called variously an offering hall (*citang*), a great descent-line shrine (*dazong ci*), and a family temple (*jiamiao*). Cheng justified the construction of the shrine in terms of the decline of the descent-line system (*zongfa*) of antiquity.[23] But he also stated that the lineage's reputation demanded a shrine. "The Liu surname is already supreme among all the various lineages." It behooved a lineage of such prominence to show the appropriate signs of success.[24] The sources therefore suggest that, initially, the activities of the Liu in the field of sacrificial ritual resemble those of other prominent families of Fuzhou and Putian. They built shrines for sacrifice both at and away from tombs and conducted collective sacrifice to their ancestors there.

In the Ming, the Liu built an ancestral hall on a dramatically larger scale. It remains an impressive sight to this day, rising out of the dense vegetation of northern Nantai. Behind this development lay the growing involvement of a few individuals of the Liu surname in the scholarly movements of neo-Confucianism and in efforts to trace the descent of all of them back to Liu Cun. This shrine then became a model that influenced the subsequent development of ancestral halls throughout Nantai.

Three brothers, descended from Liu Cun's nephews, won the *jinshi* degree in the early eleventh century. One of these was Liu Yi, whose own nephew Kangfu then earned the degree in 1088. A half-century later, a direct descendant of Liu Cun himself gained renown. Liu Zao (*jinshi* 1135) was a student of Luo Congyan (1072–1135), a minor link in the chain from the Cheng brothers to Zhu Xi.[25] The scholarly tradition of Liu Cun's descendants soon grew even more outstanding, but only through very flexible tracing of descent. According to the genealogy, Cun's great-great-grandnephew had married uxorilocally into a family surnamed Chen, and all of his sons bore that surname. Four generations later, his descendant Jiaju "returned to the original descent line" and restored the Liu surname. Jiaju's two grandsons Liu Di and Li were child prodigies who studied with Zhu Xi.[26]

Thus between the mid-eleventh and the late twelfth century there were personal connections between several individuals who traced their descent to Liu Cun and some of the most important scholars and intellectuals of the land. Though never more than peripheral themselves, these natives of

Fenggang were at the margins of what in retrospect was an important philo-
sophical movement, the Fujian school (*Minxue*), that is, the scholarly tradition of Zhu Xi. In recognition of this, in the early Ming their descendants
sought official sanction to establish a grand sacrificial shrine, which survives
today—the Shrine of the Eight Sages of the Liu Surname of Fenggang.

Two written sources discuss the history of the hall in some detail. First,
there is an inscription in the hall, composed in 1579 by Director-General of
Grain Transport Ma Sen (see Figures 4.1 and 4.2). The second is a record of
the hall written in 1606 by the prominent late Ming intellectual and grand
secretary, Ye Xianggao (1562–1627), best known to scholars for his patronage
of the Jesuit Guilio Aleni. The two sources differ on numerous points, making it difficult to be certain of even the most basic issues in the history of the
shrine. Ma's inscription records that the shrine was first constructed in the
early fifteenth century but does not say why or in what circumstances; Ye's
account explains that it was originally Liu Di and Li's study "which was converted into a shrine where they could be worshipped, and for the descendants
to make offerings to them." Numerous sources, including the two records
and also local gazetteers, report that initially only five individuals—Yi,
Kangfu, Zao, Di, and Li—received sacrifice, with Jiaju, his son, and Liu Zijie
added only later.[27] Little is known of the management or rituals of the hall
prior to the mid-sixteenth century, but, at some point, three local gentlemen who were not members of the Liu petitioned local officials requesting
that the sacrifices at the hall be inscribed in the official register of sacrifices
(*sidian*). The petition was approved, and, beginning in 1574, a functionary
was dispatched twice each year, in spring and autumn, to participate in
sacrifices held at the hall. The hall must have been endowed with some
property that was held by the descendants of the Sages, for some time later
"unscrupulous members of the lineage" sold off some of this land, leading
to the suspension of the sacrifices. Luckily, the matter was brought to the
attention of local authorities, and, after complex negotiations lasting for several years, the property was restored to the Liu and the sacrifices revived. At
the time when Ye wrote his account, "the descendants of the Sages control
the estate and personally conduct the sacrifice."[28] As an offering hall, the
Fenggang shrine obviously transcended Zhu Xi's limits on ancestral worship, for the Sages were ancestors from distant generations. Ma Sen tried to
minimize this aspect of the hall. All of the men who receive sacrifice in the
shrine "were sages, and all came from a single family. Has there ever been
a [family] more flourishing than this? So they ought to have a shrine to be
worshipped."[29]

Figure 4.1. Stone inscription commemorating the construction of the Fenggang Liu ancestral hall (photograph by author).

The Fenggang Liu hall exemplifies what I have labeled the official type of ancestral hall. Unlike later halls, the hall of the Sages was built not primarily on the principle that descendants should worship their ancestors but rather on the principle that individuals who had made extraordinary contributions to local or wider society should receive sacrifice. If they were to receive sacrifice

Figure 4.2.   Collective tablet for celebrated ancestors of the Fenggang Liu. The names were scratched out during the Cultural Revolution (photograph by author).

in their native place, then it only made sense that their descendants be involved. But these sorts of sacrifices were not purely private affairs. The wider society and the state were also involved.

THE GENTRY HALLS OF THE LINPU LIN

The second type of ancestral hall found in Fuzhou in the Ming, which I have labeled the gentry hall, is exemplified by the ancestral halls of the Lin of Linpu. A gentry hall is one constructed on the basis of the argument that those who hold high office are entitled to sacrifice to distant generations of ancestors and to do so in a free-standing ancestral hall.

Most of what we know about the history of Linpu comes from the Lin genealogy, which was first compiled by Lin Yuanmei in 1462 and has gone through a number of subsequent editions. The current edition dates from 1914.[30] There is little reliable information before the early Ming. From the early fifteenth century, the genealogy records growing involvement in the examination system and in commerce by certain individuals, and often by members of the same family, as part of a strategy of diversification.[31] The most spectacular successes were enjoyed by the descendants of Lin Guan, who lived in the mid-fifteenth century. Several of Guan's immediate direct descendants enjoyed a meteoric rise to the heights of national prominence. A seventeenth-century anecdote celebrating this rise draws attention to Guan's humble origins and, in so doing, points to the distance between his own cultural practices and those of his illustrious grandsons. On a hill just outside Linpu is the ancestral cemetery of the Lin surname. Lin Guan is said to have selected the site, whereupon a geomancer predicted great success in the coming generations. Guan replied, "I am a rustic of the wilds (*tianye ren*). Dare I hope for this?" Guan deposited in the graveyard twenty-four "jars of cremated [remains of] kin."[32] In other words, Guan's immediate ancestors had practiced Buddhist funerary rituals not the Confucian funerary practices promulgated in the *Family Rituals*.

The geomancer's prediction was soon fulfilled. Guan's son Yuanmei (1401–69) passed the *jinshi* exam in 1421 and was appointed to a series of official positions.[33] He married a woman from the Zheng surname of nearby Huangshan and had five sons, the second of whom was Lin Han (1434–1519), who passed the *jinshi* exam of 1466 and held a number of high posts in the central government, culminating with the position of Nanjing minister of war.[34] The family's success continued in the next generation. Lin Han had nine sons, two of whom also attained the *jinshi* degree. Ting'ang (1472–1541) served as minister of works, as did his younger brother, Tingji (1506–81), who in the course of his career also held the offices of libationer and minister of rites. Each of the other seven sons had less illustrious careers in the state apparatus, serving as everything from military officers to minor bureaucrats. In the next generation, two of Tingji's four sons enjoyed very successful careers. Eldest son Lian (1524–80) followed his father in holding the offices of libationer and minister of rites, while second son Jing (1540–1616) served as Nanjing minister of works. Thus Yuanmei's immediate descendants were nationally renowned, celebrated with the phrases "Five Ministers in Three Generations," "Libationers for Three Generations," and "Eight *jinshi* in Seven Examinations."[35]

While these members of the Lin family were attaining dizzying heights of official success in Nanjing and Beijing, several were also active in local affairs. To strengthen the cohesiveness of their lineage, they relied chiefly on two types of measures, genealogy and charity. Yuanmei, Han, Ting'ang, Tingji, and Jing each compiled genealogies, all of which were published, with the exception of the first, which was "kept at home." The prefaces that each of them wrote for the editions they compiled indicate their genealogical orientation to the issue of kin cohesiveness. Lin Han's preface, written in 1518, expresses his belief that genealogy could be used to strengthen the cohesiveness of the kin group. "The descendants of our line and surname pass on their virtue across the generations without limit. Rich or poor, noble or base, when they encounter one another they should not consider whose relationship is closer or more distant. Thus the compilation of a genealogy has the profound intention of uniting the agnates."[36] Han believed that a genealogy could serve to strengthen the relationship among patrilineal kin. It was a means to overcome the differentiation that resulted from his own immediate family's rise to prominence.[37] Charity was another strategy adopted to generate cohesiveness among kin. An inscription on the spirit way leading to Lin Han's tomb records that "he behaved towards the kin of his descent-line (*zongzu*) with the utmost generosity. He supported the orphaned and the poor. In cases of sons and daughters who had been sold to other surnames, he redeemed them, brought them back, and enabled them to marry appropriately."[38]

Lin Han and his descendants also built ancestral halls. But they did so not to strengthen their local leadership or to build the unity of the kin. Rather, they did so as an assertion of official privilege, which differentiated them from other villagers and the rest of the lineage. When Han returned to Linpu in 1507, he began the construction of a family temple (*jiamiao*) (Figure 4.3). As far as I have been able to determine, this was the second free-standing ancestral hall built on Nantai Island, with the Fenggang hall being the first. After Han's death, a record of the temple was solicited from Fang Hao (fl. 1506–21). In the language of Zhu Xi's *Family Rituals*, Fang writes that Han used his accumulated official salary to "construct an offering hall to the east of his ancestral house." The hall, which survives today, was of considerable size—with five chambers and two side wings. The main shrine contained five altars. In the central altar were tablets to the six members of the thirteenth generation, the founders of the six branches from which all the Lin residents of Linpu claim descent. On the remaining four altars were placed "the more junior tablets of the four generations [of ancestors] of this branch, each in *zhaomu* generational order." Lin Han's hall thus basically conformed to the ritual prescriptions of antiquity, as adjusted and transmitted by Zhu Xi, that is, four generations of ancestors, but diverged from them with the addition of tablets to the distant founding ancestors of the lineage. Fang's

Figure 4.3. Ancestral Hall of Lin Han (photograph by author).

record indicates some uncertainty about the propriety of this addition, but ultimately reconciles it with the essential meaning of ancestral sacrifice.[39]

Lin Han, who was not even the eldest son of his father, let alone the eldest son in a chain of eldest sons going back to the founding ancestor, took pains to point out that he was not usurping the prerogatives of the descent-line heir. When he first installed the tablets in the new hall and reported its completion to the ancestors, he declared, "the great descent-line (*dazong*) sacrifice will have to await [the time] when the senior branch is more powerful. They shall decide to construct a shrine and conduct [the sacrifice]." He continued:

> The [system of sacrifice by the] great descent-line [i.e., the senior branch] certainly cannot be done away with. But if we must wait until the great descent-line is powerful enough to construct a shrine and only then sacrifice, then I cannot look forward to the sacrifice myself. For this reason I have built my own shrine in order to fulfill my own heart's [desire]. The great descent-line [sacrifice] will have to wait. This does not violate ritual propriety (*li*[2]), but naturally accords with it, for it arises out of righteousness and comes from the heart.

Though Fang reports that in the spring of each year "the kin gather to sacrifice" to the founding ancestors, the sacrifices would have been performed by

Lin Han's immediate family alone. It would not have been appropriate for members of other branches to offer sacrifice to Lin Han's immediate ancestors going back four generations, for they were not their ancestors. The Lin surname family temple, as Fang Hao called it, thus occupies an intermediate position between the ancestral hall for four generations of ancestors, as prescribed by Zhu Xi, and the ancestral halls of the late Ming and Qing, in which distant ancestors were routinely worshiped. Fang's record makes clear that the construction of the hall was a public event, which conferred prestige on those responsible. "The lineage celebrates; the [people of] surrounding villages express their joy. This is indeed a major event in Fujian."[40] But it was not a place where members of the educated elite led large numbers of distant kin in rituals intended to secure a moral order; rather, it was a place for the private rituals of a narrow group of agnates within the mourning grades and a public testament to the wealth and prestige of that narrow kin group.[41]

Over the course of the sixteenth century, other members of Lin Han's immediate family constructed ancestral halls. One of these was the Shrine of Loyalty through Generations (*Shizhong ci*), first built for sacrifice to Han's son, Tingji, and Tingji's eldest son, Lian, who both died within sixteenth months of one another in 1580–81. This hall was first built sometime between 1581, when Tingji's second son, Jing, went into mourning, and 1596, when Jing resumed his official career. A record of the shrine was solicited during this period from Wang Shimao. Like his grandfather, father, uncle, and brother before him, Jing also attained the rank of minister, and, after his death, Jing's tablet was also installed in the Shrine of Loyalty through Generations and a second record was solicited from Judicial Commissioner Chen Kui.[42]

When this hall was first proposed, son and grandson sought official permission to construct the shrine. According to Wang Shimao, after the death of Tingji and his son, "the local people thought them no less worthy than [Lin Han and Lin Ting'ang]. So they requested permission from Vice-Censor-in-Chief Zhao and Acting Grand Coordinator Gong and enshrined them."[43] Chen's record outlines the rationale according to which official permission to build the hall had been solicited. "Those whose policies help the people should receive sacrifice. These five gentlemen receive sacrifice for this reason." After showing how the careers of Lin Han; his sons, Ting'ang and Tingji; and his grandsons, Lian and Jing fulfill this criterion, Chen explains that their descendants requested the right to build a shrine to commemorate them, similar to the ancestral shrine at Fenggang. The grand coordinator's subordinates approved the request and dispatched functionaries to discuss the selection of a site and the construction of the hall. Once the hall was complete, officials were sent to participate in the annual sacrifices to the five men. Chen Kui concludes his account of the hall with an interesting reflection on the benefits of having such a hall:

> Alas. The customs of gentlemen (*shi*) have been debased for a long time. Their efforts to vie for promotion and strive after profit are as numerous as the spines on a hedgehog and as chaotic as the flies. How can one bear to speak of it? If the gentry, observing this shrine, can truly learn from it and improve their conduct, such that sycophancy is no longer rewarded, and greed is extinguished, then the construction of this hall is not simply for the benefit of the Lin surname, but its connection to the ways of the world and the hearts of men will be great.[44]

The purpose of constructing an ancestral hall was not simply to make visible one's own distinctiveness but also to set an example to other members of the educated elite to encourage them to adjust their own behavior.

Between the early sixteenth and early seventeenth centuries, at least six ancestral halls were constructed in Linpu. Five of these survive to the present day and have recently been reconstructed. Figure 4.4 links these halls to the individuals in whose honor they were constructed. Besides Han's own hall, three of Yuanmei's other sons each had his own hall. Additionally, there was the Loyalty through Generations shrine, and the Jianquan hall, constructed for Han's sixth son, Tingyu (1495–1545).[45] The original tablets of one of the ancestral halls constructed in this period survive. The Jiqi hall is named for Lin Yuanmei's third son, Hu (1437–1507); Jiqi was his sobriquet. Hu held no official position but must have been a man of some means, for he purchased an honorary title. The hall contains three altars and a total of ten tablets, for Yuanmei; for Hu; for "all the descendants of Jiqi over the years who [die] without having married and lack posterity"; for Hu's only son, Tingmu (1471–1534), and for seven of Tingmu's eight sons.[46] Given this distribution of tablets, it is probable that the Jiqi hall was first constructed during the lifetimes of Tingmu's grandsons, in the late sixteenth or early seventeenth centuries (see Figures 4.5 and 4.6.).

The lineage institutions created by these prominent members of the Lin of Linpu in the sixteenth and early seventeenth centuries shared a number of features. With one significant exception, they follow the prescriptions of the *Family Rituals* in terms of the numbers of generations of ancestors whose tablets were installed. Halls were built by individual members of the

educated elite or by small groups of their descendants. In the hall built by
Lin Han, sacrifice was offered to a distant founding ancestor—though this
was recognized as being somewhat problematic. However, the builders of the
other halls recognized that sacrificing to distant ancestors was the prerogative
of the descent-line heir and chose not to challenge this prerogative.

The number of generations of ancestors who received sacrifice in a hall
had obvious implications for social organization. As long as the ancestral
hall housed tablets of ancestors going back only four generations, it was not
possible for the hall to serve as the ritual focus of larger descent groups such
as the Lin of Linpu. What, then, motivated people such as Lin Han or his
son, Tingyu, to devote the time and great expense to the construction of
not just one but a total of six halls? Why was a single hall not sufficient,
and, indeed, why was a single hall necessary or desirable at all? The surviving
records commemorating the construction of these halls, which were solicited
from other locally prominent men, suggest that the ancestral hall in the

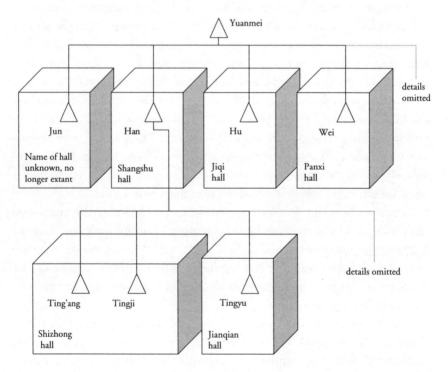

Figure 4.4. Descent Line and Ancestral Halls of Lin Yuanmei.

Figure 4.5.   Ancestral Tablets in the Jiqi Ancestral Hall (photograph by author).

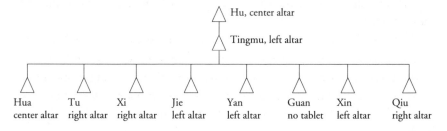

Figure 4.6.   Ancestral Tablets in the Jiqi Hall.

mid-Ming was a statement of one's prestige and commitment to neo-Confucian ideals, and thus a form of symbolic capital. This statement was directed both to the wider community as a whole and, as Chen Kui's record points out, to other members of the educated elite.

After the construction of the Jiqi hall, it would be almost a century—punctuated by the trauma of the Ming–Qing transition—before anyone in Linpu would earn another high degree or build or rebuild another ancestral hall.[47] The flurry of lineage organization and activity that would later become an important model for ancestral hall construction throughout the region had come to an end. As we will see, lineage organization took very different forms in its next phase. The ancestral hall would remain a form of symbolic capital but of a very different type. Part of the explanation for these changes lies in the changing local social and economic context.

ECONOMIC AND SOCIAL CHANGES
OF THE LATE MING

These changes can only be explored in the very broadest of detail. As I discussed in Chapter 1, the economy of the Fuzhou region underwent dramatic changes in the sixteenth century, with rising levels of agricultural production, surplus, and trade. Agriculture became increasingly specialized, and the economy of the Fuzhou suburbs including Nantai became increasingly reliant on commercial agriculture and handicraft production. Massive inflows of silver accelerated the monetization of the economy. The Ming economy was then disrupted by the turmoil of, first, a half-century of piracy and banditry, second, the Ming–Qing transition, and, finally, the early Qing coastal evacuation and trade prohibitions, but the basic economic processes were not reversed.

Trade, including foreign trade, had long been an important alternative to agriculture in the region.[48] The first half of the sixteenth century saw a rapid rise in maritime trade all along the coast of Fujian, including Fuzhou.[49] Late sixteenth century observers were struck by the volume and range of goods and the complexity of the trading patterns of the Fuzhou region:

> Not a day goes by when all these things: drawn silk from Fuzhou; lustring from Zhangzhou; indigo from Quanzhou; iron from Fuzhou and Yanping; oranges from Fuzhou and Zhangzhou; lychees from Fuzhou and Zhangzhou; cane sugar from Quanzhou and Zhangzhou; and paper from Shunchang, are not shipped across the mountain ridges dividing the two rivers or the small pass at Pucheng and from thence down into Wu and Yue [i.e., Jiangsu and Zhejiang] like flowing water. Moreover the amount that is shipped on the ocean is also beyond estimation.[50]

Fu Yiling has argued that the rising concentration of landownership was another important development during the Ming. Members of the educated elite took advantage of their special status to seize land from peasants.[51]

Because degree holders were exempt from service levy obligations and local strongmen were able to evade them, many peasant households gave over the title of their land to such people and became their tenants. Peasant indebtedness furthered the concentration of land. Moneylenders foreclosed on their debtor's property or purchased peasant holdings to convert their income to land. Wealthy landlords from Fuzhou and its suburbs came to own much of the land not only of Minxian and Houguan counties but also further afield.[52]

What were the social consequences of these changes? Xie Zhaozhe (1567–1624) wrote at length about the extravagance and conspicuous consumption of the region in the late Ming. In Fuzhou prefecture, Xie wrote, "the gentry mostly arose out of the salt business. Although they have attained positions in government and high status for their family, they are still close to trade matters." For Xie, though these interlopers might acquire the outward trappings of the educated and cultured elite, they could not help but betray their humble origins. Xie worried that status in society seemed to be determined less and less by the traditional cultural sanctions of degree and office holding and more and more by simple wealth. "These days, rank is muddled. Marriages are determined on the basis of money. People who start out as bondservants get rich and marry into exalted families."[53]

Commercialization and changing landownership patterns also strained social relations. As elsewhere in China, there were outbreaks of rent-resistance by the tenants and even armed uprisings. In the last years of the century, Governor Xu Fuyuan wrote that rent-resistance was becoming extremely serious in the counties of Minxian and Houguan, as landlords tried to collect rents on whatever terms were most advantageous to them. When the price of rice was low, they demanded rent in cash; when the price rose, they demanded rent in kind.[54] In the cities, serious tensions were created because local production of food was insufficient to meet local consumption needs.[55] There were frequent shortages and dramatic price increases, which occasionally led to outbreaks of violence.[56] In 1594, a massive rice riot shook Fuzhou, when merchants defied an order setting price caps. When a wealthy rice merchant refused buyers' demands for grain at the set price, they came to blows. The merchant's family "was very wealthy; and the hungry seized the opportunity to loot them completely." Xu dispatched local students who had gathered to write examinations to reason with the crowd, but it was no use. Several other shops were looted and riots broke out in over a dozen places in the city. Rioters even burned the examination halls. It took three days for local troops to restore order by patrolling the streets and hanging looters.[57]

The pirate threat of the mid-sixteenth to early seventeenth centuries also had dramatic effects on local society in the Fuzhou region. The genealogies suggest significant movements of population as people simply left their native villages, seeking refuge within the walls of Fuzhou city. The rural elite had the most to lose from the pirates and were best able to afford flight.[58] For those local elites who remained in the rural areas, leadership in local defense became part of the accepted repertoire of elite activity. Gu Yanwu noticed local defense structures all along the coast of Fujian when he was traveling there after the fall of the Ming.[59] Local elites took the lead in organizing these local defenses.[60] In Tangtou, just downriver from Nantai, a large fort was built in the Jiajing period in response to the pirate threat. The man behind the fort came from a poor family but had become wealthy after serving an apprenticeship with a broker of some kind. He donated the necessary funds and led the community in the construction of the fort. "When the wall was built everyone gathered within flourished, and there was no fear of bandits. The villagers entirely relied on it."[61] For men like this, local defense meant defense of one's kin. They organized their kin to build forts and form militia, and this leadership soon extended into other areas. When peace was restored, returning local elites also took the lead in rebuilding ancestral halls destroyed by the pirates, as Lin Tingji did for the ancestral hall of his father, Lin Han.[62]

Many historians have argued that in the mid-Ming the members of the educated elite grew increasingly troubled by the contradictions between their moral responsibilities and the limited means open to them to fulfill those responsibilities. In principle, a self-conscious literatus gained access to the officialdom through the examination system and then worked tirelessly for the moral and social improvement of the locale to which he was assigned. But as opportunities to hold office failed to keep pace with the rising numbers of degree holders, and as commercialization expanded the size of the local educated elite, the chance of any given individual actually obtaining an official position declined precipitously. Some fulfilled their moral imperative through education at academies and schools both in their home locality and elsewhere. Within their local society, though, many members of the educated elite found it difficult to reconcile their perceived status in the community with the lack of formal opportunities for the exercise of power.[63] From the mid-sixteenth century onward, members of the Fuzhou educated elite increasingly sought to resolve the predicament by providing local leadership and organization.

Institutions and practices connected with agnatic kinship were widely seen as the appropriate means to implement that leadership. For example, Guo Deyin wrote in 1679 that he compiled the genealogy of the Guo of Fuzhou to improve the moral shortcomings of his kin:

> Now the descendants are even more scattered. Even within the provincial capital [Fuzhou], there are some fifty or sixty lineage members within and beyond the mourning grades. Some are old, others middle-aged, others adult and others young; some are scholars, others artisans, others merchants and moneylenders. Their levels of intelligence and morality are all different. . . . Everyone has his own selfish concerns, and bears his own grudges. It has even come to the point that the generational order has been lost, and junior and senior are confused. At the extreme, there are disputes and lawsuits, and brutality towards one's own flesh and blood. Those who lack etiquette and righteousness, who are short on purity and lacking in shame, are legion.[64]

Perceptions of the appropriate functions of the ancestral hall shifted in tandem with these changing ideas. From an institution that marked difference by drawing attention to the exclusivity of the officials who were entitled to construct it, the ancestral hall gradually became an instrument for the social regulation through ritual of one's kin. Successful leadership of this new type of institution became a way of fulfilling one's perceived responsibilities as a member of the local elite.

THE INCLUSIVE HALLS OF THE NANHU ZHENG

These shifting attitudes are reflected clearly in documents relating to the Nanhu Zheng, one of two lineages that built halls on Nantai in the sixteenth century.[65] The Zheng live in Gaohu and Jiangbian villages, a short distance west of Linpu. Their first migrant ancestor, who had settled in Gaohu in the Song, had long received sacrifice at a shrine that included "an associated shrine to give sustenance to those who are without descendants."[66] In the early sixteenth century, a group of descendants began to plan for the construction of a dedicated ancestral hall. They were all members of a single branch of the lineage—not the senior branch—and apparently none were holders of examination degrees or official position. The most prominent man of the lineage at the time was Zheng Shanfu (1485–1524), a *jinshi* of 1505 and a director in the board of rites. He sent a letter to this group in which he argued for the ancestral hall as an instrument of lineage unity and cohesiveness. Shanfu noted that "[you] the Third Branch recognize that your wealth is due to the bounty of the ancestors," indicating that what enabled the group to construct the hall was not official status but financial means. However, Shanfu suggested that the hall should be inclusive rather than exclusive:

> I do not know whether after the hall is completed you will allow the descendants of each of the [other] branches to enter the gates and worship. At the autumn solstice, the descendants of each branch ought to prepare sacrifice for the first ancestors to have lived. This way the ancestors in the underworld will be pleased and will say the descendants of the Third Branch are not only rich but also righteous, and being righteous are also public-spirited. Other lineages hearing of this will also appreciate the unity of our great family. If on the other hand the branches are divided and in performing [ritual] are concerned with their own selfish interests [literally, think in terms of self and other], I'm afraid the ancestors will not appreciate this.[67]

In other words, Zheng pleaded with the men who had paid for the hall to allow it to serve as the location for collective rituals of all the descendants of the founding ancestor not just their own branch.[68]

Though the Nanhu Zheng hall was roughly contemporary with the later halls of the Linpu Lin, it was the hall of the future. Increasingly over the sixteenth and later centuries, ancestral halls were markers not of the exclusiveness of their elite sponsors but of their integration into the community and their assertion of a leadership role in the ritual life of the community. Educated elite members increasingly saw ritual as the means for building a stable and moral social order and their own leadership of ancestral hall ritual as a means for fulfilling their sense of social responsibility. Kai-Wing Chow has labeled this the ritualist orientation to local society.[69] In the Fuzhou region, this orientation grew out of factors including commercialization, which was perceived as having led to profound social decay, and piracy, which tied the rural elite more closely to their immediate community as they became involved in collective defense. Ancestral halls gradually became sites for ritual performance by all the descendants of the founding ancestors of local lineages, elements in a broad attempt to build more cohesive communities and reverse the decaying morality of rural society.

THE POPULAR HALLS OF THE HUANG OF YIXU

The Huang of Yixu present a useful case study of the complex effects of these various economic and social changes on lineage development in the Fuzhou area. The Huang had long had a certain level of corporate organization. Early sources in the genealogy refer to lineage and branch heads (*zufangzhang*) and to collective property in the form of alluvial islands. Clam beds in the Min River were endowed in the name of the founding ancestor, Zhifu, discussed in Chapter 2, and every male descendant of Zhifu was entitled to a share in the proceeds when the rights to harvest the beds were auctioned off.[70] As we shall see, lineage activists also tried to impose codes of conduct on the whole lineage membership. But for most of the Ming, no member of the Yixu Huang seems to have thought that a collective ancestral hall was the appropriate structure for institutionalizing the relationships between lineage members. Though some ancestral halls were built in the mid-Ming, these were private halls that served to mark exclusiveness rather than to build inclusiveness. It was only in the late Ming, as the effects of commercial changes and piracy penetrated local society, that lineage members hit on the ancestral hall as the essential tool to build lineage unity.

The genealogy indicates the existence of a wealthy stratum within the lineage from the early Ming. Thus Bozhen, who lived around the time of the Yuan–Ming transition "was married to a woman née Zhang who helped him get richer. He began to establish a family estate, and constructed houses and dwellings. When he died, she personally led the bondservants in the construction of his tomb."[71] Wenze, who had some education, traveled to distant provinces serving as private secretary to various officials. He became very wealthy, and, when he eventually returned home, he purchased considerable property and built a new home. His descendants became known as the New House (Xincuo) branch. Wenze also ordered the construction of four granaries to store his income from rents. When he later divided his estate among his four sons, each was given a granary as well as rights to gravesites at a cemetery he acquired.[72]

The century of piracy had a direct impact on the residents of Yixu. One intriguing biography in the genealogy suggests, as must surely have been frequently the case, that the people of Yixu were instigators as well as victims of pirate violence. Fu, who lived in the early Ming, was "short in stature and full of schemes. People said the Huang are a lineage of dwarf bandits, and everyone in the vicinity feared them. Later his descendants grew more flourishing with each day." There is also evidence in the genealogy of the negative consequences of the period of pirate activity. Five of the six grandsons of a man named Lun left no offspring. "It is said that they were drowned by the pirates at Longtanjiao."[73]

The only civil official of any distinction among the Huang in the Ming was a grandson of the wealthy Bozhen, Linzi (b. 1344), who at the age of forty was recommended for office on the basis of his virtuous reputation. The lineage could also boast a few military officers and one government student, who obtained a minor position through the intervention of his brother-in-law, a prominent general.[74] It is thus no surprise that there is no record of the construction of ancestral halls from the early to mid-Ming. As we have already seen, in Fuzhou at that time such practices were the preserve of the very upper ranks of the elite, and there were no such people in Yixu. In the late Ming, though, members of the educated elite among the Yixu Huang, holders of only the lowest examination degrees, did begin to construct small-scale ancestral halls. Tingju, who lived in the mid-sixteenth century, was the grandson of Wenze, the private secretary, and a government student like his father and grandfather. According to Qing records, he constructed a free-standing ancestral hall in which sacrifice was offered to Wenze. There is no indication that other relatives worshiped in the hall. When it was later damaged, there seemed to be no point in rebuilding it because the site was so small. This was a hall that accorded with the prescriptions of Zhu Xi: small and private, with only the tablets of recent ancestors. But much later, in the mid-eighteenth century, other descendants of Wenze became involved. In 1757, a number of holders of lower degrees donated land in another location and paid for the reconstruction of the hall on a larger scale. It became known as the branch shrine (*zhici*) of the New House Branch.[75]

In the mid-seventeenth century, despite the turmoil periodically engulfing the Fuzhou suburbs, there were two efforts to construct a more inclusive structure for ancestral worship and the organization of kin. The first of these was the family temple (*jiamiao*) of the Four Branches, referring to the descendants of the four sons of Linzi. While Linzi served in office, his wife and his concubine built up his family estate, which was later divided among the sons.[76] Neither Linzi nor any of his immediate descendants established a free-standing ancestral hall. In the mid-seventeenth century, this became a cause of concern to a group of later descendants. As one of them put it, "Our lineage in the past has never had an ancestral hall. Those who understood righteousness were constantly ashamed by this. But there was no way to meet the expenses, and the descendants were not numerous."[77] In 1651, not long after Qing forces had subdued the last remnants of Ming loyalism in the Fuzhou region, a few individuals decided the time had come to remedy this situation. The key figure involved was Baoguang, a government student of 1652. He is a classic example of the more locally engaged educated elites of the late Ming and early Qing. "Reclusive, he did not serve in office."[78] Instead, he devoted himself to the affairs of the community, initiating the construction of a communal school and Confucian shrine; compiling the genealogy; and playing a leading role in the construction of a hall in honor of his distant ancestor, Linzi.[79]

A later record stresses the official successes enjoyed by Linzi and his sons to justify the construction of a hall dedicated to them. "Their generations of virtue and official spirit were renowned in their age." It was also necessary to justify the fact that Linzi was not a descent-line heir, that is, he was not descended from the founding ancestor in a continuous line of eldest sons. The author of the record used a slippery reading of the *Liji* [*Record of Ritual*] to accomplish this:

> According to the *Li* [*ji*], if one's ancestor is a secondary son, then the descendants should have a separate descent-line. Although there should be distinctions between noble and base in the conduct of sacrifice, there is no question about this principle. For this reason, from antiquity to the present day, at spring and autumn, those who repair the descent-line temple (*zongmiao*), gather the lineage and conduct the sacrifice do so in order to express their concern and filiality.[80]

By arguing that secondary sons should establish their own descent line, the author was effectively effacing the distinction between greater and lesser descent lines. By this logic, anyone could sacrifice to distant ancestors without violating propriety.

To build the hall, Baoguang secured the agreement of the senior members of the four segments descended from Linzi. He then solicited donations from the educated elite and the wealthy within the branch (*fangnei shenfu*). A total of seventy-two individuals contributed to the project.[81] In the hall, sacrifice was offered to Zhifu, the founding ancestor to settle in Yixu; "the illustrious ancestors of this branch"; and the founding ancestor of the branch, presumably either Linzi or his father, though there was no sacrificial estate endowed to meet the costs of sacrifice. A corporate organization was created when the hall was built, the members of which were the seventy-two donors. Each owned a share in the ancestral hall by virtue of his initial investment and enjoyed certain benefits. These would have included the prestige of membership in the hall and the right to participate in its ritual activities. In the Kangxi period, funds were again solicited "from those members of the branch who had a will to requite their origins" in order to establish sacrificial property to support the hall. "They acquired property, collected rents and managed the work. The system they established was truly thorough. They exerted themselves with all their heart and as a result the rules became established." Once this corporate estate had been endowed, a rotation system was set up whereby all those who had a share in the hall collected the rents for one year in rotation. Any surplus remaining after the sacrifice had been paid for was saved for future collective expenses.[82]

The Four Branches hall was an intermediate form of the ancestral hall— between the exclusive gentry halls of the early to mid-Ming and the more inclusive lineage halls of the Qing. It is an example of asymmetrical segmentation, whereby a group of agnates define themselves as a subgroup within the larger lineage by highlighting an ancestor they share in common.[83] Though there was a tablet to Zhifu in the hall, the hall was not intended to serve as the ritual focus for all the descendants of this first ancestor who had settled in Yixu. The ritual focus was Linzi, and only people who claimed descent from Linzi were eligible to invest in the hall. On the other hand, whereas the ancestral halls in Linpu had been the private property of individuals or households, the Four Branches hall was the property of a much larger number of individuals whose kinship connections would have been quite distant. Over time, the ownership of a share in the hall became a form of property that was inherited by the descendants of the initial investors, so the number of people with a share of ownership in the hall would grow ever larger. Though the Four Branches hall might originally have been a marker of relatively high social status, this status would not have been shared generally among all the descendants of the focal ancestor but only with the descendants of those who had invested in the initial construction of the hall or its later reconstruction. Indeed, in the mid-seventeenth century there seems to have been little sense of group identity or cohesiveness among this larger group.[84]

This is not to say that there was no interest among activists like Baoguang in building greater cohesion among all the descendants of Zhifu on the basis of descent in the mid-seventeenth century—just that they did not see the ancestral hall as the chief basis for such cohesion. Rather, their focus was on moral instruction, what Chow labels the didactic approach to lineage organization.[85] Baoguang composed a set of Ancestral Injunctions intended to shape the conduct of the whole community. There were ten injunctions in all, which called on individuals to venerate their ancestors, be filial to their kin, respect their elders, educate their descendants, divide property evenly, increase the cohesiveness of the lineage, devote themselves to their occupation, practice frugality, soothe antagonisms, and guard against immorality.[86] But Baoguang's injunctions probably had little concrete effect on the people of Yixu. There was no mechanism for enforcement, no sanctions, and the injunctions on the whole were little more than vague ethical exhortations. Nevertheless, they do indicate something of the concerns of the local elite. Differentiation in wealth and status was increasing, largely due to the broader social and economic changes of the period, and it was important to counteract the resulting forces of divisiveness. Moral instruction was one way to do so.

In the late seventeenth century, the main strategy adopted to counteract these tendencies shifted. Local elite men sought to increase cohesiveness among the members of the larger community by constructing an inclusive ancestral hall for all the descendants of Zhifu. It took almost a century for the project to come to fruition. An account of the hall compiled by Fuji in 1734 explains, in the terms of a familiar trope, that although members of the lineage had served as officials for generations, they were so honest in office that they retired in poverty, while the common members of the lineage were neither sufficiently numerous nor wealthy to undertake the building of a descent-line shrine. In 1662, four members of the lineage attempted to raise funds for the construction of the hall and purchased a site in the middle of the village. However, before construction could begin, the holder of an old deed to the plot demanded further compensation. When he was rebuffed, he gave the deed to members of an official entourage, beginning a protracted lawsuit that cost the fortunes of three of the four original participants. In 1684, six members of the lineage revived the project and managed to oversee the construction of a hall, the carving of a tablet niche, and the installation of ancestral tablets (see Figure 4.7). But problems with the site persisted. In 1722, five men proposed that the hall should be repaired and rebuilt. To raise the necessary funds, Fuji's father approached the lineage and branch heads (zufangzhang) for permission to collect donations from the lineage at large. It was estimated that the reconstruction would cost over 150 taels. In a clear break from earlier traditions of ancestral hall building in the village, the bulk of this money was collected by a per capita levy on the adult males of the

Figure 4.7. Ancestral Tablets in the Yixu Huang Ancestral Hall
(photograph by author).

Huang surname. By this time, there were over one thousand members of the
lineage, and each was required to pay one mace. Fuji's father made a large
personal donation as well, and the income from collectively owned clam beds
was also diverted to the project.[87] But even after this expansion, the scale of
the hall was still thought unsatisfactory. In 1733, a small amount of rice was
again collected from every male adult in the lineage to pay for its expansion.
Finally, in 1734, Fuji was able to compose a record to commemorate the
hall's successful completion.[88] For the first time, the Huang of Yixu had an
ancestral hall in which all the descendants of their original founding ancestor
could participate.[89]

The story of the construction of the Yixu Huang ancestral hall represents
a further development in the evolving meaning of kinship and kinship organization. Its predecessors, the New House and Four Branches halls, had
been exclusive organizations—membership in which was strictly limited.
The new ancestral hall was open to all descendants of the founding ancestor
and indeed was intended to build cohesion among the entire group. The
construction of the hall was a project initiated by the local elite, and, as
we shall see in the next chapter, they retained certain privileges in its ritual
activities.

The educated elite did not give up on didactic approaches for dealing with the erosion of the social order in the late Ming and early Qing. A more substantial code of conduct for lineage members was compiled at around the same time the new hall was built by Government Military Student Yuanbin. Like the earlier version, each regulation consists of a slogan followed by an explanatory paragraph. Unlike the earlier version, the explanatory paragraphs prescribe precise regulations for personal behavior and provide sanctions to be applied should these regulations be violated. These regulations illustrate how the elite vision of the lineage both empowered them at the local level and bolstered the reach of the imperial state.[90] The managers of the ancestral hall also further expanded their authority over lineage members by asserting rights over private property in the name of protecting the geomancy of the village. A record of geography and geomancy, also written by Fuji, probably in the 1740s, provides examples of this sort of intervention. Yuliu hill served as a protective barrier to the Yixu area. Some forty years earlier, someone had felled trees on the hill. As a result, there had been several disastrous fires and outbreaks of disease. Therefore, a prohibition against cutting down any trees on the hill, regardless of whether they were on private or corporate property, was enacted. Violators were to be fined the cost of providing one opera performance in the ancestral hall, and repeat offenders were to be reported to the lineage and branch heads for punishment. Fuji praised the efficacy of this regulation. Since it was made, there had been no fires or disease in the village, and several members of the lineage had enjoyed academic success.[91] These rules can be interpreted as the assertion of new powers by the lineage leadership. Such powers included both rights over the disposition of private property held by lineage members and the power to enforce restrictions on the settlement rights of outsiders.[92] But clearly the educated elite of Yixu no longer thought about maintaining social order primarily through moral instruction and formal regulations. The inclusive ancestral hall had come to be the essential tool of this larger project.

THE LUOZHOU CHEN HALL AND THE SPREAD OF POPULAR ANCESTRAL HALLS IN THE LATE MING AND QING

The story of the Huang of Yixu illustrates how lineage organizations formalized elite control over local society from the mid-Ming. In the process, ancestral halls, which had previously been exclusive symbols of official status, became much more inclusive. The story might have ended there, were it not for the broader impact of the very changes that had given rise to the efforts by the educated elite to formalize their powers in the first place—developments such as commercialization and monetization—and the growing prestige of the gentry model of the ancestral hall. Ancestral halls spread rapidly through the Fuzhou countryside in the late Ming and early Qing, as this model was widely emulated and, in the process, markedly transformed.[93] The new halls were very different from the official and gentry type halls of the early to mid-Ming. These new halls, of which the Huang hall was one early example, may be labeled "popular halls" because they were constructed from contributions from people of different classes and often in communities where there were no degree holders.

The history of the Chen of Luozhou provides a good illustration of the shifting meaning of the ancestral hall in Fuzhou in the early Qing. We have already seen something of the Chen effort to shed their status as despised Dan in Chapter 2. The early corporate activities of the Chen of Luozhou seem to have been connected entirely to graves and sacrifice at graves. It was only in the eighteenth century that the Luozhou Chen tried to construct an ancestral hall. The hall they built was very different from the official or gentry halls of Fenggang and Linpu. It was designed to promote inclusiveness and unity of all the kin descended from the founding ancestor. Its rules and management also reflected the involvement and input of a much wider spectrum of local elites than the educated officials who built these earlier halls. Wealthy members of the lineage, whose contributions financed the hall's construction, insisted that their contribution be recognized in the ritual practices and management of the hall.

The first Chen probably came ashore by the early Ming at the latest, perhaps to work as tenants on land owned by the area's foremost lineage at the time, the Wu.[94] As we saw in Chapter 2, in the sixteenth or seventeenth century, at least some of them were still responsible for the fish tax associated with the Dan. But obviously not all of them, for by the mid-fifteenth century a few men of the Chen surname had begun to appear in the lists of successful examination candidates from Luozhou. The first of these was Chen Hua, a provincial graduate in 1459. Hua's great-grandson Chen Huai received the *jinshi* degree in 1538—one of only three Luozhou men to be so honored before the Qing.[95]

The early corporate activities of the Chen were connected with graves. In 1550, the tomb of the founding ancestor of the Chen of Luozhou and his wife was reconstructed.[96] An inscription credits "Gentleman-literatus Se of the fifth generation and others" with the reconstruction. Se was Chen Hua's grandson and Huai's father, the title being an honorary one bestowed by virtue of his son's success.[97] The construction of an elaborate hillside tomb was probably useful in the erasure of any remaining connections with Dan identity, for it is believed, even today, that the Dan are also distinguished from the non-Dan because they do not bury their dead. The reference to "others" (*deng*) is the earliest indication in the sources of any sort of collective activity by the Chen of Luozhou.

Tombs remained the focal point of whatever corporate organization existed among the Chen in the sixteenth century. The genealogy divides the descendants of the founding ancestor into five branches beginning in Chen Hua's generation, and these remain meaningful subdivisions within the lineage today. This sort of branching, based on the genealogical equivalency of brothers and cousins sharing descent from a common male ancestor, corresponds to what Myron Cohen has called associational kinship in its genealogical aspect and is very common among Nantai lineages.[98] The genealogy is silent on the question of the timing and reasons for this segmentation, and residents of Luozhou today can offer no information, but on the basis of the records on the establishment of grave estates, we can deduce that it was members of the fifth or six generation who organized the lineage in this way and that economic differentiation may have been the impulse behind it. By the time the genealogy was first compiled, of the five members of the third generation, two had been buried "beside the tomb of his father," while the tombs of the other three had been lost. The same level of detail characterizes the next generation. Then, beginning in the fifth generation, successive generations of members of what would become the Senior Branch were all buried at a place called Junbian, a hillock of Gaogai hill, the low rolling hill that dominates Nantai Island. It seems that members of this branch were wealthy enough to endow a corporate trust, in the form of the graveyard at Junbian, and perhaps additional property to support the graveyard. Ownership of the estate belonged originally to the man or men who endowed it and then later to their descendants, who as a result developed a corporate identity.

Beginning in the fourth generation, the senior branch is further subdivided into three subbranches known as the Xianwan, Fuhoudun, and Nansheng branches (Figure 4.8). The genealogy reports that this segmentation occurred during the lifetimes of the great-grandsons of the focal ancestors of the subbranches. This is probably another case of asymmetrical

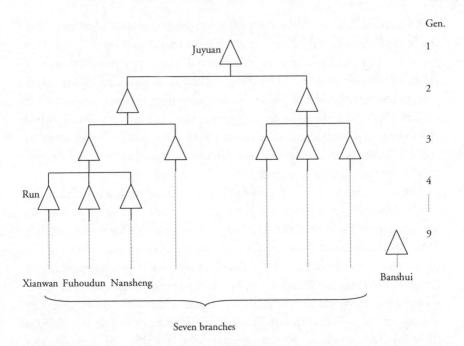

Figure 4.8. Segmentation of the Luozhou Chen.

segmentation on the basis of land property. The founding ancestor of the Xianwan branch was Run. His second son, who lived from 1528 to 1585, was a man of some wealth. He acquired another large plot of land on Gaogai hill. Eight terraces were eventually constructed there, and his descendants and their wives and concubines continued to be buried there into the mid-Qing. The site was maintained into the Republican period, when the living descendants organized themselves to protest to the magistrate about illegal burials by nonmembers of the group. Run's fourth son was a county student who married but died without posterity. He too must have been a wealthy man. According to the genealogy, "his dying wish was that he should not have posterity appointed for him, but rather that his remaining estate should be used to supplement the sacrificial estate of his father."[99] The estate was large enough to pay for the purchase of over forty *mu* of orange orchards that were leased to tenants. With the income from the estate, "the descendants of the Xianwan branch gather together as a branch and conduct seasonal sacrifices."[100]

The mid-sixteenth and seventeenth centuries were difficult years for the Chen of Luozhou, first due to piracy and then to the turmoil of the

Ming–Qing transition. But even before normalcy fully returned to local society, efforts began to be made towards the construction of an ancestral hall. While the earlier documents in the genealogy all relate to various graves and property associated with them, the later documents all have to do with the ancestral hall. Details are found in a document entitled "Record of the collection of funds and purchase of land for the family temple of our descent-line," written in the early eighteenth century by Yide, a prominent member of the twelfth generation. The record begins with a quote from the *Liji* stressing the importance of building an ancestral hall: "When establishing a palace or residence, the first task is the descent-line shrine." Yide does not address why the Chen had yet to construct one; other genealogies make clear that by the seventeenth century, not having one had become a cause for shame. Having an ancestral hall might also have served to further obscure their past as despised Dan, but of course the genealogy does not mention this. The hall was initiated by one Chen Sheng (1601–59), who identified a plot of land whose good geomantic qualities and location in the heart of the village made it an ideal site. Twenty-four individuals responded to his call for donations, raising a total of 120 taels, and the land was purchased. Most of the contributors belonged to a single subbranch, the Xianwan. Though the commemorative record of the project was written by Chen Yide, one of three members of the lineage who attained the *jinshi* degree in the early Qing, the contributors themselves were not men who attained official success. As Figure 4.9 indicates, three of the twenty-four were government students and a number of others were the sons or grandsons of holders of various lower degrees but none held an official post or earned an official salary. However, each of them was wealthy enough to make a substantial donation to promote the formal organization of their kin. They must have been landowners, moneylenders, and merchants.[101] In contrast to the pattern of the early Ming and before, in the late Ming and Qing, the men responsible for lineage activism, that is, for strengthening the ties that bound kin, were not only those at the top of local society but also those attempting to make their way there. The construction of an ancestral hall was seen as an appropriate expression of this activism. In 1677, construction was begun on the site selected by Chen Sheng of a hall "in which the spirits of the ancestors could be placed." In 1687, large double gates were added, which could be opened and closed according to schedule. Thirty years later, the initial construction was repaired, and some deficiencies were corrected. The final result was a splendid hall of which all the members of the lineage could be proud.[102]

Fifty years after the hall was completed two successful officials in the lineage called for a genealogy to be compiled as well.[103] In the preface written by one of them after the genealogy was completed, the changing focus of elite concerns about lineage building is made explicit. "If the poor and the wealthy do not get along, and the strong and the weak fight, this will inspire mockery from nearby lineages. This would result from the ancestors finding fault with people [descended from them]."[104] Clearly building ancestral halls was no longer a way to set oneself apart from one's less successful relatives. Rather, it had become a way to increase the sense of cohesiveness linking a self-professed patrilineal descent group tracing descent from a common ancestor. Inclusiveness and the unity of kin had decisively replaced exclusivity and the privileges of official status as the justification for building ancestral halls and compiling genealogies (see Table 4.1).

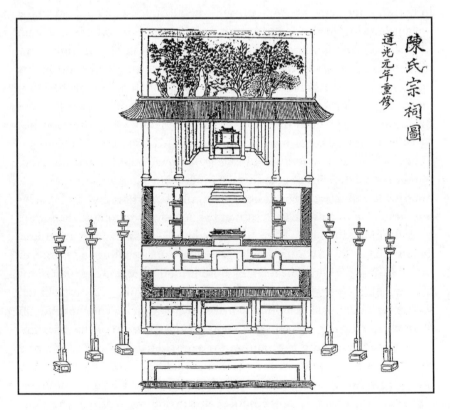

Figure 4.9. The Luozhou Chen Ancestral Hall.
SOURCE: *Luojiang Chenshi jiapu,* 1933.

TABLE 4.1
Official Status of Contributors to the Luozhou Chen Ancestral Hall

Name	Status	Father's status	Grandfather's status
Yide	Metropolitan Graduate (*jinshi*)	Tribute Student (*gongsheng*)	—
Dongbo	Government Student (*shengyuan*)	Government Student	Government Student
Faliang	—	—	—
Erzao	—	Government Student	—
Erxiang	Government Student	—	—
Riyong	—	Government Student	Government Student
Ziming	—	—	Government Student
Yongchang	—	—	—
Zishen	—	—	—
Junwei	—	Stipend Student	—
Yongjian	—	—	—
Yongji	—	—	—
Yongzan	—	—	—
Yongduan	—	—	—
Erkai	—	—	—
Juwu	Government Student (Changle)	—	—
Erzhao	—	—	—
Yonggui	—	—	—
Yongju	—	—	—
Yongtui	—	—	—
Yongding	—	—	—
Erdian	—	Government Student	Government Student
Yongguo	—	—	Government Student
Zhonghua	—	—	—
Xijiang	—	—	—

HALL MANAGEMENT AND
THE INSTALLATION OF TABLETS

The new ancestral halls of the late Ming and Qing, such as those of Yixu and Luozhou, were built not by members of the educated elite alone but by individuals from a wider spectrum of local elites, including merchants, moneylenders, and large landowners who did not necessarily hold degrees.[105] These individuals sought to have their contributions recognized, and this reshaped the operation of ancestral halls. Two issues in particular demonstrate the shifting negotiations over kinship practice and the multiple positions adopted: (1) who should have the right to have a tablet installed in the hall?

and (2) who should manage the finances of the hall? The ways in which these questions were answered illustrates another aspect of the difference between the popular halls of the Ming and Qing and earlier official and gentry halls.

The criteria by which tablets could be entered into the hall was one of the most important issues in the management of any hall. Tablets to dead ancestors worshiped on a domestic altar would eventually be discarded, usually after only a few generations.[106] In contrast, installation in the ancestral hall of a permanent tablet to an ancestor ensured the continuity of sacrifice to that ancestor in perpetuity. A tablet installed in the ancestral hall would endure for the life of the hall, and the ancestor thus commemorated would partake in the communal sacrifices periodically offered at the hall. Installing a tablet in the hall also signified a share in the ownership of the hall, entitling those descended from the ancestor to certain rights, including rights to a portion of the offerings made in the hall and a share in the income from any estate. Though the ancestral hall by the early Qing had become an institution designed to unify agnatic kin, the tablet in the hall continued to be a source of prestige and distinction, and the prestige associated with having a tablet installed seems to have been inherited by the descendants of those who installed the tablet, at least for early generations. As a result, every ancestral hall constructed on Nantai in the Qing had strict criteria governing the entry of tablets into the hall—a point noticed by Doolittle:

> At the time of erecting an ancestral hall, rules are made by the proprietor in regard to the qualifications of those who may have their tablets placed in it, or the sum of money which must be paid into the general or permanent funds of the hall, by the particular families to which the new tablets belong. These rules are very definite and strict, and are rigidly enforced, else the place devoted to holding or arranging the tablets in the halls would in a few generations become crowded.[107]

The precise criteria that were developed for the ancestral hall of the Chen of Luozhou do not survive.[108] But fortunately, as members of the Chen lineage became locally and even nationally prominent over the course of the Qing, their lineage organization came to serve as a model for other lineages constructing ancestral halls, and these lineages frequently justified their decisions by making explicit reference to the Chen hall. Indeed, the genealogies of one such lineage, the Ye of Sanshan, provide the best evidence for the actual practices of installing tablets in ancestral halls at the end of the late imperial period.[109]

Ye Guanguo was the first notable success of this descent line. He was a metropolitan graduate of 1751 and held a number of important positions in the administration of the examinations. Six of his seven sons attained the rank of provincial graduate and one went on to become a metropolitan graduate. Though none of his descendants attained Guanguo's success, several were wealthy and prominent men.[110] Guanguo's descendants were divided into seven branches, one for the descendants of each of his sons, which were further subdivided into twenty-five subbranches, one for the descendants of each of his grandsons. In the 1880s, the members of the seven branches decided to construct an ancestral hall in Fuzhou, with Guanguo as the focal ancestor. The genealogy provides extensive details on how tablets were to be installed in the hall. Tablets for Guanguo, his seven sons, and his twenty-five grandsons were all installed "without discussion." But the number of descendants in the fourth and later generations grew increasingly numerous. "If tablets were installed for all of them indiscriminately, it would be difficult to accommodate them all on the altar, and the ceremonies could almost be said to be defiled." It was therefore important to determine criteria for the further installation of tablets. Here the author of the Ye genealogy turned for guidance to the Chen of Luozhou and to another prominent local lineage, the Lin of Shangjie, west of Nantai. "Investigation of the two halls of the Lin of Houguan and the Chen of Luojiang [reveals that the criteria by which] lineage members may have tablets made and installed in the hall are office, rank, and examination success. Thus restrictions are clarified and encouragement expressed."[111] The Ye genealogy goes on to provide extremely specific criteria according to which tablets may be entered into the hall. For each rank obtained in the examination system and each rank held in the official hierarchy, certain rights to install tablets in the hall are granted. A lineage member who obtains the *jinshi* degree and then goes on to hold a top-ranking official position may install tablets for himself and his father, grandfather, and great-grandfather. A lineage member who merely passes the lowest level in the examination system or purchases a degree is allowed to install only his own tablet and that of his father. "This follows the example of the dynastic enfeoffment privileges for one, two, and three generations."

Besides official status, there are two other criteria by which members of the Ye lineage might hope to gain entry into the hall. First, those who attained the age of one hundred *sui* and earned the right to a memorial arch authorized by the state were also allowed to have a tablet installed. Second, those who contributed significant amounts to the property of the hall were eligible for this honor:

> Those who contribute or establish sacrificial estate property with a value of more than one thousand taels, regardless of office or rank, may have a tablet installed; more than two thousand taels, a tablet for oneself and one's father; more than three thousand taels, for oneself, one's grandfather and father. Although the contribution may be greater, the limit of two generations to one's grandfather may not be exceeded. This is in order to clarify restrictions. If one chooses to pass on one's qualifications to have a tablet installed to previous generations, one is allowed to do this.[112]

Similar criteria for the inclusion of tablets for lineage members who did not hold degrees are found in many Fuzhou genealogies.[113] These sources make clear that by the Qing, financial contribution alone was enough to obtain the privilege and prestige of installing a permanent tablet in the ancestral hall. It was not only examination degree holders who could arrange the installation of tablets but also members of the local elite who did not hold degrees.

A second issue confronting the builders of ancestral halls in Qing Fuzhou was how the halls and their estates should be managed. In many parts of Fujian, management simply rotated through the major segments of the lineage.[114] In Fuzhou, the large amounts of property and significant sums of money involved demanded more sophisticated arrangements. Prior to the completion of the ancestral hall of the Ye, for example, management of corporate property endowed in the name of the founding ancestor simply rotated annually among the seven branches of his descendants. In the process of establishing the hall, this estate was expanded to include several shops and houses in Fuzhou city and twenty-six separate plots of farmland earning annual rents of almost five thousand catties. When the hall was completed in 1887, the system of rotation was abandoned. The annual expenses of the hall totaled approximately 120,000 cash. The hall also employed a number of hall attendants (*ciding*) who required supervision. Managing the affairs of the hall thus called for someone who was numerate and trustworthy. As the rules for the selection of managers from the Ye genealogy make clear, this meant someone who was rich:

> A man who is upright and proper should be selected to be the general manager of the hall. The lineage and branch heads and the gentry members of the hall should collectively select him at the appropriate time. Only the filial, charitable and prosperous are suited to fill this office. The filial will not be

THE ANCESTRAL HALL   131

able to bear stealing from the hall's money. The charitable will not dare to waste the hall's money. The prosperous will not embezzle the hall's money for themselves. Those who have been selected may not evade the responsibility.[115]

The changing criteria for inclusion of tablets into the hall, the requirement that potential managers of the hall be both wealthy and numerate, and the demand for greater involvement in hall affairs by those who had made financial contributions to the hall all reflect the growing importance of commercial wealth in the institutional arrangements of ancestral halls. This was very different from the early to mid-Ming, when halls were built only by high officials and their immediate descendants. By the mid-Qing, wealthy local people were demanding and obtaining leadership roles and social status purely on the basis on their wealth, a sure sign that the ongoing commercialization of the Fuzhou area was having effects on local social organization. It was no longer necessary to convert commercial wealth into education and officeholding to claim authority in the lineage.[116]

DISCONTINUITIES AND COUNTERTRENDS

The historian researching the spread of ancestral halls in the Fuzhou countryside is naturally drawn to the greatest of the halls. Descriptions of these halls printed in the genealogy and inscribed on stone are celebratory and triumphant. It would be tempting to extrapolate the broader picture on the basis of these success stories. This runs the risk of oversimplifying the situation in two ways. First, a close reading of the sources frequently reveals that the process by which ancestral halls were proposed, financed, and brought to fruition was rarely straightforward and often long and tortured. Second, it ignores the halls that were *not* built, the lineages whose members' strategies ultimately led not to the construction of a hall but to other forms of kinship practice. This was especially true once the people of Fuzhou began to construct what I have labeled popular halls. These struggles illustrate that the meanings of lineage and lineage practice were far from monolithic in Chinese society but rather were constituted in a network of shifting representations, growing out of the multitude of strategies of individuals and groups.

The branch hall of the Chen of Langqi illustrates one of the different paths lineage development could take. At three separate moments, members of the lineage came to the decision that the immediate benefits of a continued association were not worth the costs, and the association therefore dissolved. The Chen constructed a popular hall in which all individuals descended from their founding ancestor could participate in the late sixteenth century. This was an ill-fated hall from the beginning. It was first burned down in an accident, rebuilt, then destroyed "by pirates," probably the forces of Zheng Chenggong, in 1653. A few years later, in 1661, Langqi was abandoned in the coastal evacuation. The author of the genealogy notes ironically "luckily the hall had not yet been rebuilt, or it would have been destroyed yet again, and we would have had to rebuild it again." Local society did not settle down until the end of the seventeenth century, when lineage members contributed to the construction of first a mat-shed ancestral hall and later a more solid structure.[117]

At about the same time as the lineage hall was first built, a segment within the lineage constructed its own hall, which was dedicated to a celebrated member of the segment. Jiufeng had died heroically in defense against pirates during the Jiajing period. Probably he died at sea, for his body had been lost and he had no tomb. "At the cleaning of the tombs in spring and autumn, he alone does not receive sacrifice." We do not know where the money came from, whether it was from Jiufeng's own estate or donated by his kin, but a group of his relatives decided to establish a shrine in his honor. It too was destroyed during the turmoil of 1653. More than ten *mu* of land had also been endowed in Jiufeng's name. Between 1653 and 1661, the rent from this land was allowed to accumulate to finance the reconstruction of the hall. But during the period of evacuation, the person who had been put in charge of these funds embezzled them. Furthermore, once the evacuation was rescinded, it took several years to restore the fields to productivity. In many parts of Fujian, tax relief was granted in the immediate post-evacuation period. But in the case of Jiufeng's fields, the tax relief expired before the land could yield a harvest. None of the descendants who owned a share of the land was willing to contribute his own money to pay the taxes. "So the original owners were sought and the property returned to them."[118] Now, when the descendants were pressed for tax payment by *yamen* runners or local *lijia* functionaries, they claimed the land did not belong to them but rather to whomever's name appeared in the tax register as the owner of the land. By this point, Jiufeng's estate had been reduced to the site of the former hall and some vacant land beside it. A portion of this vacant land was used for the construction of the temple to the village tutelary deity, and the kin earned a small annual rent for the use of this land. But rather than accumulate this small sum in the hopes of rebuilding Jiufeng's hall, the two main segments of descendants simply divided it among themselves.[119] Thus, the individuals who comprised the group of kin associated with Jiufeng's estate came to the decision that the immediate benefits of continued association were not worth the costs. Kinship organization, especially in its early stages, required constant deliberate renewal. In the absence of that renewal, even if there remained a material foundation for the organization, it could not survive.

The Langqi case also points to the importance that the broader context might have on local lineage organization. In Fuzhou, the period of piracy in the sixteenth century, the turmoil of the early Qing and coastal evacuation, and extremely high tax rates in the late seventeenth century all had a profound impact on the development of ancestral halls. Several Fuzhou lineages besides the Langqi Chen have legends of ancestral halls being destroyed in pirate raids or in the early Qing.[120] Extremely high rates of land tax made landownership, or at least registered landownership, very unattractive in the early Qing in the Fuzhou suburbs.[121] Inability or unwillingness to cover the tax obligations on corporate land led to many cases of estates being abandoned, with the result that the association of kin who had previously held shares in the land was necessarily threatened.[122]

Sometimes the obstacles to construction and maintenance of an ancestral hall had to do with local politics. The Yang of Huyu had no ancestral hall in the Ming. In the Kangxi period, the great-great-grandson of the one minor official in the lineage proposed the construction of a hall on the site of that official's former home. The property had since fallen into the hands of several lineage members. One lineage member had sold his share of the land to people surnamed Ye. After considerable complications, the land was recovered and the hall was constructed in 1686. "So we traced back and requited our origins, and were able to feel that the spirits were present." Sixty years later the hall required renovations, but a new dispute broke out with the Ye, who still controlled the adjoining property, and it proved impossible to begin the repairs. The dispute, perhaps better described as a feud in the making, dragged on for almost thirty years. Ultimately it degenerated into a pitched battle between the Yang and the Ye. Local elites intervened to resolve the dispute informally and found in favor of the Yang. But it was not until 1787, when the hall "was in much worse disrepair than previously," that the Yang could actually rebuild it.[123]

Another lineage that underwent a long and complicated process in the course of organizing and constructing an ancestral hall was the Ren of

Junshan. The endowment of their ancestral hall began in the mid-sixteenth century, when one Ruyuan set up a sacrificial estate to support sacrifice to his late father. Management of the property rotated annually among Ruyuan's six sons. A number of other small estates were endowed at around this time. In 1570, a group of kin proposed that the income from the separate endowments should be collected into a joint account. Though the genealogy does not mention this, the plan obviously implied that sacrifice to the individual ancestors in whose name the estates were endowed would be suspended. The money collected was to be loaned out to earn interest with the intention of raising funds for an ancestral hall. But "after a while, both the method and people's hearts became somewhat remiss. Those who looked after the money and the accounts had their own opinions; there were various factors getting in the way of the interest." Though construction of a hall began in 1587, the funds were soon exhausted. Nine individuals including the lineage head (*zuzhang*)—the senior living member of the senior generation—now set about soliciting donations to complete the project, but they met with little success, their efforts "flowering in the morning and withering by evening." Their own donations were likened to "a tie which does not bind." In 1601, a third attempt to raise funds began, under the leadership of Jingmei, the descent-line heir, that is, the eldest son in a continuous line of eldest sons going back to the founding ancestor. The rights to farm the existing sacrificial estate were auctioned off annually, and a portion of the winning bid had to be paid at the time of the auction. Jingmei took charge of loaning out this sum, called a pledge (*huaqi*), to earn interest. Through Jingmei's diligence, funds were raised and the hall brought to completion in 1607. But once the hall was finished, the direct descendants of Ruyuan successfully agitated for the return of their rights to the property he had endowed, whittling away the corporate estate of the hall. An essay from 1637 celebrating the accomplishments of the hall is an insightful commentary on the difficulties that confronted lineage organization in Fuzhou: "To increase is to flourish; to earn interest is to create. Without earning interest and without flourishing, it would have been impossible to accomplish the great matter of [building] the ancestral hall. Great is the merit of increasing and earning interest. Collective power is hard to organize, a common heart is hard to unify, common accumulation is hard to accomplish; long standing rules are hard to maintain."[124]

The difficulties that lineage activists confronted in each of the cases discussed belie the notion that the development of lineages was a natural and

straightforward process—a simple response to material or cultural factors—
and highlight the importance of individual and collective strategies. Many
groups of kin in the Fuzhou region found it advantageous to organize themselves in particular ways beginning in the mid-Ming. But individual leadership was crucial for the success of lineage building, and the individuals who
assumed that leadership role were motivated by a range of different factors
that changed over time. High officials organized the construction of ancestral halls in the early Ming to mark their exclusivity from the rest of village
society; by the late Ming, many built halls with the opposite intention, that
of using the halls to increase the cohesion of village society with themselves at
the center. Wealthy people who were not degree holders engaged in lineage
building in imitation of the educated elite, subtly changing the meaning of
the ancestral hall in the process.

The strategies of other villagers besides those who took the lead in lineage
building were equally important. Funds that were raised to build and maintain ancestral halls were by definition collective funds and could potentially
be used for other purposes. When enough of the group that was acknowledged as kin wished to divert the funds to some other purpose, such as tax
payment or education, the construction of an ancestral hall could come to
a halt. The cohesion of the group might not necessarily disintegrate as a
result, but the lineage that developed would be a different kind of lineage.
It also happened that groups sometimes lost interest or confidence in the
project, and simply chose to redistribute the funds that had accumulated.
Moreover, where collective funds were initially donated by a single man,
his direct descendants might demand that the funds be returned to them,
depriving the larger group of the funds that enabled the project of ancestral
hall construction.

CONCLUSIONS

Ancestral sacrifice in the Fuzhou region in the Song was characterized by
flexibility, eclecticism, and the quest for ritual forms that were appropriate
both in terms of contemporary social needs and the need to conform to
ancient prescriptions. While authors at the time certainly had some sense
of a social organization encompassing distant kin, and such organizations
existed in limited contexts, the ancestral hall does not seem to have been
seen as a suitable basis for solidifying or expanding such organizations. This

eclecticism in practice never disappeared, but the educated elite disavowed it in principle. The ancestral hall became accepted as the standard for ancestral sacrifice. In the early Ming, members of the highest elite constructed free-standing halls for ancestral sacrifice either because they received permission from local officials to do so or because they claimed to be entitled to do so on the basis of their own official position. These early ancestral halls, however, did not really serve to build lineages; rather, they set their builders apart from the lower orders of society—kin and nonkin. The dramatic changes of the mid-Ming—in particular, increased commercialization and the pirate threat—led members of the educated elite to bemoan the collapse of the traditional order, to search for ways to rebuild it, and to search for allies and clients to help them defend their communities. Many local elites seized upon lineage building as part of their set of strategies to achieve these goals. By constructing ancestral halls in which all residents of their village could sacri-fice and by establishing enforceable codes of conduct for their kin to follow, late Ming and early Qing elites in the Fuzhou region sought to formalize their control over local society. This period was thus one of constant ten-sion between educated elite readings of accepted neo-Confucian orthodoxy on ancestral halls and educated elite strategies for local control or, in other words, of competing representations of the forms that kinship organization ought to take.

The state weighed in on this contest more than once. The canonical text on ancestral halls, Zhu Xi's *Family Rituals*, was issued in multiple editions by official order. In 1536, Xia Yan (1482–1548) memorialized recommending that the state lift restrictions on officials' and commoners' right to sacrifice to their distant ancestors.[125] Ebrey, following the earlier scholarship of Zuo Zunpeng and Makino Tatsumi, argues that Ming law was changed to allow such practice; Zheng Zhenman believes that although memorials to this effect were indeed submitted, the recommended changes were never authorized.[126] But in any case, this development is never even mentioned in any of the local sources on the construction of ancestral halls in the Fuzhou region. Nor is there a noticeable shift in such activity centered on this date. There was a real discontinuity between official attention to kinship institutions and the activities of groups of kin on the ground. Imperial law may have adjusted to adapt to changing social realities; in the case of the ancestral hall at least, the reverse was not true.

The construction of ancestral halls may have begun with the degree-holding elite, but other groups in local society were not content simply to accept the leadership of that elite. Local commercial elites infiltrated the leadership of the lineage organization, subtly changing it in the process. Whereas in the early Ming only men who had held high official positions and their immediate relatives were eligible to have tablets installed and to receive sacrifice in ancestral halls, in most Fuzhou lineages, by the Qing, anyone who could afford to pay a set amount could enjoy these privileges. As ancestral halls became property owners in their own right, people skilled in the management of wealth emerged as leaders in the maintenance of the halls. This was not simply a struggle between two groups within the elite, for the scholarly elite and the commercial elite had close ties and in many cases were the same people. Rather, it was a struggle over different images of what the ancestral hall was and how it should function. In this new phase, construction of an ancestral hall depended on meeting the strategic objectives of all those who were involved. In other words, lineage organization depended on the convergence of the strategies of the participants. If other objectives prevailed among enough of the population of the lineage, then lineage building that centered on the ancestral hall could not work. These strategic objectives were defined both culturally and materially and were profoundly shaped by the changing local context.

FIVE

Rituals of the Ancestral Hall: New Year's Day and the Lantern Festival

The newly reconstructed ancestral halls of Nantai are usually silent and dark; their heavy gates bolted shut. They are only opened for the major ritual events of the year, the greatest of which occurs around the fifteenth day after the lunar New Year. Since the mid-1980s, on the days preceding and following this date, the roads and paths of Nantai and the surrounding countryside are busy with light trucks and motorcycle taxis ferrying villagers to and from those places where they have kin so they may participate in the ritual known in the local dialect as *beimang*, "to accompany through the night."[1] In 1993 and 1994, I observed performances of this ritual in several villages, one of which was Jingshang, a few kilometers south of Shanggan. Jingshang has a population of about two thousand, of whom about half, in three hundred odd households, are surnamed Chen. The Jingshang Chen have a handwritten genealogy, probably compiled earlier this century, that begins with their founding ancestor, whose grave is still maintained. It outlines his migration from Yuxi in Changle, probably about three hundred years ago.[2] Before 1949, the Chen were a poor lineage. Most were tenants on land belonging to wealthy landowners of the powerful Lin of Shanggan, and the villagers have many stories of their harsh treatment at the hands of the Lin. The Chen have never had an ancestral hall, though lineage members are now planning to raise funds to erect one. In its absence, the *beimang* ritual is held on a plot of wasteland between the village and the offices of the local government. The man who invited me to the ritual in 1993, a native of Luozhou and one of my most helpful informants, was cynical about the location of the ritual and indeed the performance in general, though this did not dissuade him from participating. Although he had been only a child when communal rituals were forbidden after 1949, he was sure that the Chen of Jingshang did not have a real tradition of *beimang*. "How," he asked me, "can you have *beimang* without an ancestral hall?" He suspected that the people of Jingshang had invented the ritual in emulation of other lineages that were reviving it in the area.

A theatrical troupe hired for the occasion has erected a stage beside the plot of wasteland, and villagers pass the afternoon watching theater or chatting with visitors in the meeting room of the adjacent village government office. Those who intend to participate in the ritual that evening must register and pay a fee of twenty *yuan* to the lineage association, which has set up a desk in the office. The payment of this registration fee is called buying a candle (*mai lazhu*), but many people who "buy candles" actually provide the physical candle themselves. About 1,200 candles are purchased, the majority by residents of Jingshang. In the late afternoon, a long row of tables is laid out. At the head are placed photographs of paintings of Chen Huai and Chen Ruolin of Luozhou and a red placard on which is written "Incense Place for the Generations of Early Ancestors of the Jingshang Chen." At dusk, the men feast in the courtyard of the government offices while the women lay out offerings of food on the tables. Each segment of the Jingshang Chen has its own place to lay out offerings. In 1994, fifteen groups participate; eight are subdivisions of the Jingshang lineage, and the others are delegations of between ten and thirty visitors from other villages. As darkness falls, the participants—men, women, and children—gather beside the appropriate table. While younger participants set off stupendous amounts of firecrackers, older men and women come forward from their tables to bow before the photos and placard on the head table and offer incense. When all have bowed, a great cry rises up from the head of the table. At this signal, all raise their candles and begin to walk together down the main street of the village. At the mouth of each lane, the residents of the neighborhood that is down that lane separate off and return to their homes, where they place the lit candles before their family altar. Participants from other villages bring their candles to one of the large new houses of the village that has its own courtyard. There they hold their candles before the domestic altar in the courtyard. Villagers and visitors gradually straggle back to the site of the ritual to watch opera until late into the night.[3]

In the last chapter, I discussed the spread of ancestral halls in the Fuzhou region and the changing ideas associated with them. Once an ancestral hall was built, appropriate rituals had to be devised for it and implemented. Ritual was seen as being central to ensuring that ancestral halls had the effects that they were desired and supposed to have. In this chapter, I explore the development of ancestral hall ritual with special reference to the rituals performed on the fifteenth day of the first month of the lunar New Year. I do so through three separate lines of analysis. The first relies on genealogical and gazetteer evidence to explore developments over time. It suggests that a number of different types of observances on this date were important early antecedents for the rituals devised for ancestral halls. The second relies on my observation of contemporary ritual performance in different villages of Nantai to explore variation in space. The argument here is that, although the connection is never explicitly raised in any of the written sources from Fuzhou, ritual performance in many ancestral halls can actually be linked to another set of much older rituals performed by women and dedicated to a local fertility goddess. In the third part of the chapter, I discuss in general terms how these rituals were used simultaneously to foster solidarity among and differentiation between lineage members, and I relate these functions to broader historical processes. The *beimang* ritual was a bodily expression of the new ideas and strategies of kinship practice in Ming and Qing times. Catherine Bell identifies formalization and traditionalization as important characteristics of ritual and ritual-like activities. Ritual is formalized because it makes use of a restricted set of expressions and gestures compared to informal or casual activity, and it is traditionalized in that it privileges and emulates practices from an earlier time. Though ritual is always invented, it is assumed to be invariant.[4] The discussion here shows that the development of *beimang* involved the reworking of earlier rituals to suit new contexts, new ideas, and new strategies and the formalization and traditionalization of the results. The evidence thus further demonstrates that kinship practice is not formulated in the abstract or at will but is invariably shaped by the history of the society in which it is embedded.

EARLY ANTECEDENTS

The fifteenth day after the lunar New Year has been an important popular festival in Fuzhou since long before there were ancestral halls. As lineage activists sought to bring the observances of calendrical festivals into the new ancestral halls, to bring them within the rubric of kinship practice in the Ming and Qing, they could not efface or ignore these earlier practices. Our understanding of the development of the new traditions that were invented for the ancestral hall must therefore take these older traditions into account. The activities that are described as *beimang* and that Fuzhou people are now attempting to reinvigorate actually grew out of the fusion of this range of earlier practices with new ideas about kinship ritual.

Reconstructing the historical evolution of popular ritual practice in China is a challenging task. All of the available sources are problematic texts whose different genres have specific rhetorical conventions.[5] But a careful reading of all the available sources, combined with judicious use of contemporary fieldwork, does permit a tentative analysis of the historical development of seasonal rituals in a local context. In Fuzhou, New Year's has long been one of the most important seasonal festivals of the year. During the Song, households began the day by first offering sacrifice at their domestic altar. Household members then greeted one another according to a formal sequence, with the juniors paying respects and wishing longevity to the seniors. People also went visiting their neighbors and kin to offer greetings. Some people also engaged in a practice called bowing in a circle (*tuanbai*). The Song gazetteer suggests that status distinctions were both expressed and maintained through the careful practice of these rituals. Indeed, the main point of the gazetteer description is to lament the recent decline of such clear distinctions.[6]

In the Ming, the New Year began in the home with offerings to the ancestors and gods and then the hierarchized paying of respects within the household. The 1491 Fujian gazetteer describes this as bowing in order (*xubai*): "The custom in Fujian is to greatly esteem New Year's. As soon as it is light everyone dresses in their finest clothes and makes offerings [at the domestic altar]. After, they bow in order to one another and offer best wishes, wishing longevity to the elders. Later they go to pay their respects to their kin in neighbouring areas, going back and forth visiting."[7]

Since the Tang if not earlier, in much of China the fifteenth day after the lunar New Year has been celebrated as the Lantern Festival.[8] According to the Song gazetteer, the festival was first celebrated in Fuzhou in the early eighth century. The festival in the Song included three distinct events: (1) the hanging of large and elaborate lanterns of various descriptions at the *yamens* and major Buddhist monasteries within the city; (2) a vibrant fair that drew large numbers of local prostitutes; and (3) a party thrown by the prefect for the subordinate officials under his command, with candles, dancing girls, performances of various kinds, and parades to the large monasteries where the lanterns were displayed. "The officials and common people watch and enjoy the spectacle. The powerful families and prominent lineages set up positions from which to watch outside the east and west *yamen* walkways. Along the thoroughfares and larger streets, there are spectators at every house." The festival was celebrated primarily in the city, but "from the distant rural areas and subordinate counties, visitors come throughout the night without a break."[9] A well-known story of Song Fuzhou, found in the gazetteer and also in many other sources, suggests that the popular celebration of the Lantern Festival was sponsored and even prescribed by local officials. In the late eleventh century, the story goes, the prefect ordered every household to purchase and hang ten lanterns to contribute to the overall spectacle. Sympathizing with the burden this put on the poor, a local scholar wrote a satirical poem on a large lantern that he hung on public display.[10]

Sources provide many descriptions of the splendid sights of Fuzhou and its surrounding towns during the Lantern Festival in the Ming. The mid-sixteenth century gazetteer of Fuqing reports: "On the long streets and the twisted lanes, each gate erects a pair of firs, to which [are attached] horizontal [poles of] fresh bamboo. From these are hung lanterns. The lanterns are made of cloth, porcelain, bamboo fiber, etc. They are all decorated with images of people, stories, or flowers, fruits, animals, etc. There are also things like horse lamps and dragon and tiger lamps."[11] Whereas Song sources describe considerable official influence on the celebration, by the Ming, the Lantern Festival no longer directly involved the state or its representatives. "Since the [beginning] of the current dynasty, in the celebration of the New Year among the people, some hold celebrations in their own places, so the official *yamen* no longer holds the celebration. This demonstrates the frugality and moderation promoted by the imperial ancestors."[12] In fact, local officials even tried to suppress popular celebration of the festival, especially after 1585, when lanterns caused a fire in Fuzhou that destroyed over one thousand homes.[13] But it was no use, for there was no support for the prohibitions from the usual agents of the state in local society. "The officials attempted to forbid these activities, but the gentry and scholars were unsettled for they enjoy the spectacle. In this month the people of the whole prefecture behave as if they are mad."[14]

NEW RITUALS AND THE SPREAD
OF ANCESTRAL HALLS

As I showed in the previous chapter, during the mid-Ming, new ideas and institutions connected with patrilineal kinship were spreading through regional society. The ancestral hall served increasingly as the physical setting where notions of building more cohesive kinship groups, expressions of local leadership, and the use of ritual to disseminate a particular set of values, to reaffirm and restore a moral order that was perceived as failing, were played out. Existing rituals and new ideas were part of a common process. As new rituals were developed for ancestral sacrifice in ancestral halls, earlier antecedents such as mutual greetings at the New Year and the Lantern Festival were not simply discarded but incorporated in different ways into these new rituals.

Though it did not anticipate the spread of large, free-standing ancestral halls, Zhu Xi's *Family Rituals* gradually came to be held as the orthodox standard of ritual performance. Scholars such as Patricia Ebrey and Tim Brook have shown that claims of adherence to the prescriptions of the *Family Rituals* became a touchstone of commitment to neo-Confucian orthodoxy.[15] The educated elite in Ming and Qing Fuzhou shared with elites throughout China a commitment to the *Family Rituals*. In a 1508 epitaph for a Shanggan resident, Lin Han of Linpu praised the subject for the handling of his father's funeral. "He followed the *Family Rituals*, and did not deign to invite Buddhists."[16] But the orthodox status of the *Family Rituals* as a text did not translate into its complete and unquestioning acceptance and implementation in local society. Committed to its use as a vehicle to transmit social values in an age of moral unrest, local activists created new rituals from existing ones, from widely distributed liturgies such as the *Family Rituals*, and from local needs.

CHANGING RITUALS IN LINEAGES WITHOUT HALLS

As we have seen, even before ancestral halls became common in the region, groups tracing common descent regularly practiced collective rituals that were intended both to solidify the links between them and to mark economic and social differentiation. In the Ming and Qing, such rituals were adopted and adapted, formalized and traditionalized, even among lineages that did not have ancestral halls. Many groups practiced a ritual similar to that described in the Song sources as bowing in a circle (*tuanbai*) in the home of one of their members.[17] The genealogy of the Guo of Fuzhou provides detailed information on the evolution of this ritual practice among one group. After pirates repeatedly attacked their home village in the 1550s, destroying homes and temples, most of the Guo had fled.[18] As Guo Bocang wrote in his genealogy, over the course of the Ming, "the descendants of the three branches all left [the ancestral home] because they were conscripted to serve as border guards, because they sojourned elsewhere, or in order to avoid the pirates."[19] In 1559, the first refugee arrived in Fuzhou.[20] He must have sent word that the situation there seemed at least safer than back home, for according to a later account, this man led most of the other members of the lineage to Fuzhou. Eventually all ties to the ancestral home were cut.[21]

The various members of the Guo who settled in Fuzhou at first attempted to revive a traditional New Year's custom of bowing in order. In the early seventeenth century, a lineage member named Zhike summarized the current practice:

> According to the old regulations, on the first day of the first month, the branches without regard to the distance of relationship and the individual men without regard to age go from house to house offering best wishes. This directs the descendants of the surname towards the good. Feasts of delicacies are still held. Those who can afford it hold [such feasts], and those who cannot await invitations for the kin to gather. This generates feelings of closeness between flesh and blood. Since moving to the provincial capital, more than seventy years have passed, and the rites have not been neglected in the least.

The Guo's conscientious performance of these rituals earned them the praise of the people of Fuzhou. But Zhike and others worried that as time passed and the number of younger descendants grew, participation in the ritual would suffer. They proposed to replace the individual and household rituals with a collective ritual of bowing in a circle (*tuanbai*) for all male descendants of the founding ancestor back in Fuqing:

> Every year on the fifteenth day of the first month, the home of a lineage member whose central hall is expansive is to be selected. A spirit tablet on which is written "Spirit Place of the Ancestors of the Guo of Zhongxing, Zelang, Yurong" is to be erected collectively. The incense altar is placed

above it. . . . On the eleventh day of the first month, the person responsible for collections that year prepares the sacrificial items. When the time comes, after the whole lineage is assembled, sacrifice to the ancestors, conduct bowing in a circle, and use the sacrificial items to prepare a feast.

The costs of the ritual were to be met by a small charge paid by each participant. Initially, participation would be optional. But those kin who were unwilling to pay the nominal fee were not worthy of participating anyway. Zhike was optimistic about the ritual's socializing function. "If there are young people who are willing to pay the money to study the ritual and observe the transformations, their coming should be welcomed."

This proposal did not meet with unanimous approval. The wife of one lineage member, a woman née Zheng, vigorously opposed changes to ritual practice. She believed that "the splendid rites of the lineage ancestors which have endured through the ages" should be inviolate. "If the descendants one day propose their abolition, what will there be to draw together and bring forth the ancestors?" She continued to hold a private feast, and the lineage members "did not dare go against her." Madame Zheng's objection was a subtle one. The new ritual proposed the formalization and collectivization of ancestral sacrifice. She argued that the ancestors themselves had not established this precedent, so it was not appropriate for the descendants to do so. Ultimately, it seems a compromise was worked out. The practice of individual visits and feasts continued to be held by those who wished it, and the collective *tuanbai* ritual was implemented as well.[22] But the compromise must have broken down later. A document dating from the early Qing reports that the old ritual "was converted to *tuanbai*" and makes no mention of private feasts.[23] This document explains that responsibility for arranging the ritual rotated annually through the branches of the lineage. On the fifth day of the first month, "all the adult males, regardless of age, assemble in the home of whoever is responsible for that year, to wait for the lineage head to raise incense and sacrifice to the ancestors. When the sacrifice is completed, they arrange themselves in order by age and by generation and conduct the ritual of *tuanbai*. When the ritual is over, a feast is held." The transformation of the practices associated with the New Year had now reached a new stage. A series of social visits had already been converted into a ritual of ancestral sacrifice. Now an elaborate and highly structured ritual that expressed and confirmed hierarchies of age and generation was added.

By the early Qing, lineage leaders had also pushed the ritual to a further stage by making participation compulsory. Lineage members who neither attended nor had an acceptable excuse were fined two hundred cash. Those who failed to pay within ten days were punished by being forced to kneel before the ancestral tablet for the duration that it took for an incense stick to burn down. "If there are unfilial members who deliberately claim they are too poor and thus ignore the ancestral injunctions, the whole lineage should collectively beat them and expel them from the genealogy. If in future a branch hall is erected, they will not be allowed to enter and perform sacrifice."[24] The ritual now seemed so important to the unity of the group that it was not unreasonable to require participation. Monetary sanctions, and the threat of humiliation or worse, were used to give some force to this requirement.

In the late Ming, Zhike had considered the *tuanbai* ritual followed by a communal feast to be a sufficient celebration of lineage unity at the beginning of each year. He wrote that the *tuanbai* served to "offer congratulations for the New Year and also to commemorate the Lantern Festival." It had the added virtue of offering the lineage members the opportunity to gather while limiting the expenses and inconvenience of separate feasts.[25] By the early Qing, however, his immediate descendants introduced new and more elaborate rituals intended specifically to mark the Lantern Festival. These had become well established by the time the next account of lineage ritual practice was written:

> The old regulations of the previous generations prescribe the collective cele-bration of the Lantern Festival on the fifteenth day of the first month. . . . Select the home of a lineage member which has a large main hall for the installation of the tablet to the ancestors. Gather the lineage to conduct the ritual and hold a feast. This serves to commemorate the Lantern Festival, and also as a reunion for the lineage members, which will encourage the descendants to be virtuous, and not go so far as to lose order.

Responsibility for the ancestral tablet that had been prepared according to Zhike's instructions rotated annually from branch to branch. After the *tuanbai* ritual, it received offerings throughout the year, circulating from household to household within the branch. On the last night of the year, a representative of the branch that would take responsibility in the following year accepted the tablet. This representative was also charged with collection of a "Lantern Festival fee" of fifty cash per adult male. Before the new ritual, the members of "each stove [i.e., each household] should bring with them large candles. On the night of the thirteenth, they should fully assemble in the home of the rota holder and request to have the spirit table brought out. The sacrifice is conducted. When the sacrifice is completed, the participants feast according to the appropriate order." By the time the genealogy was compiled, this ritual had also become compulsory, with a range of sanctions to enforce compliance.[26]

The ritual practices of the Fuzhou Guo, who did not have an ancestral hall until the nineteenth century, show some interesting similarities with rituals described in contemporary north China. In Yangmansa village, studied by Myron Cohen, there were no ancestral halls. The only time of the year that lineage members gathered in a ritual context was at the grave-sweeping festival of Qingming (literally, "clear and bright"), when each member family sent a representative to participate in activities at the lineage graveyard. These activities emphasized what Cohen calls the associational domain of kinship, for they were based not on particular genealogical ties but rather on the descent of all lineage members from a common ancestor.[27] By bringing together all the descendants of the founding ancestor in Fuqing, the Guo rituals also emphasized this associational domain. These similarities suggest that efforts to distinguish different types of lineage according to geography may be less useful than attempting to identify a set of possible trajectories of kinship practices and then exploring the factors that shape these trajectories and determine which trajectories are followed in particular contexts. In the Fuzhou region, significant shifts in ritual practices began when ancestral halls were built and corporate property endowed. As we have seen, this was a phenomenon of the late Ming and Qing.

CHANGING RITUALS IN ANCESTRAL HALLS

The *Family Rituals* prescribes offerings to the ancestors in ancestral halls at the time of customary festivals (*sujie*).[28] Lineage activists took this prescription seriously and, going even beyond the text, sought to relocate other observances of the customary festivals into the new ancestral halls. Gazetteers and the genealogies from the Ming and Qing suggest that lineages with ancestral halls generally practiced bowing in a circle at New Year's and the celebration of the Lantern Festival in the hall.[29] Bowing in a circle is described in the Fujian gazetteer of 1491, with reference to Xinghua prefecture, just south of

Fuzhou. On New Year's Day, household members visited the ancestral hall for a lineage assembly (*huizu*). "In Putian the hereditary families and great lineages each has a lineage shrine. On this day, after they have bowed in order in the household, they visit the ancestral hall, sacrifice to the ancestors, then conduct bowing in a circle with the lineage."[30] The earliest gazetteer source from Fuzhou prefecture to mention the celebration of the Lantern Festival in the ancestral hall is the 1547 gazetteer of Fuqing county. "All of the temples and ancestral halls are hung with [lanterns]. The lamps and the moon compete in their brightness.... The lamps are lit beginning on the thirteenth night and ending on the seventeenth."[31] Genealogies provide varying degrees of detail about the rituals performed in ancestral halls. For example, the 1680 edition of the genealogy of the Wu of Shimei explains, "The fifteenth day of the first month is the Lantern Festival. The caretakers of the hall provide lamps and candles. From each branch, eight men are selected in rotation to provide the sacrificial items. The lamps are erected and the ritual is performed."[32] A more detailed set of instructions for the performance of rituals associated with the Lantern Festival in the ancestral hall of the Pan of Sanxi, in Changle county, dated 1730, prescribes: "On the thirteenth day of the first month set up [the tablets of] the first ancestors in order.... The ten managers (*fushou*) each prepare coverings for the chairs and tables, incense, candles, fruits, flowers, and firecrackers, and arrange them in order. The hall pays for the delicacies to be sacrificed, such as a goat, wine, candles, etc."[33] Three offerings are made to the ancestors, and then a sacrificial text is read and burned. When the ritual is over, the instructions continue, "perform the parade of lanterns (*yingdeng*). When the parade of lanterns is over, hold the feast and accompany the spirits (*banshen*) [i.e., perform *beimang*]."[34]

These earliest references in the genealogies to New Year and Lantern Festival rituals in the ancestral hall date from the late seventeenth century. But such rituals must have undergone a lengthy period of development before that time. From the eighteenth century on, the regulations regarding ritual performance become increasingly elaborate and specific. Two genealogies from the island of Langqi, one from the late eighteenth or nineteenth century and one from the early twentieth, contain very precise accounts of these ritual complexes. The Chen of Langqi, whose genealogy is the earlier of the two, practiced bowing in a circle early in the year in the ancestral hall. The lineage member responsible for administering the ancestral sacrifice for the coming year purchases fruits, tea, wine, paper money, incense, and candles. At the specified time, the members of the lineage gather at the ancestral hall. They offer incense to the tablets of the ancestors and bow in unison four times. Then, "in order of seniority each performs the ritual of bowing in a circle." After the bowing, the participants are served tea, congratulate one another, and return home.[35] Doolittle provides a brief account of this ritual in the nineteenth century: "On the fourth or fifth day of the first month . . . they worship in a circle. This takes its distinctive name from the circumstance that all the representatives of the families who are present *stand in a circle* before the tablets in the main room of the hall, with their faces toward the *inside*, and, at a given signal, each having grasped his own hands, make their obeisance once, after Chinese fashion."[36]

The Langqi genealogies also give a description of the Lantern Festival, for which the term used is *banye*, meaning "to accompany through the night." The rituals of the Lantern Festival were the most complex annual observances in the ancestral hall of the Dong of Langqi aside from the festival of the local tutelary deity, a topic discussed in the next chapter.[37] Instructions in the genealogy explain that the outgoing managers of the ancestral hall post a notice on the first day of the year outlining the division of responsibilities for the ritual. This is their last act as managers, for early in the new year they are replaced by the members of the incoming cadre, whose first duty is to inspect the preparations. The next day, the lineage members must bring their offerings for inspection by the new managers. "If anyone provides an insufficient amount, he is to be punished in accordance with the regulations." The Dong conduct the ritual by branch. The genealogy includes a schedule of the specific nights on which each branch and subbranch performs the ritual separately. On the appropriate night, the members of the branch sacrifice to their ancestors in the hall. Every adult member of the branch is entitled to prepare one decorated lantern, which is displayed around the village while feasting goes on in the hall. Besides the separate rituals carried out by each branch, on the first night the lineage as a whole slaughters four pigs—one per branch. The sacrificial offerings are inspected by two lineage members known as lineage officers (*zuzheng*).[38] After the festival is over, on the nineteenth day of the New Year, the sacrificial meat from the pigs is distributed to the lineage members. The other offerings remain in the hall for two more days, after which the managers prepare packages of offerings for distribution. The descendants gather again and take leave of the spirits, and then the offerings are removed.[39]

The Langqi Chen are also divided into four branches, which perform the ritual separately on the two nights prior to and following the fifteenth day of the first month. "According to the old regulations, each night in rotation the descendants of one branch prepare incense, candles, lamps, wine and firecrackers and come to the hall to bow and make offerings. When this is over, a feast is held." On the night of the fifteenth, members of the four branches gather together in the hall. A whole pig is offered, and everyone lights lanterns. The Chen genealogy, as with other mid-Qing genealogies from Fuzhou, provides a detailed liturgy for the celebration of *beimang* in the ancestral hall—testimony to the formalization and elaboration of the ritual. The liturgy is clearly based on that essential source of ritual authority for lineage ritual specialists, Zhu Xi's *Family Rituals*. The Chen liturgy consists of instructions to a cantor (*tongzan*), who calls out instruction to all those assembled, and a precentor (*yinzan*), who instructs the presiding man on the intricacies of his role. The ritual begins with a series of collective bows. The spirits are invoked. The presiding man purifies himself and then offers food and wine. A sacrificial text is read aloud. The second and third offerings follow the same form. At each step, the presiding man steps forward, bows, makes the offering, bows, and then retires. The spirits are then urged to eat, the door to their niche is closed and opened again, the sacrificed foods are collected, and the remains are cleared away. This script can be compared to Ebrey's translation of the relevant sections of the *Family Rituals*, which it follows closely in structure and content.[40]

Doolittle provides a brief account of this ritual in the nineteenth century. The third of the six annual sacrifices in the ancestral hall was held

> from the eleventh to the fifteenth of the first month, in the evening. At these times the halls are brilliantly lighted. Frequently a pair of huge candles for each of the living male descendants is burned before the tablets, each person sometimes furnishing his own candles. The one whose turn it is to superintend the affairs of the hall for the current year usually has his candles placed in the centre. Mock-money is always burnt at these times for the benefit of the dead. During this period, they feast together in the evening from two to four times after worshipping the tablets. This is called keeping company with the spirits of the dead by night.[41]

The formalization and elaboration of these rituals is evident not only in their liturgies but also in the body of other texts that became associated with them. For example, the genealogies contain guides for many required documents such as the notices that were to be posted outside the ancestral hall each year to inform the lineage members of the upcoming ritual.[42]

The gazetteer and genealogical evidence, to sum up, shows that early antecedents, such as domestic rituals to commemorate New Year's and official celebrations of the Lantern Festival, were reworked into a lineage idiom by elite activists of the Ming and Qing. These rituals were transplanted into the ancestral halls, where the liturgies of the *Family Rituals* were incorporated. But as I show below this did not mean the displacement of earlier local practices.

VARIATIONS: THE EVIDENCE FROM CONTEMPORARY
PRACTICE AND ORAL HISTORY

The ritual guides in the genealogies, on which the previous account of the rituals has been based, are liturgies, that is, rules about how the rituals ought to be performed rather than ethnographic accounts of what people actually did. To get a better sense of practice, it is essential to turn to other sources, such as observation of the contemporary performance of these rituals, which are presented explicitly as attempts to re-create ritual practices before 1949, and oral tradition, interviews and casual conversations with men and women in Nantai villages. These sources suggest that there was considerable variation, even within Nantai, in the performance of rituals and the language used to describe them. There are a number of elements that appear in ritual performance but that are never mentioned in written liturgies. At least some of these noncanonical elements can be linked to a local fertility cult—the cult of Chen Jinggu. Variations in the performance of these elements is consistent with variations in the timing and circumstances of the construction of an ancestral hall in the particular village, suggesting in other words, that there is a close connection between the type of ancestral hall and the way non-canonical elements were incorporated into its rituals. In villages where gentry halls were built in the mid-Ming, hall rituals known as *tuanbai* correspond most closely to the liturgies of the *Family Rituals*, and the fertility rituals of the cult of Chen Jinggu have no connection to the ancestral hall. In villages where popular ancestral halls were built in the late Ming or early Qing, *beimang* is the term used for rituals in the ancestral hall, and these rituals do not seem to have any association with Chen Jinggu. However, in villages that built ancestral halls only in the late Qing, *beimang* is a fertility ritual linked to Chen Jinggu, which is performed in the ancestral hall. Thus, considering all the villages of Nantai together, it is clear that the performance of ritual in Qing and Republican times did not simply follow the prescriptions of the *Family Rituals*. Rather, it combined and integrated elements of the early antecedents discussed above—popular rituals that had been associated with the first days of the year since the Song or earlier and the worship of Chen Jinggu on her birthday by rural women—with Ming concerns about creating rituals that corresponded to those prescribed by Zhu Xi, and served strategies of building lineage cohesion. The precise form that this combination took depended on the timing and context of lineage building.

Chen Jinggu—also known as *Linshui Furen*, the Lady by the Water—is both an important local goddess and a central figure in the wider Lüshan tradition[43] (Figure 5.1). The historical Chen Jinggu, if there was one, probably lived in the late seventh century and was born to a family of shamans in Fuzhou prefecture. She is associated with a wide range of miracles, including relief of drought and the suppression of a snake demon in Gutian. In recognition of her miracles, the people of Linshui erected a temple in her honor. According to the earliest surviving written account of the temple composed by Zhang Yining (1301–1370), the god and her temple received a number of honorary titles from the Song court, including the title Favorable and Virtuous (*shunyi*).[44] By the Ming at the latest, Chen Jinggu had become associated with children and especially with childbirth. A Ming gazetteer explains that she deliberately miscarried her fetus to perform rituals of prayer for rain during a drought and subsequently died while delivering the dead fetus. On her deathbed, she declared "After my death, should I not save the people of the world from the difficulties of childbirth, I will be no divinity." A Ming hagiographical compendium describes how Chen Jinggu assisted an empress of the Later Tang in labor. By the mid-Ming, Chen Jinggu's reputation for helping women in matters having to do with children and childbirth was well established. According to Xie Zhaozhe, "Women pray to protect their unborn children. When the children grow up, they give thanks on a grand scale. . . . The gods they worship all belong to local crones and village matchmakers."[45]

In the Ming, the temple of Chen Jinggu at Gutian was at the heart of a network of affiliated temples, of which there was at least one in Fuzhou that is recorded in the gazetteers. But the gazetteers record only a fraction of the total number of temples in an area. Xie Zhaozhe wrote that there were many temples of the cult in Luoyuan and Changle counties. In the nineteenth century, Doolittle wrote that the deity "is believed by some to be the most

Figure 5.1. The Goddess Chen Jinggu (photograph by author).

frequently worshiped of all the gods and goddesses" in the Fuzhou region.[46] Elderly villagers in most every village today can locate the site of a former temple or smaller shrine in their own village, and many of these temples have been recently reconstructed.

The Ming sources may disagree about when Chen Jinggu lived, but there is general agreement that her birthday fell on the fifteenth day of the first month of the New Year, and this was therefore the date of her annual festival.[47] This day had also come to be associated with a particular set of ritual activities in which only women participated. According to the 1547 gazetteer of Fuqing, "In the morning the women of the whole town worship the Buddha and the various gods, and at night they watch the lanterns, cross over the bridges with new wheat and then return home." There was a taboo against men and women encountering one another during these processions. Men were required to yield the road when they came across women at these times and were punished if they failed to do so.[48] Xie Zhaozhe's account of the Lantern Festival in Fuzhou also mentions ritualized movements through the town by women of all social classes at the time of the festival, an activity known as "crossing the three bridges."[49] These rituals are not linked in the sources explicitly with the cult of Chen Jinggu, but I think it is reasonable to make that link, since these rituals involved only women, and they took place on the birthday of a goddess particularly associated with women and childbirth.

The worship of Chen Jinggu plays a variable role in the rituals of the Lantern Festival in different villages of Nantai, and this variation is remarkably consistent with variation in the construction of ancestral halls and other lineage-building activities in the village. The ritual traditions of the Linpu Lin, whose ancestral halls are the classic example of the gentry model, stick closest to Zhu Xi's prescriptions. Unfortunately, their genealogy provides little information about ritual practice, and the limited evidence available is ambiguous. When Lin Zhichun compiled the genealogy in 1746, he indicated that participation in ritual was an essential criterion for lineage membership. The question of whether people whose ancestors were recorded in the genealogy but who had moved away should themselves be recorded was to be determined on the basis of whether they returned for sacrifices in the ancestral hall.[50] This suggests that by the mid-eighteenth century, there was some kind of communal ritual in the halls. Perhaps such ritual had arisen in imitation of the rituals of the popular halls built nearby during the centuries since the Linpu halls were first built. According to interviews with the oldest members of the current ancestral hall committee, prior to 1949 communal rituals were held three times annually. In spring and autumn, sacrifice was performed in one of the six halls by the lineage and branch heads. A ritual called *tuanbai* was performed on the second day of the year in one of the halls by the senior surviving members of each generation. The Lin had no communal sacrifice in which all members of the lineage participated and held no ritual of ancestral sacrifice on the fifteenth day of the first month. But elderly residents, both male and female, do know the term *beimang*. By it they mean the festival of Chen Jinggu. In honor of her birthday, the image of the goddess used to be carried in a procession, accompanied by lanterns, to the neighborhoods of the village to receive the offerings and prayers of the local women. The goddess spent one night in each neighborhood, being kept company by all the women of that neighborhood. On the night of the fifteenth, the goddess was returned to her temple, and many village women spent the night there with her.[51]

Ritual performance in the town of Yixu is described in a guidebook in the Huang genealogy, and male informants can confirm the broad details. At New Year's, lineage unity was expressed through a candle-lighting ritual that involved representatives of each branch of the whole lineage. In contrast, a ritual called *beimang* marked distinctions within the lineage. The descendants of the fifteen investors in the construction of the ancestral hall, followed by the different branches of the lineage, performed *beimang* according to a specific order. Larger branches performed the ritual on their own, and smaller branches grouped together to perform the ritual. The ritual involved members of the branch spending the night in the hall, offering sacrifices to the ancestors, and feasting. Women in Yixu, as elsewhere in the Fuzhou region, were forbidden to enter the hall. But village women also perform a separate ritual, which they call *panye*, at the same time as the men perform *beimang* in the ancestral hall. On the night of the Lantern Festival, the women of every household in the village participate in a parade of Chen Jinggu throughout the village. Only women may participate in this parade. The procession ends with the return of the image of the goddess to her temple. Women remain in the temple the whole night, accompanying the goddess and making offerings of chickens; eggs; dumplings; long-life noodles; fruits; and pig's head, stomach, and feet.

The meaning and performance of *beimang* is very different in a third village, Taiyu. This town has about one thousand households, most of which share the surname Chen. Although they have long considered themselves to share common descent, the institutionalization of the lineage clearly took place much later than in the previous two examples.[52] The Chen lack important elements in the cultural repertoire of lineages in Fuzhou. They claim common descent, for example, but are unable to identify a common ancestor or any ancestors of distinction. They are not mentioned at all in the detailed list of Great Surnames in the Minxian gazetteer. Nor do they have a printed genealogy known as a *zupu* or *zongpu*.[53] The Chen do have an ancestral hall, but it is of uncertain, probably recent, date.[54] In Taiyu, the term *beimang* is used to describe the parade of Chen Jinggu from her temple to the ancestral hall at the time of the Lantern Festival. The hall is known at this time as the temporary palace (*xingyuan*) of the goddess. Each household offers a rooster to the goddess. The roosters are killed according to strict rules and then laid out in a specific way on a large and complex wooden rack that is installed in the hall for the duration of the festival. Informants recall that in their youth seven to eight hundred roosters were offered at this time. Households reclaim the roosters the following morning using numbered tickets. Lanterns are also brought into the hall and the men and women of each household pray to Chen Jinggu for the safety of their children. Participation in this ritual, signified by the bringing of a rooster, used to be compulsory for Chen households with immature children and optional for those with adult children, though most households participated. The older women of the village, that is, women who have married into the Chen lineage and borne sons and daughters bearing the Chen surname, spend the night in the ancestral hall, praying to the goddess for more children and performing the ritual known as requesting flowers (*qinghua*) to guarantee success. As long as they are childless, women whose natal family belongs to the Taiyu Chen and who have married out to other villages also return to Taiyu and visit the ancestral hall to request children of their own. In Taiyu, the *beimang* ritual appears to be primarily a fertility ritual, strongly associated with women and the goddess Chen Jinggu, which has been relocated into the ancestral hall.

The different meanings of *beimang* for men and women in different villages of Nantai can thus be explained by reference to variation in the timing and pattern of lineage organization and ancestral hall construction. In Linpu, where ancestral halls were constructed in the mid-Ming by high officials who were able to enforce adherence to the *Family Rituals*, *beimang* is a festival centered on Chen Jinggu, with no connection to the ancestral hall, whereas *tuanbai* is a ritual emphasizing the associational domain of kinship, the shared descent of all the branches from a common ancestor. In Yixu, where ancestral halls were constructed only later, and for different reasons, the *tuanbai* ritual is much the same, and *beimang* is also a ritual of ancestral sacrifice that celebrates the special contributions of wealthy lineage members to the organization. A different term is used to describe the rituals of

Chen Jinggu, which have no connection to the ancestral hall. But in Taiyu, where lineage organization was very late in developing, *beimang* is a fertility ritual associated with Chen Jinggu. Thus, where lineages were organized by members of the upper educated elite in the mid-Ming who were able to more effectively create rituals in accordance with the canonical prescriptions, the Lantern Festival is not associated with the ancestral hall, with ancestors, nor with men, but remains a festival for women, associated with Chen Jinggu and fertility. In the early popular halls that developed later in the Ming and early Qing, whose initiators were more humble members of the local elite, we see efforts to capture the popular intensity of the Lantern Festival in the ancestral hall. Such efforts were not completely successful. *Banye* consists of two quite different rituals for men and for women: the men sacrifice to the ancestors in the hall, whereas the women sacrifice to Chen Jinggu in her temple. In communities where lineages have only begun to organize more recently, *beimang* is clearly a fertility ritual in which both women and men participate and that has been transposed into the ancestral hall, but which has little to do with the ancestors and certainly no connection with the orthodox rituals prescribed in the *Family Rituals*.

RITUAL UNITY, RITUAL LEADERSHIP

An outside observer might try to analyze the rituals of the ancestral hall in any one of a number of different ways. The structure of these rituals could be interpreted in terms of the category of rites of passage.[55] They also served a specific social function—the maintenance of an accurate census of lineage membership.[56] More generally, the rituals were clearly also intended to foster lineage solidarity, while at the same time serving as a venue for strategic competition between different types of local elites. Rules for the performance of the rituals in a given lineage, that is, rules of who could participate and who should hold leadership positions, reflect these various functions at least some of which were recognized by participants.

The integrative function of rituals was a common feature of the elite discourse on ritual. In the mid-Ming, the builders of the ancestral hall of the Gongxi Huang lineage of Putian understood well that the significance of the ancestral hall lay not just in the relationships between the living and the dead ancestors but also in the community formed by the tracing of descent from the ancestor in whose name the hall was endowed: "How could not building an ancestral hall harm the ancestors? But the living uncles and brothers would then have no place to elegantly gather at the time of the festivals. Then if they run into one another in the lanes and villages, they would simply pass by ill-manneredly without adjusting their clothing, just as if they were strangers."[57] In the early Qing, a prominent member of the Fuzhou Guo expressed concern that since the kin had fled to Fuzhou from Fuqing in the Ming, they no longer visited the ancestral tombs and shrines. The resulting lack of lineage rituals would diminish the cohesion of the group. "The descendants of the branch have scattered like stars of the sky. [Access to] the ancestral shrine has been obstructed. Feasting and enjoyment [of sacrifice] are not heard of. In the future, lineage members will meet and not even recognize one another."[58] Educated elites of the time were well aware of the instrumental aspects of ritual, that is, of its potential usefulness as a tool for social integration.

Ancestral hall ritual was clearly viewed as an important means by which lineage solidarity was fostered. In Chapter 2, I argued that many prominent lineages of Nantai in the late Qing formed through fusion through the tracing of descent. Lineage ritual was important to the creation and solidification of the ties between different groups in the lineage. The Lin of Shanggan, which grew rapidly in the Qing into one of the largest and most powerful lineages of the region, provides a clear example. A nineteenth-century observer speculated that the extremely rapid rise in the Lin numbers might be explained by their having fabricated descent relations. "At present in this locality the Lin are the most flourishing. I do not know whether or not in fact all of them are the descendants of [the founding ancestor]."[59] For ritual purposes, the lineage is now divided into twenty-four subdivisions, known locally as sectors (*jie*). These sectors are defined geographically as well as genealogically.[60] In the genealogy, all of the sectors can be linked back to the common founding ancestor, but many of the links are obviously fabricated.[61] What all the sectors do share is the right to participate in the *beimang* rituals of the ancestral hall (Figure 5.2). There is a precise schedule according to which the subdivisions of the lineage perform their own collective rituals. Every one of the twenty-four sectors of the lineage has a specific date for the performance of *beimang*. The narrative of lineage expansion and development is largely the story of the acquisition of this right of participation. According to the author of the village history, the members of the Houcuo sector did not at first enjoy the right to participate in the *beimang* ritual in the ancestral hall:

Figure 5.2. The Beimang Ritual in Shanggan (photograph by author).

I do not know why, but they were excluded by the senior [branches], who would not allow them to enter the hall to perform *beimang*. Each year they were only able to arrange their candles in front of their household altars. This went on until there appeared a distinguished [man] in the Fangtingli sector. Only in that year did the elder lead the younger, saying, "Younger brothers of Houcuo, come with your elder brothers in Fangtingli to perform *beimang* in the ancestral hall!" This saying has been passed down continuously to the present day.[62]

The story of how the Houcuo sector came to convert their previously domestic rituals into participation in the communal rituals at the ancestral hall is actually the story of the acceptance by one group of the lineage of another group's tracing of descent back to a common ancestor.[63] Thus the Lantern Festival rituals promoted the integration of the lineage, but this was not simply a matter of creating ties between a genealogically determined group of people. The Lantern Festival ritual, presented in the genealogies as following the rules laid down by Zhu Xi, was less the simple rote repetition of fixed expressions of predetermined relationships than a discourse about the possibilities of social relationships.[64]

Elite commentators in the Ming and Qing also appreciated the ways in which ritual could serve to reinforce political and social differentiation, by establishing or legitimating hierarchical relations.[65] As the rituals of the New Year developed and were elaborated over time, they became not only a force for cohesiveness but also, simultaneously, a vehicle for the expression of social differentiation and strategic competition over local leadership. This competition took a variety of forms. The most obvious example was the widespread practice of distributing the sacrificial meat at the end of the sacrifice according to a graded hierarchy of status. Among the Pan of Sanxi, for example, in addition to the basic per capita division, extra shares were given to the lineage head, the descent-line heir, men above certain ages, and degree holders.[66]

In Yixu, it is possible to trace an ongoing negotiation about who should preside over rituals. According to a ritual guidebook of 1730, a ritual of mutual greeting, a version of bowing in a circle, was performed on the fifth day of the New Year when the gates of the ancestral hall were reopened. When the ancestral hall was first constructed, the ritual was performed by the fifteen shares (*fen*), which refers to the fifteen individuals who had originally contributed to the construction of the hall—four in 1662, six in 1684, and five subsequently—and to their direct descendants.[67] The use of the term share, and the absence of any discussion of what would happen after one of these individuals died, suggests the initial contribution to the ancestral hall project became the justification for a claim to share in hall leadership, a right that would be transferred through inheritance to the descendants of the individual contributors. But this claim to leadership was contested, for a commentary in the genealogy records, "now the members of the gentry, and the lineage and branch heads worship together." The founders of the hall asserted ritual leadership on financial principles. They had contributed money for the construction of the hall; they and their descendants had thereby earned the right to run its affairs. But this approach conflicted with other principles of village organization. Degree holders and their descendants also claimed the right to lead the ritual. Genealogical principles justified the inclusion of the lineage and branch heads, that is, the senior living members of the senior living generation. Degree-holding members of the lineage also became involved in the day-to-day management of the ancestral hall, in which capacity they no doubt often dominated the lineage and branch heads who were recruited purely on the basis of seniority. "Every month at the new and full moon the heads of the lineage and the branch burn incense, worship the ancestors and look after lineage affairs. The gentry take it in turns to be in charge of the incense."[68]

Competition over rights of participation also arose in the performance of rituals of the Lantern Festival in Yixu. During the whole first month of the year, the Huang lit enormous candles in the hall. On the last night of the year, the lineage and branch heads each lit the candles. Beginning on the first day of the year, "candles are lit in rotation in order according to the generational sequence of the lineage and branch heads." Each branch was responsible for contributing one pair of candles. The candles were allowed to burn through the night, and the larger ones would burn for two, three, or four nights. Thus this ritual was performed first by the representatives of the whole lineage and then by representatives of each branch. The second element to the celebration of the Lantern Festival was the ritual of *beimang*: "On the night of the fifteenth, the fifteen shares conduct the sacrificial ritual. On the night of the sixteenth it is the turn of the Lower House branch. This was decided originally and the various branches all follow the rule. The other [branches] each have their turn to *banye* according to the generational order and seniority. The smaller ones group together into two or three to perform *banye*." A Republican era commentary to the original regulations indicates that since the lineage now numbers nearly ten thousand members, the ritual continues to the very end of the month.[69] According to a seventy-year-old member of the lineage whom I interviewed in the Huang ancestral hall, the ritual of *banye* serves three functions: (1) to commemorate the ancestors, (2) to inform the ancestors of the branch of the current situation of their descendants, and (3) to meet with one's relatives. But here again, the lineage members who were descended from the initial donors to the hall asserted a special right—to perform the ritual themselves in the hall on the very night of the Lantern Festival. Although the arrangements recorded in the genealogy must have been the outcome of disputes and struggles between individuals— for example, members of the lineage holding official titles claiming that they rather than the descendants of the original investors in the hall should officiate at lineage rituals—the competition was also between the principles governing village organization. Were the ritual leaders of the lineage to be determined by genealogy, by status conferred by the state, or by economic contribution and thus indirectly by wealth? Discussion of and dispute over this question was an ongoing theme running through lineage politics in the Fuzhou region in the Ming and Qing.

Competition frequently broke out over the right to manage ritual matters, in particular, the financing of ritual. Recall that the Luozhou Chen was divided into five main branches beginning in the third generation, and the senior generation was further subdivided into three subbranches a few generations later.[70] This made a total of seven segments, comprising the three subbranches of the senior branch and the four other branches. According to Chen Ruolin:

> Previously, the seasonal sacrifices have been managed by the seven branches in rotation. Although there are nominally seven branches, in actual fact there are five. . . . The order of branches is decided by the relative seniority [of their founding ancestor]. Even though it is fixed that there are five [branches], the rotating administration of the sacrifice has long been divided into seven, because some of the descendants see service [in this regard] as something that is glorious.[71]

Chen Ruolin is writing here about the juxtaposition of two different dimensions of agnatic kinship, one genealogical and the other rooted in economic differentiation.[72] The five main branches of the lineage are affiliated on the basis of genealogical branching. The three subbranches of the senior branch reflect asymmetrical segmentation based on exclusive ownership of a corporate estate. Though it was clear to Ruolin according to the logic of genealogy that the sacrifice should be administered by the five main branches in rotation, members of the three subbranches of the senior branch had asserted that they should share equally in the responsibility. The conflict was probably not between genealogical principles and formal social status, that is, the demands of the educated elite for power and prestige within the community, for if this were the case, Ruolin would have said so.[73] Rather, it appears the dispute was between genealogical principles and financial ones. The contributors to the ancestral hall came primarily from the senior branch. Presumably, the members of that branch felt that their greater financial stake earned them a greater right in the management of the hall and claimed a three-sevenths share rather than the one-fifth share that was owed them on strictly genealogical principles. This share was then divided among the three subbranches. Members of the subbranches had contributed significantly to the costs of building the ancestral hall; later they or their descendants claimed certain rights of ritual leadership on that basis. The greater wealth of certain members of the senior branch, if this reconstruction is correct, was at the heart of the issue.[74]

To participate in the complex ceremonies prescribed in the *Family Rituals* required knowledge and experience. When the Langqi Dong performed their rituals of ancestral sacrifice, in addition to the person who presided over the sacrifice and the masses of lineage members who gathered in the hall to watch, the genealogy assigned seventeen specific roles to individuals, including: one for holding the ancestral tablet, one for handling the sacrificial text, one cantor, one precentor, one attendant for the washing basin, nine attendants for the wine vessels, and one attendant for the tea.[75] For at least the first few of these tasks, performance required at a minimum literacy and at a maximum a close familiarity with the ritual classics and a sense of judgment for appropriate ritual performance. These roles were probably filled informally, by whomever was considered the most qualified in the lineage. But they were a source of prestige nonetheless. The frequent references in Chinese biographies to the act of "leading the kin in the performance of ritual" probably refers to this kind of leadership. Only those who had received a Confucian education could fulfill the most important roles as ritual specialists. Thus leadership of the ancestral hall rituals was part of the larger claim to status and leadership by the educated elite in lineage society. Competition also arose over the issue of who should preside (*zhu*) over the rituals, that is, who should actually make the offerings. The *Family Rituals* prescribed that the descent-line heir, the eldest son of the eldest son going back to the founding ancestor, should serve as the presiding man. Respect for the elderly and generational distinction sanctioned the lineage head, who was the senior surviving male of the senior surviving generation. Degree-holding members of the lineage asserted their own right to serve as presiding man based on externally determined status. Qin Huitian wrote in the mid-eighteenth century: "The *Family Rituals* is a book that the gentry at home cannot afford to be without for even one day. . . . But there are also some areas where it is difficult to put into practice. . . . At present, the descent-line heir may not be an esteemed man, and an esteemed man may not be the descent-line heir. What about when the branch heir is a member of the gentry and the descent-line heir a farmer?"[76] When Justus Doolittle visited an ancestral hall in Fuzhou, it was the descent-line heir who presided over the ritual, assisted by a ritual specialist:

> A professor of ceremonies was present directing the worshipers when to kneel, bow, and rise up. The faces of these worshipers were turned toward the tablets. The head person among them was a lad some six or eight years old, being the eldest son of the eldest son of the eldest son, etc., of the remote male ancestors from whom all the Chinese having his ancestral name living in this city claim to have descended. He was the chief of the clan, according to the Chinese law of primogeniture. This lad, instructed by the professor of ceremonies, took the lead in the worship.[77]

The canonical justifications notwithstanding, ritual leadership by the descent-line heir must still have been galling for members of the educated elite. According to the 1923 gazetteer of Pingtan, in some lineages, "the first offering is performed by one with rank, because the descent-line heir is foolish and simple and cannot carry out the ritual."[78] Degree holders proposed different means by which their status could be acknowledged in ritual leadership. Li Guangdi (1642–1718), an advisor to the Kangxi emperor whose home was in Anxi county, in southern Fujian, proposed that the conflicting claims to ritual leadership should be resolved by having the claimants preside over the ritual together, the descent-line heir on the left, the person holding official rank or title in the center, and the hall administrator on the right.[79] A more common solution, described in many Fuzhou genealogies, was to have each of the three offerings presided over by a different person, with lineage or branch heads performing the first, the descent-line heir the second, and degree holders the third. One guide gives the right to preside over the third offering to degree holders of the lineage together with the descent-line heir, probably in anticipation that the lineage would not always have a degree holder in its ranks. In other lineages, claims by the educated elite to prestigious lineage leadership won out entirely. Among the Jin'an Du, at the *tuanbai* and other calendrical sacrifices to the ancestors, "the descendant in the provincial capital [i.e., residing in Fuzhou and not serving in office elsewhere] with the highest official rank presides over the sacrifice."[80]

The liturgical scripts and other documents in the genealogies suggest a number of ways of analyzing the rituals. In terms of ritual structure, they can be seen as corresponding to the category of rites of passage. In terms of their social functions, they ensured the maintenance of accurate lineage membership records to facilitate the assignment of tax responsibilities and the compilation of genealogies. At the same time, the rituals were also used to foster lineage solidarity and cohesiveness and served as a venue for strategic competition between different types of lineage elites. The rules for the performance of the rituals in a given lineage, rules of who could participate and who should hold leadership positions, were in part a product of such efforts and such competition.

CONCLUSIONS

This attempt to historicize and consider variations in the rituals performed in ancestral halls in the Fuzhou region demonstrates a number of aspects of Chinese ritual practice. Far from the simple reenactment of a script provided by an authoritative text written in the twelfth century, rituals of ancestral worship were inherently flexible and fluid.[81] Though Zhu Xi's *Family Rituals* sanctioned offerings to the ancestors at the time of popular seasonal festivals, and considerable intellectual labor had been expended throughout China in modifying Zhu Xi's prescriptions to suit local contexts, the fundamental problem that the orthodoxy of the text raised for literate members of Fuzhou lineages was the profound noncanonicity of the social practices that surrounded them. Many of the intellectuals who compiled genealogies were deeply troubled by the disjuncture between orthodox ideal and practice. One common response was to argue for the importance of following canonical practice in ritual, while at the same time acknowledging that following the practices established, and paid for, by the ancestors agreed with even more fundamental concerns. Thus the author of the ritual guide section of the genealogy of the Pan of Sanxi notes that there is some uncertainty about the canonicity of their sacrificial practices. However, he continues:

> the fields, gardens and hills accumulated and left behind by the ancestors [yield] extremely prodigious amounts of grain, which enable the descendants who follow to enjoy the fruits for a long time. To transfer them, or to dare to trifle with them or endanger them, would be to commit offenses against the ancestors. Carefully maintaining the ancestral estate, taking on the sacrifice at the four seasons, and respecting the sacrificial regulations is to express the desire to requite one's origins. Thus the ceremonial rites are recorded.[82]

Confronted with the various practices associated with *beimang*—burning of lanterns in the ancestral hall, keeping company with the ancestral spirits through the night, and so forth—some elite commentators simply threw up their hands in exasperation, recognizing that there was no way to eliminate or even reform popular noncanonical practice. The compiler of one nineteenth-century Fuzhou genealogy wrote of *beimang*, "it is not known in which classic (*dian*) it is found. Nevertheless, it [is performed] in all of our [area of] Min. It must be that it comes from popular custom (*su*)."[83] Local culture had been incorporated into the local version of national culture.

The content of the *beimang* ritual complex as it developed in the late Ming and Qing incorporated two older traditions, those of the Lantern Festival and the festival of Chen Jinggu, into a new tradition centered on ancestral sacrifice in the ancestral hall. In the genealogies, this tradition is portrayed in terms of adherence to the *Family Rituals*. This vision emerged in the Ming in part as a reflection of elite concerns about deteriorating status differentiation and changing notions of the appropriate role of different types of elite in local society. Involvement in ancestral ritual was one of the means used to increase their power and prestige, but ritual activities were transformed in the process. As ancestral halls spread in the Fuzhou countryside, existing popular practices were brought under the aegis of the halls, transformed into rituals of ancestor worship, masculinized, and Confucianized. In this process, the women who were the original practitioners of some of the earlier rituals, and Chen Jinggu, the object of their ritual, were excluded from the new forms, and women reinvented their own set of rituals outside the orbit of the ancestral hall. But no Nantai lineage, not even the Linpu Lin, was really able to put the *Family Rituals* into practice, for their context and their purposes were just too far from what Zhu Xi had envisioned. Whereas the *Family Rituals* was underpinned by the principles of genealogical precedence, lineage ritual was influenced by different principles: of differentiation within the lineage, of *per stirpes* rights, and of financial rather than genealogical principles. Agnatic principles could frame very diverse modes of organization. Thus, from another perspective, the *beimang* ritual also diverged from neo-Confucian orthodoxy as it was shaped by prior popular practice and various and contesting understandings of it. The ritual became more popularized as it became more orthodox. The *beimang* ritual complex illustrates several of the key elements in the invention of tradition in late imperial China. To spread and to persist, invented traditions had to appropriate or harmonize with existing social practices; to conform, or appear to conform, to state-sanctioned models; and to meet current social needs. *Beimang* spread through the Fuzhou region because it met all three of these criteria, though there were always tensions between them.[84]

I began this chapter with a discussion of the *beimang* ritual in Jingshang village, to which I now return briefly. Of the fifteen groups that participated in the ritual in 1994, only eight claim any genealogical connection to the founding ancestor of the Jingshang Chen. Four other groups come from villages in the vicinity of Jingshang, but do not claim any genealogical connection with the founding ancestor of the Jingshang Chen. Members of the Chen of Luozhou say they participate because of a bond established between the two lineages in the eighteenth century. Chen Ruolin of Luozhou once came to Jingshang to borrow money to go to Beijing to participate in the examinations. Someone in Jingshang lent him the money, and, although

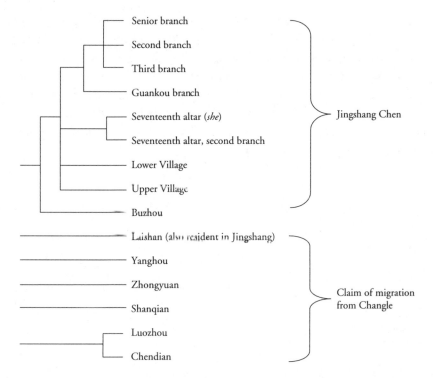

Figure 5.3. Genealogical ties between groups participating in the Jingshang ritual.

Ruolin failed at this first attempt, he never forgot their trust in him, and when he eventually did pass the exams, he came back to Jingshang to report this to the ancestral tablets. The Chen of Chendian participate because they are related to the Chen of Luozhou (Figure 5.3).

Recall that my informant from Luozhou was suspicious that the *beimang* ritual in Jingshang may have been a new invention. After several visits to the village, I learned that his suspicions were well founded. Residents of Jingshang explained that there is actually no tradition of communal *beimang* in the village. Before 1949, people simply performed a ritual in their own homes, keeping company with the ancestral spirits at the domestic altar. In the mid-1980s, the Chen of Jingshang were invited to participate in the revival of the *beimang* ritual of the Lin of Shanggan. They did this for several years, until they learned that they were being charged more to buy a candle, that is, to participate, than people surnamed Lin. When the organizers in

Shanggan refused to treat them more equitably, they decided to hold their own ritual. At first, the scale of the ritual compared unfavorably with the Shanggan version. So they decided to invite other groups to increase the ritual's size and prestige. By the mid-1990s, several other groups of Chen had accepted the invitation. The Chen of Jingshang were hopeful that they could attract more participants in the future. Even in contemporary China, ancestral rituals can serve not only to solidify preexisting groups but also to create new ones.

SIX

The Local Cult: *Lijia*, Lineage, and Temple

It is not only the ancestors who are worshiped in the ancestral halls of Nantai; it is also the gods. A few days after the performance of *beimang*, the Chen of Luozhou celebrate another major event in their ritual calendar, the annual festival of the local tutelary deities—the Great Liu Kings.[1] On the twentieth day of the New Year, the incense burners and images of the deities are brought out from the temple that they share with the deity Taishan and paraded to the ancestral hall, accompanied by giant puppets known as *tagu*, which represent the subordinate cults of the gods. The caretaker of the ancestral hall leads the procession, striking a gong to draw the villagers. The main incense burner is carried proudly by the elderly woman who in the late 1980s was responsible for organizing the revival of the festival after its prohibition in the early years of the People's Republic. As the procession enters the ancestral hall, the senior member of the management committee of the hall stands in the doorway announcing the arrival of each deity to the ancestors, represented by their tablets at the back of the hall. The deities enter and are directed to their allocated spaces, with the Great Kings in the center, their backs to the tablet niche, facing the main chamber and outer doors of the hall, and the *tagu* flanking on

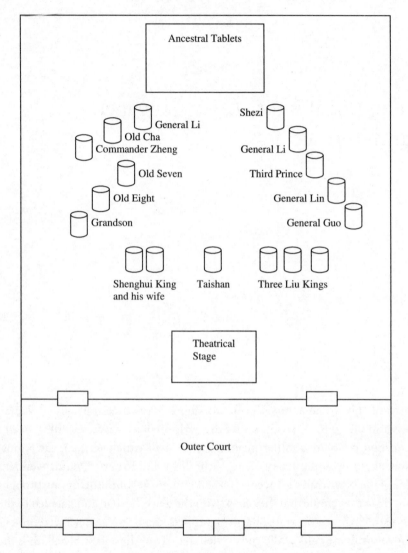

Figure 6.1. Arrangement of Deities in the Luozhou Chen Ancestral Hall.

either side (Figures 6.1–6.3). The gods remain in the ancestral hall for several days, receiving nightly performances of opera and other local cultural forms and sacrifices from the households of the Luozhou Chen. On the twenty-eighth day of the first month, or in the event of rain on the first clear night following, the deities are then paraded with great spectacle, including musical bands and other performers, around the town. The gods are carried in sedan chairs that are decorated with colored electrical lights and followed by a cart supporting a generator. As they walk, the musicians play over a cacophony of firecrackers and fireworks. The villagers stand in front of their houses to watch the parade go by. As each deity passes by, the women of the household place sticks of lit incense in the deity's incense burner, exchanging them for a few sticks that they take out of the burner and place before their home altars. The procession visits the ancestral hall of the Lin of Zhouwei—at the opposite end of the town from the Chen settlement—where the gods enjoy rich offerings and operatic performance; then it continues its tour of the town, which lasts through the night, before the gods are finally returned to the temple at dawn.

Most every village in the Fuzhou region today boasts a temple to a local tutelary deity like the Three Liu Kings of Luozhou, and most every household in the village participates in some way in the cult of the god. During the annual festival of the deity, revived in many villages in the late 1980s and then suppressed again in the mid-1990s, rituals bring good fortune to and expel evil influence from the whole community; operas are performed that all may enjoy, and processions wind through lane and alley past every doorway. For the villagers, the shared memory of the miracles of the gods, the gods'

Figure 6.2. The Great Kings of Luozhou receive offerings in the Chen Ancestral Hall (photograph by author).

Figure 6.3. Attendants of the Great Kings (photograph by author).

ties to the ancestors, and the faithful transmission of history and ritual from the ancestors are important to establishing the legitimacy and validity of the cult, which to the outside observer might therefore appear to be a locus of identification for the village. But this is not to say that the cult is an eternal, unchanging expression of territorial community. Both cults and community are shaped by the changing context in which they are embedded, and organized agnatic kinship is an important part of this local context.

The preceding chapters have discussed the histories of institutions and practices within groups of patrilineally related kin. Looking at local popular religion provides a fruitful line of entry into analysis of the relations between

different groups of kin as well as another approach to the question of relations between lineage organization and the state. I argue in this chapter that
the history of the organization and meaning of the cults of the Fuzhou area
is the result of complex interaction between state policy and local society
and that changing strategies and models of kinship played an important role
in this interaction. The early Ming state implemented an official religious
system that extended down to the rural community and was complementary
to the tax system, discussed in Chapter 3, and prohibited all other forms of
religious expression. This chapter explores how these regulations played out
on the ground in rural Fuzhou, restructuring both cult forms and norms. In
response to state policy, existing local cults were reshaped, manipulated, and
represented to bring them in line with the official system. The close connection that had developed between registration and kinship was now extended
into local religious life. Although the Ming official system never functioned
as intended, conformity, or claims to conformity, with the norms of the
system became a cultural resource that could be deployed in local struggles
and in relations with the state. As ancestral halls spread through the Fuzhou
countryside, it became common practice to parade the deities associated with
a lineage to its ancestral hall, as manifest expression of the lineage's claim to
the special protection of the deity. Issues of affiliation or disaffiliation with a
given temple, of temple financing, and of ritual organization became matters
determined not by individual preference, or by place of residence, but by the
registered household to which one belonged, which over the course of the
Ming had become virtually synonymous with the lineage. Thus in Fuzhou,
state attempts to regulate local religious practices, the emergence of the strategies and models of kinship that are associated with the lineage, as well as issues
of ethnic labeling and differentiation all came together to shape the social
history of local cults. The local cult, its temple, and its rituals became part
of kinship practice, shaped by the kinship strategies of actors in local society.

Scholars of Chinese religion have become increasingly interested in the
role of local cults in the integration of the village into Chinese society and in
the organization and reproduction of village society itself. The arguments of
Stephan Feuchtwang on the "imperial metaphor," of Steven Sangren on the
attribution to cult deities of the function of mediating order and disorder,
and of James Watson on the "standardization of the gods," for example, all
look to religion as part of an explanation for how the local community fit
into the larger society. Wang Mingming and Ken Dean have looked at the
question from the perspective of local society in different parts of Fujian.[2] But

little attention has been paid to the precise connections between local cults and lineage organization. In this chapter I consider the complex relationship between lineage organization and state policy in the history of local cults in the Fuzhou region.

BACKGROUND: THE RELIGIOUS LANDSCAPE IN THE SONG

Song sources from Fujian describe a religious world that may seem quite familiar to twentieth-century observers of Chinese popular religious practice.[3] The cults of the popular religion were in the Song and remain today, as Overmyer puts it, "personalized, devoted to deities who had once been human beings."[4] The gods were represented in human form, housed in temples, credited with a wide range of powers to influence local affairs, and paraded through the community periodically to ensure their protection, just as they are today. But these similarities should not lead us to overlook the long and complex historical processes that distinguish the religious life of the Song from that of later periods.

Song sources frequently use the term *she* to describe the physical sites of religious ritual. In antiquity, *she* were open altars where the abstract gods of the soil received offerings, and *sheji* altars where the gods of soil and grain received offerings together. The terms would come to have much wider meaning. Song sources use them to describe both open shrines to anonymous cosmic forces and enclosed temples housing anthropomorphic deities. Ken Dean has pointed out the difficulties created by the flexible use of these terms. Elite writers made deliberate use of the ambiguities and frequently "played with the frame of reference of these terms, quoting classical texts in defense of diverse popular religious practices."[5] For example, besides the officially sanctioned altars associated with administrative divisions, where officials made offerings to the cosmic forces as part of their official duties, temples in rural communities were also known as *she*.[6] The *Sanshan zhi* offers a wealth of detail on these religious sites, for which it uses the term *lishe*, or community *she*. There were many such temples. "One country may have several hundred. It would be impossible to count them all."[7] Xu Xiaowang has argued that the indigenous peoples of the region had offered cults to animals such as the snake, the frog, and the dog, and representations of these cults were gradually reworked to correspond to ideas about the *she*. This suggests that the history of local cults in the Fuzhou region must also take into account the complex ethnic history of the area, the cults of the indigenous peoples of the region, and the reshaping of these cults by the growing Han presence.[8]

In the Song, the efficacy of local deities became a matter of state interest. Complicated procedures were enacted to investigate, verify, and report miracles performed and to reward deities of proven efficacy with titles and other prerogatives.[9] But not every cult received state sanction, and the attitudes of elite writers, who were conscious of the tension between the ancient *she* and contemporary practice, remained ambiguous. Liu Kezhuang (1187–1269) justified the construction of popular temples known as *she* because of the positive motivations of worshipers. "What is this *she*? It is not the same as the prefectural or county *she*, consisting of an unenclosed altar, with a title but no image. In a market of three families, or where several dozen households gather, there is invariably a shrine for prayers for good fortune, at which there is an image. This is called the community *she*. To sacrifice to a local gentleman here implies both venerating virtue and serving the spirits."[10] Other Song officials were less sanguine about popular religious practice. Li Kan, for example, an official in Gutian county, ordered the destruction of some 315 illicit shrines there.[11] In the early Ming, the relationship between the state, its officials, and the local cults became more complex, with the promulgation of a set of laws designed to impose a greater degree of orthodoxy and control over local society.

NEW OFFICIAL REGULATIONS IN THE EARLY MING

In Chapter 3, I discussed the effects of the first Ming emperor's introduction of the *lijia* system to coordinate fulfillment of services to the state. Zhu Yuanzhang also ordered the implementation of a comprehensive official religious system. Two cults of this system were intended to permeate rural society, extending down to the *lijia* hundreds. The people of every *li* were ordered to perform sacrifices to two cults, known as *sheji* and *litan*.[12] The *sheji* was an altar for worship of the anonymous spirits of the soil and grains. Each year in rotation, the representative of one household in the *li* was to serve as the head of the assembly (*huishou*). He was charged with maintaining the altar and making preparations for the sacrifice, which was held twice each year, in the second and eighth months. At the sacrifice, animals were ritually slaughtered and offered to the cult, along with wine, fruit, incense, and candles. After the ritual, a member of the community was to recite the Oath to Restrain the Strong and Support the Weak, a call for community self-regulation.[13] The second official cult, the *litan*, was an altar for the hungry ghosts, the dead who were not otherwise cared for by their descendants. The *litan* sacrifices, to be held thrice annually at the Qingming festival in the third month, on the fifteenth day of the seventh month, and on the first day of the tenth month, would reduce the danger that these ghosts posed to the living.

Aside from these officially authorized sacrifices, all other organized popular religious practices were forbidden. The Ming code specifies harsh punishments for "shamans who summon false gods" and members of cults that "secretly hide images, burn incense and congregate, meeting at night and dispersing at dawn." Procession festivals such as those described in the Song record are explicitly prohibited. "Should members of military or civilian households dress up as images of deities, beat the gongs and drums in processions and meetings to welcome the gods, they shall receive 100 strokes of the heavy bamboo."[14]

Romeyn Taylor has commented that together these two authorized cults, "for all their differences, had the intended effects of reinforcing communal solidarity and integrating the communities into the hierarchical structure of the state."[15] But how and to what extent these regulations were actually put into place and enforced in local society in the Ming and how they affected the existing network of local cults has as yet received little scholarly attention. The sixteenth-century gazetteer of Fuzhou prefecture reports only that, "in the rural areas, there are some [communities] which have established *she* altars and *li* altars."[16] From the very start though, these altars merged with existing popular temples, where anthropomorphic deities were worshiped in enclosed chambers. For example, in the early Ming, the ancient temple of the Duke of the Peaceful Sacred Precincts (*jing*) in Fuzhou "was converted to a *li* altar."[17] The Zhuyi temple of Hongtang, which was established no later than 1388, was reconstructed "by the people of the *she* altar" in 1490. But the deities worshiped in this temple were not anonymous cosmic spirits. They were three generals who had come to the village in the form of a talismanic stone, "whereupon the people of the locality [built a] temple and sacrificed to them."[18]

Terminology and organizational practices drawn from the official regulations were in use in many parts of Fujian in the late Ming, but clearly in contexts rather different than what was envisioned by the regulations.[19] The provincial gazetteer of 1491, the *Bamin tongzhi*, suggests that there was considerable variation in the extent to which the official system actually replaced existing popular religious practices. In northwestern Jianning prefecture, local communities held a semiannual feast at their *she*. "Every year on the day of the spring and autumn *she* festival, chickens, piglets, wines and food are provided to sacrifice to the gods of the soil and grains. When this is completed they hold an assembly feast, and when the feasting is done they retire."[20] But Jianning appears to have been the exception rather than the rule. Elsewhere in the province, the solemn rites prescribed in the Ming ritual texts had merged with, been displaced by, or perhaps had never supplanted earlier popular practices. A late-fifteenth-century gazetteer of Xinghua prefecture, to the south of Fuzhou, laments that "the rites of the village *she* have long been abandoned." In fact, the account continues, the *she* still existed, but the term was now used to describe something very different from what was prescribed in the Ming regulations. "The head of every *she*, just before or after the first full moon, gathers together the people to worship at an annual *jiao* ritual, and carry the god of the *she* in a procession around the territory. Drums and music lead the way, and lanterns light the path. There is not a single family that does not participate."[21] Ming authors frequently complained at the wastefulness of popular religious expression and the trickery of those who extorted from the people the money to pay for this extravagance. The editor of the Changle gazetteer of 1637, county magistrate Xia Yunyi, complained that, "The custom is that there are many illicit cults. Every village holds sacrifices at Qingming, Middle and Late Origin. For the sacrifice at the *she*, the amount of money wasted for these annual sacrifices can reach 2,500 *jin*. The *li* head bullies this out of each household."[22] Ye Chunji (1532–95) also traced the decay of the early Ming system further south, in Hui'an county: "At present the officials only sacrifice at the county *sheji* altar, and those in each *li* have mostly been abandoned. Licentious shrines have been erected, with a single *li* having several dozen. They all claim the names of [altars] of the gods of the soil and grain, and house shamans and mediums who receive sacrifice without measure."[23] In these temples, which Ye distinguishes from legal altars with the remark that "state regulations prescribe that the altar be unenclosed," various offenses including extravagant rituals and theatrical performances were perpetrated.[24] Of course, there is also the possibility that what is presented in all of these sources as a falling away from official standards reflects simply a failure to adhere to those standards and that the Ming rites had never been successfully implemented in the first place.

On Nantai, later traditions represented the late Yuan and early Ming as a time when immigrants to the commercially developing areas just south of Fuzhou city began to organize themselves into communities for religious purposes. These communities are described in terms of *she* (altars) or of sacred precincts (*jing*) under the protection of the god of the altar. In the Tengshan area, where Western traders would settle in the nineteenth century, "in the late Tang and early Song, there were very few residents. After the southward flight of the Song, refugees from turmoil gradually moved to Teng[shan]. Only in the Yuan did villages begin to form. From this, one hundred families combined together to constitute one *li* altar. The *li* altars were then converted into *jing*."[25] Perhaps the distinction between *li* and *jing* has to do with the conversion of open-air altars to enclosed temples. The actual construction of *li* altars and temples must have taken into account both local realities and the demands of the Ming regulations. One area of Tengshan, said to have developed beginning in the Yuan, is known as Ten Sacred Precincts (*shijing*). "In the Yuan there were first ten *li* altars. Later the names were changed to ten sacred precincts." The names of the ten precincts are still well known to long-time residents of the area as the main geographic divisions, though not to the large number of inmigrants since 1978. The residents of the ten precincts constructed a temple together in the late Yuan. "But the site was small and unsuitable. In the Zhizheng period (1341–68), local people surnamed Pan opened up the hills and donated land for the shrine. The [people of] the ten sacred precincts gathered funds and constructed the temple."[26]

It thus appears that although the official religious system did take effect at least to some degree, by the mid-Ming there was a widespread consensus in elite discourse that the system had fallen apart.[27] The simple and dignified *she* altars within the local communities had fallen into disuse and were replaced by lavish enclosed temples to deities who had not received official sanction, with the communities putting on extravagant and wasteful rituals. In fact, as we shall see in the next section, the real situation was much more complex, and closely tied to changes in another aspect of the Ming administrative system, the *lijia*.

THE 'LIJIA,' THE VILLAGE TEMPLE,
AND THE LINEAGE

As we saw in Chapter 3, when the *lijia* was first implemented in the early Ming, each registered household may have been something like a household in the modern sense of the term, a domestic unit engaged in shared production and consumption. But over time the heads of the original households became the progenitors of patrilines transmitted through multiple generations. The original *lijia* household gradually became both a fiscal unit bearing no fixed relationship to population and an umbrella group comprising all the descendants of the original registered progenitor. As a result, the group associated with a given *li* altar would come to consist not of one hundred domestic units engaged in shared production and consumption, but perhaps many times that number. Furthermore, the Ming regulations equated the worshipers at the village altars with the households registered under the *lijia* system. But as we have seen, this was not the whole of the rural population. Village residents who did not belong to registered households may have had some rights of participation in worship at the *she* altar, but they would not have been able to fulfill the office of head of assembly, a position that rotated among the one hundred registered households attached to the altar. Nor, presumably, would a member of a nonregistered household have been selected for the honor of reading the oath at the conclusion of the sacrifices. Full participation in the *lishe* was a privilege that was jealously guarded by the registered households of the *li*.

By the mid-Ming, demographic pressures and social differentiation had transformed the *she* altar and the *lijia* hundred with which it was initially associated. Individual registered households, in many cases corresponding to lineages, began to construct their own *she* altars and temples, or to claim that their own altars and temples were in fact *she* altars. This process might be labeled the devolution of the *she*. Devolution also meant a reconfiguration of the role of the *she*. It became common practice to parade the deity of a particular *she* to the ancestral hall of the lineage associated with the *she*, as manifest expression of the lineage's claim to the special protection of the deity. Issues of affiliation or disaffiliation with a given temple, of temple financing, and of ritual organization became matters determined not by individual preference or by place of residence, but by the registered household to which one belonged and thus to lineage organization. The local cult and its rituals became a part of kinship practice, part of the ways ideas and concepts related to kinship were implicated in social relations and institutions.

The history of religious sites in Yixu illustrates the processes of the devolution of the *she*. The Light of Samādhi Monastery (*Dingguangsi*) originally served as the *she* for a *li* located in the vicinity of the village of Yixu. The monastery was destroyed after 1949, but an eighteenth-century description survives in the genealogy of the Huang lineage of Yixu. The monastery, also known as the Gaoguantang "serves as the *she* school (*shexue*) of the first ward (*tu*) of Renfeng subcanton (*li*)." How are we to interpret these terms? Recall that the Fuzhou region had since the Song been divided into territorial divisions called subcantons, of which a county might have several. By the Ming, these named subcantons had lost their earlier administrative significance, but they remained in common usage as an indicator of location, and indeed they remain so today. The term ward (*tu*) was in use in the early Ming as a measure of land corresponding in theory to the area of taxable land belonging to a single *lijia* hundred.[28] When the *lijia* system was introduced, the same character *li* was used to refer both to the preexisting subcantons and to the *li* hundreds of the *lijia* system. This must have caused considerable confusion. The term ward (*tu*) appears to have been used as a synonym for *lijia* hundred to minimize the confusion.[29] The account uses the term *she* school, perhaps because according to Ming regulations every *she* altar should have a school attached, but clearly what is described is the local version of the *she* altar itself.

> The main hall is the Temple of the Sage [Confucius] (*shengmiao*). To the left is the Wenchang hall. Later it was destroyed by fire, but the tablet of the god still survives. The lower hall is where the monks worship Rulai [Tathāgata] and the various Buddhas. In the eastern kiosk, the Heavenly Immortal Great Emperor (Tianxian dadi) is worshiped. Half of the front hall serves as a roadside resting place, where Mituo is worshiped.

The description of the structure and the deities worshiped in it shows that this altar was something very different from what was prescribed in the Ming regulations. This was an enclosed temple in which deities from all the major religious traditions were worshiped and in which Buddhist monks resided.

The description continues, "although this monastery is the collective property of the first ward, the expenses for repairs and for the maintenance of the monks are all met by our lineage."[30] This comment points to the effect of demographic pressures and social differentiation on the *she* altar associated with a *lijia* hundred and hints at the underlying causes behind the devolution of the *she*, that is, the construction by individual *lijia*-registered households of their own temples, which they also called *she*. The Huang of Yixu were only one of the hundred *lijia* households that belonged to the *she*, but because they were so numerous they found themselves paying all its expenses. In places such as Yixu where the descendants of a single *lijia* household dominated the local population, members of this household frequently claimed the right to have their own *she* altar, to assert their dominance of the *she*, to confirm their *lijia*-registered status to the exclusion of those who could not claim this status, and to justify the orthodoxy and legality of their temple in the face of repeated official campaigns against heterodox cults.[31]

In Yixu, this devolution took the form of the temple of the Venerated Kings of Water and Land (*Shuilu zunwang*), which was probably built in the fifteenth or very early sixteenth century. The history of this temple, recorded in an eighteenth-century inscription by Huang Fuji, illustrates several important elements in the relationship between popular religious organization and local society. The inscription begins with the assertion that although the temple contains images of deities in an enclosed chamber, it is actually a legitimate *she* altar. "Our village has had a temple for the altar to the god of the soil and grains (*sheji miao*) for a long time already." The temple's long history and conformity with the classical model of antiquity demonstrate that its credentials were not open to question. But the inscription also notes that the image of one of the three deities is said to have floated up to the river's edge at Yixu, suggesting that this cult probably originated in the placation of a hungry ghost, to which the ideology of the *she* had been attached later. Much of the text of the inscription details the process of financing and reconstruction of the *she*. "It was proposed to rebuild and enlarge the temple.... The lineage members with one voice agreed. The Lin surname and the various sojourners who lived here and belonged to the same altar also agreed."[32] The construction process was overseen by the lineage head (*zuzhang*), assisted by ten lineage members. Thus this *she* had devolved from the original *lijia* hundred to a single registered household in the *lijia* hundred, that of the Yixu Huang lineage. The final lines of the inscription illustrate how the orthodoxy of the shrine was socially useful, serving as a mark of distinction separating Yixu from other communities in the area. "The momentous scale [of the temple] is foremost among the *she* of the neighbouring villages. It reveals the spirit of the gods and the health of the people."[33] The text asserts the special role for the Huang in the history of the temple, which was constructed under the auspices of their lineage organization. This *she* belongs not to the whole of the *li*, as did the Light of Samādhi Monastery, but to the village of Yixu and primarily the Huang lineage of Yixu. Other residents of the community have only a secondary role to play.

Many similar cases of *lijia* household/lineages constructing their own *she* in the mid-Ming can be found. For example, the genealogy of the Yang of Huyu records:

> When our distant ancestor Tingyi first moved to Huyu, he originally worshiped the god of the soil and grain at the Palace of Seven Precincts (*Qijing gong*). Afterwards he established a *she* at the summit of Jade Hill, the site of a former *she*. He called it the Jade Hill Flourishing Precincts (*Yushan shengjing*). He divided incense from the Palace of Seven Precincts and worshiped there. For many generations we enjoyed the protection of the god.[34]

According to the Yang genealogy, Yang Tingyi was the first generation or founding ancestor of the lineage. He lived from 1297 to 1379. When he first settled in Huyu, or as is more likely, when he first registered in the *lijia* system, his family participated in the ritual activities of the *lishe* altar.[35] Over the course of the Ming, the individual registered households who worshiped at this altar established their own *she* altars. Yang Tingyi is described as having established his own *she* altar through division of incense from the original *lishe*, suggesting that there may have been a hierarchical network linking the original *she* that belonged to the whole *li* and the later *she* that belonged to the individual registered households of the *li*.[36] We know that the deity worshiped at the Huyu altar was not an anonymous cosmic deity but an anthropomorphic one, because, in 1463, the god appeared in a vision to a member of the lineage who was in Beijing to sit the examinations.[37]

Read in isolation, the descriptions of these temples might suggest that the Ming official system had completely broken down, with social groups of all kinds able to construct enclosed temples housing personalized deities at will. But the texts make clear that this was not the case. Both authors are careful to justify the establishment of their local temples in terms of their derivation from a prior *she* in the official system. In other words, the legitimacy of these temples rested on precedent. Many descriptions of local temples constructed after the mid-Ming make similar claims, suggesting that a link to the Ming official system remained an important source of legitimacy for local cults.

Some groups were unable to lay claim to a *she* altar established by the order of the Ming, for example, because they had never been registered in the *lijia* system. In such cases, it was also possible to claim the right to establish a legitimate temple by purchasing this right.[38] The Lan of Wangchuan provide an example. Recall that the Lan are a She group living in Lianjiang county. In 1692, the magistrate of Lianjiang had imposed the policy of "allocating tax households to the descent line," according to which residents of Lianjiang were to identify the *lijia*-registered household from which they were descended or had been affiliated to facilitate the administration of tax payment. The Lan had been unable to comply, for they had not previously been registered in the *lijia* system. So the Lan together with twelve other surnames had purchased the registration of a certain Wu family. The share of ownership of the registration of each surname was expressed as a unit of account called the official fiscal male (*guanding*). The Lianjiang Lan acquired fifteen of the 114 *guanding*, or shares.[39] Immediately after the purchase was complete, the thirteen surnames established a *she* altar, the ownership of which was allocated according to the shares for which each surname group had accepted responsibility. The contract recording the purchase of the registration, introduced in Chapter 3, organizes the thirteen participating surnames into five groups. Each group was associated with a particular annual sacrifice, at Qingming in the third month, on the fifteenth day of the seventh month, during the eighth month, on the first day of the tenth month, and during the second month. For each group, the date of the sacrifice is identified, followed by the name of the founding ancestor of each of the participating surnames, the number of shares held by the surname, and the ancestors of the lineage in whose name the shares are endowed.[40] The activities of the altar show clearly that it was a combination of the *sheji* and *litan* prescribed in the early Ming. The dates on which sacrifices were scheduled are precisely those of the Ming regulations for sacrifice at the *she* altar and the *litan*. By purchasing a *lijia* registration, the Lan and the other "friendly households," each corresponding to a lineage, thus purchased the right to erect their own *she* altar and perform rituals there.[41]

Once a link was established between *lijia* registration and the legitimacy of a local temple, affiliation or disaffiliation with a given temple became a matter decided not by individual preference or place of residence but by the *lijia*-registered household to which one belonged. Since by the mid-Ming a single *lijia*-registered household had often become equivalent to a lineage, kinship organization thus became a critical factor in determining temple affiliation. Ye Xianggao of Fuqing county provides a clear example from the late Ming. In an essay titled "Record of the Neighbouring Descent Lines," Ye discusses the population of the villages near his home. All of the surrounding villages were inhabited by residentially concentrated descent groups, many of which were surnamed Ye but did not necessarily belong to the same descent line as Ye Xianggao. His account explains the household registration situation of each village. For example, the village nearest his own is called Qiangli, and its residents are all surnamed Ye. They are registered in seven *lijia* households, five of which are commoner households and two salt-manufacturing households. To the west of Yun hill live the Shijing Ye, divided into three registered households.[42] Originally, all of these groups, and several others, had worshiped at a single *she* altar, the Yun hill shrine:

> All these families were our close neighbours, and shared a common *she*. The *she* altar consists of a shrine for the worship of the gods of the soil and grain. There is also a temple to the Heavenly Consort [i.e., Mazu]. These were built in the early years of the [Ming] dynasty. With each reconstruction and each decay, the site was moved. Now it has been returned to the original site and enlarged. I record that [the villages] from the centre and to the west of the hill [formerly] shared a common altar. But the people were numerous and fractious. Each year when the god was invited and requited, the assembly of the altar was held. There would suddenly be liquor and cursing, and it even came to fighting. The villagers were troubled by this. When the *she* shrine collapsed and was to be rebuilt, the elders proposed that not a single cash be accepted from [the residents of the villages] west of the hill, and we should not associate with them. The [villages] west of the hill constructed their own shrine, and did not come anymore to the assembly. The avoidance of fighting at the assembly of the altar began with the division of the altar.[43]

Here members of several different *lijia*-registered households/lineages had originally worshiped together at a single shrine. But because of conflicts between the different groups, one group of lineages excluded another when the shrine was rebuilt. The excluded Shijing Ye, who made up three of the households/lineages, were forced to construct their own temple, their members forced to disaffiliate with the original cult by virtue of their kinship situation and collectively shift their affiliation to a new temple.

The close connection between registration, lineage, and the local temple also had a major impact on ritual practices. As ancestral halls spread through the Fuzhou countryside beginning in the mid-Ming, it became common practice in single-lineage villages to parade the deities to the ancestral hall at the time of their annual festival. The earliest evidence I have found for this development comes from the 1680 genealogy of the Shimei Wu of Fuzhou, which calls on the caretakers of the ancestral hall to prepare "incense, candles, wine and grass mats" for their deity, who is paraded on the sixteenth day of the first month.[44] The current practice in those villages in the Fuzhou region that have an ancestral hall is for the main rituals of the annual festival to take place in the hall. The villagers of the Fuzhou region find it unnecessary to explain why the deities visit the ancestral hall. Their deities protect the people of the lineage, so it is natural that the lineage should honor them. This is simply the way things are done. In some villages, Daoist priests are hired to perform a *jiao* ritual in the ancestral hall at the time of the annual festival. A document that is posted outside the Temple of the Generals (*Jiangjun miao*) in Yixu each year, and that I collected in 1995, provides a more formal explanation for why this should be done.[45] The proclamation serves as notification for the community of the upcoming festival and is posted by the temple managers in the name of a subordinate deity of the Generals. In language rich with bureaucratic and historical allusions, it describes the tour the gods will make of the lanes of the village and of the surrounding communities. The destination of the tour is the "Auxiliary Station" (*xingtai*), which refers to the Huang ancestral hall.[46] In other words, for the purpose of the festival, the gods, who are perceived in terms of the bureaucratic metaphor, visit the ancestral hall, reinvented as their temporary bureaucratic office. There they receive the submissions of the people with whose welfare they are charged, the members of the lineage.

In multilineage communities with more than one ancestral hall the situation could be more complex. The lineages might share a common temple, in which case precise regulations would be spelled out delimiting the rights of each lineage to participate in the ritual. Thus in the town of Gantangbao, Fu'an county, whose population is divided into four lineages, a contract dated 1920 includes the following regulations for the annual procession festival:

> On the morning of the fourth day of the first month of the year, the spirits of the gods descend. First the gods receive offerings from the [ancestral] hall of the Zheng of Inner Lane (*Lijie Zheng ci*). Next, they go to the [ancestral] hall of the Zheng of Upper Lane (*Qianjie Zheng ci*) and the halls of the Old Chen and the New Chen. When the gods are taken out, the Zheng surname of Upper Lane will start. On the same day, the Zheng surname of Inner Lane

take out the gods immediately afterwards. Everyone must respect these old regulations. No one should disrupt the order.[47]

In Luozhou, rather than the three dominant lineages sharing a single temple, each lineage has its own temple. The earliest temple is in the center of the Wu settlement, adjoining the Wu ancestral hall. The Chen did not build their own temple until the early nineteenth century, a century after the ancestral hall and just as the stream of high officials began to emerge from among the Chen.[48] Each lineage, and each temple, performs a separate procession ritual in the course of the first month of the New Year. In each case, the deities are brought from their temple to the ancestral hall, whereas they receive offerings for several days, before their procession. All three processions tour the entire town, but the procession performed by the Wu visits no other ancestral hall, whereas the gods of the Chen and the Lin visit one another's hall for several hours in the course of the procession. My informants from the Luozhou Chen explain that the gods visit the Lin ancestral hall because the wife of one of the deities in the temple is a woman of the Zhouwei Lin, so the parade is also a visit to her natal home. But lineage politics obviously played a role in this tradition, for the Chen and the Lin were traditional allies against the greater strength and numbers of the dominant lineage in Luozhou, the Wu.

The close connection between lineage organization and local temple also had implications for the financing and organization of temple activities. The costs of ritual activities were often met from lineage corporate funds. In the list of annual expenses of the Sanshan Ye lineage in their 1890 genealogy is a set of costs associated with the Wansuipu sacred precincts. These include the costs of the procession festival of the deity and of theatrical performances held on the birthdays of the deity, his wife, and a subordinate deity in the temple. These expenses were met out of the income from the ancestral hall's estate, which consisted of land and other rental properties.[49] Lineage organization principles might also be implicated in the funding of the temple, even if the lineage estate itself did not contribute directly to temple expenses. The Dong of Langqi venerate the Respected King of the Golden Island (*Jinqi zunwang*), who is paraded through their village on the tenth day of the year. Their genealogy instructs that the costs of the festival be divided among the four branches of the lineage and, in turn, among the households that make up each branch, and charge the ancestral hall managers with collecting funds each year.[50] Ancestral halls themselves often became major sponsors of temple reconstruction. An inscription commemorating the 1928 reconstruction of the temple of the Great Kings of Linpu lists some fifty donors, of which the largest were the six ancestral halls of the village.[51]

The links between *lijia* registration, lineage organization, and ritual practice is further illustrated in two Qing contracts from the genealogy of the Lan of Wangchuan. The first, dated 1836, resulted from a dispute over responsibilities for the expenses of ritual performance at the altar. The contract was drawn up in the name of three household heads, the senior member of each of three of the segments into which the Lan lineage is divided. It begins by restating the account of the purchase of *lijia* registration under the leadership of Zeng Mingsheng:

> Fifteen shares were acquired [in the name of] Lan Gongzhi. Four shares [were allocated to ancestors of the lineage segment settled at] Gangli; seven to Beiying, of which three were given to Jutai, and four to Danyang Houwan, making a total of fifteen.[52] Whenever it came time for a sacrifice at the altar, the expenses were allocated according to the shares. But the distribution of the shares was not clear. . . . At the time of the sacrifice in 1836, Wenyu went to observe the sacrifice. Upon inspection of the general accounts of household head Zeng Mingsheng, he found that four shares were held by the Gangli [branch], in the names of Chaoren, Chaojing, Chaoming and Chaogong. Beginning in 1836, when the sacrifice was held, the Gangli [branch] should be responsible for four shares [of the contributions for expenses].[53]

The original shares in the altar had been endowed in the name of individual members of the Lan surname. These shares would eventually come to be the collective property of the descendants of that individual.[54] The individuals named were the founding ancestors of the branches of the lineage, so the shares were divided among these branches. The dispute in the contract arose because one branch was not fulfilling its obligations. By referring to written documents that laid out the ownership of the registration, the other branches were able to persuade the members of the errant branch that they were responsible for participating in the rituals of the altar and meeting the expenses associated with that participation.

A second contract, titled "Contract on the Division of the Sacrifice at the Altar of the *She*," dates from 1854:

> The makers of this contract are Cai Yuandao, the household head of Kangyuan; Lan Luzhi, the household head of Gangli; Lan Zuxin, the household head of Beiying Houwan; Lan Jicai, the household head of Danyang

Houwan; Lan Changtong, the household head of Yuyao, and others of the fifth *jia* of the second ward. At the time of the Qingming sacrifice on the eighth day of the third month of 1854, each of the surnames came to the sacrificial altar at Kangyuan Xiangwei. There were too many people. The Cai surname had to provide shelter and funds for the wine, and the requests were considerable and complicated. The burden was truly difficult to fulfill. Now it is collectively decided through the mediation of the descendants of Household Head Zeng to divide the sacrifice.

The Lan surname hold fifteen shares total . . . and the Jiang two. In all this makes seventeen shares. [When it is their turn to hold the] sacrifice, the two surnames agree that two people per share may attend the feast, and no more. If [this agreement] is ignored and there are too many people, a fine should be assessed in proportion to the number of shares held. It is also agreed that the household heads of the ten placards should [be seated at] two tables of the feast, and receive ten catties of cooked meet, one pig's liver, and ten bottles of wine. The Zeng family household head should receive two catties of fresh meat in thanks for his [ancestor's] contributions. At the time of the sacrifice to the lord of the soil of the precincts (*jingtuzhu*), and the holding of communal feasts, any beggars should be [allowed to sit at] one table.[55] The expenses of the sacrifice are to be allocated according to the shares owned. The Cai are not liable for any of these expenses. . . .

The Cai family hold four shares. [When it is their turn to hold the] sacrifice, they must invite the household heads of the Qiu and the Zhuang to attend the feast. After the sacrifice is divided, the Cai need not invite the descendents of the Lan or Jiang or others, but they must not neglect the sacrifice. We only desire the descendants to flourish and enjoy good fortune. Fearing that an oral agreement is unreliable, we have prepared this contract in five copies, with each party holding one copy, to serve forever as evidence.[56]

This contract was drawn up to resolve a dispute between three surname groups who in the original agreement of 1708 were supposed to take responsibility for one of the five annual sacrifices at the altar. The solution was to set up a rotation by lineage. Two of the three groups shared responsibility for certain ritual performances, and the third group took responsibility for the remaining performances on their own. Together the contracts illustrate some of the possible long-term consequences of the purchase of the right to construct a *she* altar by internally and externally differentiated lineage organizations. The altar had come to resemble a corporation, one in which disputes arose over the rights and responsibilities associated with share ownership. Here local religious organization played an important role in structuring interaction between different groups in local society.

The connection between lineage and temple by way of *lijia* registration
did not mean that all members of the lineage, that is, all the descendants
of the registered ancestor, participated in temple affairs on an equal basis.
The sources indicate considerable strategic competition over control of local
temples and their construction and management. The two chief temples of
Yixu provide a good illustration. The history of the Temple of the Generals
was retraced in 1866 by Huang Yongnian. After providing a description of the
deities as martial heroes, Yongnian considers the provenance of their temple,
which was first constructed early in the Qianlong period:

> The early management of the temple is unknown. It was first managed by
> five gentlemen [names omitted]; after they grew old, they resigned and were
> replaced by ten gentlemen [names omitted]. After only a short time because
> of being old or too busy, they also resigned in favour of the lineage and
> branch heads. Afterwards it was collectively decided that the local gentry
> should manage the temple in rotation. This has now become the rule.[57]

The Temple of the Generals thus seems to have been first constructed and
managed by common people whose identities were not important enough
even to be recorded. Then gradually there was a transition toward elite
management. A similar transition marked the history of the Temple of the
Venerated Kings of Water and Land, discussed earlier. When the temple
was first built, the project was undertaken by common people, not members of the educated elite who would be expected to have left some record.
"Those in charge were old and there was no one to record their biographies." But the eighteenth-century reconstruction was under the authority
of prominent members of the lineage, such as Fuji himself, a *jinshi* of 1733.
The appropriation of control over the temple by the educated elite had
an impact on popular religiosity. Huang Fuji records the discomfort that
some in the village felt at the placement of deities after the temple of the
Venerated Kings of Water and Land was reconstructed. Besides the Venerated Kings, the temple housed images of Guandi and Marshall Tian in
the gatehouse. "To have Guandi and the various gods all in the doorway
made some uncomfortable." Probably what made people uncomfortable,
and here he clearly meant the educated elite, was to have an imperially
sanctioned deity in a subordinate position to a local one, whose orthodoxy
was actually open to some question. So when the temple was next reconstructed, Guandi was removed and installed in his own dedicated temple,

constructed from the materials salvaged from the original temple when it was torn down.[58]

The use of territorial temples and their gods as arenas for elite production and deployment of local power is well illustrated in the biography of Chen Yongsheng in the Houguan county gazetteer. Chen, a resident of Qishan, upriver from Nantai, was a man of local influence in the Qing and frequently mediated local disputes. A woman villager intended to bring charges of unfiliality against her son to the magistrate. Chen urged her not to go to the officials, but ordered the younger villagers to seize her son and take him to the temple of the territorial god (*shegong miao*). There he faced the god and declared, "This is the god of the soil. Our whole locality worships him. He is no less important than the magistrate. How will it be if today I stand to the side and issue proclamations on the god's behalf?" He interrogated the mother, ordered the son be punished with a beating, and oversaw their reconciliation.[59] Parallels to this kind of judicial and regulatory activities by local elites could be found in various community pacts and lineage regulations surviving from the Fuzhou region and point to the self-regulation of local society in the late imperial period.[60]

BEYOND THE 'LIJIA' AND THE 'SHE'

The examples discussed earlier illustrate some of the practical consequences of the *lijia* registration and *lishe* system on the ground in Fujian in the Ming and Qing. The connection between *lijia*, lineage, and temple should not be overstated. Some formerly local cults in Fujian came to have regional and even national followings.[61] Even at the local level, temples and their cults could serve as the foci of territorial alliances that extended beyond the single lineage or *lijia* household. Such temples were often involved in matters of concern to larger territorial units, such as irrigation and reclamation or public works and charity. A typical example is the cult of two subordinate deities in the temple of the Xu Immortals at Qingpu, Generals Wei and Zhao, who served as the ritual focus for a land reclamation project involving ten different villages.[62] Moreover, the lineage temple rubric does not nearly encompass all the organizational and associational forms of the individual lineage village in the Fuzhou region. Within the one temple, groups of individuals might form their own voluntary organizations, known as *bashe*, similar to the *shenming hui* found in Taiwan and elsewhere in China, each oriented around a subordinate deity of the temple.[63] But the lineage organization to which villagers, even members of *bashe*, belonged or did not belong, and the position of that lineage in the *lijia* system, would still have had important consequences for their own religious life.

The cases so far discussed involve the strategies of people who belonged to households that had been registered with the authorities. We saw in the case of the Lan of Lianjiang that some household/lineages had to buy their way into registration. But what about those members of groups labeled as ethnically different, migrant laborers, and others living on the margins of Han society who were never willing or able to register in the *lijia* system? In this section, I discuss one example of how such groups might develop their own religious practices and organization. The Temple of the Minister (*Shangshu miao*) is located in Yangqi village south of Fuzhou. The chief deity is Chen Wenlong (1232–77), a famous Song martyr.[64] According to the current managers of the temple and many older residents of the surrounding area, the vast majority of worshipers at the temple are Dan. The high point of the ritual activities of the temple is a biannual ritual known as "parading the boat" (*yingchuan*). It involves the procession of a large wooden boat, specially built for the purpose, through 193 villages over six days, accompanied by a crowd of worshipers.[65] Chen Wenlong is greeted outside each village by the god of the village temple and escorted to the temple to receive offerings there before pushing on to the next village. Men of the host village carry the boat through their own village, handing it off to the men of Yangqi who carry the boat between communities. Finally the procession returns to Yangqi, and the ritual culminates with the boat being launched, set alight, and then allowed to drift off down the river.[66] Though the people of the villages that participate in the ritual whom I spoke with told me they are Han, and many have genealogies, ancestral halls, and other evidence of lineage organization, two stone inscriptions at the temple suggest that this is a recently acquired identity and that in the past some or all of the people of these communities were Dan (Figure 6.4).

The first is a simple tablet commemorating the reconstruction of the temple at a cost of almost three thousand taels in 1840. It records the names of thirty-nine donors, thirty-eight of which are corporate entities of some kind, villages (*dun*), market towns (*jie*[2], *pu*), or associations or flotillas (*bang*). In Fuzhou, the term *bang* refers to a fleet of Dan fishing boats that moored close to one another. There were at least three *bang* in the Yangqi area in the early twentieth century. One of them, the Ferry boat *bang*, was made up of

Figure 6.4.   Stone inscription at Yangqi recording granting of tax relief to Dan fishermen (photograph by author).

Dan who monopolized the ferry crossings between Yangqi, its surrounding villages, and the south shore of the Min River.

The second tablet presents a somewhat different picture of the ethnicity of the temple's adherents and of the temple's political and social functions. The inscription was erected in 1804 to record a judgment by the magistrate of Houguan county in response to a petition from a number of residents of the county. The litigants declare themselves to be fishermen households (*yuhu*), some of whom continue to live afloat while farming rented land. "As a result, they have come to moor their boats at Xinqi, Suqi, Gaoqi, Tuniu, Nanyu and other harbours in Houguan." All of these are places visited by the contemporary procession festival of the cult and all places that appear in the first inscription as donors to the temple's reconstruction. The contents of the inscription are mostly concerned with taxes. The petitioners accept their liability for the fish tax but deny liability for another tax, the tax on boatmen (*shuifu*), that derived from a former service levy obligation. "We reflect that for fishermen households there has always been a distinction between tax payment and service levy obligations. This has long been established in the regulations. The law is strict and manifest. How can it not be known that [the petitioners] are liable for the payment of the tax, and not for the fulfillment of the service levy?" But recently, the petition continues, the head of the boatmen (*shuifu tou*), "relying on bullies in the locality, in violation of the old regulations, dares to act on his own authority with no regret." In other words, he was pressing the fishing households to pay the tax on boatmen. Ultimately, the magistrate ruled in favor of the fishing households, and the inscription was erected at the temple to demonstrate this.[67]

The petition distinguishes between two taxes, the fish tax and the boatmen tax. Recall from Chapter 2 that the fish tax was a levy on nonregistered Dan households in the Ming. The tax was abolished in the Qing, but clearly it continued to be levied—probably according to the Ming amounts adjusted by customary surcharges—and collected by a subbureaucratic functionary. The tax on boatmen must have been a legacy of the Ming service levy, which in the Qing was collected by a local figure who held the subbureaucratic position of head of the boatmen. Clearly this was a position held by a local bully who extorted rather than collected the tax. By the mid-Qing, no one in Fuzhou was actually liable for the service levy surcharge.[68] The inscription blames the head of the boatmen for repeatedly trying to extort additional money from the Dan on the principle that the service levy surcharge should be added to the original fish tax. The fishermen resisted the additional levies and turned to the magistrate. One option might have been to register themselves with the magistrate as land dwellers and thereby claim exemption from the fish tax.[69] But this group had not yet acquired the cultural resources or credibility to deny their Dan background. All they could do was request that the extortion of the fish tax be more reasonable. What is most significant here is that in the absence of formal registration, it appears to have been the Temple of the Minister, and the organization behind it, that served as the political institution through which they interacted with the state, an institution whose community was solidified annually through the ritual procession of the god.[70] As the *lijia* household became increasingly synonymous with the lineage for those registered in the system, the lineage served increasingly as the institution through which relations with the state and its officials were mediated. Religious organization played an important role in structuring local society for all; for those outside the *lijia* system, it also played an important role in structuring relations between society and the state.

Since the worshipers of Chen Wenlong no longer consider themselves to be Dan, the tablet at the temple to Chen Wenlong stands as a trace of a particular stage in a process of transformation of ethnic identification, a process whose later stages involved the erasure from the collective memory of the earlier stages. In the long run, as I have argued earlier, it often made sense for groups of Dan to adopt strategies aimed at redefining their ethnic identification, strategies such as the tracing of descent to ancestors who had migrated from the Chinese heartland, the formalization of registration with the state, and the adoption of cultural practices such as the ancestral hall that marked one as Han. As the people whose communities contributed to the maintenance of the temple came to consider themselves non-Dan, and as that claim came to be widely accepted, the temple's role as a political institution structuring their relationship with the state may have declined.

Interestingly, the ethnic aspects of early temple affiliation persist in the ritual practices of the cult. Before 1949, in the procession ritual of Chen Wenlong, the boat itself was carried by Dan from boats that moor in the vicinity of Yangqi, organized by the headmen of the two flotillas into which they were divided. This practice is common elsewhere in the Fuzhou region, even where the local temple is clearly under the control of a powerful lineage whose members included prominent degree holders. For the parade festivals of the Three Generals of Yixu, the responsibility of carrying the sedan chairs of the gods themselves falls on the local Dan fishermen. The explanation offered to me both by elderly members of the Huang lineage and by local Dan people is that the Dan were the first to welcome the gods ashore when their images floated to Yixu. But perhaps this is also a lingering relic of a time when the Huang were not so different from the Dan, that is, of an earlier ethnic identification now almost entirely suppressed.

CONCLUSIONS

Though efforts to control popular religious practices were not new, the early Ming state's efforts were singularly ambitious. The Ming official religious system, complementary to the tax and service levy system, extended in theory down to the rural community and prohibited all other forms of religious expression. It is not clear to what extent this system was actually implemented as planned in Fujian, but we have seen that it had a major impact on local society. Existing local cults were reshaped, manipulated, and represented to bring them in line with the official system. A persuasive claim of adherence to the Ming regulations became a cultural resource to be preserved, pursued, and contested.

The Ming system tied local popular religion to the *lijia* system and hence to the lineage. When the right to construct a *she* altar, whatever that might mean on the ground, devolved to the individual *lijia* household, the construction and maintenance of a *she* altar could become the mandate of a single lineage group. Kinship then came to define issues such as temple affiliation and to shape the ritual practices associated with the temple and its gods. But even as the local temple was brought within the ambit of lineage activities, it remained a venue for strategic competition by different types of elites within the lineage.

Cults that could demonstrate adherence to the Ming system did not define the limits of religious life. There was a wide variety of other patterns of association, especially for people like the Dan, who remained outside the Ming registration system. Such groups developed their own associational forms, and not surprisingly these forms came to fill crucial roles in their relationship with the state, roles that the *lijia* system filled for the registered populace. As Dan groups came ashore, effaced their ethnic difference, and registered for the tax, which also meant organizing themselves into lineages, these forms may have lost their effectiveness, but they did not disappear. Thus the rise of the lineage as a tax-paying institution, as the unit by which relationships with the state were mediated, and as an expression of educated-elite ideals reshaped by commercial interests and other local concerns—all of which were a product of the early Ming—had a profound impact on local religious life.

Comparing the evidence from Fuzhou with other studies on the relationship between lineage organization and local religion suggests that the situation may have been quite different in different parts of south China. In his study of the transformations or mutations in the *she* altar system, Dean identifies a process wherein "the *she*-altar and the local temple system gradually replaced lineage centred domination of local space." Although not dismissing lineage organization, Dean limits its influence to the promotion of Confucian learning through support of schools.[71] But the evidence from Fuzhou suggests that lineage organization continued to play an important role in the local religious system and, indeed, that lineages were in some ways the basis of cult organization. In the Pearl River Delta, Faure sees the process occurring in the reverse order from Dean, with "groupings that were focused on places of worship and sacrifice replaced by those that were registered for tax, and then by lineages that accepted the scholarly mode of lineage organization as the ideal to aspire to."[72] In Fuzhou, groupings based on worship, groups registered for taxation, and lineages in the "scholarly mode" became one and the same organization. This chapter has thus shown that neither of these linear trajectories is sufficient to explain the situation in the Fuzhou region, where the history of lineage organization remained inseparable from that of local cult organization. Not only did the two continue to shape one another throughout the Ming and Qing period, but they also had a profound impact, which endured into the twentieth century and beyond, on local life.

SEVEN

Conclusion: Flexible Strategies of Kinship Practice

Guo Bocang and other educated compilers of lineage genealogies in Ming and Qing Fuzhou knew that they were describing an institution very different from the kinship system of antiquity. Still, they felt that the corporate lineages to which they belonged and which they had helped to build were manifestations of universal, eternal, and natural principles that had been made explicit in the neo-Confucian canonical texts. These principles would have included patrilineal descent and surname fidelity, patrilocal residence, sacrificial obligations to patrilineal ancestors according to state promulgated standards, and ties of locality expressed through sacrifices to the local gods of the soil and grain. In the preceding chapters, I have outlined some of the ways in which these principles were negotiated, manipulated, and appropriated in the history of organized patrilineal kinship in the region. Rather than the simple implementation of a set of unchanging principles or rules, kinship in the Fuzhou region was a form of strategic practice in which resources both material and symbolic were accumulated and deployed in pursuit of diverse interests. Because institutionalized patrilineal kinship was strategic, because it was practiced, the set of practices and representations connected with kinship could never be unitary. Rather, patrilineal kinship was understood and used differently by different people and at different times. Thus, kinship took shape in a network of alternative representations, sometimes cooperating but more often negotiating, appropriating, and contesting. The institutionalized forms that resulted were always strategic, multivocal, and flexible. There are not merely two stories of the Chinese lineage, the written and the oral, the national orthodoxy and the local variation, but countless versions each with its own uses in practice. This study both attests to this variation and also in its own way offers one more version.

The contrast between multiple versions of genealogy is but one striking example of the multiple representations of kinship and descent in the Fuzhou region in the Ming–Qing period. Although most genealogies do more or less precisely what they set out to do, that is, to record agnatic descent with reference to the compiler, we also find in the oral tradition clues that direct us toward the larger setting in which claims to kinship took on specific local meanings. The widespread practices of cross-surname adoption and uxorilocal marriage could be useful tools in the construction of narratives of origin and descent. The construction of such narratives was extremely common in Chinese history, but one particularly important strategy behind the construction of such narratives in Fuzhou was to differentiate one's ancestors from the indigenous peoples of the region. Many of the most prominent lineages of Qing Fuzhou, whose members held high office and who celebrated their unity in elaborate printed genealogies, were descended from ancestors who had been labeled as Dan or She. Tracing descent to a migrant from north China was a way to deny any connection to Dan or She and to build a connection with national culture. The written genealogy was in part a way of making claims about ethnic labeling.

Though the surviving written genealogies were compiled by the educated elite, it was not only the educated elite who engaged in strategizing about kinship. Kinship took on new meanings for all during the Ming, as state household registration and taxation systems drove groups of kin to organize themselves. It was precisely those groups which could not claim tax exemptions on the grounds that one of their members held an examination degree which had the most at stake in such strategic practice. Descendants of families registered with the state as hereditary military households, or as ordinary commoner households, were forced to develop complex institutional mechanisms—to remake their kinship practice—to ensure that the obligations for which their ancestors had registered were met.

The most visible change in kinship practice in the villages of the Fuzhou region was the proliferation of free-standing ancestral halls in the Ming and Qing. This proliferation has sometimes been treated by historians as evidence for a process of cultural integration under the leadership of the degree-holding elite. The situation in Fuzhou was more complex, for the history of the ancestral hall is also a history of shifts in meaning and in strategy. From the first ancestral halls of the Fuzhou region, markers of exclusivity constructed by prominent officials, to the ubiquitous halls of the late Qing—arenas for strategic competition over local power—there were fundamental shifts in how the functions and meanings of ancestral halls were understood and used.

Literati writings, prescriptive and descriptive, tend to present the rituals performed in the ancestral halls that proliferated in the Fuzhou countryside in the late Ming and Qing as if they were straightforward reenactments of a script provided by the authoritative twelfth-century text of Zhu Xi. Educated elites promoted the implementation of Zhu Xi's prescriptions, but the rituals of the hall actually incorporated aspects of two popular traditions, the Lantern Festival and the cult of Chen Jinggu. Popular practices were transformed, masculinized, and Confucianized as they were brought in line with elite understandings of Zhu Xi's vision. But ancestral hall ritual also diverged from neo-Confucian orthodoxy as it was shaped by prior popular practice and various and contesting understandings of it. Orthodoxy could only implant itself stably in local society through compromise with popular practice.

The practices of organized kinship also affected other realms such as local religious life. As ancestral halls spread through the Fuzhou countryside, it became common practice to parade the deities associated with a lineage to its ancestral hall, as manifest expression of the lineage's claim to the special protection of the deity. Issues of affiliation or disaffiliation with a given temple, of temple financing, and of ritual organization became matters determined not by individual preference, or by place of residence, but by the registered household to which one belonged, which over the course of the Ming had become virtually synonymous with the lineage. Indeed, the organization and activities of local cults came to rest on a foundation of kinship ideas and institutions.

ETHNICITY, ELITES, AND THE STATE

A more full understanding of the changing meaning of organized kinship thus requires considering its relations with other aspects of the broader social context. Three aspects in particular have arisen repeatedly in the preceding chapters as factors shaping kinship practice, namely ethnic differentiation, shifts in the composition and objectives of local elites, and the role of the state.

Though the arguments here challenge the notion that the highly organized lineage was a function of Fuzhou's location on the frontier of state authority, it is true that the region was a place where ethnicities were fluid. Dan and She were distinguished on the basis of a range of attributes, including language, customs, and occupation. All of these bases for differentiation could change; persons identified as Dan and She could shed that identification, and Han farmers sometimes took to the waters or the hills. Ethnicity itself was a kind of frontier, which individuals and groups could cross and recross. Tracing descent back to immigrants from north China, and fixing that descent in the written or printed genealogy, was part of a complex of strategies to cross that frontier, which also included registering for taxation, building an ancestral hall, and performing the appropriate rituals in the hall. But deployment of this strategy necessarily destabilized and disrupted the straightforward chronological narrative of the genealogy. Kinship strategies were part of the complex process by which the people of the Fuzhou region became Chinese. But at the same time, these strategies could serve other goals besides that of transforming one's ethnic identification.

Shifts in the composition and interests of local elites is a second factor that profoundly shaped many kinship strategies. The earliest ancestral halls on Nantai were built by members of the scholarly elite and their immediate descendants, in accordance with state prescriptions and in the style advocated by Zhu Xi, in part to demonstrate their distinctiveness and exclusivity from the rest of local society. Over the course of the Ming and Qing, there was a significant shift in the reasons why ancestral halls were constructed. First, the relative decline in opportunities to hold formal office as the number of degree holders grew turned many members of the educated elite toward strategies of involvement in their local community. Commercialization of the economy seemed to be leading to a breakdown of the local moral and social order, a perception reinforced by the real violence of the sixteenth and seventeenth centuries. These factors shaped elite strategies in which the ancestral hall became a tool for local social control, characterized by inclusiveness of larger and larger groups of kin. Second, commercial prosperity vastly increased the material resources of members of other types of rural elites, who used them to behave in a manner befitting the educated elite in the hopes of narrowing the social distance between them but with the unanticipated result that, in terms of leadership and organization, halls increasingly reflected the input and interests of those whose claim to elite status was based purely on wealth.

The most complex issue shaping the meaning of kinship and kinship organization was the changing relationship between the imperial state and local society. The history of kinship organization in southern China was not the result of the lawlessness of the frontier nor the hegemonic imposition of state-sanctioned orthodoxy, but was much more complex, involving state policies that ranged from the taxation system to the promotion of certain texts and the ideas contained in them to the implementation of the official religious system and the local responses to all of these policies. Much of the history of kinship in representation and practice in the Fuzhou region was due neither to the absence of the state nor to the state's overwhelming dominance over local society but rather to the complexities of the partial or incomplete state presence. Organized kinship developed in the Fuzhou region in the interstices of this partial state presence; these spaces could be very wide indeed. The population registration and taxation systems of the Ming state encouraged groups of kin to organize themselves, to endow corporate holdings, and to establish permanent organizational structures to minimize or apportion their tax responsibilities. Lineages in Fuzhou were as adept as any modern corporation at taking advantage of the loopholes in the tax law; indeed, the parallel can be pushed even further, for many corporate groups that organized on the basis of patrilineal descent did so precisely in order to minimize tax obligations. We have also seen how Zhu Yuanzhang's vision of strictly regulated religion reshaped local religious life, not by bringing it in-line with the vision but rather by creating incentives to claim adherence to it. The link between tax-paying unit and state-religious unit played out on the ground as a link between lineage and local temple, affecting the history of both but not as the makers of the law had intended.

State policies such as the *lijia* or *she* systems were not intended to have implications for kinship organization, but in practice they often did. On the other hand, where the state did deliberately intervene to shape kinship practice, it rarely succeeded in attaining the desired effects. Successive dynasties established laws restricting the right to construct free-standing ancestral halls. But such laws were never strictly obeyed. Local officials tried to promote the use of the *Family Rituals* as the liturgy for local ritual performance, but other ritual traditions continued to be practiced, and even the *Family Rituals* could be adapted to suit local contexts and local concerns. In fact, state laws and policies aimed at enforcing kinship orthodoxy tended to become themselves resources to be deployed by the very individuals and groups who were breaking those laws. In formulating new policies, local officials might even be forced to take into account local permutations that had developed in response to earlier policies by reimposing those permutations in ways more satisfactory to state interests.

At various times, intellectuals and officials argued for more direct intervention of the state in kinship practices, sometimes to support those practices and sometimes to suppress them.[1] From the early Qing onward, many of these arguments were based on the idea that powerful lineages should be enlisted in support of a stable social and political order.[2] William Rowe's research has shown that in the mid-eighteenth century the governor of Fujian, Chen Hongmou, granted to lineage leaders the power to maintain internal discipline among their kin, charging them to investigate, apprehend, punish, and if necessary turn over to the magistrate any criminals in the lineage.[3] But as we have seen, individuals and groups in rural society had been asserting the right and responsibility to organize, control, and discipline their kin since well before the mid-Qing.

In the twentieth century, political leaders' visions for shaping kinship practice grew much more grandiose. As David Strand has shown, Sun Yatsen imagined the construction of a national polity based on the lineage. Concern over the extinguishing of descent lines could be reimagined in terms of the racial threat to the Chinese people, giving modern applications to traditional cultural practices.[4] This vision was incorporated into the genealogy of the Lin of Shanggan, which counted the premier of the Republic of China, Lin Sen, among its members. In his preface to the lineage genealogy of 1931, Lin Sen wrote:

> The meaning of genealogy lies in clarifying the generational numbers, ordering the generations, creating feelings of kinship among the relatives and uniting the agnates. I would dare to go further. The establishment of the nation is based on the lineage system (*zongfa*). From the lineage (*jiazu*) is formed the descent-line (*zongzu*); from the descent-line is formed the people of the nation (*guozu*). . . . When understanding of the lineage is clarified and strengthened, then there is a common belief, a strong determination,

a morality of sacrifice, a culture of encouragement. This is the particular characteristic of our Chinese people. When promoted and encouraged, it becomes national spirit (*minzu jingshen*). . . . For recovery of national spirit, there is no way better than to effectively unify by means of the lineage.

Claiming to go even further than Sun, Lin concluded that the function of the genealogy was none other than the creation of a national polity.[5]

The most ambitious attempt to shape the meaning of kinship came with the establishment of the People's Republic of China. Mao's early writings, such as the *Hunan Report* or the *Report from Xunwu* contain many descriptions of his perceptions of the power of organized patrilineal kinship in traditional rural society.[6] The new regime was determined to break that power through confiscation of lineage properties, destruction of ancestral halls, and, at a deeper level, eradication of the structures of authority that underpinned the lineage. As Potter and Potter have written, "With the disappearance of their property base, the lineage and lineage branches effectively ceased to exist as corporate groups. Their economic, political, legal, military, religious functions were taken over by the state and its local cadres."[7] Despite these measures, there was considerable continuity between rural social organization before and after 1949. At the organizational level, work teams tended to be coterminous with lineage segments, and many brigades were simply old lineages. At a deeper level, the principles of kinship organization, which placed control of land and resources in the hands of patrilineally related men and which conceived of women largely in terms of their relation to men and of the individual in terms of the group to which he or she belonged, all persisted in the new collective order. Thus the Maoist state, more powerful by far than its predecessors, unwittingly replicated some of the very structures it sought to eliminate. Many scholars have noted that in their efforts to control local society, rural cadres were the heirs to the degree-holding elites, though they derived their authority from much narrower channels than their predecessors' cultural nexus of power. But as with late imperial elites, modern cadres were unable to fully impose integration on local society, and the seeds of local strategizing remained dormant until after 1978. When overt control began to relax in the reform period, and social networks were reconstituted, the durability and persistence of local strategizing about kinship became clear.

No state effort, including those of Sun Yatsen and Mao Zedong, to impose order on kinship in Fuzhou was ever totally effective. The underlying flexibility of kinship representations and practices enabled local actors to appropriate and manipulate hegemonic pressures, subverting them or converting them to new purposes. The close analysis of the meaning of kinship in local contexts may thus provide new insights into the complex relationship between state and society in China. Looking at factors not normally considered in connection with kinship—ethnic differentiation, elite composition and objectives, and state policy—may help shed new light not only on kinship itself, but also on broader historical processes at work in local society.

PRACTICING KINSHIP: ORTHODOXY AND INTEGRATION

Throughout this work, I have argued for understanding organized patrilineal kinship in Chinese history in terms of flexibility and multiplicity. The Chinese lineage was constructed from an array of representations and practices, which emerged out of a vast number of individual and group strategies. These in turn were shaped by widely shared ideas about kinship as well as immediate local contexts. As Prasenjit Duara has written of north China: "As the 'official' ideology of kinship . . . patrilineal descent does not exhaust the ways in which kinship was practically used and understood in northern villages. But just as the actual functioning of kinship and lineage organisations is incomprehensible apart from the practical deviations from the norm, so, too, they can hardly be understood without reference to this official model."[8] I have tried to argue in this work that local distinctiveness must be considered as more than just deviation from Confucian conceptions and the systematic ordering of Chinese society. Strategizing in the context of local constraints and opportunities was central to the lived experience of Chinese people at all levels of society. The results of this strategizing appear in the historical sources—be they written, spoken, or performed—in a language of orthodoxy, but this should not fool us into confusing the orthodoxy for the culture. Few would claim that Chinese society in late imperial times was characterized by universal adherence to orthodoxy (correct belief) or even, to use James Watson's term, universal orthopraxy (correct practice). What was more or less universal was the practice of strategies in which conformity, or the appearance of conformity, to orthodoxy played an important role.

Orthodoxy, adherence to the universal principles made manifest in the canonical texts, permits no strategizing. Strategies that involve creating the appearance of conformity to orthodoxy necessarily conceal their own effects. In their own writings, the elites who are credited with building lineages describe their objectives in terms of the institutionalizing of ancient principles or at most their adaptation to current realities. Regardless of the diverse local circumstances that as we have seen could give rise to the construction of a given ancestral hall—circumstances that could give rise to strategies varying from elite efforts to distinguish themselves from their community to elite efforts to build local power, or to commercial elite efforts to portray themselves as members of the educated elite—the sources invariably represent the ancestral hall as the triumph of a single neo-Confucian vision. The rituals in a given ancestral hall might incorporate diverse earlier practices, including not only ancestral sacrifice but also popular celebrations of seasonal holidays and even worship of a local fertility goddess; local ritual performance might also be the venue for all manner of strategic competition between different types of local elite. But the descriptions of the rituals in the sources invariably attempt, with varying degrees of success, to cast them in terms of a single, unified, national standard of orthodoxy, Zhu Xi's *Family Rituals*. Strategizing in the language of orthodoxy is precisely what ties together all of the different approaches to kinship discussed in this work, tying as well the cultures of elites and common people alike into a single system. The Chinese lineage emerged out of the cumulative strategies of multiple agents, degree holders, merchants, and peasants, responding to their circumstances and using the language of eternal principle in representation of their strategic practice.

Because of its microhistorical approach, the findings of this study are of greatest relevance to the history of the Fuzhou region itself. But its conclusions bear on the broader issues of the integration of Chinese society in the late imperial period and the complex role of kinship and other cultural factors in that integration. This study has tried to elaborate on Watson's suggestive argument that "the state intervened in subtle ways to impose a kind of unity," or standarization, on local culture by exploring how the outcomes of that intervention could differ from what was intended.[9] Historians of China are increasingly aware that careful attention to local history presents opportunities to move beyond overly broad generalizations about cultural hegemony and the standardization or superscription of interpretations. Several studies have suggested that though imperial control systems imposed from beyond the village had important effects on local popular culture, they did not necessarily serve the straightforward end of cultural integration. Wang's finding that "popular imitations [of the imperial system] derived from nothing but an attempt to authenticate and disguise unofficial kinds of social spatial conceptions and grass-roots protests" rings true for the Fuzhou region.[10] But popular imitation, what I have labeled elsewhere as the illusion of standardization, was not simply a mechanistic reaction to state pressure. It could actually become a tool in the service of particular local interests. Microhistorical approaches make it possible to see institutions not simply as forms imposed by the state but as the outcome of the interaction between those forms and local dynamics. The relationship between the forces of state and local kinship organization in late imperial China did not reflect a straightforward dichotomy of state and society but rather an ongoing negotiation and contest over meanings. As I showed in the discussion of the relationships between lineage and taxation and between lineage and local religious structures, contested meanings in one domain of social life could also become relevant to other domains. The lineage in the village served not just as the expression of communal identity but also as a domain of negotiation and contest within village and local society. Local elites were important actors in this domain, neither simply representing state interests nor opposing them but rather manipulating the system to serve their own interests. But they were not the sole nor always the decisive actors. Nor was the contest simply a bilateral one between a unitary state and a unitary, hermetically sealed locale. Rather, it was a multi-stranded relationship between a complex state and many different groups and interests within local society. Organized kinship played an important and complex role in the structuring of both the relationship between the state and local society and local life itself, as a venue for strategic negotiation and competition over local power. Attention to the individual and group strategies that shaped local meanings of lineage suggests a complex and dialectic relationship between integrative forces of the imperial state and local communities. The contests over meaning were never fully resolved; kinship in late imperial China was always multivocal and negotiated.

The advantage of thinking of kinship strategically is in highlighting the production and historicization of cultural phenomena. From this perspective, the spread of the lineage was not simply the inevitable permeation of a fixed repertoire of lineage activities that had first appeared in the Song throughout local society but also a long-term negotiation and contestation over meaning. Far from being a simple matter of permeation, the development of lineage organization in Fuzhou was characterized by twists and ruptures and personal decisions. Far from being inevitable, the spread of lineage organization was actively resisted when it conflicted with other strategies. This approach may be helpful to discussions of kinship in modern as well as late imperial China. Because kinship is a form of strategic practice, the contests over meaning within it can never be completely resolved. Large-scale patrilineal kinship organization is reappearing in Fuzhou and elsewhere in south China in new forms and for new purposes. Some of these purposes seem quite similar to the strategic goals of villagers and elites in the Ming and Qing, to revive morality and social cohesiveness in a time of bewildering change or to demonstrate pride in a past identity and social distinctiveness. Other purposes, such as the desire to renew links to Overseas Chinese kin to enlist their charity or their investment, are quite new. Though in recent years the state has certainly withdrawn somewhat from rural social life, it remains a presence that shapes the forms that kinship organization can take, the limits of strategizing, and the language of orthodoxy in which strategizing goes on. In turn, state efforts are appropriated and manipulated as part of that strategizing. Thus, kinship practice, the ideas and institutions that become attached to the principles of kinship and reshape those same principles, continues to be an important part of the endless process of cultural production and strategizing that characterized and still characterizes Chinese society.

Religious Inscriptions from the Fuzhou Region

INSCRIPTION ON THE TEMPLE OF THE THREE VENERATED LIU KINGS
OF LUOZHOU (DATE UNKNOWN)

On the banks of the Luojiang River is [the temple of] the three Liu brothers. They are from the Huai region [modern Henan and northern Anhui] and are the descendants of Liu Dewei of the Tang. During the Ganning period (894–8), when rebels created disturbances, the brothers supervised the militia and cleared up the rebels. Their merit was very great, but they died before they could be rewarded. The people of [Fujian] erected a temple for them and offered sacrifice at the site. Whatever was asked of them, they invariably responded. During the Shaoxing period (1131–62), villagers Wu Zhizhong and others responded to the calls from navy officers to defend against pirate incursion. Carrying the incense fires [of the gods] they went to Zhenjiang. The pirates arrived in large numbers. The commander ordered the captains to attack. The enemy was fierce and could not be withstood. Zhizhong silently prayed to the gods. Suddenly a large flag with [the characters] Three Liu appeared among the boats. The officers and soldiers grew more numerous. The pirates were terrified and [fled] to the north. Zhizhong subsequently earned a commendation. This came to the attention of the Gaozong emperor, who rewarded [the deities] with the title marquises of Min.

In 1221, there was a plague of locusts, which piled up on the pathways to a depth of over one *zhang*. The elders (*fulao*) of the village prayed to the gods. Under the gods blessing, the locusts did not enter the precincts. So Sheng, Qi, Pei, and

Lu [all settlements in the vicinity of Luozhou] vied with one another to welcome the gods and request [aid] according to the proper etiquette (*ying er li qing*). During the Qingyuan period (1195–1200) local men of the altar (*shemin*) Zhang Keming and Xie Kexian slept in the temple. They dreamt the gods gave them an efficacious charm. They were able to cure the sick and revive the dead in countless numbers.

During the Duanming reign [probably an error for Duanping (1234–36)], there was Yu Deming, a drafter from Hantou in Xinghua. Yu Deming and others were shipping salt. As they passed by Luojiang, a great wind blew up and threatened to capsize the ship. Deming prayed to the gods, vowing he would erect a stone pillar, a row of stone columns, and a stone veranda [in gratitude for their aid]. They were saved. Since then, many people made vows promising [to repay the god's favor with a donation of] stone. In the Chunyou period (1241–53), local man Lin Qingda was shipping grain to Zhejiang when he encountered pirates. He called on the gods to help him and suddenly an unusual wind blew from both banks so the pirate ship could not proceed. The wind filled the sails of the grain ship, which sailed away.

In 1239 there was a great drought. The flood was exhausted and the young rice was drying out. The people of the village paraded the gods and prayed for rain. As this was happening, a sweet dew fell heavily and the people obtained a harvest. In 1259 there was a great fire in the village; the wind was blowing it toward the temple when suddenly a wind blew up in the other direction and extinguished the fire. At that time, local *jinshi* Chen Yingliu and others reported this to the authorities. The authorities transmitted this upward, and the gods were rewarded with the title Venerated Three Liu Kings who Protect the State and are Manifestly Responsive. They were permitted to wear robe and crown, and their attendants on either side were also given titles.

Source: *Luozhou zhi* (1863), 1:23b–24a.

RECORD OF THE TEMPLE OF THE VENERATED KINGS OF WATER AND LAND,
BY HUANG FUJI (*JINSHI* 1733)

When the ancients established a state they invariably established a *she*. The "Monthly Ordinances" ["Yueling," a chapter of the *Liji*], in the second section [contains the phrase] "the people are ordered [to sacrifice] at the *she* [altar]." Thus the *she* [sacrifice] has extended both high and low since long ago. The "Datian" section of the "Xiaoya" chapter and elsewhere in the *Shijing* [*Book of Odes*] [contains the phrase] "ancestor of the field". The ancestor of the field is the [spirit of the] grains (*ji*). Thus the altar to the spirits of the grains and the *she* are equally important. Those who walk upon the soil and eat the grains, enjoying their benefit, ought all to requite this merit. Looking back, [we note that] the ancients for their *she* used a square mound and chose a tablet made from a suitable wood for the sacrifice to the spirits of the grains. They made offerings in prayer, [lit] candles, and made sacrifices. They also proceeded in an orderly fashion through the country. For the tablet they used millet. Although they erected an altar, there was no temple, nor was there an image. Building a temple and carving an image belong to the [ritual] systems of the Han, Tang, and later eras.

Our village has long had a temple for the altar to the god of the soil and grains (*sheji miao*). It is located in the center of the village, facing the ancestral hall. It is truly an auspicious site. The ancestral hall faces south and the temple of the altar to the gods of grain faces north. This obtains the benefits of *yin* and *yang*. The deities are called the Venerated Kings of Water and Land. Perhaps this is because the soil and the grain do not go beyond water and land, so they have been given this new name. Or else perhaps it is because our village is near to the sea, and the people either live on the land or earn their living on the water, so they link their benefits with the gods of land and water. The gods of soil and grain are certainly only two gods, so the gods of water and land should also be two gods. But there are three of our venerated kings. It is said that in a previous dynasty the image of a God of Supervising the Way (*fasi*) floated up to the bank of the river south of Liu hill. The rising tide pulled at it but it would not float away. So it was sacrificed to at the edge of Fourth Branch Hill, in the present Ancestral Palace of the Great King (*Dawang zudian*) south of Liu hill. The deity was extremely heroic, numinous, sympathetic, and responsive. So the villagers cast another image of the deity and sacrificed to it in the Temple of the Venerated Kings. So there are three venerated kings, and the Master of the Way (*fashi*)[1] is in the middle. He has no wife.

It is no longer known when the old temple was first built or by whom. In 1561, the temple was reconstructed in three chambers. The front chamber was the gatehouse. In the east and west side halls, Guandi and Marshal Tian (Tian Yuanshuai) received sacrifice, facing south. The center chamber was the auxiliary palace (*xingdian*). In the east and west side halls, Guanyin and Linshui Furen received sacrifice, facing north. The rear chamber was the main palace, devoted to the sacrifice to the three Venerated Kings. Their subordinate deities were arrayed to either side. The person who was responsible [for the temple] was old and there was no one able to replace him.

Two hundred years passed, and the wind and rain beat down on the temple. It was inevitable that there would be some damage. Also, the scale was too small and could not be considered worthy. Furthermore, having Guandi and the various gods all in the doorway made some uncomfortable. In 1733, the harvest was exceptionally good. The people [gathered] with great joy on the fifteenth day of the seventh month. It was proposed to rebuild and enlarge the temple. The three halls would be torn down and replaced with two halls. The front hall would serve as the gatehouse, and the rear hall as the main palace. In the central chamber the Venerated Kings would receive sacrifice, and in the left pavilion Linshui Furen. In front and back there would be an open space, and a brick wall would surround the temple on four sides. The scale was to be grand, and identical to the ancestral hall. As for Guandi and the various other gods, a new temple would be built for them at Changtang Weijingdou, using the building materials from the old palace. The lineage members with one voice agreed. The Lin surname and the various sojourners who lived here and belonged to the same altar also agreed. So a levy of five *fen* per *mu* of fields was assessed on both landlords and tenants. This raised over four hundred taels. To this was added over forty taels raised from auctioning off the rights to harvest the clam beds. It is said that the Venerated Kings exert their efficacy, every family contributes money and every person contributes his efforts. Work began on the twenty-sixth day of the eighth month, and the main beam was raised on the seventeenth day of the tenth month. The work was completed by the end of winter. There was music and theater. The gods were carried into the temple. This labor was overseen by lineage head Yuanbin. Those in charge of collecting the money and supervising the work were [ten named men, all members of the Huang lineage]. The chief manager was the unworthy Fuji, who respectfully obeys the orders of his father and follows behind these men encouraging their efforts.

The momentous scale [of the temple] is foremost among the *she* of the neighboring villages. It reveals the spirit of the gods and the health of the people. The harvest is good and material needs are satisfied, the whole *jing* receives the bounty of the god for all eternity.

Source: "Shuilu zunwang miao ji" (n.d.), inscription in the Shuilu Zunwang temple, Yixu. The text is virtually identical to an essay entitled "Shuilu zunwang miao zhi," by Huang Fuji, at *Huqiu Yishan Huangshi Shipu*, 1:23a–b.

UNTITLED INSCRIPTION (1804)

Magistrate Wang of Houguan, in the matter of illegal extortion. . . on 9/26 of the current year (1804) ordered the following:

> On 9/14, in Min county, a petition was received from Lin Shou, Chen Wei, Liu Shi, Wang Xinlian, Lin Anlian and Silian, Deng Wengcheng, Ou Ba, Zheng Degui, Lin Chang Yang Wu, Lin Xingshou and others which claimed:
> Shou *et al.* are fishermen households (*yuhu*) of Tanwei and other harbours in this jurisdiction. We make our living from ferrying, fishing, and gathering. Every year, we pay the fish tax to Lin Dawei and others of Tai[jiang] jurisdiction. Because the land is limited and the people are numerous it is hard to make a living. Some bid on auctioned alluvial land and each year pay the owner of the island the full [rent]; some [rent] fish beds, in which case they pay the owner of the bed. As a result, we have come to moor our boats at Xinqi, Suqi, Gaoqi, Tuniu, Nanyu and other harbours in Houguan. . . . Those who are temporarily moored pay the fish tax at Tai[jiang]. In Houguan County, there is also a payment surcharge of 4 fen 8 li per household. . . .

The collection registers are incontrovertible and have been for many years up to the present day. Moreover, [these people] are not responsible for fulfilling [the levy] for the boatmen of Houguan. How can it be that the new head of the boatmen of Houguan, Zhang Zaikai, and others, relying on bullies in the locality, in violation of the old regulations, dare to act on their authority with no regret? His gang is very numerous....

Petition: Shou *et al.* pay the money [they owe], but the gang's followers are reckless [in their demands]. It is too miserable to bear. We reflect that for fishermen households there has always been a distinction between tax payment and service levy obligations. This has long been established in the regulations. The law is strict and manifest. How can it not be known that Shou *et al.* are liable for the payment of tax and not for the fulfillment of the service levy? How can [Zhang and his gang] be allowed to violate the regulations... at their own will and rampantly consume us?...

Moreover, the previous head of the boatmen of Houguan, Lin Jing, in 1797 falsely extorted payments [in fulfillment of] service levy [obligations] from Zheng Chengshun. [Cheng]shun brought suit and the former magistrate endorsed his claims, [and ordered] a stone [be erected] at Hongjiang prohibiting this.

Recently, fisherman household Zheng Tianxiang and others had [suffered] illicit extortions.... According to precedent, they petitioned... and were blessed with the issuing of a prohibition. All of this is recorded in the precedents.... [Zhang Zai]kai *et al.* now dare to oppress with rage and do not fear death.... [The Magistrate] of Houguan county issued a prohibition to relieve forever.... According to Zheng Tianxiang's petition, Zhang [Zai]kai extorted the service levy charges for the boatmen [from the fishermen]. Now Zhang [Zai]kai and others again dare to ignore the prohibition and recklessly distribute [tax assessments]....

In response to these various requests, according to this prohibition, boatman head Zhang [Zai]kai and others are not permitted to extort funds from the various fishermen households Lin Shou *et al.* as they have done in the past....

Source: Untitled inscription (1804), outside the Shangshu temple, Yangqi, Fuzhou. Ellipses indicate illegible characters on the inscription.

Reference Matter

Character List

Bai Yuchan 白玉蟾

baiye 拜夜

bang 幫

banshen 伴神

banye 伴夜

Banzhou 牛洲

baojia 保甲

baozheng 保正

bashe 把社

beimang (Fuzhou dialect) 陪盲

Cai Hai 蔡海

Cai Xiang 蔡襄

Cangshan 倉山

Changle 長樂

Chen Baochen 陳寶琛

Chen Baoji 陳保極

Chen Changlie 陳長烈

Chen Chun 陳淳

Chen Feng 陳逢

Chen Guling 陳古靈

Chen Hua 陳華

Chen Huai 陳淮

Chen Jiangong 陳建功

Chen Jinggu 陳靖姑

Chen Jingliang 陳京亮

Chen Jiufeng 陳九峰

Chen Juyuan 陳巨原

Chen Kangxun 陳康旬

Chen Kui 陳奎

Chen Run 陳潤

Chen Ruolin 陳若霖

Chen Se 陳澀

Chen Sheng 陳升

Chen Shengshao 陳盛韶

Chen Wenlong 陳文龍

Chen Xiang 陳襄

Chen Ximan 陳希滿

Chen Xuanyi 陳宣議

Chen Yan 陳衍

Chen Yide 陳依德

Chen Yongsheng 陳永盛

Chen Youliang 陳友諒

Chen Yuanguang 陳元光

Chendian 陳店

Chengmen 城門

Chengshanding 城山頂

Churong gongyi 處戎公議

ci 祠

ciding 祠丁

cishe 祠社

citang 祠堂

Dan 蛋

daxing 大姓

dazong 大宗

dazong ci 大宗祠

deng 燈

deye jun 得業軍

dian 典

Dianqian 店前

dibao 地保

difang zhi 地方志

diming lu 地名錄

ding 丁

Dingguangsi 定光寺

Dong Yingju 董應舉

du 都

dun 墩

fang 房

Fang Dacong 方大琮

Fang Hao 方濠

fangnei shenfu 房內紳富

fashi 法士

fasi 法司

fatang 法堂

fen 份

Fenggang 鳳崗

fengshui zhi mei 風水之美

Fenyang 汾陽

fubing miba 夫兵米八

fulao 夫老

Funing 福寧

funong 富農

Fuqing 福清

fushou 福首

Futang 福唐

fuxing 復姓

Gantangbao 甘棠堡

Gaogaishan 高蓋山

Gaoguantang 高觀堂

Gaohu 高湖

gongji tang gongsi 公積堂公司

gongpo 公婆

Guandi 關帝

guanding 官丁

Guanyin 觀音

Guangzhou 光州

guizong hehu 歸宗合戶

guniang 姑娘

Guo Biao 郭彪

Guo Bocang 郭柏蒼

Guo Boyin 郭柏陰

Guo Guiqing 郭貴輕

Guo Jianlang 郭建郎

Guo Tang 郭鏜

Guo Wei 郭尾

Guo Yao 郭耀

Guo Yuanxian 郭元顯

Guo Zhike 郭志科

Guo Ziyi 郭子儀

guoji 過繼

Guozhai 郭宅

guozu 國族

Gushi 古始

Gutian 古田

He Qiaoyuan 何喬遠

Hebo suo 河泊所

Hongshan 洪山

Hongtang 洪唐

Houcuo 後厝

Houguan 侯官

hu 戶

Huai'an 懷安

Huang Baoguang 黃葆光

Huang Bozhen 黃伯震

Huang Dun 黃敦

Huang Fuji 黃輔極

Huang Gan 黃榦

Huang Guangrong 黃光榮

Huang Guorui 黃國瑞

Huang Keying 黃克英

Huang Kun 黃焜

Huang Linzi 黃麟子

Huang Shenliang 黃什良

Huang Shujing 黃述經

Huang Tingju 黃廷舉

Huang Tong 黃統

Huang Wenze 黃文澤

Huang Xi 黃樀

Huang Xiuqing 黃秀卿

Huang Yiliang 黃炅良

Huang Yinglin 黃應麟

Huang Yongdong 黃永棟

Huang Yuanbin 黃元斌

Huang Yuanzhi 黃元旺

Huang Zhifu 黃之復

Huang Zhong 黃仲

Huang Zhongyuan 黃仲元

Huang Zhulang 黃諸郎

huaqi 花契

Hudong 湖東

hui 會

huishou 會首

huizu 會族

Huji 湖際

Huqiu 虎丘

hushou 戶首

Hutou 湖頭

Huyu 壺嶼

ji 稷

jia 甲

jiamiao 家廟

Jiangbian 江邊

Jiangjun miao 將軍廟

Jiangzhong 江中

Jianquan 見泉

Jianzhou 建州

jiao 醮

jiazu 家族

jie 節

*jie*² 街

jin 金

jing 境

Jingpu 境浦

Jingshang 鏡上

jingshe 精舍

jingtuzhu 境土主

Jinqi zunwang 金岐尊王

jinshi 進士

jinzhu 進主

Jiqi 濟齊

jisiquan 祭祀圈

junhu 軍戶

junyu 軍餘

juren 舉人

keliangzhang 課量長

kyōdōtai (Japanese) 共同体

Lan 藍

Lan Chaocan 藍朝

Lan Yaoye 藍耀冶

Langqi 琅岐

Lei 雷

li 里

*li*² 禮

Li Hengchu 李衡楚

Li Kan 李堪

li qiyu yi 禮起于義

lianghu guizong 糧戶歸宗

liangmin 良民

Lianjiang 連江

lijia 里甲

Lijie Zheng ci 里街鄭祠

lilao 里老

Lin Cai 林材

Lin Guan 林覲

Lin Guangchao 林光朝

Lin Han 林瀚

Lin Haosheng 林昊生

Lin Hu 林澯

Lin Jing 林烴

Lin Lian 林煉

Lin Run 林潤

Lin Sen 林森

Lin Ting'ang 林庭昂

Lin Tingji 林庭機

Lin Tingmu 林庭模

Lin Tingxuan 林廷選

Lin Tingyu 林庭榆

Lin Yuanmei 林元美

Lin Yaohua 林耀華

Lin Zexu 林則徐

ling 靈

Linpu 林浦

Linshui furen 臨水夫人

lishe 里社

litan 厲壇

Liu Cheng 劉俛

Liu Chu 劉楚

Liu Cun 劉存

Liu Di 劉砥

Liu Jin 劉瑾

Liu Kangfu 劉康夫

Liu Kezhuang 劉克莊

Liu Li 劉礪

Liu Xingquan 劉行全

Liu Yi 劉彝

Liu Zao 劉藻

lizhang 里長

lizheng 里正

Luoyuan 羅源

Luozhou 螺洲

Lüshan 呂山

Luxia 臚夏

Ma Sen 馬森

mai lazhu 買蠟燭

Menkou 門口

Miao 苗

Min 閩

MinYue 閩粵

mingling 螟蛉

Minhou 閩侯

minhu 民戶

Minqing 閩清

Minxue 閩學

minzu jingshen 民族精神

Mituo 彌陀

mu 畝

mudai pu 墓代譜

Nanhu 南湖

Nantai 南臺

niangniang she 娘娘社

nüxu jun 女婿軍

paimang 排盲

paizhu 排主

penghu 朋戶

pin 品

pu 舖

Putian 莆田

qi 岐

Qiancuo 前厝

Qianjie Zheng ci 前街鄭祠

qijia 旗甲

qijing gong 七境宮

qinghua 請花

Qingming 清明

quti 曲蹄

ren 仁

Ren Jingmei 任敬美

Ren Ruyuan 任汝源

ru 儒

Rulai 如來

rumin shizu 入閩始祖

Shanggan 尚乾

Shangjie 上街

Shangshu 尚書

Shangshu miao 尚書廟

shanshui zhi sheng 山水之勝

Shaoqi 邵崎

she 社

She 畬

shebao 社保

shegong miao 社公廟

sheji 社稷

sheji miao 社稷廟

shemin 社民

shengmiao 聖廟

shenming hui 神明會

sheshou 社首

shetan 社壇

shexue 社學

shezhong 蛇種

shi 士

shijing 十境

shijing ci 十境祠

shiqianzu 始遷祖

shitou 勢頭

Shizhong ci 世忠祠

shuhang 叔行

shuifu 水夫

shuifu tou 水夫頭

Shuilu Zunwang 水陸尊王

shunyi 順懿

sidian 祀典

siding 私丁

sizhi 四知

Song Lian 宋濂

su 俗

sujie 俗節

tagu (Fuzhou dialect) 塔骨

Taishan 泰山

Taiyu 臺嶼

Tangfeng 唐峰

Tangyu 唐嶼

Tanshishan 曇石山

Tengshan 藤山

tianding 添丁

Tianxian dadi 天仙大帝

tianye ren 田野人

tongxing jun 同姓軍

tongzan 通贊

tu 圖

Tu Zhiyao 涂之堯

tuanbai 團拜

tudigong 土地公

Wang Chao 王潮

Wang Shenzhi 王審知

Wang Shimao 王世懋

Wang Yingzhong 王應鐘

Wangchuan 網川

Wanshou qiao 萬壽橋

Wenchang 文昌

wokou 倭寇

Wu Chaoxian 吳朝羨

Wu Fu 吳復

Wu Hai 吳海

Wu Qianzhang 吳乾長

Wu Shandan 吳善玼

Wucuo 吳厝

Wushan 吳山

xijin 喜金

Xia Yan 夏言

Xiadu 下渡

xianci 先祠

xianci[2] 賢祠

xiang 鄉

xiangtang 享堂

xiangyue 鄉約

xiangzu 鄉族

xianying 顯應

Xianyou 仙游

xiaozong 小宗

Xiayang 下洋

Xie Zhaozhe 謝肇淛

xiedou 械斗

Xincuo 新厝

Xing Yongchao 興永朝

xingdian 行殿

xinggong 行宮

Xinghua 興化

xingtai 行臺

Xu Fuyuan 許孚遠

xubai 序拜

xungen 尋根

yamen 衙門

Yan Fu 嚴復

yang 洋

Yang Shi 陽時

Yang Tingyi 陽廷詒

Yangqi 陽岐

Ye Chunji 葉春及

Ye Guanguo 葉觀國

Ye Xianggao 葉向高

yinci 淫祠

ying er li qing 迎而禮請

yingchuan 迎船

Yingchuan 潁川

yingdeng 迎燈

yingtang 影堂

yinzan 引贊

Yixu 義序

Yongfu 永福

Yue 越

yuhu 漁戶

yuke 魚課

Yuncheng 雲程

Yunshan 雲山

Yushan shengjing 玉山勝境

Zelang 澤郎

Zeng Mingsheng 曾明生

Zhang Boyuan 張伯源

Zhang Jianmeng 張肩孟

Zhang Jing 張經

Zhang Masi 張馬賜

Zhang Yintao 張尹燾

Zhang Yuncha 張雲槎

Zhang Zongben 張宗本

Zhanglin 漳林

Zhangpu 漳浦

Zhangzhou 漳州

zhaofu 招撫

zhaomu 昭穆

Zheng Chenggong 鄭成功

Zheng Ji 鄭紀

Zheng Mu 鄭穆

Zheng Shanfu 鄭善夫

zhengming 正名

Zhengshi Lang 徵仕郎

Zhengyi 正一

zhici 支祠

zhifu 知府

zhixian 知縣

zhizhou 知州

zhizu 知足

Zhong Dakun 鐘大焜

zhou 洲

Zhou Ximeng 周希孟

Zhou Zhikui 周之夔

Zhouwei 洲尾

zhu 主

Zhu Xi 朱熹

Zhu Yuanzhang 朱元章

zhuiyuan 追原

Zhuti 築堤

zhuxian ci 諸賢祠

Zhuyi 朱異

Zhuzhai 朱宅

zirancun 自然村

zongci 宗祠

zongfa 宗法

zonghui tang 宗會堂

zongmiao 宗廟

zongpu 宗譜

zongtu 宗圖

zongzi 宗子

zongzu 宗族

zu 族

zuci 族祠

zufangzhang 族房長

zupu 族譜

zuzhang 族長

zuzheng 族正

Notes

1. Guo Ziyi was elevated to noble rank for his part in the suppression of the rebellion of An Lushan.

2. *Fuzhou Guoshi zhipu*, j.6 passim.

3. Preface by Guo Dayun, dated 1572, in ibid., 1:12b. For Chinese primary sources cited in the text, I provide as much information as possible to help identify the source, including, wherever helpful, the details of individual texts contained within a larger work. Genealogies often lack or have irregular page numbers, so this information is not always provided. For rare works, I include page numbers that have been added by the libraries and archives that hold the work.

4. Preface by Guo Bocang, dated 1874, in ibid., 1:21a.

5. The two men were in many ways also typical members of the local educated elite. Boyin, a Metropolitan Graduate (*jinshi*) of 1832, had the more distinguished official career, rising to the position of governor-general of Huguang. When not holding office in distant provinces, they taught in local academies, organized and led militia groups, contributed to flood relief and irrigation works, compiled local gazetteers, and made large charitable donations to various causes. Biographies of the brothers can be found in *Minhou xianzhi*, 69:24a–25b and 72:15b–16a; and Gao Rong, 52–56.

6. I follow convention in using the term "late imperial," both because of and despite its ambiguities and vagueness. Since it was first introduced by Frederic Wakeman to cover the period from the late Ming to the 1930s, the term has gained wide acceptance, though it is defined differently by different scholars. See Wakeman, 2;

Rowe, "Approaches to Modern Chinese History," 241–42; and Rawski, "Economic and Social Foundations," 3–11.

7. My use of the term "practice" has been influenced most obviously by Bourdieu, *Logic of Practice*, and the discussion by Ortner, 144–57.

8. Faure, "Lineage as Cultural Invention," 5–8. Arthur Wolf offers another, equally inclusive definition of the lineage—as a corporate group, that is, as a group that acts as a group and is so regarded by others, that recruits members by way of descent. Wolf, "Origins and Explanations," 243. Also see Chen Qi'nan, 131–36.

9. Freedman, *Lineage Organization* and *Chinese Lineage and Society*.

10. James Watson, "Chinese Kinship Reconsidered," 594.

11. Wolf, "Origins and Explanations," 243; Cohen, "Lineage Organization in North China," 532; Brook, "Must Lineages Own Land?" 78–79.

12. Faure, "Lineage as Cultural Invention." The lack of meaningful fit between the Chinese terms and the English language terms used by anthropologists is evident in Patricia Ebrey and James Watson's introduction to an edited volume on kinship organization in late imperial China. Ebrey and Watson provide two sets of definitions, one Chinese and one English, whose relationship with one another is never made clear. Thus there is a definition for lineage, which mainly follows Watson's earlier definition, and a separate definition for the Chinese term *zu*, which is often but not always used to refer to a lineage as defined by Watson. "The core meaning seems to be 'agnates' as a set of people.... In particular contexts these can be very close relatives, but a common use is for those beyond the realm of specific kinship terms." (Ebrey and Watson, 8). This lack of fit should itself provoke questions. Do the difficulties arise because the two sets of definitions are trying to define different things or because the Chinese terms are vague about things the English definitions try to define precisely? Or do the problems arise from efforts to fix meanings that were inherently unstable and contested?

13. Arthur Wolf includes in his account of the "invariant aspects of the Chinese kinship system," the point that "agnates who lived in close proximity almost always constituted themselves as a descent group," or *lineage* in my terminology. Wolf, "Origins and Explanations," 242–43.

14. Ebrey, *Confucianism and Family Rituals*; trans. *Chu Hsi's Family Rituals*; "Education Through Ritual." See also Rowe, "Ancestral Rites"; and Xu Yangjie for similar arguments in the Chinese literature.

15. Twitchett, 130–33; Chow, 223–28; Esherick and Rankin, 11; Beattie, 127–32. Other important examples include the essays in Ebrey and Watson. In Chinese as in Western scholarship, recent attention to intellectual and cultural strategies responds to earlier focus on material issues, exemplified by the classic work of Zuo Yunpeng. Japanese scholars led the way in integrating these different approaches. For an early effort, see Makino, *Kinsei chūgoku sōzoku*.

16. In distinction to the model of lineage organization in south China that is based on extensive anthropology in Taiwan and the New Territories of Hong Kong, historians have also identified a Huizhou lineage model and a north China model. Key works on south China include: Ahern, *Cult of the Dead* and "Segmentation in

Chinese Lineages"; Baker, *Chinese Lineage Village* and *Chinese Family and Kinship*; Cohen, "Agnatic Kinship in South China"; Pasternak, "Role of the Frontier" and *Kinship and Community*; Potter, "Land and Lineage in Traditional China"; James Watson, "Agnates and Outsiders"; Rubie Watson, "Creation of a Chinese Lineage" and *Inequality Among Brothers*. On Huizhou, key works include: Hazelton; and Zurndorfer, *Change and Continuity*. On north China, see Naquin, "Two Descent Groups"; and Cohen, "Lineage Organization in North China." For reviews of recent scholarship on the Chinese lineage, see Chun, 429–50, and Ruskola, 1616n.45 and 1622n.68.

17. My research approaches though are certainly shaped by the fruitful links being forged between history and anthropology by other scholars of south China. The essays in Faure and Siu, eds., for example, combine analysis of a wide range of historical texts with ethnographic fieldwork, oral history, documentation of ritual performance, and so on. This work shares many similarities, and indeed is often collaborative, with scholars from the People's Republic of China. In Fujian, similar approaches were developed by the research group at Xiamen University under Fu Yiling, whose concept of the lineage-village (*xiangzu*) has shaped much of this literature. For the application of this formulation to the history of Fujian, see the essays in Fu Yiling and Yang Guozhen, eds. For a discussion of the term *xiangzu* and its relation to the influential Japanese term *kyōdōtai*, see Mori, 1–8.

18. In his study of Chinese nationalism, Prasenjit Duara has argued for the importance of recognizing the "polyphony of voices, contradictory and ambiguous, opposing, affirming and negotiating their views of the nation." Since ancient times the kinship group had been seen as related to the state through a complex homology, so it should come as no surprise that polyphony also characterizes the ideas and institutions of Chinese kinship. Duara, *Rescuing History*, 10.

19. Readers already familiar with the history of the Fuzhou region may wish to move directly to the more specific account of Nantai which begins on p13.

20. Archaeological evidence suggests that ten thousand years ago, the mouth of the Min was well upstream from the modern city of Fuzhou, in the vicinity of the town of Ganzhe. Zheng Lipeng, 3 ff.

21. Wang Zhenzhong, 3–13, 38–41.

22. Doolittle, *Social Life of the Chinese*, 1:24.

23. Trade was facilitated by the transport infrastructure established by the early Ming state and lubricated by the silver that flowed from Japan and South America. The growing export market further encouraged the commercialization of agricultural and other commodity production. Market towns expanded in number and size. State revenues were increasingly monetized, with tax in kind and labor services commuted to payment in silver, culminating in the Single Whip reforms of the late sixteenth century. See the essays in Twitchett and Mote, eds., *Cambridge History of China*, vol. 8, and Brook, *Confusions of Pleasure*, 65–79, 191–218. The paradigm has grown out of the work of Japanese scholars such as Nishijima Sadao on the Ming economy and the Chinese scholarship on the "sprouts of capitalism." Fu Yiling, who wrote extensively on the socioeconomic history of Fujian, was a leading figure in this

approach. Rawski's *Agricultural Change* is an early example of Western language scholarship to adopt this approach.

24. The region's involvement in maritime commerce has been comparatively little studied, perhaps because it was consistently overshadowed by the more important ports of southern Fujian, first Quanzhou in the Song and later Yuegang in the Ming and Xiamen in the late Qing. See Tang Wenji, 389–91.

25. Song authors looked back to a past when Fuzhou had little hinterland. "Agriculture only extended to the areas around the walled towns; elsewhere were deep forests and caves, overgrown with plants. Rarely did people's footsteps reach there; it was a wasteland belonging to the tiger, leopard and monkey." *Sanshan zhi*, 33:1b. But times had changed dramatically since the Tang, and by the Song the high population relative to arable land is a concern noted in countless sources. See Wang Xiangzhi, 130:11a–b; Fang Shuo, 3:15; Liu Kezhuang, 93:80a. A comprehensive list of citations is in Clark, *Community, Trade, and Networks*, 145–48, 231 n.86. Also see Liang Gengyao. On commercial crops, see Fang Dacong, 21:4b. The most celebrated local crop was the lychee, which already had a long history of cultivation as a cash crop. Cai Xiang's essay on the fruit, written in 1059, describes large commercial orchards, mass processing, and shipments to domestic and foreign markets. See "Lizhi pu," in Cai Xiang, 35:646–47.

26. Tang Wenji, ed., part 4; Zhu Weigan, chap. 17.

27. Tobacco became an important cash crop in southern Fujian; in the Fuzhou region, the appearance of the sweet potato seems to have had important though complex implications. It provided a measure of security for cultivators of commercial crops; if the crop failed or its price fell, peasants could still live off the sweet potato planted on marginal lands. On the sweet potato, see Chen Shiyuan, 1:2a; *Huangli hepu*, 30; *Min shu*, 150:34a. On technical developments, see Zhu Weigan, 2:26–28. The fundamental practices of the fruit business seem to have changed little over the centuries. Cai Xiang's eleventh-century account of outside merchants seeking advice from local experts when bidding on the lychee crop in advance is remarkably similar to a nineteenth-century description. "Lizhi pu," in Cai Xiang, 35:646–47; Zhou Lianggong, 1:16–17. The sixteenth-century *Minbu shu* records that "travelling south from the river, for a distance of several dozen *li*, lychee and longan trees lie along the road providing shade. Amongst them are pomelos, bananas and *weifei* arching between them." It also describes the large-scale production of other commercial crops, such as olives, that "the local people carry into the city to sell, but [which] are not accounted a delicacy." Also sugar cane, which was both produced and processed for transshipment in the area, as was indigo, produced everywhere in the prefecture but "especially in Minxian, Houguan, and Changle. . . . From south of Fuzhou comes the greatest indigo in the empire." *Minbu shu*, 3a, 4b, 22a–b; *Bamin tongzhi*, 25:512–13. *Fuzhou fuzhi* (1613), 8:7b–8a.

28. Zhu Weigan, 2:207–10; *Minxian xiangtuzhi*, 70a–b; *Huangli hepu*, 27a–b. Early in the seventeenth century, Xie Zhaozhe (1567–1624) of Changle looked back on the Jiajing reign period as a time of killing and slaughter all along the coast from Guangdong to Fujian. He listed several county and prefectural towns that had

been sacked, including Xinghua, Fuqing, and Ningde. Xie Zhaozhe, 4:34b–35a. On official efforts to deal with the indigenous causes of violence and unrest using the Village Pact (*xiangyue*) and Mutual Responsibility (*baojia*) systems, see Miki, 67–100.

29. In the early seventeenth century, Dong Yingju wrote that the current pirate threat was no less severe than it had been fifty years earlier, and pirate exactions were as regular as state taxes. "Fuhai shi," in Dong Yingju, 39. Even in midcentury, kidnapping remained a constant concern. *Luojiang Chenshi jiapu*, 3:6b.

30. The apparent paradox of rising trade and rising piracy in the sixteenth century may have to do with changing Chinese policies concerning trade. When Portugese merchants were ejected from Canton in 1521, they had begun furtive trading all along the coasts of Zhejiang and Fujian. This trade was prohibited in midcentury, and pirate violence intensified, as merchants and traders who found their livelihood cut off turned instead to violent raids on coastal settlements. The writings of Zhu Zhe (1486–1552) of Putian illustrate that economic conditions in Fujian were largely responsible for the fluctuations in pirate activity and that pirate success depended on close contacts between the pirates and local informants, who provided details about potential targets who could be kidnapped for ransom. Lin Renchuan, *Minqmo Qingchu Haishang maoyi*, 40–84, and *Fujian duiwai maoyi*, 104 ff.; Zhu Zhe, 4:20a–b.

31. Haiwai sanren, 4–14; Struve, 86. The coastal evacuation is discussed in Chapter 3.

32. Skinner, "Structure of Chinese History," 271–92; Vermeer, "Decline of Hsing-hua," 130–31.

33. Ng Chin-keong (*Trade and Society*, 60 ff.) makes the same argument about the length of the downturn for southern Fujian. The economic activities of Fuzhou merchants even during the tumultous seventeenth century are richly detailed in the writings of Hayashi Shunsai (1618–80) and his family, who gathered reports from Chinese merchants visiting Nagasaki in their *Ka-I Hentai*. The stationing of officials and soldiers is described in "Suichan migu" in Zheng Guangce.

34. *Minxian xiangtuzhi*, 345a. Neither the wood nor paper industry was dependent on foreign exports. In 1771, lumber merchants from Zhejiang built a large guild hall just south of the city. Documents from Chinese merchant ships shipwrecked in Japan illustrate the operation of the lumber trade in eighteenth-century Fuzhou. One such document describes the experience of Fuzhou shipowner Li Zhenchun, whose vessel carried lumber from Nantai to Shandong, where a return cargo of mung beans was loaded aboard. "Anlan huiguan beiji," Inscription; "Letter of thanks."

35. Ng has shown that in southern Fujian, the sweet potato fulfilled much of the food deficit. But in Fuzhou, the sweet potato was rarely eaten. According to Doolittle, "It is considered a hardship and a mark of excessive poverty to eat potatoes except as luncheon. Immense quantities of the sweet potato are grated into coarse slips and dried in the sun, for use as food among the poor in case rice can not be procured. This dried potato is called potato-rice." The implication is that in ordinary times, most of the people of Fuzhou were prosperous enough to afford imported rice. See

Wang Yeh-Chien, 86; Ng, 131 n.151; Doolittle, *Social Life of the Chinese*, 1:45; and Gardella.

36. In Qing times, Fuzhou prefecture consisted of ten counties. To the east, the more prosperous commercialized counties of Lianjiang, Changle, and Fuqing were situated on the coastal plain, whereas the remaining counties, including Gutian and Minqing, lay in the poorer mountainous regions surrounding the plains to the north and west. The Qing county of Houguan included the territory of its Ming namesake, as well as most of the former county of Huai'an, which was dissolved in 1579. *Fuzhou fuzhi* (1754), 2:5a–b.

37. For the sake of clarity, I use the term *Nantai District* to refer to this urbanized area, reserving the term *Nantai* for the island. Residents of the island today do not generally think of themselves as such, and the term *Nantai Island* is rarely used. The earliest maps on which I have seen this term date from the early twentieth century. See, for example, the maps in Nogami.

38. For example, in the low-lying areas of the eastern section of the island lie the villages of Hutou (Lakehead), Huji (Lakeshore), and Hudong (Eastlake)—villagers can point to the former boundaries of the marshy lake that their ancestors reclaimed as fields. The names of many villages throughout the island include terms for island (*zhou, qi*), for stream (*pu*), or for alluvial land (*yang*), and in most cases the term no longer bears much connection to the local topography. Former islands are now joined to the larger Nantai Island; streams have been filled in, and villages on alluvial land pushed inland by further alluvial reclamation out into the Min River.

39. This area developed rapidly from the late fifteenth century, largely as a result of changes to the salt distribution system. To raise revenues, the government authorized the sale of salt trading vouchers for silver, abandoning the old policy of requiring merchants to supply grain to the military on the northern borders in exchange for the right to trade salt. Merchants in salt-producing areas became more involved in the salt trade and made use of their salt distribution networks to trade in a range of goods. In the Cangshan district, salt merchants built over one hundred storehouses in the mid-sixteenth century, giving the area its name. In the river in front of Cangshan, according to one sixteenth-century source, "the salt boats are lined up like the scales of a fish." In the nineteenth century, Cangshan would become the site of the foreign community in Fuzhou. See Heijdra, 515; *Mindu ji*, 14:3b; *Minbu shu*, 3a; *Tengshan zhi*, 2:4a.

40. See Wang Ance, "Chongsi lidai zaoqiao zhugong luwei ji," in *Hongtang xiaozhi*. These economic patterns have long been reflected in administrative arrangements. In late imperial times, the two halves of Nantai, as with the two halves of Fuzhou city, were under the administration of different counties, Houguan in the west and Minxian in the east, with the dividing line running south from the Wanshou bridge and along Gaogai hill. The division was broadly followed during collectivization, when four communes were set up on Nantai Island. The northwestern half of the island was organized into Jianxin commune, with the commune government at Hongtang. The more populous southwestern half of the island was divided into two communes, Gaishan, with the commune seat at Xialian, and Chengmen, the seat of

which was the town of the same name. Cangshan was the fourth commune, corresponding to the commercial district of the same name. When the communes were dissolved in the mid-1980s, Cangshan was incorporated into Fuzhou city proper, and the remainder of Nantai Island was placed under the administration of the Fuzhou Suburban Area Government.

41. By way of contrast, the most recent gazetteer, the *Fuzhou diminglu*, compiled in the early 1980s, lists 298 "natural villages" (*ziran cun*) for the same region. This is a gazetteer in the true English sense of the word, a geographical index (*diminglu*) rather than a local record (*difang zhi*), for which Western scholars use the term gazetteer. Few new settlements have been established in Nantai this century; the explanation for the discrepancy in numbers is probably that the compilers of the early twentieth-century gazetteers followed local usage in defining settlements, whereas the modern gazetteer follows administrative divisions imposed by the state. There are also some ambiguities and inconsistencies in the earlier gazetteers.

42. There is no explanation of the criteria for lineage, but the implication is that these were social groups whose male members had, or claimed to have, kinship connections, that is, that they were lineages in my terminology. The data from the Houguan gazetteer is summarized in Zheng Zhenman, *Ming-Qing Fujian jiazu zuzhi*, 152.

43. Zhanglin and Chengshanding are examples of the first type; Guanlu and Jiangdian are examples of the second.

44. This explanation is certainly accepted by the authors of the gazetteer: "The population of Ganyuanzhou is extremely small, because of [the need] to avoid the disaster of flooding." *Houguanxian xiangtuzhi*, 6:14b.

45. For example, Zhuzhai (Residence of the Zhu) is now populated entirely by a group of people of the Chen surname, who are said to have settled only in the Qianlong period. Geyu (Island of the Ge) is inhabited by a lineage surnamed Li. This material has also been analyzed by Kuribayashi in "Shindai Fukushū." Because he accepts the foundation legends of Fuzhou surnames at face value, we have come to rather different conclusions.

46. See *Houguanxian xiangtuzhi*, 6:15a; *Minxian xiangtuzhi*, 264b-65a, 269a, 277a,b. Numerous other examples of commercial activities could be cited for the hinterland surrounding Fuzhou. In Houguan's Shati, "there are over a thousand households of the Zhao surname, who work in agriculture, weaving and commerce." In Zemiao, "there are over a thousand households of the Zhang surname, who work in agriculture and commerce. The village produces mainly oranges." In Dawanshang, "there are about six or seven hundred households, all of the Chen surname. There is little land for fields, so they all make earthenware. There are about eighteen earthenware kilns." *Houguanxian xiangtuzhi*, 6:1 aff.; Fu Yiling, "Qingdai Fuzhou jiaoqu."

47. According to a sixteenth-century source, "from outside the south gate of Fuzhou to as far as ten *li* down to the Nantai River, the people's houses stretch unbroken." *Minbu shu*, 2b.

48. Overlooking the town, on Nine-Twists hill, is the Monastery of the Auspicious Footprint, founded in 860. Some years earlier a resident of the village of Lianpu was

visiting Nine-Twists hill when he saw an image of a silver Buddha, who left a footprint on a large stone. A small stone shrine to Guanyin, located just below the present site of the monastery, contains an untitled inscription commemorating the event that bears the date 852. In the twelfth century, judging by the size of its endowment, the monastery was a humble one. Lianpu and Linpu are one and the same place. Local tradition holds that the name of the village was changed as the Lin became the most numerous resident kinship group. According to a fifteenth-century source, "in the Five Dynasties period, our distant ancestor moved from Gushi to Fujian and settled here. He named the stream by the village for our lineage and called it Linpu . . . in order to commemorate the first migration of our line." *Sanshan zhi*, 33:28b; Lin Yuanmei, "Tianshun renwu (1462) xiupu xu," in *Lianjiang Linshi jiapu, shou*: 1a.

49. From the west of the island, ferries ran to neighboring Yixu and Yinqi, where a charitable ferry to points further west had been endowed in the Yuan. Yinqi was also known as Celery Island because it was a center for the commercial production of vegetables to feed the city's markets. Another ferry crossed the Wulong at Xiabei, linking Luozhou to the main southward routes of the province—along the coast through the southern counties of Fuzhou prefecture to Putian and beyond to Quanzhou and Zhangzhou. Poetic works describing passage on this ferry survive from as early as the Song. Several stone roads and bridges had been built in Luozhou, facilitating communication upon the island, and from Luozhou to Nantai Island, from whence routes passed through marshy lowlands to the southern suburbs of Fuzhou. Early in the sixteenth century, a new temple to Taishan was constructed in the center of the village, one of four that Luozhou would eventually boast. In 1594, a new monastery was built. The village temple to Confucius, which was said to date back to the Song and had certainly been in existence by the late fifteenth century when a prefectural official had lodged there on a visit to the island, was reconstructed twice in the sixteenth century and further enlarged in 1607. *Luozhou zhi*, 14 aff., 33a, 21a–22b; *Mindu ji*, 14:13b.

50. The people of Luozhou tell an amusing story about the past enmity between the Chen and the Wu. The two groups had once fought violently over a dispute connected with the racing of dragon boats on the fourth day of the fifth lunar month. The side that was defeated, and of course this depends on who tells the story, painted the words "Remember 5/4" on the wall that separated the settlements. When Japanese troops occupied the village, they treated the villagers very harshly, believing the sign referred to the May Fourth demonstrations.

51. "Zhizuzhai shifang jiushu." Jingliang's descendants remained in the pawnbroking business until 1949. See Zhuang Jiazi, 37.

52. A fragment of the plaque commemorating the passing of the *jinshi* examination by one of Baochen's younger brothers in 1876 can still be seen serving as a window shutter nearby.

53. I use the term *in situ* to reflect my experience in Luxia village, where I was instructed to climb a ladder into the loft of the ancestral hall to consult the genealogy. Rotten floorboards in one part of the loft gave way, and I narrowly avoided falling onto the ancestral tablets in their niche.

54. The two counties that traditionally made up the city itself, Minxian and Houguan, are rather badly served by the gazetteers, with only a late-Qing edition of a county gazetteer for each and a Republican gazetteer of Minhou, the county into which the two were combined. This shortcoming is more than made up for, however, by the great wealth of subcounty and institutional gazetteers from the surrounding area. This study makes use of four monastic and academic gazetteers and over a dozen gazetteers at the neighborhood or village level. It may well have been Fuzhou's political and social centrality that explains this skewed distribution of the gazetteers. Ambitious compilers tackled provincial and prefectural projects; the less ambitious contented themselves with gazetteers celebrating the history of their own towns and villages.

CHAPTER 2

1. This tradition appears as early as the seventh-century *Chenshu*. See Yao Cha and Yao Silian, 35:486.

2. The kingdom of Min fell in the middle of the tenth century, and Song rulers had asserted effective authority over the region by the end of the century. The period has been studied by Schafer and by Xu Xiaowang, in *Minguo shi*.

3. *Minxian xiangtuzhi*, 231a.

4. Some families claim to have migrated to Fujian at some time prior to the ninth century, moved back to central China for some reason, and then returned to Fujian with the Wang brothers. Among the Chen, for example, "In the early Tang, Chen Zheng opened up Zhangzhou in the capacity of general, and settled there. His descendant Yong served as adjutant in Guangzhou [Henan], remaining there and dwelling at Gushi. His descendants then followed Wang Chao and migrated to Fuzhou." Ibid., 236b, 231b–32a.

5. Freedman, *Chinese Lineage and Society*, 31; Meskill, "Chinese Genealogy," 139–61; Baker, *Chinese Family and Kinship*; Hui-Chen Wang Liu, 21–46; Rubie Watson, *Inequality Among Brothers*.

6. Meskill briefly discusses the construction of genealogical narratives, but this line of analysis also recalls the work of Gu Jiegang, who long ago observed that in many texts, the material presented as most distant chronologically is often the most recently added. See Meskill, "Chinese Genealogy," 155–59; and Gu Jiegang, 75–82.

7. The lineage choronym arises from the story of Dun's death in 911. While walking in the hills around his home, Dun encountered a tiger and died of fright. The body was discovered some time later, in perfect condition, by his eldest son, who was unable to move the corpse and so built a tomb mound around it. "Ever after, the descendants flourished, and in the current [Song] dynasty, countless numbers of them serve in office." One of Dun's grandsons built a Buddhist monastery near the tomb. Lands opened up by Dun and his descendants were converted into charitable fields for the community, and two hundred *mu* was set aside to serve as his sacrificial estate. By 1196, descendants were gathering at the tomb to perform sacrifice there. Huang Xingjian, "Rumin puzhi" (ca. 1195–1224), and Huang Kao (*jinshi* 1010),

"Husang gongbei ji," in *Huqiu Yishan Huangshi shipu*, 1:1a–b, 1b–2a. Thus, at least some of Dun's descendants displayed many of the elements of what Ebrey has labeled the cultural repertoire of lineage practices: the tracing of common descent, corporate property, and ritual unity. See Ebrey, "Early Stages."

8. Zhang also explains the importance of tracing the descent line accurately:

> The origin of men is their ancestors. If countless thousands and hundreds of years have passed since they were alive, and the [number of descendants] is also countless thousands and hundreds, what can later descendants do in order to know and record [their ancestry] in a genealogy? But the more recent generations which can be known should be recorded. As for the more distant generations which cannot be known, how could one falsify these and detail them? Good people in the world find that there are people who will use force to take advantage of what they do not know, dragging them in and appending them [to their genealogy] in order to bully others.
>
> Zhang Jianmeng, "Yuan xu," in *Huqiu Yishan Huangshi shipu*, 1:2a–b.

9. Huang Tai, "Yuan xu," and Huang Yong, "Yuan xu," in ibid., 1:2b–4a.

10. Huang Zhong, "Yuan xu," in ibid., 1:5a.

11. Wang Yingzhong, "Yuan xu," and Huang Yinglin, "Yuan xu," in ibid., 1:5a–6a.

12. Huang Xi, "Yuan xu," in ibid., 1:6a.

13. Huang Xi, "Yuan xu," in ibid., 1:6a–b.

14. Compare Faure, "Lineage as Cultural Invention," 6.

15. It was probably Keying who added the following note to Xi's preface: "The account in this preface of the history of migration is different than all the other genealogies. This must be because he was unable to obtain the old genealogy, and thus based it on legend. [This preface] is personal opinion only, so it does not accord [with the facts]." Huang Xi, "Yuan xu," in *Huqiu Yishan Huangshi shipu*, 1:6b.

16. Huang Keying, "Yuan xu," in ibid., 1:6b–7a.

17. Huang Guorui, "Yuan xu," in ibid., 1:7a.

18. Huang Fuji, "Yuan xu," in ibid., 1:7a–8a.

19. Other examples of Fuzhou and Nantai genealogies in which chronologically distant material has clearly been added at a later date include *Baxian Liushi Guizhifang zhipu*, *Nanyang Chenshi zupu*, and *Yingyang Sanxi Panshi zupu*.

20. The latter term is used in this way in Chen Fangkai, "Qianlong guimu (1763) xinxiu jiapu xu," in *Luojiang Chenshi jiapu*, 1:1a.

21. For examples of foundation legends for whole lineages or lineage branches that explicitly involve uxorilocal marriage, see "Qianmin shici tupu shu," in *Baxian Liushi Guizhifang zhipu*, 1:22a–b; *Taojiang Linshi zupu*, 2:3a; *Minyi Huyu Yangshi Tingqifang pudie*, 42; and *Lianjiang Linshi jiapu*, 4:6a. For examples of foundation legends involving adoption, see "Fuqing Darangxiang zongzhi shixi," in *Jin'an Dushi zupu*; and *Yuban Liushi zupu*, 13:14b–15a.

22. Waltner, 60.

23. Hong Mai, *zhigui*: 3:1238. For historical perspectives on adoption, see Waltner. On the nineteenth and twentieth centuries, see Wolf and Huang.

24. "Weishi shipu xu," in Wu Hai, 1:20–21.

25. *Minshangshi xiguan diaocha baogaolu*, 1601.

26. A 1709 document of household division from Houguan is explicit about the concern that agnates might interfere with cross-surname adoption. Lin Lichang, who had no sons of his own, had previously adopted a newborn infant named Wushi, who had now grown to adulthood and had a son of his own. "Even if the son is considered to be adopted, one could not say further that the grandson is adopted. Now I am ill and will soon die. In accord with reason and in the presence of all the relatives, I bestow all of the property that is my lot to Wushi to control and manage. The younger brothers and nephews of the lineage should not engage in wishful thinking and contest this [decision], claiming that they are my designated heir or making some such excuse." ("Lin Lichang yishu.") Lin Lichang worried that his agnatic relatives would contest the inheritance rights of his adopted son Wushi, and so he made sure to specify clearly that Wushi was designated heir to his estate. The term used for adoption here is *mingling*, the mulberry wasp. See Waltner, 74–75, and Wolf and Huang, 110, on how this animal became a metaphor for adoption. On both adoption and uxorilocal marriage, see Chen Qi'nan, 169–87.

27. State authorities today classify the Lan as She not Miao, in keeping with official definitions of minority people distribution.

28. The Lan genealogy warns against cross-surname adoption, but grudgingly accepts it:

> Our family is mean and humble. There are amongst us cases of adoption. The man may be already dead and his name and tablet already arrayed among the ancestral tablets. When the whole lineage sacrifices collectively, they must all be allowed to attend the feast.... Continuity of the descent-line and numerous descendants offering sacrifice can be said to be no offense to the ancestors. But all must be warned not to give up their offspring.
>
> "Jiagui," in *Chongxiu Lianjiang Lanshi zupu*, 3a.

29. For an overview of uxorilocal marriage, see Pasternak, "Causes and Consequences," and on the practice in the Song, see Ebrey, *Inner Quarters*, chap. 14.

30. Hong Mai, *bingzhi*:13:474.

31. "Wushi shipu xu," in Wu Hai, 3.

32. Doolittle, *Social Life of the Chinese*, 1:99–100. The practice of uxorilocal marriage could give rise to some extraordinary kinship structures, exemplified in the Fuzhou region by joint-surname genealogies such as that of the Huang and Li of Tangfeng. According to a preface of 1601, Huang Youcai had married uxorilocally into the Li family in the Yuan dynasty and had agreed with his father-in-law that his third son should be brought up with the Li surname. "After that the Huang and Li families both had descendants who became increasingly numerous. The Huang descendants felt that their origins were with the Li so it would be wrong not to

treat them as relatives. The descendants of the Li also said, 'Our origins are with the Huang, so afterwards we Li do not dare treat the Huang as strangers.' This is the reason why the genealogy is compiled jointly." Although both groups of descendants later constructed ancestral halls, each had a shrine for the installation of a tablet to the founding ancestor of the other surname. *Huangli hepu*, 5–7.

33. *Fuzhou Guoshi zhipu*, 10:3a.

34. For a biography of Jing, see *Fuzhou fuzhi* (1754), 50:37b–40b.

35. Zhang Jing, "Hongzhou Zhangshi shixi zongxu," in *Hongzhou Zhangshi shixi*, 1a–5b.

36. Zhang Jing, "Zou," in ibid., 6a–7b.

37. *Chunqiu*, 5:19a. The quote is at Legge, 5:156–57. See Waltner, 67

38. "Xifeng Zhang gong zhuan," in *Hongzhou Zhangshi shixi*, 8a–11b.

39. Zhang Jing, "Hongzhou Zhangshi shixi zongxu," in ibid., 1a–5b.

40. Zhang Jing had little time to enjoy his newfound ancestry. In 1554 he was appointed supreme military commander of the southern coast, and charged with suppressing the endemic piracy. The following year, he was blamed for delays in attacking pirate bases in Zhejiang and executed.

41. An example of a foundation legend that depends on the idea of restoring the surname is the Baoceng branch of the Nanyang Chen. The most recent edition notes that this branch was not included in previous editions of the genealogy. "Baoceng was a fourth generation descendent of [the Nanyang Chen's founding ancestor]. He went out to serve as the heir of [a man surnamed] Lin of Xinshang. . . . Afterwards, he [or his descendants] restored the original surname." (Chen Zhi'an, "Xiupu ji," [1933], in *Nanyang Chenshi zupu*). Sometimes the reversion of surname is only implicit. Lin Ling of Linpu married uxorilocally into a family surnamed Liu. His sons either retained or restored the Lin surname, and "[their descendants] are the Zhongting branch." One of Ling's grandsons also married uxorilocally, into the Ye surname. His sons either retained or restored their father's surname, for "[his descendants] are the Tanwei branch." *Lianjiang Linshi jiapu*, 4:6a.

42. On the meaning of ethnicity in early modern China, see the discussion in Crossley. Eberhard considers but rejects the use of the term caste to describe the Dan (Eberhard, *China's Minorities*, 94). On non-Han becoming Han, see Eberhard, *China's Minorities*, 105–147, and Wiens, 130–226. For a discussion of ethnic labeling in southern Fujian in more recent times, see Gladney.

43. Xu Shen, j.13 *shang*. Historical records describe a MinYue settlement known as Ye in the vicinity of modern Fuzhou. A Stone Age culture that has been given the name Tanshishan and that may correspond to the historical MinYue has left shellfish mounds west of the modern city. Tang Wenji, ed., 31–33. For a more comprehensive discussion, see Wu Chunming and Lin Guo.

44. Sima Qian, 114:2984; Bielenstein. Hugh Clark's characterization of the immigrant society of southern Fujian by the sixth century is probably equally valid for the Fuzhou region: "an overlay of immigrant families with some claim to membership in the elite society of post-Han China; a class of agriculturists, which may have included the descendants of an intermediate warrior class; a small artisan class of undefined origin; and possibly the descendants of an intermediate warrior class

connected with the old northern elites and also of northern origin." As Clark has pointed out, the Han evacuation must have been imposed only on the local elite, if at all, and much of the population must have remained. Clark, *Community, Trade, and Networks*, 14.

45. Yue Shi, 100:1a; Lin Yuxi, "Tang gu Fujian dengzhou du tuanlian guan-cha.... Xie gong shendao bei," in Dong Hao, 609:12b.

46. Yue Shi, 100:3a; 102:2b. At least one individual boat person from the late Tang can be identified. Chen Feng, a Daoist poet, was originally a "boat captain who came from the sea... he was known as the Sage of Whitewater." *Sanshan zhi*, 6:9b–10a; *Xiapu xianzhi*, 38:1a–b.

47. Cai Xiang, 34:621, 5:92.

48. *Bamin tongzhi*, 1:7. An elaborate tradition in southern Fujian, studied by Li Yiyuan, explains the establishment of Zhangzhou prefecture as the result of the pacification of aboriginal peoples in the highlands by the semilegendary general Chen Yuanguang. The legend is also found in *Zhangzhou fuzhi* (1613), 12:1b–4a.

49. Liu Kezhuang, 93:5b–8a.

50. *Min shu*, 39:970–71.

51. *Minhou xianzhi*, 29:1b; *Min shu*, 51:1311.

52. Studies on the Dan include: Anderson; Luo Xianglin; Chen Xujing; Hansson. On the She, see *Shezu shehui lishi diaocha*. In the Ming, Xie Zhaozhe wrote that, "in the mountains of Fujian there is a kind of people called She. They have five surnames, including Gou, Lei and Lan. They do not wear hats or shoes; they marry amongst themselves. They are most numerous in the mountains of Fuzhou, Minqing, and Yongfu." In the late Ming, the magistrate of Luoyuan county enlisted the aid of She hunters armed with poison arrows to kill marauding tigers, and She people were blamed for uprisings and rebellions in the Xinghua region south of Fuzhou. See Xie Zhaozhe, 6:32b; *Luoyuan xianzhi*, and Chongzhen era *Xinghua xianzhi*, cited in *Shezu shehui lishi diaocha*, 328.

53. For a survey of these stories, see Anderson, 3 ff.

54. Yue Shi, 101:2b.

55. According to Sima Guang (259:8427), when Wang Shenzhi marched north from Quanzhou to lay seige to Fuzhou, the fall of which would lead to the establishment of the kingdom, "the [registered Han] people volunteered food to support the army, and the Dan barbarians living on lakes, in caves, and by the sea assisted him with their warships."

56. *Huaxu dafu*, 1:3a. Chen was the son of a family of fishermen from Hubei and began his career as clerk to a rebel commander before becoming a military leader in his own right. From 1357 to 1359 he established a power base in the Central Yangtze with the support of the people of the fishing villages of Anhui. By 1360, he was strong enough to establish the Han dynasty, which became the main challenger to Zhu Yuanzhang's new regime based at Nanjing. See Goodrich and Fang, eds., 185–88; Dreyer, 65–77, 82–88.

57. See Ye Xian'en, 85.

58. *Houguanxian xiangtuzhi*, 5:1a–b.

59. *Minxian xiangtuzhi*, 228a–b.

60. *Houguanxian xiangtuzhi*, 6:14a.

61. *Huamei bao*, 4/1899 cited in *Shezu shehui lishi diaocha*, 364. Just as members of these two distinct groups might shed their identity and become Han, Han sometimes adopted the attributes of Dan or She. The Dutch sinologist de Groot observed in the nineteenth century that in times of trouble, whole families of land dwellers of south Fujian moved into boats and survived by fishing and piracy (cited in Blussé, 245). In certain contexts there were thus opportunities and constraints that led people to identify themselves as Han and not Dan, and in other contexts there were reasons to renounce carefully cultivated Han identity and accept other identifications.

62. For discussion in different contexts, see Chen Zhiping, *Kejia yuanliu*, chap. 4; Eberhard, *Social Mobility*, 37–40; Leong, 78–79.

63. Chen Yide, "Qianlong guimu (1763) xinxiu jiapu xu," in *Luojiang Chenshi jiapu*, 1:3a–5a.

64. Chen Fangkai, "Qianlong guimu (1763) xinxiu jiapu xu," in ibid., 1:1a.

65. Chen Fangkai, "Qianlong guimu (1763) xinxiu jiapu xu," in ibid., 1:1b.

66. Chen Baochen, "Sanxiu zupu xu" (1933), in ibid., 1a.

67. The Yingchuan choronym is a claim to descent from Chen Shi of the Han, posthumously marquis of Yingchuan.

68. *Chitoufang zupu*, 2a–b, 5a–b.

69. Chen Jiancai, ed., 18.

70. Charles Hucker (*Dictionary*, 366) translates *baozheng* as Security Group Head and defines it as the leader of a unit in the *baojia* local community defense system. Since I have found no other evidence on the implementation of the *baojia* system in Luozhou, I prefer the less specific term headman.

71. See Chapter 4 for an exploration of the meaning of the term *tu*.

72. *Luozhou zhi*, 2:16b–17a.

73. *Fenggang Zhongxian Liushi jiniantang zhi*, 8:1a.

74. See Waltner, 1–4, 76; Fisher, chap. 3.

75. But even in these sources, the tradition of including previous prefaces in subsequent editions sheds light on the process of constructing narratives of descent. Recall the early versions of the Yixu genealogy, tentative and inconsistent, handwritten but never printed, "preserved in the family, to await a later time, when an earlier genealogy can be obtained and compared for consistency." There must have been many such tentative genealogies in rural Fuzhou before 1949. But at the same time, other versions of the foundation legend persist in the oral tradition.

76. See *Minyi Huyu Yangshi Tingqifang pudie*, 88a. Unfortunately I was not able to locate the Minghang genealogy.

77. Several centuries earlier, Fang Dacong (1183–1247) of Putian wrote of his curiosity about the ubiquitous legends of Gushi origin. His research found that, "Wang Shenzhi pacified Fujian with the support of troops [from Gushi]. So he gave special treatment to people from Gushi for reasons of native-place solidarity. Thus to the present day, when people of Fujian discuss their lineage, they always mention Gushi. This is because at the time of Wang Shenzhi, people of Gushi were favoured. It is actually inaccurate." "Bashu changguan qianpu shishi," in Fang Dacong, 32:1a–2a. See Makino; and Aoyama, 1–18.

78. *Fujian tongzhi* (1737), 66:49a.

79. Guo Tang, "Guo Tang zishu," in *Fuzhou Guoshi zhipu*, 2:5a–b.

80. See Siu and Liu, 6–7. For an interesting exploration of developments in Hakka genealogy, see Chan, 64–82.

81. Hobsbawm, 1.

CHAPTER 3

1. Agnatic kinship continues to play an important role in structuring economic activity in contemporary Nantai. For example, when collectively owned property was auctioned off in the 1980s and early 1990s, it was frequently brothers and cousins who formed consortia to bid on it, and many of the new small factories that have been set up to produce plastic footwear, shopping bags, and other light consumer products are the joint investments of male cousins. More informally, kin help kin in various ways to find jobs, gain acceptance to schools, and raise capital. Villagers with whom I stayed frequently found themselves called on to pay for unexpected expenses of their agnatic kin and dependents. The most important of such expenses are funerals, fines assessed for births outside the limits allowed by family planning, and, increasingly, costly medical treatment. Since I first began visiting the Fuzhou region, an important new form of economic cooperation has arisen. Groups of patrilineally related kin often pool their resources to pay expenses associated with legal and illegal emigration. The persistent importance of agnatic solidarity in contemporary China is discussed in many works, including Potter and Potter, who show particularly effectively how patrilineal kinship remained economically important even during the period of collectivization. For a more recent account, see Ruf.

2. Freedman, *Chinese Lineage and Society*, 159–64. This argument was challenged from a different angle by Burton Pasternak ("Role of the Frontier"), who agreed with Freedman that the demands of frontier conditions could encourage the formation of corporate groups, but noted that these groups could well be organized on the basis of principles other than those of patrilineal kinship.

3. See Esherick and Rankin, 11.

4. The Ming regulations on hereditary occupations actually borrowed from more complex Yuan models. Ho, 55.

5. *Min shu*, 39:958.

6. *Minxian xiangtuzhi*, 232b; *Nanyang Chenshi zupu*, 7:25b; *Pingyang Chenshi zupu*, 6a.

7. See earlier, Chapter 2. In the mid-eleventh century, Cai Xiang (21:369–71) had noted that the great nautical skill of the boat people made it impossible for the coastal military to keep them under control, and he sought to involve them in coastal defense. In 1099, in response to a multiple murder that was blamed on boat people, the prefect of Fuzhou issued a proclamation noting that "in every country there are boat dwellers who go to the remote streams to plunder, rape and kill." He urged that each household of boat people be required to register with the authorities

at the nearest garrison, so the authorities could keep track of them. *Sanshan zhi*, 39:7a–b.

8. *Ming shilu*, 143:1383. Gu Yanwu (27:11b–12a) records a similar policy, also in Guangdong, a few years later in 1391.

9. *Minxian xiangtuzhi*, 197a–b.

10. Zheng Ji, "Yu Pang Dacan shu," in *Fujian tongzhi* (1871), 49:21b–22a; see Ray Huang, 76, and Hucker, *Censorial System*, 75–77.

11. Ray Huang, 33. For a summary of recent Chinese scholarship on military registration in the Ming, see Yu Zhijia, 635 n.1.

12. Tu Zhiyao, "Guxiang fengwu," in Yu Dazhu, ed., 225.

13. The document gives us a fascinating glimpse into the dynamics of an ordinary household in the late Yuan and early Ming. The will was prepared at the behest of Yuanxian's widow, Madame Yang. Guo Yuanxian and Madame Yang had three children, two sons and a daughter. Yuanxian had been engaged in some kind of commerce and traveled frequently to inland Jianning prefecture, where he had a son with another woman. When the woman died, Yuanxian brought the boy, whose name was Jianlang, back with him to Fuqing. There were thus three sons who had claims on Yuanxian's estate. Yuanxian appears to have inherited no property from his ancestors, but on the basis of his commercial success he was able to arrange a good marriage for his eldest son, Guiliu. Guiliu's wife brought with her a substantial dowry in the form of fields and other property. Guiliu in turn invested the income from this land into his father's business and reinvested most of the profits from the business in land. At the time of Yuanxian's death, his estate consisted of a house, eighty taels of silver, and fields earning rent of 25.4 piculs per year. Dealing with the house was easy; it was divided into three sections, with each son taking ownership of one section. Guiliu was given twenty taels of silver and ownership of fields earning 3.5 piculs in rent. This may have been equivalent to the original contribution of his wife's dowry; it may also have been because he was the eldest son. The three sons each took an equal share of the remaining sixty taels. The remaining fields were also divided into three equal shares, and the three brothers drew lots to see who would assume ownership of which share. "Yuanxian gong bi Yangshi jiushu," in *Fuzhou Guoshi zhipu*, 7:1a–2a.

14. Guo Zhike, "Lishu junyou," in ibid., 10:6a–7a.

15. Guo Zhike, "Tianfang Zhike gong dierci chongxiu zhipu xu," in ibid., 1:14a–b. For another analysis of this case, see Zheng Zhenman, *Ming-Qing Fujian jiazu zuzhi*, 244.

16. Besides Lin Tingxuan's, there is another preface that is illegible but that likely comes from the subsequent compilation of the genealogy. The 1535 version cannot be the most recent compilation, for the genealogy also includes a copy of a contract dated 1570, and the date 1579 appears elsewhere. This tentative dating is suggested on the basis of the general practice in the Fuzhou region, which seems to have been to recompile editions of a genealogy approximately every sixty years.

17. Huang Tingxuan, "Fuxing shu," in *Changle Zhuti Linshi zupu*, 2.

18. "Churong gongyi," in ibid.   19. "Churong gongyi," in ibid.

20. Ray Huang, 36.   21. Liu Zhiwei, 9.

22. Of course, this was in addition to the familiar use of the term *li* as a measure of length, meaning that the same term is thus used in different contexts to represent length, area, and population.

23. In the early to mid-Ming, the territorial divisions of the counties were shaped by prior administrative units. All three counties were subdivided into cantons (*xiang*), which had existed since the Song. In the Ming, the cantons were territorial divisions that defined physiographic regions and served no administrative function. As Brook has observed for China in general, by the Ming the canton had become too populous to serve as a useful unit for the county magistrate, and subdivisions of the canton became more relevant to his administration (See Brook, "Spatial Structure," 14). Subcantons (*li*) had already been established in the Song; their precise function in the Ming is not clear. The 1612 Yongfu county gazetteer mentions that they were eliminated there (1612 *Yongfu xianzhi*, cited in ibid., 15). In Minxian, the subcanton continued to be a unit of the sub-county administration, but in Houguan and Huai'an, subcantons were eliminated and replaced with sectors (*du*). Sectors were numbered rather than named and were primarily units for land registration purposes. Houguan had thirty-six sectors in mid-Ming, and Huai'an had twenty-five. In 1579, Huai'an was reincorporated into Houguan county, and the sectors of the new county were renumbered (*Fuzhou fuzhi* [1754], 2:5a–b). Given that the various forms of sub-county administration resulted from local officials devising different ways to deal with what were essentially the same responsibilities and problems, it is likely that the subcanton in Minxian and the sector in Houguan both served the same function, as a basic unit for tax and service assessment.

24. "Thus we may think of a ward, in south China at least, as a unit having a population of about a thousand people and embracing something between three and six thousand *mu* of land under cultivation." (Brook, "Spatial Structure," 25). To make this discussion more concrete, consider how these various systems were applied on the ground in Nantai in the late Ming. The situation in the less-populous northwestern parts of the island is simplest. The westernmost tip of the island was part of Houguan county. It comprised one canton, which was made up of a single sector, that in turn was made up of nine wards. This ratio of wards to sectors was much higher than the average; probably the explanation lies in the rapid development of the market town of Hongtang in the early Ming. To the south and east was Huai'an county's Yifeng canton—made up of two sectors, which between them consisted of five wards. Moving into the more densely populated southeastern half of the island, the situation becomes more complicated, even though this whole section fell under the administration of one county, Minxian. This part of Nantai was made up of portions of three different cantons, two of which were themselves subdivisions of former Song cantons. Due south of Fuzhou city was Gaogai South canton, which encompassed the commercialized area of Cangshan, across the marshes to Gaogai hill and beyond to the town of Yixu. To the northeast of Gaogai South canton was a portion of Anren canton, and to the southeast was a portion of Kaihua West canton. Gaogai South canton was divided into three subcantons and fourteen wards. Anren canton straddled the Nantai River. The portion of Anren on Nantai Island was divided into

242 NOTES TO PAGES 71-78

three subcantons and eleven wards. The towns of Linpu and Chengmen were located in these wards. Kaihua West canton was divided into three subcantons and six wards. At least two of these subcantons were on Nantai and included the land around Luozhou. I have not been able to determine the precise location of the third subcanton.

25. *Min shu*, 39:962–63.

26. *Lianjiang xianzhi*, 8:33b.

27. *Min shu*, 39:958.

28. See Liu Zhiwei, 8–10; Katayama, "Shindai Kantonshō," 2–11.

29. "Hehu shimo," in *Zhangzhou fuzhi*, 14:20a. John Dardess (75–76) has argued that in the Ming "official registration as a [*lijia* registered] household was a social honour for families to cling to as long as they could."

30. Zheng Zhenman, *Ming–Qing Fujian jiazu zuzhi*, chap. 5. The situation was somewhat more complicated, since in principle the household was the unit of labor service assessment, but households were actually assessed in terms of their property and fiscal males. In terms of the labor service, therefore, the ideal for an individual family was to belong to a registered household with a large membership, reducing the family's individual liability, but a small number of registered males, reducing the household's total liability.

31. Brook, "Spatial Structure," 35; *Min shu*, 39:958.

32. Zheng Ji, "Xin lijia mulu xu," in *Xianyou xianzhi*, 48:8b.

33. We have already come across the Li in the previous chapter, as an example of the unusual kinship structures to which uxorilocal marriage could give rise. See Chap. 2, n.32.

34. Tangfeng has since been transferred to the administrative control of Changle county.

35. Li Hengchu, "Hujie jishi," in *Huangli hepu*, 119–21.

36. The text actually says it was in 1523, but this is clearly a mistake. Cai appears in the national *jinshi* lists for 1583.

37. It is not clear from the genealogy whether the Nominal Named Household Head referred to an actual living individual or to a deceased ancestor who served as a corporate symbol for some or all of his living descendants.

38. Li Hengchu, "Hujie jishi," in *Huangli hepu*, 119.

39. Ray Huang, 117.

40. Li Hengchu, "Hujie jishi," in *Huangli hepu*, 121.

41. *Zhangpu xianzhi*, 20:1589–91. The explanation offered is that accurate assessments were made impossible by the rebellion of Geng Jingzhong.

42. Zheng Zhenman, *Ming-Qing Fujian jiazu zuzhi*, 190–94.

43. *Shezu shehui lishi diaocha*, 92–93. The She origins of the Lan were discussed in Chapter 2.

44. "Disishi gongzu Chaocan gong . . . he zhuan," in *Chongxiu Lianjiang Lanshi zupu.*

45. It may be that they did attempt to affiliate with some *lijia*-registered household but were unsuccessful, perhaps because of their ethnic difference or perhaps because the demands made of them in return for registration were considered excessive.

46. The genealogy records that a certain Wu Chaoxian "has sent a notice to the officials that because there are [in his family] few fiscal males and little tax bearing property, it is difficult for him to fulfill the labor service levies." "Yueye zhuan" in *Chongxiu Lianjiang Lanshi zupu*. It seems likely that Wu Qianzhang was the name of a person who had originally registered in the *lijia*, and Wu Chaoxian was his descendant, speaking on behalf of all the other descendants.

47. The contract begins:

In 1692, the county magistrate Master Zhang Yuncha implemented the policy [of allocating tax households to the descent line]. In 1708, household head Zeng Mingsheng [arranged the] purchase of [the registration] of Wu Qianzhang of Xiagong for twenty taels. Then this was reported to the authorities at a cost of 67 taels. The friendly households (*penghu*) of the thirteen surnames Zeng, Zheng, Cai, Zhu, Wu, Zhuang, Qiu, Huang, Chen, Guo, Zhou, Hong, Lan, etc., collectively donate two catties of meat to thank Zeng Mingsheng for his efforts. Each friendly household should respect this.

"Hetong guiyue" (1836), in *Chongxiu Lianjiang Lanshi zupu*.

48. "Hetong guiyue" (1836), in ibid.

49. This is how additional expenses associated with the registration, for example, at the performance of rituals tied to the purchase of registration, were allocated. This topic is discussed in Chapter 6.

50. The most detailed evidence comes from Qing Taiwan. For a discussion, see Zhuang Yingzhang, 178–90.

51. *Zhangpu xianzhi*, 20:1606–7.

52. Wakefield, chap. 3, provides the most detailed study of family division practices in late imperial China.

53. Freedman suggested a relation between complex irrigation works and corporate property. "In some cases, a joint investment of labor may have led to the establishment as an undivided estate of the land on which the labor had been expended." Freedman, *Chinese Lineage and Society*, 160.

54. Zheng Zhenman has argued that the financing and administration of land reclamation and irrigation projects in Fujian became increasingly a private concern during the Ming–Qing period. The earliest projects in the Fuzhou region were indeed the work of powerful local officials, able to mobilize large amounts of labor and funds (see Zheng Zhenman, "Yanhai shuili"; for evidence from Fuzhou, see *Bamin tongzhi*, 21:444; *Houguanxian xiangtuzhi*, 1:14a; and *Sanshan zhi*, 16:1a–b). From the late Tang to the Ming, Buddhist monasteries, which were becoming more numerous and more important to the local economy as a whole, played a major role in irrigation and reclamation. In the Song, monasteries provided funds, land, leadership, and labor to different projects. This seems to have been a form of taxation, since monastic lands were otherwise exempt from the usual taxes (*Sanshan zhi*, 16:9b–10a; Huang Minzhi, 318–36, Chikusa, *Chūgoku bukkyō*). By the Ming, neither local officials nor the Buddhist monasteries could support irrigation and reclamation to the previous extent. The simplification and monetization of taxes made tax revenues considerably

more liquid and thus more easily extracted by higher levels of the administration, leaving the county magistrates impoverished and unable to mobilize labor. With a few exceptions, monasteries grew weaker and weaker as their holdings were encroached on by powerful local interests while their obligations stayed constant and even increased when the state tried to shift onto them the costs of coastal defense. T'ien Ju-K'ang, 92–100.

55. Reclamation of alluvial sands began by driving stakes into and piling rocks on the river shallows to encourage silt retention. At this stage, shellfish could be cultivated on the deposits, which were known as clam beds (*xiancheng*). When the level of silt was raised above the level of high tide, the new island was cultivated with grasses, which strengthened the deposit, and which could also be harvested and woven into mats, while the foreshore continued to be cultivated with shellfish. Finally after years of effort, the alluvial island could be cultivated with rice or other crops. Compare *Sanshan zhi*, 6:3b–4a; *Minxian xiangtuzhi*, 273 b; Huadong junzheng weiyuanhui tudi gaige weiyuanhui, ed., 136 ff.

56. In a village of Xiapu county, "they treat the sea as a field. Over three hundred households support themselves by catching fish with nets and raising [shellfish]. In the past the seawater was fertile and the [shellfish] that were cultivated tasty. They were gathered and sold in various markets." Commercial cultivation of oysters is said to have begun in the county as early as the fifteenth century. *Xiapu xianzhi*, 18:12b–13a.

57. "Kecheng dijie," in *Xiaojiang Qiushi zupu*, 3:12b. I was not able to conduct fieldwork in the coastal village of Xiaojiang; I wonder whether the Qiu like so many other lineages of the Fuzhou region have undergone the process of sloughing off Dan identity in the course of registering with the state authorities.

58. Skinner, "Structure of Chinese History," 278. The coastal evacuation has not yet been studied in sufficient detail. See Xie Guozhen, and more recently Chang Hengdao. The consequences of the evacuation are vividly described by a seventeenth-century diarist.

> On the very day of the order, supporting their wives and carrying their children, [the people] took to the roads. The homes and dwellings in the area were set alight and burned, until not a tile or stone remained. More than half the people died, [their corpses] lay about on one another in the road. Of the one or two who were able to make it to the interior, none of them had even a picul of rice. The corpses of the starving are really still before my eyes. . . . Of the twenty four districts of Changle, only four [were not affected]. The fires burned for two months, the misery was unspeakable.
>
> Haiwai sanren, 22.

59. Zhu Weigan, 2:412 ff.; *Xiapu xianzhi*, 3:17b; "Lu qixing nicheng tucheng heyue," in *Gongtou Duimen Linshi zupu*.

60. See Wakefield, chap. 3. Of course there could be many complications to the ideal type presented here.

61. Land reform work teams despatched to Yixu were told that flooding in 1947 had wiped out over 600 *mu* of alluvial land, or about thirty percent of the total alluvial land around the town. Huadong junzheng weiyuanhui tudi gaige weiyuanhui, ed., 137.

62. "Kecheng dijie," in *Xiaojiang Qiushi zupu*, 3:12b.

63. A nineteenth-century account of the Lin of Shanggan says that their conduct is "ferocious," and identifies the town as "the most difficult place in Minxian to administer." This reputation was due at least in part to their frequent seizures of alluvial islands, as numerous local legends and stories make clear. Zhou Lianggong, 3:43.

64. Huadong junzheng weiyuanhui tudi gaige weiyuanhui, ed., 140.

65. The owners of Sanxing Island came from the village of Shibu. Fearing attack from Shanggan, they invited residents of Luozhou and Chengmen to take a share of the ownership of the island. Ibid., 138.

66. According to a Republican-era contract drawn up by the three groups, "This island is owned collectively by the Lin, Zhao, and Chen surnames of this locality. The number of shares of ownership is in accordance with the flourishing of each lineage. The Lin surname is the largest, so 260 shares are allocated to them. The Zhao surname is smaller, so 150 shares are allocated to them. The Chen surname is the smallest, so 40 shares are allocated to them. In all there are 450 shares. Each share is worth 1 yuan, which can be converted to one half picul of rice. The capitalization is therefore 450 yuan, or 225 piculs, which has been collected." Ibid., 138.

67. "Every five years a contract is drawn up. Shares are allocated to married couples and households. Youths inherit their father's share. In addition, when a man marries he is given one share in the clambed. Those who become students, widows who keep chaste, those without offspring, and young girls whose parents have died all receive a share." *Changle xianzhi* (1763), 10:29b–30a.

68. They traced their descent back to the Song neo-Confucian Huang Gan and even further back to the brother of Huang Dun, the founding ancestor of the Tiger Mound Huang.

69. "Jiushu" (1906), in *Wenshan Huangshi jiapu*.

70. "Gongji tang gongchan lunnian gongyue" (1920), in ibid. On diversification strategies followed by Chinese families, see Ho, 73–86, 267–318; Cohen, *House United, House Divided*, 120–30.

71. "Although he did not come to Fuzhou with the Wang, in fact it was because the Wang had pacified the region that he was able to establish a school and teach students." "Yingchuan Chenshi zongyuan," in *Langshan Yaqian Chenshi zongpu*, 26. On the Yingchuan choronym, see earlier, Chapter 2, n.67.

72. The pronunciation in Fuzhou dialect is similar.

73. This must have been one of the exactions to which *li* heads were liable; it is not clear from the genealogy whether the money was actually used for the purposes of recompilation, or whether it was simply a customary charge.

74. "Yingchuan Chenshi cimu guiding," in *Langshan Yaqian Chenshi zongpu*, 51.

75. "Yaqian Chenshi Julang zumu ji," in ibid., 37.

76. "Changjiling Xuanyi gong mu ji," in ibid., 30–31.

77. Faure, *Structure of Chinese Rural Society*, 179.

CHAPTER 4

1. For a description of over one hundred restored ancestral halls, see Chen Qingwu.

2. In the early 1990s, I recorded fees ranging from 50 to 500 *yuan* in the Fuzhou region.

3. Faure, *Structure of Chinese Rural Society*, 148–65; Ebrey, *Confucianism and Family Rituals*, 202–19.

4. Chow, 86–97.

5. *Sanshan zhi*, 40:5 a.

6. In Huang's own time, the monastery had been taken over by the family of a female cousin to whom Huang's father had lent the use of one room as a residence. The presence of her and her family made visiting the monastery to make offerings most inconvenient for the Huang. For years the two families had engaged in brawls and lawsuits over the use of the monastery. ("Yu Xiwai Zhizong xu tongqing fendi bing shimu," in Huang Gan, 28:34b.) Other examples include a Ming account in the genealogy of the Sanxi Pan, which records that a Song ancestor, the sixth-generation descendant of their founding migrant ancestor, constructed a monastery "to sacrifice to his ancestors." (Lin Cai, "Ci ji," in *Yingyang Sanxi Panshi zupu*, 17b.) Oral traditions of many local lineages today also include legends of Buddhist monasteries, situated beside ancestral graveyards, that were charged with the performance of rituals to commemorate the ancestors. The people of Shanggan point to Zhenfeng hill near the former ferry crossing to Fuzhou as the site of the tomb of their founding ancestor and describe the endowment of a monastery there in the Song. There was indeed a Zhenfeng monastery established in 960; it is described in the twelfth-century gazetteer as "the place where travellers wait for the tide" for the crossing to Fuzhou. (*Sanshan zhi*, 33:33 b.) For a study of these institutions, see Chikusa, "Sōdai funji kō."

7. "Shizu jitian guanyue," in Huang Gan, 34:14a. Lineage head presumably refers here, as it would in later times, to the senior surviving male in the senior surviving generation.

8. Other Song sources from Fuzhou itself are sparse, but these can be supplemented with a number of important inscriptions collected by Dean and Zheng from Xinghua, immediately to the south of Fuzhou prefecture, including documents connected with the Fang kinship group that has been studied by Hugh Clark (in "Fu of Minnan" and "Private Rituals"). According to an inscription by Liu Kezhuang, dated 1265 and reportedly based on earlier writings by a local magistrate, the descendants of the founding ancestor had constructed a spirit hall (*jingshe*) within the Guanghua Buddhist monastery in Putian. "Collective sacrifice is performed. The descendants of the six branches all come reverently and respectfully; the gathering numbers several thousand people. For three hundred years since the establishment of the hall, the incense fires burned as if a single day had passed" (Liu Kezhuang, "Jianfu yuan

Fangshi citang ji," in Dean and Zheng, 49). The ancestors were worshiped in the form of painted portraits. ("Fangshi zupu xu," in Fang Dacong, 31:2b). Fang Yansun (1213–76) tried to promote collective sacrifice at the graves of the ancestors. He built an offering hall (citang) by the graves and endowed a small estate to support sacrifice. "If the fields remain, the shrine will remain; if the shrine remains, the sacrifice will remain" "Putian Fangshi lingyin ben an ji," in Lin Xiyi, 11:4a–6a.

    9. Huang Zhongyuan, "Huangshi zuci sijing tang ji," in Dean and Zheng, 51–52.

    10. For example, there was an offering hall to Fuzhou's Chen Guling (jinshi 1042), celebrated in an essay by his friend Liu Yi (1017–86), that was located in the prefectural school of Changzhou, where he had served in office. (Liu Yi, "Chen xiansheng citang ji," in Chen Guling, 25:27a–37b). In the twelfth century, an offering hall was constructed in honor of Lin Guangchao (1114–78) of Putian, who had served as libationer, that is, as head of the directorate of education, and was a prominent teacher in his home county. According to Chen Junqing, a few years after Lin Guangchao's death, a new prefect arrived in Xinghua. A group of local notables paid the prefect a visit to sing Lin's praises. As they told him, "people reflect on his restraint and model behaviour, and wish to erect a shrine for him, at which he may receive sacrifice annually." The prefect agreed, selected a suitable plot of land south of the city and, when the hall was completed, led the local students in sacrifice at the shrine. "All the people of the prefecture rushed to pay their respects" (Chen Junqing, "Aixuan citang ji," in Dean and Zheng, 29). According to an essay by Huang Hao, dating from the late twelfth century,

> The way of sacrifice is that those who have earned merit for the people should all receive sacrifice. The offering hall (citang) of the present is in accordance with this. Either on the basis of merit, or of virtue, or reputation, without restriction according to whether they are exalted or base, venerated or degraded, or on the basis of rank, all those who are admired by people in their hearts should have [an offering hall].
>
> (Huang Hao "Xinghua jun mingxian hesi ji," in Bamin tongzhi, 84:977.)

Also see Ebrey, "Early Stages," 51.

    11. Indeed, some of the Song accounts read remarkably like descriptions of ancestor worship in north China in more recent times. See Cohen, "Lineage Organization in North China," 519–28.

    12. Ebrey, trans., Chu Hsi's Family Rituals, xxi–xxiv, 8–10, 167n. 43; Confucianism and Family Rituals, 160–62. On ancestral halls, see Makino, "Sōshi to sono hattatsu," and Zuo Yunpeng.

    13. He praised one such hall in the following terms: "To the east of his bedchamber, Wu Yuanyu set aside a hall to serve as an offering shrine (cishe). The walls encircling it are majestic; the gates and chambers deeply hidden away; it is clean and silent—a suitable dwelling place for the spirits. His ancestors from his great-grandfather down to his father are worshiped there." "Yongsi tang ji," in Wu Hai, 2:32–33.

14. In fact, sacrifice for this purpose was meaningless. If sacrifice was performed "to the highest standards of etiquette, and without transgression, how then could the spirits not accept the offering? But on the contrary, if the hall is constructed, the embellishments beautiful, the sacrifice abundant, the animals rich and the wine clear, yet one is not filial, the spirits will spit out [the offering]." ("Houyan," in ibid., 1:28–29.) The Lin had an offering hall in which tablets of ancestors going back twenty-one generations received sacrifice. Wu felt that although the sentiments underlying the practice were admirable the sacrifice itself was actually a transgression, which usurped the privileges of the ancient nobility. The common people were restricted to making offerings to their immediate ancestors at home. Wu had the excessive tablets buried and a genealogical chart drawn up that could be displayed in the hall at the winter solstice and at New Year's. Lineage members in strict order led by the descent-line heir were to bow before the chart. ("Zonghui tang ji," in ibid, 2:41–42.)

15. At some time prior to Song Lian's record, a shrine to the ancestors (*xianci*) had been constructed. It contained five tablets, each four feet high. The central tablet was dedicated to a prominent Song official, Lin Yuan, his father, his grandfather, and his three sons. Other tablets were dedicated to the collective ancestors of three branches descended from the Tang founding ancestor. "All those descended from the three branches have their names added when they die." In the late Song, the hall had been endowed with considerable wealth, which was used to support collective sacrifice in the hall, "so the seasonal rituals were particularly abundant when compared with other lineages." Song's inscription was composed in honor of the expansion of the hall, which lineage members had decided was "poor and small, and not sufficient for intercourse with the spirits." (Song Lian, "Guoqing Linshi chongxiu xianci ji," in Dean and Zheng, 78–79.) See also Ebrey, "Early Stages," 53.

16. *Houguanxian xiangtuzhi*, 339–40.

17. As I show below, over the Ming–Qing period, groups of Liu living all over Fujian used Liu Cun's father as a common ancestor in tracing a genealogical connection with one another. As a result, much information about the Fenggang Liu was copied into genealogies of Liu lineages living in other places, and these can now be used to supplement the Fenggang genealogy. For three generations, Cun's line was transmitted through a single line of descent, until we reach the fourth-generation ancestor Wenji, who had eight sons. According to a document of unknown date but certainly no earlier than the Ming, descendants of six of these sons moved away from Fenggang, throughout Fujian province and even beyond. Descendants of Wenji's third son, for example, are said to have moved to Hongtang and Gaohu on Nantai, to Fuzhou city, to Changle and Minqing counties, and to Xinghua prefecture. The descendant who moved to Minqing was one Kang. Kang was the founding ancestor of the Liu of Yuban. This document reads like a retrospective attempt to link several descent lines. "Zongzhi fenpai kao," in *Baxian Liushi Guizhifang zhipu*, 1:87a–b.

18. Chen Baoji (*jinshi* 928), "Huaisou muzhiming," in ibid., 1:1a–2a.

19. No doubt the magistrate simply gave official recognition to the de facto situation. *Yuban Liushi zupu*, 15:4b. Compare Meskill, *Chinese Pioneer Family*, 253–71.

20. *Yuban Liushi zupu*, 15:1a ff.

21. Liu Yin, "QianMin shishi" (1141), in *Baxian Liushi Guizhifang zhipu*, 1:80a–b.

22. ibid., 1:106a. The shrine consisted of two halls surrounding a well and survived at least into the early nineteenth century, when it was recorded in the genealogy of the Liu of Yuban. *Yuban Liushi zupu*, 12:1a–b.

23. "The ancients established the descent-line for their lineage; because they respect the line they venerate the sacrifice. For the sacrifice to the ancestors there is the shrine; for uniting the kin there is the surname. . . . Since the way of establishing the descent-line has fallen into decay, the method for uniting the kin has deteriorated." Cheng was also responsible for the establishment of a sacrificial estate in support of the shrine. Liu Cheng, "Zupu xu," in *Baxian Liushi Guizhifang zhipu*, 1:78a–79a.

24. Just over one century later, the hall was clearly the site of large-scale collective sacrifice to the ancestors, for when a member of the lineage returned home from taking the examinations in the 1130s, he participated in the sacrifice and then enjoyed a feast together with "all the younger brothers." We know nothing of the rituals that were performed in the hall, but we do know that the ancestors were represented in the form of tablets, for a later preface explains that the information on these tablets was used in compiling the Liu genealogy. Liu Cao, "Xuxiu zupu zhi," in ibid., 1:81a.

25. We have already encountered Yi as the author of the commemorative record of Chen Guling's offering hall. See earlier, n.10. Both Yi and Kangfu were minor figures in the intellectual currents of the latter half of the eleventh century. Yi was a student of Hu Yuan (993–1059), who was part of "the first stream in the rise of Song learning." Yi enjoyed a successful official career and wrote a number of works of philosophy and administration. By the early Shaoxing period, he was prominent enough to be included in a "Shrine to the Five Gentlemen" in the prefectural school. (Huang Zongxi, 17; *Bamin tongzhi*, 62:457–58; and Liu Shuxun, ed., 85 ff). Kangfu studied under Zhou Ximeng and, though he never served in an official capacity, enjoyed a long career and some renown as a teacher in the Fuzhou area (*Bamin tongzhi*, 62:459). According to Zhen Duxiu (1178–1235), the line of scholarly transmission that linked the Cheng brothers to Zhu Xi began with Luo Congyan's teacher Yang Shi (1053–1135). When Yang returned home to Fujian, Cheng Hao is reputed to have said "Henceforth, my teachings are going to the south." Yang passed these teachings on to Luo Congyan and Li Yanping (1093–1163). The genealogy records that Zao came to the attention of the court for his great filiality. He is said to have written commentaries on the *Book of Changes* and the *Record of Ritual*. Zhu Xi once named Zao as one of three scholars who, "among the previous generation [of scholars] from Fuzhou, understood rites." *Bamin tongzhi*, 62:459; *Minhou xianzhi*, 70:2a; and Huang Zongxi, 48:846.

26. *Baxian Liushi Guizhifang zhipu*, 1:109a. Jiaju's son Shi'nan was in turn a student of Lin Zhiqi, another prominent neo-Confucian of the Fuzhou region. Liu Di seems to have been the more outstanding of the two brothers. An anecdote relates that after reading Buddhist and Daoist works he sighed and said "this is not worth studying." He then devoted himself to preparation for the examinations but soon came to the same conclusion. He abandoned his aspirations to officialdom

and became a student of Zhu Xi, who was most impressed with his abilities. Liu Li was also a student of Zhu Xi and a close friend of Huang Gan. By the Qing, the sources record that both he and his brother attained the *jinshi* degree in 1166, but Ming sources make no mention of this and their names do not even appear in the Song gazetteer. Liu Di is said to have written two works, an investigation into ancient court ritual and an explication of the *Analects* and the *Mencius*, but these were never published. (See *Fuzhou fuzhi* (1754) 58:3b; and *Bamin tongzhi*, 62:461–62.) Liu Zijie, whose father was either Liu Di or Li according to different sources, was another prodigy. He was born after the death of his father and was raised by his natal family; at the age of six he "mourned his uncle like a grown man." When he grew older, he became a student of Huang Gan and maintained a strict code of personal conduct. "He had no intercourse with anyone who was not a renowned scholar, and would not keep a book if it was not concerned with righteousness and principle." He was a man of some means, leaving a legacy of several hundred *mu* of fields to his sons and nephews. *Bamin tongzhi*, 62:461–62.

27. This change was reflected in the renaming of the shrine from Shrine of the Sages (*xianci*[2]) to Shrine of All the Sages (*zhuxian ci*). Probably this change took place in the sixteenth century, for Ma records it as a recent development.

28. Ma Sen, "Liushi zhuxianci beiwen" (1579), in *Baxian Liushi Guizhifang zhipu*, 1:1a–2a. The three outsiders must have been held in some esteem to be able to petition officialdom directly; presumably they were minor local notables who did not enjoy the sorts of success that would have led to their names being recorded in local gazetteers. According to Ye, one of them also carved a plaque for the lintel of the shrine and donated land to pay for the sacrifices. Ye Xianggao, "Baxian citi ji" (1606), in ibid., 1:5a–b.

29. The Liu hall in Fenggang may have been modeled on a late-fifteenth-century shrine to five illustrious members of the Liu lineage of Jianyang. In a record written in 1490 about this shrine, the problem of worshiping distant ancestors was addressed directly.

> In the past, these five gentleman never had a shrine. Because they are from distant generations, they are not able to enjoy the sacrifice given to four generations of ancestors. But for such ancestors, if their descendants followed [the regulations], and neglecting them did not offer sacrifice, would they not feel ashamed in their hearts? So in 1489 [reading *ji* for *yi*, otherwise the date makes no sense] my younger brother-in-law Liu Ze, the twelfth generation descendant of Jia, built the hall to the right of the Pingshan shrine, installed the tablets and offered sacrifice. . . . The virtues of the ancestors are venerated, the descendants are enlightened, the illumination continues without limit. The intentions are profound and distant.
>
> [Liu?] You, "Jianyang Liushi yuanshi xu" (1490), in ibid., 1:3b–4a.

30. According to Yuanmei's preface, his father claimed that a genealogy had once existed going all the way back to the founding ancestor, but it had been destroyed

in the turmoil of the Yuan–Ming transition. As a result, when Yuanmei set about compiling the genealogy, he had only fragmentary material to work with. Indeed, the earliest generation for which he can provide any details is the eleventh. There were three members of this generation, whose relationship with one another is unclear and who are known only by ordinal numbers. Between them, they had four sons, whose names only are known. These four men had six sons, who are the founding ancestors of the six branches into which the Lin of Linpu are divided to the present day. This arrangement is very similar to the branches of the Huang of Yixu, suggesting that the Lin of Linpu might also be a lineage constructed by the fusion of several lineages.

31. Lin Ben, for example, was a tribute student and served as an assistant instructor in Guangdong. His grandson Lin Chao (1487–1559) was originally a scholar but gave up his studies and became very wealthy as a salt merchant. Commercial success could be converted into other types of success, for in 1540 Chao was honored as the senior guest at the Community Drinking Ritual of the prefecture. His son returned to scholarship and was successful enough to be able to reward his father with several honorary titles. *Lianjiang Linshi jiapu*. 1:1a, 6a.

32. *Mindu ji*, 13:5a. Guan receives not even the briefest of biographies in the Linpu Lin genealogy.

33. He held the offices of county magistrate (*zhixian*), subprefectural magistrate (*zhizhou*), and prefect (*zhifu*) in succession. In 1460 he asked for leave to retire and returned home, whereupon a friend remarked that he also knew when to be satisfied (*zhizu*) and called him a man of "Four Knowings" (*sizhi*). Yuanmei gave this name to the residence he constructed in Linpu on his retirement.

34. Han's career was interrupted and he was stripped from office as a result of the opposition of the powerful eunuch Liu Jin. After Liu Jin's fall, Han was invited to return to his position, but chose retirement instead.

35. Zhang Tingyu, 163:4428–31; *Shangshu li*; *Lianjiang Linshi jiapu, zhuan*.

36. Lin Han, "Zhengde wuyan (1548) chongxiu xu," in *Lianjiang Linshi jiapu, shou*:2b.

37. These themes are echoed in the prefaces of his sons and grandsons. In his preface of 1540, Ting'ang explains that the previous edition had been destroyed in a fire two years earlier. He was deeply troubled and ordered his son to gather the surviving material to compile a new genealogy. "Compiling a genealogy is the fullest [expression] of a heart which wishes to unite the agnates, so that all will conduct themselves in a filial and fraternal way without regard to success or failure, and there will be warm feelings among the kin without regard to the closeness of their relationship." He pointed out that his immediate family was considerably wealthier than their kin and warned them neither to take advantage of those less fortunate nor to attempt to enrich themselves at the expense of others. Tingji makes the same claim in his preface to the 1577 edition. "A genealogy serves to unite the agnates." Lin Ting'ang, "Jiajing gengzi (1540) chongxiu xu," in ibid., *shou*:3b; and Lin Tingji, "Wanli dingchou (1577) chongxiu xu," in ibid., *shou*:4a.

38. Yang Tinghe, "Taize taibao libing erbu shangshu yi Wen'an Lin gong shendao beiming," in ibid., 1:54b. The charitable endeavors of elite members of the

Linpu Lin extended beyond their immediate kin to the wider community. Tingji's grandson Shiji (1547–1616) held a minor post in the ministry of revenue, which he attained through the inheritance privilege, but left his official career to return home, where he founded a poetic society with a group of prominent Fuzhou men. He was instrumental in raising funds for the reconstruction of the main bridge linking Nantai Island with the city. "Up to the present day, those who use the roads praise his virtue." He also sold grain at reduced prices in times of famine. Lin Qing was also known for his charitable works. He would wander the streets of Fuzhou at night and leave money anonymously at the gate of households where he heard sounds of sorrow and misery from within. Ibid., 1:32a.

39. Fang Hao, "Linshi jiamiao ji" (1518), in ibid., 1:71b:

Sacrifice comes from the heart, and ritual arises out of righteousness (*li qiyu yi*). Only the virtuous are able to avoid losing their heart, so only the virtuous are able to attain the limits of the righteousness of sacrifice. Sacrifice must be performed to only four generations [of ancestors] and cease [for generations beyond four]. But as for my first ancestor who migrated, how can I bear to forget him? If I cannot bear to forget my own first migrant ancestor, how can I order my kin to forget theirs? In this lineage, the first migrant ancestors are numerous. How could each have their own shrine? Thus they are united together in one shrine, and united together in receiving sacrifice. In this way, the wish to venerate the ancestors and unite the agnates is expressed to the limit.

40. Fang Hao, "Linshi jiamiao ji" (1518), in ibid., 1:71a–b.

41. No details survive on the financing of rituals in the hall constructed by Lin Han, but some sense of Han's thoughts on the subject can be gained from an essay he wrote on the establishment of sacrificial fields for a descent group in southern Fujian. He begins by stressing the importance of endowed property to ensure that sacrifices are performed regularly over time. The lineage had endowed fifty *mu* of fields to support sacrifices both at the tombs and at an ancestral shrine. Sacrifices at the numerous graves were to be restrained and less elaborate than in the past. "The rituals at the tombs of the various ancestors for a long time down to the present have had rituals performed in an excessively splendid way. This cannot remain unchanged." Rituals at the shrine were to be performed in accordance with the *Family Rituals.* "Jinjiang Zhuangshi jitian ji," in Lin Han, 15:2b–4a.

42. Chen either did not know or chose to ignore the fact that there were two distinct phases in the development of the hall, its initial construction by Jing and Shiji, and the inclusion of Jing's tablet after his death. He includes Jing in the list of illustrious ancestors on whose behalf the hall was initially constructed, but of course Jing was not yet an ancestor when this took place.

43. Wang Shimao, "Shizhong ci ji," in *Lianjiang Linshi jiapu,* 1:65a–66b.

44. Chen Kui, "Shizhong ci houji," in ibid., 1:67a–68a. The hall earns a brief mention in the prefectural gazetteer of 1613, which confirms official participation in sacrifices. *Fuzhou fuzhi* (1613), 17:7a–b.

45. Tingyu's career was utterly undistinguished. Themselves finding it curious that such an obscure individual should have his own free-standing ancestral hall, contemporary villagers believe that he considered himself entitled to one by virtue of being the elder brother of a minister.

46. The sons had varied careers, with two provincial graduates, who held posts as high as prefectural vice-magistrate, two government students, and one holder of a title by purchase. It is not clear why one son has no tablet.

47. There were two other ancestral halls built on Nantai prior to the late sixteenth century. One of these was the hall of the Wu of Luozhou, who claim descent from Wu Deguang. He migrated from Henan to Changle in the northern Song and then married uxorilocally to a woman from Luozhou. As would be expected with a uxorilocal marriage, most of Deguang's progeny were given the surname of his wife's natal family. Wu Fu was Deguang's eighth-generation descendant, the eldest of the surviving members of that generation, whose descendants comprise the seven branches of the lineage today. He held a number of offices in the early Ming before retiring in 1463 to Luozhou. A century later, in the Jiajing period, after a temple in the center of the village of Luozhou was destroyed in an official campaign against illicit cults (*yinci*), Deguang's direct descendants, who were themselves officeholders, purchased the site and constructed an ancestral hall in his honor. There are biographies of Wu in *Fujian tongzhi* (1938), 34:18:22a–b and *Minhou xianzhi*, 66:4b. Also see *Luozhou zhi*, 1:6b, 32a ff. It appears that the Wu hall, as with that of the Linpu Lin, was also constructed by the immediate descendants of a high official in fulfillment of a prerogative exclusive to that status and thus as demonstration of high status and commitment to neo-Confucian orthodoxy.

48. As the governor of the province wrote in the last years of the sixteenth century, "The flat land of Fujian is narrow and its people are pressed together; there are few possibilities to grow grain, so those living along the coast make their homes in boats and their fields in the sea, living by trading with foreigners." *Ming shilu*, 262:4864 (7/1593).

49. Early in the seventeenth century, Dong Yingju (*jinshi* 1598) described the people living in the mouth of the Min River in the following terms. "Previously they had contact with the pirates; now they have contact with the foreigners . . . they aspire to the profits of three hundred percent that can be made on [trade in] small goods; all of them are so [rich] that they are too proud to farm. The crafty ones among them make themselves ships' captains. When the merchant's money is in their hands, they spend it frivolously." ("Yu Jiadeng li wen," in Dong Yingju, 51.) The implication is that the trade was sufficiently sophisticated for a division of labor to have developed, with merchants entrusting their cargoes to ship captains for a fee. In the Ming, Hongtang was the most important port for merchants involved in overseas trade: it was said of a temple to Wang Shenzhi located near Hongtang that "those who cross the sea in boats all pray here." *Mindu ji*, 19:4b.

50. *Minbu shu*, 22a. A memorial on the elimination of certain commercial taxes by Xu Fuyuan mentions merchants involved in the following trades in Fuzhou in

the sixteenth century: black sugar export merchants, lumber export merchants, pig merchants, cotton merchants, ship's brokers, indigo brokers, yellow and white silk brokers, cotton export brokers, woven cloth brokers, tea and oil export merchants, white sugar brokers, export brokers for different kinds of paper, hemp brokers, metal brokers, black sugar import merchants, porcelain brokers, salt brokers, copper export merchants, oxen boat brokers, and lumber boat brokers. "Zhuomian shangshui xing Fuzhou fu," in Xu Fuyuan, 9:43b ff.

51. Fu Yiling, "Minqing minjian dianyue." Xie Zhaozhe provides evidence in support.

In central Fujian, the land tax is light and the price of rice is moderate. So the officials and rich households vie with one another to accumulate land. The corrupt officials and powerful lineages have fields and marshes in neighbouring areas. As for the property beyond the boundaries, they encircle and appropriate it; as for land without a proprietor they solicit and beg for it; as for the land to support temples and monasteries they use force and seize it. . . . Thus the rich get richer and poor get poorer. (Xie Zhaozhe, 4:36b.)

For analysis of Xie's writing on landownership, see Kataoka, 42–49. There are numerous examples of gentry seizure of land from monasteries in the mid-Ming. The most celebrated case involved the theft of over 2500 *mu* belonging to the Gushan Monastery by local landlords. The abbot brought a lawsuit against the offenders, but they proved so recalcitrant that it dragged on for years without any resolution, until finally the land was "donated" to local academies. Many of the monks, having no means of subsistence, were forced to leave the monastery. "Fuzhoufu sixue xinli xuetian ji," Inscription; and *Wushishan zhi*, 5:10b–11a.

52. In Minqing, "the tenants refer to their landlord as Strongman (*shitou*). . . . It is said that in the Ming the levies for military expenses were heavy, and were collected twice annually. Most of the common people who owned land sold it cheaply to the noble and powerful, hoping to cultivate it for them." (*Minqing xianzhi*, 8:zalu: 8a–b.) Zhou Zhikui (b. 1586) wrote that villagers were often forced to borrow grain from local grain merchants to see them through the winter and for seed grain in the spring. When the harvest came in, they had to repay the grain they had borrowed, with interest. Peasant proprietors were forced further into debt, and tenants, unable to pay their rents, were forced to turn to the moneylenders again. ("Guangji gu yi gu Min hanyi," in Zhou Zhikui, *wenji*:5:10a–17b.) According to one county magistrate, "Nowadays, the wealthy have proficient methods to loan money to the peasants. . . . they collect the interest and then make a new loan. In a year they double their money, over several years their profits grow accordingly. After ten years, they expand their property and enrich their descendants." (*Xianyou xianzhi*, 20:1b–2a.) In Minqing during the Ming there was a market village known as Little Nantai, after the commercial center of Fuzhou, because so many rich landlords from Nantai District had built temporary granaries there for the storage of rental income from nearby tenants. This is confirmed in the writings of Zhou Zhikui:

"The landlords and powerful families living in [Fuzhou] city establish granaries in the outer villages or other counties. Aside from the consumption needs of a few families, they ship the remainder to the city to sell. The big households in the villages do the same." *Minqing xianzhi,* 8:*zalu*:8a; "Guangji gu yi gu Min hanyi," in Zhou Zhikui, *wenji*:5:11a–b; "Tiaochen Fuzhou fu zhihuang luyao yi," in Zhou Zhikui, *wenji*:5:22b.

53. Xie describes a fellow native who passed the examinations, attained the rank of prefect, and accumulated a huge fortune, which was used to build the finest dwelling in Fuzhou prefecture. But the official and his wife died before they could enjoy the palatial dwelling, and their descendants squabbled so much over the inheritance that the house had to be sold off. Extravagant spending on funerary ritual and especially on geomantic burial sights was particularly offensive to Xie. "Some rich and high class families acquire land but worry about its shortcomings, and lose sight of its beauty. They build up the soil into a hill, open up fields into mounds to make a surrounding wall, draw in water, build bridges and pavilions, spending vast sums and ten years in the construction. Not only do they fail to get good fortune, but they rapidly bring on disaster and misery." (Xie Zhaozhe, 15:51b, 3:42a, 6:18b, and 13:31b.) On conspicuous consumption, see also "Tiaochen Fuzhou fu zhihuang luyao yi," in Zhou Zhikui, *wenji*:5:22b.

54. As soon as they arrive in the fields they act like bullies, taking 60 percent, planning to hoard grain until price rises. If they do not get exactly what they want, they try a hundred schemes to harm [the tenants], falsely claiming they are robbers and forcing them at knifepoint to send [grain] to the storehouses. Because the villagers are afraid of their power and do not know what to do they have come to the *yamen.* . . . We have even learned that there are cases of the tenants arming themselves, forming into gangs, ignoring principle and the law. When it is time to divide the crop they steal it first, or they pay the rent in sand, or if they are to pay rent, they do not pay for the whole year, or even ignore their life and plan riot.

"Zhaogu shouzu xing bafu yizhou," in Xu Fuyuan, 9:21b–22b.

55. "Yu nan Ertai Gongzu shu," and "Mijin," in Dong Yingju, 34–35, 41; "Tiaochen Fuzhou fu zhihuang luyao yi," in Zhou Zhikui, *wenji*:5:18a–21b. See Wang Yeh-Chien for a discussion of food supply problems from a later time.

56. On violence, see Fu Yiling, "Ming Wanli . . . qiangmi fengchao," 140–47. Fu notes that sixteenth-century officials blamed environmental constraints for outbreaks of violence in Fuzhou. But this is hardly a satisfactory explanation. Both rent-resistance and rice riots have to be situated historically. Overpopulation, rising land concentration and chronic food shortages were part of broad economic changes of the sixteenth century, changes that were widely recognized in the writings of Fuzhou natives of the time.

57. In 1593, the harvest had failed and rice prices in the city began to rise. More concerned about meeting official and military payroll, the obtuse prefect of Fuzhou

refused to release what grain was available in the granary without receiving approval from higher authorities. Some officials called for measures to encourage more private merchants to import rice, but these could hardly be effective when rampant piracy made any sea venture risky. Nor could this eliminate the problem of hoarding, an issue also addressed by Xu Fuyuan. "In the capital of Fujian the land is limited and the population dense. For grain supply they always rely on other places. With repeated poor harvests, the poor have an increasingly hard time to eat. Oceangoing grain boats then come... but the powerful brokers and rich households purchase all the grain and do not sell it, so the price becomes very expensive, and the poor can not buy a peck or a bushel of rice." ("Guangji gu yi gu Min hanyi," in Zhou Zhikui, *wenji*:5:10a–17b; and "Ban zhengsu bianxing geshu," in Xu Fuyuan, 8:15b.) On the riot, see *Fuzhou fuzhi* (1613), j.75, and Fu Yiling, "Ming Wanli... qiangmi fengchao," 140.

58. On population movements recorded in the genealogies, see *Fuzhou Guoshi zhipu*, discussed in Chapter 5. The writings of Zhu Zhe of Putian suggest that the elite were singled out for attack by pirates, who identified them with the help of local informants. "If they come in the dark of night, how can they be defended against? So several families who in ordinary times were known for their wealth have each moved into the city." Zhu Zhe, 5:12b–13a; for another example, *Minxian xiangtuzhi*, 107a–b.

59. He wrote of Zhangzhou: "Since 1561, the people have built walled forts and walled buildings in ever-increasing numbers, especially in the regions along the coast." (Gu Yanwu, 26:104b.) The Qing gazetteer of Funing prefecture, to the north of Fuzhou, records the construction of almost sixty defensive forts in the mid- to late sixteenth century as a result of pirate incursions. Lin Aimin, "Chi'an baoji," in *Funing fuzhi*, 39:6a.

60. In some strategic areas, state aid financed the construction of defensive fortifications. At the important port of Haikou, devastated by pirate attacks in 1555 that left half the population dead, the Surveillance Censor disbursed large amounts of relief, which the people used to build a wall that enabled successful defense against later pirate attacks. *Mindu ji*, 27:7b.

61. The same man was also active in his community in other ways. He established a charitable granary that lent out grain in spring and summer and did not charge interest when the grain was repaid after the harvest. He supported members of his kin who could not afford the costs of funerals and weddings. ibid., 13:6b; and *Minxian xiangtuzhi*, 108b.

62. *Mindu ji*, 13:5a.

63. As Tim Brook has written,

> To put their predicament simply, the mid-Ming gentry had to make sense of who they were in local society in the absence of formal opportunities to undertake public action. In relation to the emperor, they were his obedient servants whose conduct conformed to Confucian principles. But with reference to the local context, they held no formal franchise. Their social mobility gave

them an informal power, but that was hard to justify in terms of Confucian ideals of deference and obligation to the imperial order that the magistrate represented.

(Brook, *Confusions of Pleasure*, 140.)

Scholars have identified a number of different effects arising out of this predicament. Miki Satoshi has argued that Ming officials were aware of it and occasionally tried to turn it to the advantage of the state by involving the gentry in leadership of subcounty organizational schemes such as the village covenant (*xiangyue*). (Miki, 99–100.) Chow Kai-Wing has linked it to what he considers the major intellectual trend in China from the late Ming to the Qing, Confucian ritualism as expressed in ethics, classical learning, and lineage discourse. Chow, 223–28.

64. Guo Deyin, "Tianfang Deyin gong disanci chongxiu zhipu ji," in *Fuzhou Guoshi zhipu*, 1:15b.

65. The other sixteenth century hall was that of the Luozhou Wu, discussed earlier, in chap. 4, n. 47.

66. Zheng Shanfu, 9:5a. The choronym South Lake (Nanhu) comes not from any geographic feature of Nantai, but because they claim to be descended from the South Lake Zheng of Putian, one of the most prominent families in the region in the Song.

67. Zheng Shanfu, 17:8b. Unfortunately I was not permitted to consult the genealogy of the Nanhu Zheng, so I cannot explain the kinship connection between Zheng Shanfu and the Third branch.

68. By the nineteenth century, Zheng Shanfu had come to be considered the prime impetus behind the hall, perhaps because he was the only member of the lineage to enjoy an enduring reputation. In 1826, a later descendant named Bingwen made a donation to support the ancestral shrine, the property of which had been embezzled by unscrupulous descendants. Bingwen's friend Lin Zexu wrote an inscription commemorating his donation, which begins, "The Zheng of Nanhu have had sacrificial fields since [Shanfu] in the Ming first donated funds, proposed construction of the ancestral hall (*citang*) and donated his own fields to serve as the sacrificial estate.... [Zheng Shanfu] built the hall and established the sacrifice, later Bingwen continued the virtuous practice." "Nanhu Zhengshi jitian ji," (1827) Inscription.

69. Chow, 86–97.

70. Huang Fuji, "Zongci zhi" (1734), in *Huqiu Yishan Huangshi shipu*, 1:18a–b.

71. *Huqiu Yishan Huangshi shipu*, 1:30a. Shi, born in the Yongle period, "had many schemes, and people were afraid of his power.... He married a woman née He of Yingshan who brought a very large dowry. Then he married a woman née Zhang of Xixia, who gave birth to a son. Then he married a woman née Deng of Nantai, whose dowry was also very large. As a result of this, he became very wealthy." ibid., 1:34a.

72. Wenze's father had endowed a small estate to support his widow. The income from the estate rotated between his two surviving sons. The son who received the

income in a specified period was also responsible for providing meals for the mother. But there was tension between the mother and the younger son, and she preferred to sleep in the home of the elder, Wenze, regardless of whose turn it was to provide her meals. One evening she left the home of the younger son after the evening meal but was caught in a violent storm. When she did not arrive promptly at his house, Wenze, assuming that she would not venture out on such a night but had remained at his brother's house, barred the gate for the night. His brother meanwhile did the same. As a result, their mother passed the whole night exposed to the storm and by morning was dead. The two brothers were reported to the authorities for their appalling lack of filiality and were ruined. It was in hope of regaining his fortune that he sought employment elsewhere. ibid., 1:35a–b.

73. ibid., 1:33b. More telling evidence for the effects of the sixteenth-century turmoil is the high percentage of males listed in the genealogy who failed to reach adulthood, marry, and have posterity. It is also seen in the convoluted efforts of the compilers of the genealogy to trace the frequent and varied adoptions that took place, perhaps only nominally, to ensure that sacrifice was maintained for the many members of the lineage who were left without posterity because either they themselves or their descendants had fallen victims to the pirates.

74. As his biography explains, this was at a time when social mobility among the local elite was much more fluid than it became later. "Military officials were respected in the Yongle era, and a government student could become a ministry official." ibid., 1:29b.

75. Huang Xiangcao, "Xincuofang zhici zhi" (1867), in ibid., 1:22b. This hall was reconstructed in 1867 and again in 1918, but no longer survives.

76. ibid., 1:30a.   77. "Sifang zhici ji," in ibid., 1:21b.

78. ibid., 1:14a.   79. ibid., 1:33a.

80. Huang Zunjiu, "Tuojian Sifang Pingpu gong jiamiao ji" (1932), in ibid., 1:22a.

81. These contributions were insufficient to construct the hall, so Baoguang matched the total amount donated.

82. "Sifang zhici ji," in ibid., 1:21b. When Lin Yaohua did his research in Yixu in 1935, the Four Branches hall had just been reconstructed four years earlier. It owned property amounting to sixty-six *mu*. The annual income from the property was more than one thousand *yuan*. A portion of this was used to meet the hall expenses; the remainder went to the rota holder. Lin Yaohua, 32, 52.

83. See Rubie Watson, *Inequality Among Brothers*, chap. 2.

84. Recall Huang Fuji's relative's comment that he did not know the relationship between the different branches of the lineage. See above, chap. 2. n.18.

85. Chow, 14.

86. Each injunction is followed by a brief paragraph explaining its content. For example, the elaborating paragraph on the injunction to divide property evenly begins by noting the need to have sufficient property to sustain oneself and then quotes Confucius: "Do not worry about scarcity; worry about inequality." In concrete terms, this meant that one should not expropriate land belonging to others. When households divided their property, one should not take more than one's

share. Other injunctions were more vague. One praises the practice of large un-divided households of antiquity, in which ten or more generations lived together. Though this was no longer possible, the spirit behind it could be maintained. "All the members of our lineage (*zu*) enjoy mutual conviviality and mutual sympathy. The wise do not bully the foolish; the noble do not humiliate the base; the wealthy do not reject the poor; the brave do not trouble the timid; the many do not exploit the few." Huang Baoguang, "Zu xun," in *Huqiu Yishan Huangshi shipu*, 1:19a–b.

87. At the ceremonial raising of the main beam of the new hall, the secret to the difficulties that the Huang had encountered in the construction process was revealed. In the decaying walls of the existing hall, a talisman consisting of two pieces of red paper held down by a copper coin was discovered. An elderly craftsmen explained that this was a curse left by a previous workman.

88. Huang Fuji, "Zongci zhi" (1734), in *Huqiu Yishan Huangshi shipu*, 1:18a–b.

89. When Lin Yaohua visited Yixu in 1935, he reported that this hall contained approximately twenty rows of ancestral tablets, each row containing twenty-seven tablets for a total of about 540. Obviously this meant that only a small fraction of all the ancestors of the lineage going back to Zhifu had their own tablet in the hall to receive sacrifice, but unfortunately there is no information on the criteria for the admission of tablets. Moreover, these tablets would have been installed after a major reconstruction project in 1866. We have no way of knowing how many tablets were installed when the hall was first built. Lin Yaohua, 32, 46 n.11.

90. The first regulation is "Recite the Sagely Instructions," referring to the moral code in sixteen sections promulgated by the Kangxi emperor. One regulation calls on lineage members to restrain the wild and unruly, "those who think only of profit and fail to consider reason," the danger being that their criminal conduct might come to the attention of the local *dibao*—or constable in the mutual surveillance *baojia*—and get the whole group into trouble. Thus lineage organization had become entangled with two of the chief structures of imperial control below the level of the county—the community pact and the *baojia* mutual security system. Another regulation forbade a lineage member from bringing lawsuits against other members of the lineage to the magistrate. He was required to submit first to the adjudication of the lineage elders, who according to the instructions had the power to make determinations and even impose punishments. If the guilty party did not submit, the lineage elders would then themselves bring a complaint to the local official, presumably greatly strengthening the case of the claimant. The stated aim of this regulation was to reduce the number of lawsuits, which "if major lead to bankruptcy and waste money, and even if minor bring trouble and shame to the kinfolk." William Rowe ("Ancestral Rites," 387–97) has shown that in the mid-eighteenth century Chen Hongmou tried to promote lineage judicial authority by empowering ancestral hall elders as a kind of judicial body below the formal mechanism of the magistrate's court. But the Huang injunctions make no reference to official sanction of the authority of the hall managers. Another regulation prohibits wives from bringing disputes to the attention of the ancestral hall. Husbands and sons of women who were so bold as to ignore this regulation were to be punished severely. So too were those accused of lacking filial

piety. Thus the lineage regulations also bolstered the patriarchal household. Other regulations address more directly and attempt to reverse what the author considered to be the negative changes affecting local society. There are prohibitions against drinking and gambling and a call for the literati to be respected, for "the scholars are at the head of the four classes of people." The third regulation, "encourage harmony," suggests Yuanbin's concern that the whole local social order was deteriorating due to greed and selfishness, with traditional restraints collapsing. A major cause was the rising frequency of transfers of land ownership. The final regulation illustrates that when the breakdown in the social order grew too serious, the ultimate recourse was violence. It was strictly forbidden to beat the large drum located in the ancestral hall without just cause. There is no explanation of this regulation in the text, but elderly villagers in Yixu know instantly to what this refers. It was a call to arms for the men of the lineage, to be used only when violent feuding broke out. Huang Yuanbin, "Jiamiao shigui," in *Huqiu Yishan Huangshi shipu*, 1:20b–21b.

91. Another case had to do with Golden Carp (*Jinli*) hill, which also had great geomantic significance. Foolish villagers had established private orchards on the hill and, when disputes broke out, built walls on it to strengthen their claims, "which made it impossible for the fish to flourish." On one slope of the hill, sojourners had constructed tombs. This too harmed the geomantic properties of the hill. Further construction and the felling of trees were therefore prohibited. Huang Fuji, "Shanchuan fengshui zhi," in ibid., 1:26a–b.

92. On settlement rights, see Faure, *Structure of Chinese Rural Society*, chap. 3.

93. Among the halls now found in Nantai for which the date of construction can be verified with documentary evidence, a few examples suffice to demonstrate the spread of halls in this period. The Chengmen Lin hall, according to a reconstruction tablet dated 1885, was first constructed three hundred years previously. A modern reconstruction tablet does claim that the hall was first built in 1380, destroyed by pirates in 1535, and rebuilt in 1583, but as the Chengmen Lin were not a lineage of particular note in the Ming, it seems more likely that what was destroyed in 1535 was an ancestral home in which sacrifice was performed rather than the imposing free-standing hall built in 1583 and rebuilt in 1885. The Zheng of Huangshan converted a monastery into an ancestral hall in the Wanli period. Another hall on Nantai that dates from the early Qing is that of the Yan of Yangqi, to whom belonged the late Qing author and translator Yan Fu, first built in 1691. Untitled Inscription (1885); "Chongjian houlou Linshi zongci zhujuan timing ji," Inscription; "Fengtang guji," in *Daicaotang Fengshan Zhengshi zupu*; and "Chongjian Yanshi zongci beiji," Inscription.

94. The most numerous surnames on the island in the early to mid-Ming were the Wu and the Lin. The Lin claim as their founding ancestor Lin Wenmao, a native of Putian, who is said to have retired to Luozhou, his wife's native village, from a minor official post in Guangdong in 1195. Lin Wenmao appears in the lists of founding ancestors in the late Qing county gazetteer, but, of course, this information may well have been provided to the compilers by the Lin themselves. The construction of Luozhou's first ancestral hall by the Wu must have cemented

their position as the town's first family. *Minxian xiangtuzhi*, 231b; and *Mindu ji*, 14:13b.

95. After his examination success, Hua had an undistinguished career as instructor in a Confucian school in a northern county. Lin Han, the most prominent native of Fuzhou in the early sixteenth century, wrote a brief approving biography, which notes Hua's commitment to scholarship and makes no mention whatsoever of his origins or family—unusual in a Ming biography but hardly surprising if Hua's immediate ancestors had been Dan boat people. A painting of Chen Hua's great grandson Huai that still hangs in the Luozhou Chen ancestral hall shows a thin, pale man with distinguished whiskers and a serious demeanor. Huai cannot have spent long in office, for he enjoyed a retirement of forty-three years before dying at the age of ninety-three. Lin Han, "Chen Xiaolian shuming xiansheng zhuan" (1513), and Zheng Renda, "Luojiang Chen xiansheng zhuan," in *Luojiang Chenshi jiapu*, zhuan: 1a–b, 2a–b.

96. The identity of this ancestor, who according to the oral tradition of the village was Chen Youliang, was discussed in Chapter 2.

97. The inscription has been copied into the front section of *Luojiang Chenshi jiapu*.

98. Cohen, "Lineage Organization in North China," 511–12. See also Freedman, *Lineage Organization*, chap. 6.

99. Here was the tension between the personal and the lineage dimensions of kinship in stark form. The executors of the estate, for it was probably they rather than the man himself who made the real decision about the estate's disposition, had to make a choice between using the estate as a lure to attract an adoptive heir—thereby ensuring the continuity of sacrifices at a household altar—and using the estate to build a common fund that would benefit all, for all would have a share in the income from the estate and its existence would heighten the prestige of all. Whatever the deceased himself may have wanted, the latter option was chosen.

100. By the nineteenth century, the income from the estate that remained was only sufficient to pay for the collective annual feast for all of the descendants. This annual feast was said to have been held continuously for three hundred years. ("Yunde gong jichan yuanshi ji qi guanli shuolue" in *Luojiang Chenshi jiapu*). Older villagers still remember this feast being held before 1949.

101. Chen Yide, "Benzong jiamiao jiujin goudi ji" in *Luojiang Chenshi jiapu*. Unfortunately, the genealogy does not include biographies for any of the twenty-four. However, we know more about several other activists in lineage formation. One was Chen Jiangong, the son of one of the twenty-four contributors and the last man to be buried at the cemetery at Gaogai. He was known as a philanthropist, and his biography in the genealogy praises him for all manner of meritorious behavior. He assisted the poor, forgave the debts of his tenants, looked after his kin, donated sacrificial land, and established a free ferry. Jiangong himself held no official position, nor did any of his immediate ancestors. He was probably a prosperous merchant looking for ways to climb the social ladder through culturally appropriate expenditures on charity and social welfare. All seven of Jiangong's sons were county students

at a time when competition for advancement was increasing. In the early eighteenth century, certain members of the educated elite from the upriver county of Minqing visited Fuzhou in connection with the repair of the county school and temple to Confucius. They contacted Jiangong and promised in return for a donation of two hundred taels to arrange registration for his sons in Minqing, where presumably the competition for places in the county school was less than in the Chen's home county of Minxian. Thus Jiangong's son Gaishan was registered as a military student of Minqing in 1720, and three years later he passed the provincial military examination. A similar figure from the same period was Tongxuan, who moved from Luozhou to the city. "Although his ancestors left him no property to inherit, through careful management and accumulation his became a family of tremendous wealth." His biography also speaks approvingly of his decision to divide the household estate evenly with his elder brother, including the "great capital he had accumulated over the course of several dozen years." Tongxuan's wealth no doubt came from trade and moneylending, for the genealogy also relates an anecdote concerning a storm that arose while he was returning by ship along the coast from Suzhou and praises his habit of burning the mortgage deeds of those who fell indebted to him. While in Fuzhou, Tongxuan became renowned for his acts of charity to his relatives. "He was particularly virtuous when it came to aiding and encouraging warm feelings among his relatives and associates. Whenever there were weddings and funerals, he made a point of providing assistance diligently." (ibid., *zhuan*: 39a; and *zhuan*: 50a–b.) Biographies of men like Jiangong and Tongxuan only rarely found their way into the gazetteers, even the local ones. But the details of their lives recorded in the genealogies reveal them as the real lineage builders of the time.

102. The final appearance of the hall after all of these efforts is described in detail in the following passage:

> The site of the shrine is over sixty *zhang* deep and thirty wide. The layout of the shrine consists of three halls flanked by two wings. In front of the hall is the main chamber and the east and west side-rooms. In front are the gates for the rites. There are three gates; one enters and exits through those on the right and left. Beyond the gate is the front courtyard and the east and west verandas and stalls. Continuing on, there is the main gate . . . which extends to the road. Behind the hall are two stalls used for cooking and cleaning for the sacrifice. Beyond the [rear] wall is the garden, which takes up half the remaining space. The garden is planted with fruit trees of various kinds. The income from the annual harvest is used to meet unexpected expenses of the hall. From front to back it is surrounded by an encircling wall. Although much time elapsed until the hall was finally completed, the shrine's atmosphere is dignified; the scope is expansive; the eaves and rafters are impressive; the ancestors are commemorated as if they were present. This will bestow limitless good fortune on the descendants.
>
> Chen Yide, "Benzong jiamiao jiujin goudi ji" in ibid.

103. This project was described in Chapter 2.

104. Chen Fangkai, "Qianlong guimu (1763) xinxiu jiapu xu," in *Luojiang Chenshi jiapu*, 1:1b.

105. See Esherick and Rankin for a useful exploration of the connections between these different types of elite.

106. This not only accorded with Zhu Xi's prescriptions but, as Doolittle noted, was the result of practical concerns about space. "After the third or fifth generation has passed away, the tablets which represent it are sometimes taken away and buried in or near the graves of the persons they represent, or they may be burned to ashes; at least they must be removed from the niche, to furnish room for the tablets representing the individuals of a less remote period." Doolittle, *Social Life of the Chinese*, 1:222–23.

107. Ibid., 1:226.

108. Nor is there a complete list of the tablets that were found in the hall before its destruction during the Cultural Revolution, a problem that troubled the committee in charge of reconstructing the hall in the 1990s. Such a list might have permitted the reconstruction of the criteria by inference. In the end, the reconstruction committee gave up on the idea of reinstalling all the tablets that had once stood in the hall and established a single criterion for the installation of new ones. Any member of the lineage who wished to was able to install a new tablet on payment of a fee, and several hundred did so, but those in charge of the project recognized that this was not in accord with the original practice of the lineage.

109. According to the Great Surnames section of the Qing gazetteer of Minxian, "in the beginning of the dynasty, [the Ye] moved from Fuqing to this locale. In the Qianlong period [there was] Guanguo, whose descendants were numerous and now extend to eight or nine generations." Guanguo, great-grandson of the founding ancestor in Fuzhou, was the compiler of the first edition of their genealogy, which appeared in 1791. His preface traces the early history of his ancestors, according to a pattern that will by now be familiar. Originally a native of Gushi in Henan, one of them followed Wang Shenzhi to Fujian and settled near modern Xiamen. "The generations are distant and the place is far away, so the generational order is not known in detail." In the twelfth century, an ancestor moved from southern Fujian to Fuqing. Guanguo identifies this individual as his lineage's "founding ancestor." *Minxian xiangtuzhi*, 239a; Ye Guanguo, "Yuan xu" (1791), in *Sanshan Yeshi sishi lu*, 1:1a.

110. Shenjie, one of Guanguo's twenty-five grandsons, was a major book collector with a reputation for charitable works. Shenjie's son Yichang (*juren* 1828) is said to have inherited several thousand *mu* of land. Because the land was mostly of poor quality, his tenants were always falling into his debt. Recognizing their inability to pay, he burned the records of their loans. He also set up a charitable graveyard where several hundred of the poor were buried. *Minhou xianzhi*, 68:3b–6b.

111. "Rusi tiaoli," in *Sanshan Yeshi sishi lu*, 4:4a. The identical wording appears in several other nineteenth-century genealogies from Fuzhou, which suggests either that the same author was employed by different lineages to assist in the compilation of their genealogy or, more likely, that authors of genealogies in the late nineteenth

century used locally available styleguides or other formal or informal models. See, for example, "Jinzhu tiaoli," in *Pingyang Chenshi zupu, jiaju*: 1a.

112. "Rusi tiaoli," in *Sanshan Yeshi sishi lu*, 4:4a–b.

113. See, for example, "Jinzhu tiaoli," in *Pingyang Chenshi zupu, jiaju*: 1a; and "Jintang Wangshi zhici guizhi," in *Jintang Wangshi zhipu*, j.2. As it so often seems, Doolittle again turns out to be a highly accurate observer of custom in Fuzhou: "Some require that a large sum of money shall be paid into the funds of the hall for the privilege of entering a tablet, or that all those who become graduates of the second literary degree, or officers of the government above a certain rank, may have their tablet placed in it gratis, etc." Doolittle, *Social Life of the Chinese*, 1:226.

114. Thus, reported Chen Shengshao, a nineteenth-century magistrate:

> The gentry and common people of Jianyang all have rotating rental income for sacrifice. Members of great descent-line branches have the right to collect the rent once every five or six years; for lesser descent-line branches, the right to collect rents rotates through fifty or sixty years. Whoever's turn it is in the rotation to collect the rent is responsible for paying the tax, for repairs to the ancestral hall, for the supply of sacrificial items to be sacrificed to the ancestors in spring and autumn, and the sacrificial meat which is divided [and distributed]. If there is any left over, it belongs to the rota holder.
>
> Chen Shengshao, 60.

115. "Zhici tiaogui," in *Sanshan Yeshi sishi lu*, 4:1 a–b. Lin Yaohua provides some details on the management of their ancestral hall in the early twentieth century. He lists the names, ages, and qualifications of the forty-three members of the hall management committee. The average age of the members was just under sixty. Fifteen of the members held the position on the basis of their status as heads of individual branches. A second criterion for officeholding was education or official position. Two of the members were holders of minor Qing degrees, one had been an administrative clerk, another four had graduated from modern educational establishments, and one was a returned overseas student. Four members were described as "Confucian scholars" (*ru*). Most of the remaining positions were held on the basis of wealth and property ownership. There are eleven members described as "wealthy merchants," landlords, or both. Of this number, one was a moneyshop owner, one was a salt merchant, one was a lumber merchant, and one was described as chairman of the Commercial Discussion Society (probably a village Chamber of Commerce). Two managers of distilleries, a wealthy farmer, and a landlord round out the list. The remaining member is described as a wealthy farmer (*funong*); he held office by virtue of his brother's position as a naval officer. Lin points out that this is an informal rather than a formal list, but that real authority over lineage affairs was indeed vested in this group. Obviously the management of the hall was not the same in the early twentieth century as it had been when the hall was first built in the early eighteenth century, but the general principles by which the management was selected may not have been entirely different. Lin Yaohua, 46 n.11.

116. This was inevitably a challenge to neo-Confucian ideas, a challenge that Yu Yingshi argues created the possibility for more permissive and tolerant visions of social relations. Yu Yingshi, 161–66.

117. Chen Kangxu, "Yaqian Chenshi zongci ji" (1714), in *Langshan Yaqian Chenshi zongpu*, 28–29.

118. This may mean that the purchase of the land by Jiufeng's kin had never been registered with the authorities.

119. Chen Kangxu, "Yaqian Chenshi zhici ji" (1714), in *Langshan Yaqian Chenshi zongpu*, 29–30.

120. See, for example, Untitled Inscription (1885) and "Chongjian houlou Linshi zongci zhujuan timing ji," Inscription, both in the Chengmen Lin ancestral hall; and *Dayi xiangzhi*, 1:9a–b.

121. An anonymous diarist records that in this period:

> There were two brothers whose family was rich and had much land. After some years, because of military disturbances everywhere, their land yielded no income but their tax obligations were heavy. One day the younger brother died. His wife wanted to remarry. The elder brother explained "That is for you to decide, but you must take two thousand taels worth of land with you. Otherwise, I will not allow the marriage."
>
> Haiwai sanren, 25.

122. There are several examples in the history of the Huang of Yixu. The tombs of two ancestors on Gaogai hill were surrounded by lychee orchards. "Later, because of unrest, the plot became wasteland and declined in value. The trees were cut down, and the land sold off illegally by the grave tenants to the Yang of Xiadu to construct tombs." In another case, a substantial estate of one hundred *mu* was abandoned because of tax obligations. "In the early Qing, taxes were heavy and rice cheap, so this land was not particularly valuable. It was also quite far away. It was agreed to have son-in-law Jiang Peishu control the land. Lineage members saw it as public property, so no one was willing to exert himself [to recover it]. [Now], there is no way to be sure of the names of the tenants or the identification of the property." Huang Fuji, "Fenshan zhi," in *Huqiu Yishan Huangshi shipu*, 1:25 b.

123. Yang Zhou, "Huyu Yangshi citang ji," in *Minyi Huyu Yangshi Tingqifang pudie*, 29a–30a.

124. Ren Jingshi *et al.* "Fanxi ji" (1637), in *Junshan Renshi zupu*, 2:126a.

125. Qin Huitian, 115:27a–29b.

126. Zuo Yunpeng, 5–6, 103; Makino, "Sōshi to sono hattatsu," 193; Ebrey, *Confucianism and Family Rituals*, 152; and Zheng Zhenman, *Ming–Qing Fujian jiazu zuzhi*, 228–29. Chow (108) calls the memorial "a plea for official recognition of existing practices," but does not explicitly address the issue of whether the plea was accepted.

CHAPTER 5

1. For simplicity's sake, I use the term *beimang* throughout, as the most common term used by the villagers to describe this ritual. The term *banye*, which means to lay out [offerings] at night, is also used at times. These vernacular terms are represented in writing with a number of different terms, including *baiye, banye, paibu, paimang,* and *paizhu.* See Szonyi, "Village Rituals," 85 n.10.

2. The genealogy is kept in the home of a member of the lineage who was born in 1906 and is a twelfth-generation descendant of the founding ancestor.

3. The performance of this ritual by the Shanggan Lin is described in a history of the lineage written over a period of several decades by a local Daoist priest:

> In past times in Shanggan, beginning on the twelfth day of the first month, the Lin surname performed *beimang* on successive days, each branch in order according to seniority from first to last. This illustrated how each branch had multiplied and passed through the generations, how it had declined and flourished, grown poor or rich, strong or weak. Because conditions are now poor, it has been decided that [the ritual] will only last one night. Each year on this day, lamps, peace [eggs], longevity [noodles] and other things are prepared. A representative from each branch enters the hall, lights candles, burns incense and sets off firecrackers for the ancestors in order to express sentiments. This is done every year in order to express *beimang.* When conditions are right, on this day we will really be able to cook the communal meal and stage operas and so forth. . . . Each branch will distribute [sacrificial] meat and candles, etc. This will depend on how much sacrificial property there is. Those who have moved away and settled in other areas should every year on this night all willingly return, to assemble with the agnates and sacrifice to the ancestors to demonstrate their filial hearts. After dinner, the branch [members] enter the hall according to seniority. Each adult male from each household takes his proper place. They light candles, burn incense and facing the ancestors demonstrate their filiality. Afterwards, each takes a candle in order and exits the hall. Lighting firecrackers on the way, each returns to his home and taking the candle places it in front of the ancestral tablets (*gongpo*). [The term suggests parents, but in Fuzhou and other Fujian dialects refers to ancestral tablets.] Those from other villages may ask to go back to the tablet room [in the home of the founding ancestor of] their particular sector (*jie*), or go back to the sector's neighbourhood.
>
> (Lin Yidong, 20b–21a.)

Lin was unwilling to be interviewed, but I was able to observe performance of this ritual in Shanggan in 1993. On sectors in Shanggan, see below, n.60.

4. See Bell, 76. James Hevia has criticized Orientalist scholarship on Chinese ritual for adopting a sociological approach that treats ritual as a "typical feature of archaic or premodern societies" and thus indicates "an absence of fully conscious rationality." Hevia also objects to the functional–instrumental analysis of ritual in this literature, which depends, he argues, on a claim to "knowledge . . . superior to

that of historical Chinese subjects." (Hevia, 19–20.) Hevia's dissatisfaction with an assumed dichotomy between ritual and rationality as essential characteristics of traditional and modern societies, respectively, is well founded, and his theories of ritual as strategic practice, adapted from Catherine Bell, inform this chapter. But his criticism of instrumental treatments of ritual may be overstated. The genealogical and gazetteer evidence shows that the people of Fuzhou were well aware of the instrumentality of ritual, and indeed this awareness was fundamental to their strategic use of ritual; to probe the workings of that instrumentality involves no claim to knowledge superior to that of the people of Fuzhou who created and participated in these rituals.

5. For example, gazetteers, which have long included descriptions of annual festivals, typically stress the distant origins of the names and dates of specific events, linking ancient texts to contemporary life and identifying practices that were shared by Chinese everywhere. In the very first phrases of his account of Fuzhou's festivals, the author of the twelfth-century gazetteer articulates his intention to record local distinctiveness in the context of conformity to universal cultural patterns. "Calendrical observances have existed since antiquity. It is not possible that the customs in the four quadrants should be without differences." According to Susan Naquin, "the annual calendar genre cannot be taken even remotely as a kind of anthropological account derived from fieldwork. It is not simply that the authors have selected and omitted and tailored their facts to suit their audiences and their ideals. It is that the genre itself smooths out differences, veils omissions, stresses what is shared, masks change, denies development, and encourages the conflation of past and present." *Sanshan zhi*, 40:1a; Naquin, "Annual Festivals," 873.

6. *Sanshan zhi*, 40:1a–2a. As noted in the previous chapter, the domestic sacrifice was not the most elaborate ritual of ancestral sacrifice; this took place at the graves at the Cold Food festival.

7. The gazetteer continues that on the second and third day of the year, "the prominent families and large surnames lead the young and the old to worship at the tombs." (*Bamin tongzhi*, 3:40.) Visits to tombs are also described in an account of Fuzhou from about a hundred years later. "The custom in Fujian is to attach great importance to the New Year. The people do not open their main doors until after the festival of celebration, when they all go together to worship at the tombs." *Minbu shu*, 6a–7a.

8. A Tang emperor is recorded as having left the palace accompanied by a large entourage of women to watch lanterns in the year 710 (Liu Xu, 7:149). Nakamura Takashi has identified two alternative explanations for the origins of the Lantern Festival that were current in the Song. One traced the festival back to Han era sacrifices that Wolfram Eberhard links to fertility. The other located the origins of the festival in the introduction of Buddhism to China. (See Nakamura, *Chūgoku no nenchū gyōji*, 33–36, and *Chūgoku saishishi*; and Eberhard, *Chinese Festivals*, 64–65.) In the Daoist tradition, the fifteenth day of the first month is devoted to the celebration of the first of the Sanyuan, or Three Origins. The Sanyuan are primordial forces, the three supreme gods of the body, "personified forces of the cosmos who govern its

various spheres." Fifth century texts in the Daoist canon explain the idea of the Three Origins; Tang scriptures provide a basis for thrice annual celebration of them, and Song liturgical texts describe how these rituals were actually carried out. *Taishang dongxuan lingbao sanyuan pinjie gongde qingzhong jing*; Du Guangting; and Teiser, 37.

9. *Sanshan zhi*, 40:3b–4a. A Song gazetteer of Quanzhou, apparently no longer extant, also explains the elaborate celebration of the Lantern Festival as originating with the officialdom. "At the New Year there is the ceremony of congratulations. The officials dwelling in the localities arrange to gather and greet one another. In order to reduce the inconvenience of coming and going, the two prefectural officials ordered all their subordinates to assemble [at the prefecture]." (Cited in *Min shu*, 38:948.) This passage was copied into a nineteenth-century account of Fuzhou festivals, the *Rongcheng suishi ji* (Dai Chengfen, 2a), with no mention of Quanzhou. Obviously the editor of this work thought it applicable to Fuzhou as well as Quanzhou.

10. The poem reads: "The rich family's single lantern is [to them] no more than a grain to the imperial granary/The poor family's single lantern, however, is what father and son come together to weep over/Does our lavish prefect know about this? I am only sorry that my song lacks a fine tune." (*Sanshan zhi*, 40:4a.) See also *Fuzhou fuzhi* (1520), 1:19a, for a more thorough examination of the date of this incident.

11. *Fuqing xianzhi*, 1:2b. Xie Zhaozhe thought Fujian, particularly Fuzhou and Putian to the south, had the most elaborate celebration of the Lantern Festival anywhere:

There is nowhere under heaven where the celebration of First Origin with lamps and candles is as elaborate as in central Fujian. Beginning on the eleventh day of the first month, there are already people hanging out lanterns. By the thirteenth, every household is lit with lanterns, as bright as daylight. In the households of the rich, there are lamps in every [chamber], numbering in the thousands. The main doors are opened and people amuse themselves. In the city streets, every household hangs two lanterns. Groups of ten families construct a lantern shed. . . . The celebration only ends on the twenty-second. So while in the rest of the empire, [the Lantern Festival only lasts] five nights, in central Fujian it lasts ten.

Xie Zhaozhe, 2:3b–4a.

12. *Fuzhou fuzhi* (1520) 1:19b.

13. Xie Zhaozhe, 2:4a.

14. *Minbu shu*, 7a. For other Ming descriptions of the festival in Fuzhou, see *Fuzhou fuzhi* (1596) 4:3a; and *Fuzhou fuzhi* (1613), 7:3a.

15. Brook, "Funerary Ritual," 474–80; and Ebrey, *Confucianism and Family Rituals*, chap. 4.

16. *Taojiang Linshi zupu*, 2:3a–4b.

17. For example, according to the genealogy of the Ren of Junshan, in 1601, lineage members gathered in the home of one of them to perform this ritual. It was after the ritual took place that a number of lineage members first discussed

the construction of the ancestral hall, beginning a process whose culmination was explored in the previous chapter. Ren Jingshi *et al.* "Fanxi ji" (1637), in *Junshan Renshi zupu*, 2:126a.

18. "Difang Wenyuan gong biji" (1559), in *Fuzhou Guoshi zhipu*, 10:4a.

19. Guo Bocang, "Fuzhou Guoshi diliuci xinshou zhipu xu," in ibid., 1:22a.

20. Others fled to Yong'an, Gutian, Putian, Xianyou, and even Nanjing. Ibid., 2:14a ff.

21. "Qing Shidun gong ji," in ibid., 10:7a–b. One of the refugees wrote

> In 1558, the chief pirates attacked the interior. The brothers in my uncle's generation all moved one after the other to the provincial capital. Only Dayou, Lu and Qian remained to look after the old place. When these three gentlemen died, the houses started to fall into ruin. They were lent out to other people to occupy, and the planks, doors and windows were completely destroyed. . . . So I sighed and said: "If there is not a major change in the situation, there can be no major renewal. The estates of the brothers have all been moved to the provincial capital. The wood from the ancestral home is being stolen by robbers. Conflicts arise frequently, and there is the expense of going back and forth. It would be better to give up the old to start anew." So my younger brother Ruiwo and I decided to sell off the wood and bricks. In all we obtained less than six taels.
>
> "Ming Tianfang Zhike gong liu ji," in ibid., 10:5b–6a.

22. Zhike took note of the compromise in the conclusion to his discussion of the invention of the new ritual. Of Madame Zheng, he wrote,

> Bravo, how virtuous! With one word she turned back wild madness. Would that the handsome men of the lineage be as vigorous as our Auntie in promoting the reputation of the lineage. How can adjusting rules be considered? But the ritual of bowing in a circle actually rescues the bad [and converts them to] good. These rules certainly cannot be abandoned. So this preface has been recorded. It will endure the passage of numerous generations. . . . Those who attend and conduct the ritual will observe the depth and extent of the provisions made by previous generations for ten thousand generations.
>
> "Ming Tianfang Zhike gong yixing tuanbai li," in ibid., 7:4a–5b.

23. As Hobsbawm noted, traditions have probably been invented in every time and place in history, but "we should expect it to occur more frequently when a rapid transformation of society weakens or destroys the social patterns for which 'old' traditions had been designed . . . or when such old traditions and their institutional carriers and promulgators no longer prove sufficiently adaptable and flexible, or are otherwise eliminated." Hobsbawm, 4–5.

24. "Qing Tianfang liyusheyushushu liufang gongzhi sichan yuezi," in *Fuzhou Guoshi zhipu*, 7:6a–7a.

25. "Ming Tianfang Zhike gong yixing tuanbai li," in ibid., 7:4a–5b.

26. "Qing Tianfang liyuesheyushushu liufang gongzhi sichan yuezi," in ibid., 7:6a–7a.

27. Cohen, "Lineage Organization in North China," 521.

28. See Ebrey, trans., *Chu Hsi's Family Rituals*, 17.

29. By the late Ming, the sacrifices at the ancestral graves at the Cold Food Festival, which in the Song had been the most important rites of ancestral sacrifice in the ritual year, had been displaced by the *beimang* rituals in the ancestral hall at the Lantern Festival. Xie Zhaozhe disapproved of this change, writing that "people of the south use the [Cold Food] sacrifice as an excuse to visit the countryside for amusement. Even before paper money has been burned, shoes are already [removed for feasting] in disarray and everybody gets drunk. . . . It is disgraceful." Xie Zhaozhe, 2:9a–b.

30. The ritual of bowing in a circle seems to have been unique to the New Year celebration. Visits to the ancestral hall are mentioned in connection with another seasonal festival, the winter solstice, for which the entry reads: "this is similar to the ritual at New Year's, except that there is no bowing in a circle." *Bamin tongzhi*, 3:50–51.

31. *Fuqing xianzhi*, 1:2b.

32. "Tiaoyue," in *Shimei Wushi zupu*.

33. The lists of items to be prepared by the ten managers are detailed and complex. The first manager, for example, is required to provide "one lamp to hang in the middle of the front passageway, one length of silk to hang over the door of the inner chamber, and all of the containers for noodles and the handkerchiefs." Yingyang Sanxi Panshi zupu, 5:73.

34. The sacrificial text reads:

We remember that our ancestor was born in Nan'an. He moved to and settled north of Sanxi, facing the hills and overlooking the water. His high office was glorious. Because of two adversities, he moved his abode. In four lines, his descendants have continued. Adorned by the headdress of official position, generation after generation they maintain their literary tradition. The descendants have grown numerous; the source is far away and the river is long [i.e., the lineage is flourishing]. The requiting of the favour of the ancestor must not be forgotten. Now is the time when we [offer] this poor sacrifice of platters and goblets. May his spirit in heaven descend upon this shrine, protect us and shelter us, [bestowing] prosperity, longevity and health, as the dragon rises and the phoenix emerges, spreading our literary reputation far and wide. What the descendants celebrate is the glory of their ancestors. We hereby make this offering.

ibid., 5:13.

35. "Cimu guiding," in *Langshan Yaqian Chenshi zongpu*, 50.

36. Doolittle, *Social Life of the Chinese*, 1:228–29. Doolittle does not provide the Chinese term for "worship in a circle," but presumably it is *tuanbai*.

37. These are the rituals to which the "Record of the Ritual Calendar" in the lineage's genealogy devotes the greatest amount of text. The Record describes four

major calendrical rites. The entries for sacrifices at the Winter Solstice and Middle Origin consist only of the sacrificial text to be read, and the entry for grave sacrifices at Qingming consists of the ritual text and one line of instructions. The entry for the Lantern Festival consists of the sacrificial text and eight lines of instructions. "Jidian zhi," and "Dongshi zongci . . . " in *Langqi Dongshi pudie*.

38. Elderly villagers explain that the job of the *zuzheng* was to determine which branch had raised the fattest pig, as this would be a sign of good fortune in the year to come. In 1757, the Qianlong emperor ordered that *zuzheng* be selected for every lineage to investigate and report on the conduct of lineage members. But the connection here is not clear; *zuzheng* in Langqi seems to be a local term for ancestral hall manager. It is not widely used in Fuzhou. *Da Qing huidian shili*, 158:4b; and Hsiao, 349.

39. "Jidian zhi," and "Dongshi zongci . . . " in *Langqi Dongshi pudie*.

40. "Cimu guiding," in *Langshan Yaqian Chenshi zongpu*, 54a ff.; Ebrey, trans., *Chu Hsi's Family Rituals*, 155–66.

41. Doolittle, *Social Life of the Chinese*, 1:228–29.

42. The 1887 genealogy of the Ye of Sanshan contains one such text, for the *tuanbai* ritual. ("Yuanxiao tuanbai zhidan," in *Sanshan Yeshi sishi lu*, 4:12a.) The development of texts such as these was part of a larger phenomenon in mid-Qing China. Ritual codification, including the search for ritual origins, the study of past practices, and the preparation of authoritative ritual texts was an important part of many aspects of intellectual practice in the eighteenth century. The great imperially sponsored ritual compendia such as the *DaQing tongli* represent this trend at the highest levels, signs of a general project to "establish and promote proper ritual to restore order to a world perceived as increasingly guided by vulgar and heterodox customs." The same project also shaped lineage practice in the humble villages of the Fuzhou region in the Qing. See Esherick, 149, and Zito, 69–78.

43. Her tradition has been described as a "local particularism, founded on an ancient shamanistic tradition, supplemented across the ages, and especially since the Song, by borrowing from other traditions, leaving its origin uncertain." (Baptandier-Berthier, "Kaiguan Ritual," 533.) Since the earliest sources on the cult date from some centuries after the time when it was reputedly founded, reconstruction of the history of the cult and its influence is a difficult task, requiring the use of a wide range of sources including gazetteers, popular fiction, local scriptures, and theatrical scripts. The most comprehensive study of her cult is Berthier, *La Dame-du-bord-de-l'eau*. Fujian scholar Ye Mingsheng has published two extensive collections of ritual texts and ethnographic description of the cult in modern-day northwestern Fujian, *Minxi Shanghang Gaoqiang kuilei yu furen xi* and *Lüshan jiao guangjitan keyiben*. Song sources on the cult are limited. In the *Sanshan zhi*, there is only a vague reference to a temple to the Maiden (*guniang*), who may be Chen Jinggu (*Sanshan zhi*, 8:24a). The dearth of material may well be explained not because the cult was not yet important locally, but rather because it had not yet received the sanction of local Daoists. In his discussion of the various schools of Daoism that flourished in Fujian in the Song, the Daoist master Bai Yuchan (fl. 1200–1224) criticized the Lüshan tradition

as heterodox and shamanistic. "In the past, the methods of sorcery included the school of Bangu, the school of Lingshan and also the school of Lüshan. In fact these are all ways of sorcerers." (Bai Yuchan, 1.) As with so many other local traditions of southern China, Daoist masters gradually made peace with the Lüshan tradition, part of the ongoing process of channeling what van der Loon labels China's "shamanistic substratum." By the late imperial period, Daoist scriptures and liturgies had been composed for the tradition and the cult of Chen Jinggu, though none are found in the *Daozang*. The cult does appear in the Canon, though, in a hagiography of Chen Jinggu in the *Sanjiao yuanliu soushen daquan*, a Ming version of the *Soushen ji*. See Dean, *Taoist Ritual*, 30–32.

44. Some sources describe her as living in the tenth century, at the time of the kingdom of Min, with which several of her legends are associated. (See Baptandier-Berthier, "Kaiguan Ritual," 530.) On the snake demon story cycle, see, for example, *Gutian xianzhi*, 7:8a–b. Since the snake was the object of a cult by native groups prior to the Han incursion into Fujian, this raises the interesting possibility that the legends of the cult are also an expression of the subordination and integration of local peoples as Han power in the region grew. Her titles are described in "Gutian xian Linshui Shunyi miao ji," in Zhang Yining, 4:48b–50a.

45. On the story of the aborted fetus, see *Bamin tongzhi*, 58:373–74; and *Gutian xianzhi*, 5:12b. The Tang legend is found at *Sanjiao yuanliu soushen daquan*, 183–84, the dating of which is discussed in Dudbridge, 109n.105, and ter Haar, "Genesis and Spread," 359 n.25. Xu Xiaowang questions the veracity of this legend, since the cult is not mentioned in the *Sanshan zhi* written two centuries later (*Fujian minjian xinyang*, 348.) Also see Xie Zhaozhe, 15:19b–20a. A Ming source from Jianning county describes her rescue of women suffering from difficulties in pregnancy:

> Xu Qingsou was from Pucheng. His daughter-in-law was pregnant for
> seventeen months without delivering. Suddenly a women came to the door. She
> said she was named Chen and was a specialist in obstetrics. Xu happily retained
> her, and explained the situation. She said: "This is an easy matter." She ordered
> the construction of an elevated structure, with a cave-like chamber in the centre.
> She put the pregnant woman in the structure. She also ordered that several
> servants should hold sticks and await below. If anything fell to the ground, they
> should beat it to death. Then [the woman] gave birth to a small snake.... It
> found a hole and went down. The group of servants beat it to death.

While the woman refused the gifts offered by the family, she did accept a piece of cloth on which she asked Xu to write the message: "Bestowed by Xu to Chen who protects in childbirth." Sure enough, Xu later become prefect of Fuzhou, and discovered the banner already hanging at her temple. So he requested titles for her and paid for the temple's enlargement. From *Jianning fuzhi*, 21:20, cited in Xu Xiaowang, *Fujian minjian xinyang*, 346.

46. *Mindu ji*, 10:12a ff.; Doolittle, *Social Life of the Chinese*, 1:204–5.

47. For example, the Ming hagiography mentioned earlier explains the miraculous circumstances of her conception through the intervention of Guanyin. The snake demon that many legends describe Chen Jinggu as slaying received a cult from the people of Gutian, who sacrificed two young people each year to assuage the appetite of the demon. Guanyin impregnated Chen's mother with her own essence, and the mother gave birth to Jinggu on the fifteenth day of the first month. (*Sanjiao yuanliu soushen daquan*, 183.) Other sources that mention this date include the Qing novel *Mindu bieji*, much of which is devoted to tales of the goddess, and a ritual song sung by mediums in the Fuzhou area in the early twentieth century. Liren Heqiu; and Wei Yingqi, 41.

48. *Fuqing xianzhi*, 1:2b.

49. Xie Zhaozhe, 2:3b–4a.

50. Lin Zhichun, "Puli shizi," in *Lianjiang Linshi jiapu*, 1:10a. Several lineage members are said to have taken particular interest in communal ritual. Lin Jinghu "led the lineage members in the performance of ritual. All entered the shrine with reverence, and none dared to play games." Lin Huipu contributed extra whenever there was a shortfall in the funds contributed by lineage members for rituals. Ibid., 2:42a, 45a.

51. In the past, the parade from neighborhood to neighborhood followed a fixed route and was conducted entirely by the women of the village, all of whom belonged to the Society of the Mother (*niangniang she*), that was divided into residential segments. When the festival was revived in the mid-1980s, those most active in the cult drew lots to determine a new parade order. Since so many groups now wish to participate, the procession now lasts for two full months, ending on the third day of the third month with a spectacular parade around the village. Many new elements have been added to the parade, including groups of thirty-six women who dress up as the goddess' assistants, each carrying a doll to indicate her connection with childbirth and fertility, and much theater outside the temple.

52. The temple of the village tutelary deity was rebuilt in 1920, and a number of beam inscriptions commemorating donations are of the form "Follower So-and-so, of the X Branch." Residents of Taiyu with the Chen surname all belong to one of five branches (*fang*), though the genealogical relationship between the branches in unclear.

53. What they do have is a number of handwritten descent-line charts that are called "genealogies of the generations [descended from the ancestors buried in] tombs" (*mudai pu*) and that are brought to the ancestral hall at the time of sacrifices. These documents are considered private, and I was not permitted to examine them. But lineage elders explained that they contain lists of descendants of particular ancestors. These are not ancestors common to the whole lineage, and the genealogical relationship between the different ancestors is unknown.

54. The only inscription in the hall is a record of imperial gratitude bestowed on one Chen Huai in 1458 for his donation of two hundred piculs of rice, probably in relief of local famine. Interestingly, no one in Taiyu claims descent from Huai.

55. The Lantern Festival marks the end of the celebrations of the Spring Festival that began on the last night of the year when the Stove God was dispatched heavenward to report on the conduct of the household in the previous year. This initiates a phase of transition, signified by the suspension of official matters and commerce. After days of feasting, visiting, and other celebrations, the Lantern Festival precedes the return to normality. The ritual observances of the first fifteen days of the year as a whole call to mind Bourdieu's writings on the concatenation of the calendar in Algeria. They begin with the New Year's celebrations that are private to the household, they expand in scale as neighbors and immediate relatives are included in the following days and they culminate with lineage rituals and the village temple festival—discussed in the next chapter—in the middle of the month. *Beimang* thus takes place at the end of a process from private to public observance, which marks the reincorporation of individuals first as members of their family, and then as members of their lineage. The Lantern Festival also marks a key transition in the agricultural cycle. The economy of Nantai in the Qing was largely based on commercial agriculture, mainly the growing of fruit, especially oranges. There are two imporant periods for agriculture labor in fruit orchards, the harvest in the tenth or eleventh month of the year and the trimming of the buds in the second or third. The first month is thus the time of respite between the end of one stage in the agricultural cycle and the beginning of the next. See van Gennep, 3–4; and Bourdieu, *Logic of Practice*, 204–9.

56. Genealogical accounts of the ritual indicate that the rituals of the New Year were times when the major life cycle transitions of the lineage membership in the previous year were recorded. Births of sons, marriages, passages of sons to adulthood, and deaths were all to be reported to the ancestral hall management. The first three events often also required the payment of a small sum of money (*xijin*) to the ancestral hall. Births were the most important events to be recorded, and informants report a number of prerogatives that households to which sons had been born in the previous year enjoyed at the Lantern Festival. These included the right and obligation to suspend a special kind of lantern in the hall, to donate one of the massive sticks of incense that burned through the night in the hall, and to carry candles and lamps back from the ancestral hall using a special, elaborate candelabrum. Xie Zhaozhe (2:3b–4a) in the late Ming explained the connection between the celebration of births, candles and lamps, and the Lantern Festival in Fuzhou. "In Fujian dialects, the word for lamp (*deng*) has the same sound as the word for male individual (*ding*). Everyone who hands out a lantern is said to have added a male (*tianding*)." Many of my informants recall the rituals as a time when the affairs of the lineage were reported to the ancestors in the hall, of which the careful recording of events in the households of the lineage was an important part. The lineage census may originally have been tied to taxation issues. Once the registered household (*hu*), registered in the name of the founding ancestor of a lineage, became simply a unit of account through which taxes were paid, the allocation of the tax obligations of the *hu* became an internal matter for the lineage. As we have seen, genealogies from the mid-Ming frequently contain details about how this allocation should be done. Obviously, fair allocation

depended on the lineage leadership having precise details of the population. In terms of social function, then, the *beimang* ritual facilitated the maintenance of an accurate census to permit tax allocation within the lineage. Of course, maintaining accurate records would also have facilitated the compilation of the genealogy. Such practices were common throughout south China. For Fujian, see Zheng Zhenman, *Ming–Qing Fujian jiazu zuzhi*, 65.

57. Cited in Zheng Zhenman, *Ming–Qing Fujian jiazu zuzhi*, 239.

58. "Qing Tianfang liyuesheyushushu liufang gong zhi sichan yuezi," in *Fuzhou Guoshi zhipu*, 7:6a.

59. Zhou Lianggong, 3:43. See also Kuribayashi, "Shindai Fukushū," 32–33. The Shanggan village history notes that the Lin were not the first people to settle there. When the Lin's founding ancestor arrived, "the town was known as Daiyu or Shangyu. There were formerly eight surnames, of which the Zhu, He and Yan were the most flourishing." Some of these lineages even had their own ancestral halls; the ruins of several can still be seen in Shanggan. But the other surnames are said to have died out or to have moved away, although no one knows to where they moved. (Lin Yidong, 9b–10a.) It remains an open question whether, as the Lin grew ever more powerful, people of other surnames traced their descent to ancestors of the Lin lineage and thus became lineage members themselves.

60. Thus there are sectors named Qiancuo, "before the [founding ancestor's] home," and Houcuo, "behind the [founding ancestor's] home." These sectors are inhabited by "the descendants of Shishen, [who make up] the senior branch descended from Wenzhai" and "the descendants of Shiyu, [who make up] the branch descended from the fourth son of Wenzhai," respectively. There used to be a Buddhist nunnery at the foot of the hill overlooking the town. "In this area lives the branch descended from Kezhao. It is known as Below the Nunnery sector." (Lin Yidong, 21b.) The character *jie* originally meant a peak or an upright tablet often serving as a boundary marker.

61. Lineage members are familiar with many legends of feuds, vendettas, and violence between sectors. One such feud took place in 1856. A member of Below the Nunnery sector was accused of chopping firewood on land belonging to one Daozhun, of the Shoreline sector. When Daozhun confronted the offender, he was dragged into the fields and beaten. The people of the two sectors both vowed to exact vengeance and fixed a date to fight the matter out. Allied groups also got involved. "At that time, the most powerful was Qiancuo . . . which had more than 120 fighters armed with staffs." The battle ended with two dead and eighteen injured. Such a serious altercation naturally came to the attention of the local magistrate. The culprits were identified as men of a wealthy family who paid bribes to have the blame transferred to three members of another sector. Enmity persisted between the two groups, and there were reports of fights and killings. Most of the members of the weaker Below the Nunnery sector and their allies eventually fled the village. Ibid., 13a–14a.

62. Ibid., 14a–b.

63. In the same way, the members of the Banshui branch in Luozhou became part of the Luozhou Chen lineage when they were allowed to participate in the

rituals of ancestral worship in the lineage hall. The Banshui branch was said to have descended from ancestors who had moved to Luozhou from Houguan county. They claimed that all of their own genealogical records had been lost:

> When the ancestral hall was being built [in the 1670s], they ordered their sons and younger members to come and contribute their labour with enthusiasm. As a consequence, they asked to place the tablet of their ancestor, Zi, in the hall. From this time on, when there were sacrifices, they would always participate. Over the years this came to be considered appropriate. The members all work at the essential occupation, labouring in the fields. They have the pleasant reputation of being frugal and flourishing. They are close to us and we look after them. So they came to be of our lineage and of our surname.
>
> ("Banshui tu" in *Luojiang Chenshi jiapu*, 8:1a.)

It is possible that the Banshui branch members may have originally been bondservants of other members of the lineage, but there is no historical evidence that can shed light on this question.

64. As Hevia puts it, "Within the space between what ought to occur and what is realizable under the circumstances, ritual becomes radically historical, grounded, as it were, in the materiality of life as the actions of human beings shape the world they inhabit." Hevia, 132.

65. The provincial gazetteer of 1491 notes with approval the strict rules observed when people of different status visited one another during the New Year's festival. The author quotes from an unnamed older source, "As for visiting at the time of seasonal festivals, from the gentry on down, the scholars and the common people, *yamen* clerks, merchants and lictors, all had distinctions in their clothing, and consistency in their terms of address; they did not dare transgress even in trifling matters." This situation had obtained at the height of the Song, but unfortunately things had been deteriorating since. "Over the years to the present, although the tone of this custom still survives here and there, it is nothing compared to the flourishing time of the Song." The author of the gazetteer reinforces the point that correct performance of ritual was fundamental to the maintenance of appropriate social distinctions.

> I have heard the village elders say that several dozen years ago, in the areas between villages, when a junior met a member of the gentry, in action and speech he was regulated, respectful and careful, not daring to relax. When members of the lower orders encountered [a member of] an old family or hereditary lineage, they behaved with etiquette, in an orderly way according to the rules, and did not dare make the least transgression. This was the old way.
>
> (*Bamin tongzhi*, 3:40–41, 50.)

Appreciation for the integrative function of ritual was, of course, nothing new in Chinese thought; it was one of the fundamental principles of the Confucian perspective on *li* [2] (ritual/etiquette). See Schwartz, 67.

66. *Yingyang Sanxi Panshi zupu*, 5:73.

67. See earlier, Chapter 4, "The Popular Halls of the Huang of Yixu".

68. "Jiu gui," in *Huqiu Yishan Huangshi shipu*, 1:18b. The distinction between leaders selected on genealogical principles and leadership claimed on the basis of official status was first discussed long ago, but mainly in a synchronous way. See, for example, Freedman, *Lineage Organization*, 67 ff; and Baker, *Chinese Family and Kinship*, 55–64.

69. A precise schedule for the branches follows. "Jiu gui," in *Huqiu Yishan Huangshi shipu*, 1:18b.

70. See earlier, chapter 4, "The Luozhou Chen Hall."

71. "Puli shize," in *Luojiang Chenshi jiapu*.

72. This distinction invites comparison with Cohen's, that is, between the associational mode and the fixed genealogical mode of agnatic kinship. Cohen's argument is that, in the fixed genealogical mode, "patrilineal ties are figured on the basis of the relative seniority of descent lines." So far, this seems to match the Luozhou situation. But, Cohen continues, "the unity of the lineage as a whole is based upon a ritual focus on the senior descent line." Thus in Cohen's field site the ritual focus of the lineage is always the senior descent line, whereas in Luozhou the ritual focus rotates through the different descent lines according to the relative order of seniority of the founding ancestor of the descent line. See Cohen, "Lineage Organization in North China," 510.

73. The spate of high officials of the lineage in the mid- to late Qing came mostly from the senior branch, but this glorious future would not have been evident at the time of the construction of the hall, so it is not surprising that this is not invoked as the reason for the confusing arrangement.

74. Asymmetrical segmentation is also discussed in early anthropological studies of the lineage but not, to my knowledge, in a diachronous way. See, for example, Freedman, *Chinese Lineage and Society*, 37 ff; Baker, *Chinese Family and Kinship*, 54–55, 61–64; and Chen Qi'nan, 188–202.

75. "Jidian zhi," in *Langqi Dongshi pudie*.

76. Qin Huitian, 115:3b–4a.

77. Doolittle, *Social Life of the Chinese*, 1:234.

78. *Pingtan xianzhi*, 21:12b.

79. "Shizu ciji li lue," in Li Guangdi, 6:14a–b.

80. "Guanli guiyue," in *Jin'an Dushi zupu, fuji*:3b.

81. Bell's description of rituals as sites for the production of "nuanced relations of power, relationships characterized by acceptance and resistance, negotiated appropriation, and redemptive reinterpretation of the hegemonic order" seems apposite. Bell, 16.

82. *Yingyang Sanxi Panshi zupu*, 5:73.

83. *Fuzhou Gongshi zhipu, zongci*:4b.

84. The rituals of the Lantern Festival retained their creative potential into the twentieth century. During the Republican period, they became implicated in an attempt by the weak and small villages in the hills between Linpu and Chengmen to form an alliance to resist the stronger lineages surrounding them. One of these small villages is Cheng Mountain Summit, Chengshanding, whose residents are all surnamed Zheng. A young man from the village "worried that the village was small

and its population weak, and so suffered the imprecations of neighbouring villages." He proposed the formation of an Association of the Lineages of the Thirteen Villages of Cheng Hill. Each lineage was asked to dispatch a representative to the humble ancestral hall of the Chengshanding Zheng on the thirteenth night of the first month, for "discussions, *beimang*, and sacrifices. . . . The representatives could decide various issues." *Chengshan Daicaotang Zhengshi zupu*, 228–29.

CHAPTER 6

1. This discussion is based on my observation of the festival in 1993 and 1994. Local authorities have prohibited most festival activities since 1996. There has been a cult to the Great Liu Kings in the region since Song times. The Kings are three brothers, the eldest of whom was named Liu Xingquan—a historical figure. According to the *Xin Tangshu* (Ouyang Xiu and Song Qi, 19:5491), Xingquan was a henchman of Wang Xu, the military chieftain under whose leadership Wang Shenzhi first entered Fujian. After a diviner warned Xu that rebellion was brewing among his troops, he found pretexts to kill off the prominent members of his army. Liu Xingquan then conspired with several others to ambush Xu. The rebels wanted to make him their leader, but he yielded to Wang Shenzhi's brother. According to the *Sanshan zhi* (8:18b), Liu Xingquan did not survive long enough to lead the conspiracy against Wang Xu, who is identified as his brother-in-law, but was executed by Xu in Zhangzhou. The earliest written record of the cult of the Great Liu Kings in Luozhou village comes from a fifteenth-century provincial gazetteer, which notes the existence of the Temple of Manifest Responsiveness dedicated to the three Liu brothers, who had answered prayers for rain (*Bamin tongzhi*, 58:366). In private, Luozhou residents explained to me repeatedly that the Three Liu Kings were originally local bandits who had been given offerings in an attempt to placate them. The most detailed account of their cult is an inscription that was copied into the nineteenth-century gazetteer of Luozhou. The text has been included in the Appendix.

2. As Wang Mingming has pointed out, all of these scholars are in a sense rethinking the work of William Skinner, who saw marketing and individual rational choice as the logic underlying a hierarchy of regional systems in China. (See Feuchtwang; Sangren, *History and Magical Power*; James Watson, "Standardizing the Gods"; Wang, "Place, Administration and Territorial Cults," 34–38; Dean, "Transformations of the *She*"; and Skinner, "Marketing and Social Structure." Other relevant works include: Schipper; Faure, *Structure of Chinese Rural Society*, 70–86, and "Lineage as Cultural Invention"; ter Haar, "Local Society and Organization of Cults"; and Katz, "Temple Cults and the Creation of Hsin-chuang." Taiwanese scholars, in particular Lin Meirong, have developed the notion of the ritual sphere (*jisiquan*) as a tool for the analysis of the relationship between popular religion and spatial hierarchy.

3. In a letter to Zhao Rudong, prefect of Zhangzhou in southern Fujian from 1211 to 1213, Chen Chun (1159–1223) criticized the procession festivals to local deities, an important form of religious activity at the time. According to Chen, local hooligans

gathered money to pay the costs of such festivals, in which prominent members of the community as well as local *yamen* functionaries held various positions of authority. A dozen images of deities were paraded, each preceded by a guard of honor. "All around one can hear the sound of the drums... and troupes of actors vie to respond. Everyone is dressed all in new clothes of gold and blue silk, trying to please the god. Some secretly spur on their horses and let them gallop, saying that the god rushes the horse; others secretly urge [the bearers of the] sedan chairs to run, saying that the god rushes the chair." (Chen Chun, 43:13a-14a.) The colorful details could easily come from the pen of a modern ethnographer or, for that matter, a contemporary local official. See Feuchtwang, 76–79, for a discussion of the essential elements of temple cults and festivals in contemporary Taiwan.

4. Overmyer, "Attitudes Toward Popular Religion," 192.

5. Dean, "Transformations of the *She*," 22. A further complication is that the term seems also to have been used on occasion to refer to the ubiquitous altar to the god of the earth (*tudigong*). In this chapter, I have tried to avoid any evidence in which there is ambiguity whether *she* refers to a regulation altar or community temple and a shrine to the god of the earth.

6. Kanai Noriyuki has discussed the history of the *she* in the village since ancient times in a series of articles. See "Nansō ni okeru shashokudan to shabyō," "Sōdai no sonsha to sōzoku," "Shajin to Dōkyō," "Sōdai no sonsha to shajin," and "Sōdai Sekisei sonsha to dojin." ter Haar, "Local Society and Organization of Cults," 10–11, points out some problems with Kanai's analysis.

7. *Sanshan zhi*, 9:18a.

8. Xu Xiaowang, *Fujian minjian xinyang*, 14 ff. Several gods who were worshiped in Fuzhou in the Song originated as snake deities, which had probably long received cults from indigenous peoples. For example, two anonymous subordinate deities of the temple to the ancient king of Min in Fuzhou, said to be generals of the king, were strongly associated with snakes, and their Song cult probably derived from an earlier snake cult. Snakes also figure in a number of stories and legends that might be interpreted as accounts of the long-term conflict between Han and indigenous cultures, including the story cycle of Linshui Furen discussed in Chapter 5. Another story in the late Qing collection *Mindu bieji* tells of a local woman who marries a snake and produces several children who are slain or subordinated by the woman's brother, a Daoist adept. Such stories are probably also legacies of the long period of interaction between the local people and Han immigrants. The establishment of a cult at the place where aboriginal enemies were defeated is a common trope in Fujian popular religion. Snake cults persist in modern Fujian, often but not always associated with She and Dan groups. The best known is the Zhanghuban temple, upriver from Fuzhou, that Xie Zhaozhe described in the Ming, but there are many others. On the temple of the King of Min, see *Sanshan zhi*, 8:11a. For the Linshui Furen story, see Xu Bo, *Jin'an mianzhi*, in *Rongyin xinjian*; and Liren Heqiu, 85:429. For other examples, see *Min shu*, 11:253; and Dean, *Taoist Ritual*, 120; and on the Zhanghuban temple, see Chen Cunxi *et al.*

9. See Hansen, chap. 4.

10. "Yanyun si Yuyang xiansheng Han gong citang ji," in Liu Kezhuang, 93:11a.

11. *Sanshan zhi*, 9:22a. On the history of state campaigns against cults in Fujian, see Kojima.

12. Shen Shixing, 94:15–16. See Kuribayashi, *Rikōsei*, 5–10; Overmyer, "Attitudes Toward Popular Religion"; and Wada, "Rikōsei." There is a slight discrepancy in the official regulations between the 110 households of the *lijia* system and the 100 households per *li* in the religious system, but the two systems were clearly intended to be coterminous in practice.

13. Yu Ruji, 30:30a–b; the text is translated in Taylor, "Official and Popular Religions," 145.

14. *DaMing lü*, 181; the translation is from Farmer, "Social Regulations," 125.

15. Taylor, "Official and Popular Religions," 145. Official policies toward popular religion in the Ming are also discussed in Overmyer, "Attitudes Toward Popular Religion."

16. *Fuzhou fuzhi* (1613), 9:12b.

17. *Mindu ji*, 5:11a–b. *Jing* is a complex term with a wide range of meanings. In a generic sense, it refers to precincts under the protection of a deity. The term is discussed in Wang, "Place, Administration and Territorial Cults;" 56 ff.

18. This is probably an example of the familiar pattern whereby a cult originates in the placation of a hungry ghost who has died an untimely or mysterious death. Over time, the legend is sanitized into a tale of a mysterious object that floats ashore. See Harrell, 193–206; ter Haar, "Genesis and Spread," 353; and Katz, "Demons or Deities," 202–3. A Ming poem refers to the temple as the Temple of the Generals. *Jinshan zhi*, 4:3b–4a.

19. For example, in Jianyang an annual *she* festival was held, at which the guardian of the *she* (*shebao*) gathered funds, slaughtered a pig and officiated over the sacrifice to the god. The next morning, the rota holder prepared a special broth that was distributed to each household. (*Jianyang xianzhi*, 1:86b.) ter Haar (in "Local Society and Organization of Cults," 14–15) notes that altars were often built in the vicinity of existing local temples. Faure writes of Foshan in Guangdong that in the early Ming, the town consisted of neighborhoods called *she*, organized around local deities, and that it was precisely these neighborhoods that became the *lijia* units. Faure, "Lineage as Cultural Invention," 16.

20. *Bamin tongzhi*, 3:44.

21. The problems are not universal: "In Shuinan of Putian the Fang, Xu and Qiu lineages build earthen altars for the *she* altar of the soil, and carry out rites in spring and autumn. They do not pursue the frivolous ways of the village lanes. Their rites can be taken [as a model]." From *Xinghua fuzhi* (Hongzhi edition), j.15, cited in Dean, "Transformations of the *She*," 35.

22. *Changle xianzhi* (1637), 1:13b–14a.

23. Ye Chunji, 10:343.

24. Worshipers were also tricked by mediums and phony priests, wasting their money and endangering their health. "At the extreme, men and women mix together

inappropriately, and unspeakable things happen." Ye "completely eradicated [these illicit temples], and erected *lishe* altars as of old." But he was sanguine about the possibility of the bad practices recurring. "I have heard that the people still secretly conceal [the images of the gods]. When they hear that I have left the city, the demons are returned to the temples. Alas!" Ibid., 10:347, 10:343, and 9:337.

25. *Tengshan zhi*, 1:3b.

26. Ibid., 2:5b.

27. See Dean, "Transformations of the *She*," 22–29, 33–41, for a discussion of this discourse.

28. Brook, "Spatial Structure," 25.

29. Zheng Zhenman has offered a different explanation, suggesting that the *tu* was an intermediate unit between the *lijia* hundred and the individual household, which was introduced in populous areas of Fujian. But Zheng does not explain how the intermediate unit fit into the structure of the system. Zheng Zhenman, "Shenmiao jidian," 40.

30. Huang Fuji, "Dingguangsi zhi," in *Huqiu Yishan Huangshi shipu*, 1:23b.

31. If a temple derived from the officially mandated *lishe* system, then presumably it could not be threatened with destruction. For a summary of Ming campaigns against local cults, see Kojima. There is evidence of such campaigns in the immediate vicinity of Yixu. An illicit temple in nearby Luozhou was destroyed by the order of the magistrate in the Jiajing period. *Luozhou zhi*, 1:28b.

32. According to the foundation legend of the Huang, their first ancestor married uxorilocally to a woman of the Lin surname of Yixu. As a result, relations between the Huang and Lin are especially cordial. There are now only a few families with the Lin surname in the village.

33. "Shuilu zunwang miao ji," Inscription. The text is virtually identical to an essay entitled "Shuilu zunwang miao zhi," by Huang Fuji, at *Huqiu Yishan Huangshi shipu*, 1:23a–b. The full text is included in the Appendix.

34. Yang Zhou, "Yushan shengshe ji," in *Minyi Huyu Yangshi Tingqifang pudie*, 31a.

35. Faure notes that in Han lineages in the Pearl River Delta the first generation of settlement is often recorded from the early Ming because this was the time when contact with the officialdom through the *lijia* system created documents that granted title to settlement rights. Faure, "Lineage as Cultural Invention," 14.

36. That the center of the cluster should be known as the Palace of Seven Sacred Precincts is interesting, for Dean and Zheng found in Putian a number of temple clusters which also consisted of seven constituent units and had similar names. Dean translates the term *qijing* as Seven-fold Sacred Territory. See Dean, "Transformations of the *She*," 42; and Zheng Zhenman, "Putian pingyuan," 588.

37. Yang Zhou, "Yushan shengshe ji," in *Minyi Huyu Yangshi Tingqifang pudie*, 31b.

38. There was also a third broad method by which claims to the legitimacy of a *she* temple could be made. Since the *she* altar had originally been the prerogative of the nobility, the legitimacy of village temples could also be affirmed on the basis of

the status of worshipers. The Huyu account begins:

> Of old, the first kings established shrines to the god of the five soils and called these *she*, and shrines to the god of the five grains and called these *ji* .... Just as the state has the altar to the soil and grain, so in the countryside there are the gods of the soil and grain. According to the Book of Rites, the *she* of the king is called the great *she* or the royal *she*. The *she* of the various princes are called the state *she* or the princely *she*. The *she* of the nobility and below who form a group and establish a *she* are called established *she*. We Yang are originally a noble family. According to the Rites we are entitled to have a *she*.

Thus the Yang lineage also claimed the right to establish a *she* altar on the basis of their ascribed privileges as descendants of the ancient nobility. Yang Zhou, "Yushan shengshe ji" in ibid., 31a–b.

39. See Chapter 3.

40. Thus the first group, associated with the Qingming sacrifice, includes four names representing four lineages. Lan Zhigong, the founding ancestor of the Lan of Wangchuan, is the first of these names. His entry reads: "Lan Zhigong: 15 shares equivalent to the tax obligations on a single adult male [i.e., an official fiscal male (*guanding*)] [in the names of] Chaoren, Shengchu, Zhichu, Zichu, Dachu, Bojiu, Bocai, Chaochao, Zechu, Chaocan, Fanwen, Chaogong, Chaoying, Fanjie, Youqian." "Hetong guiyue" (1836), in *Chongxiu Lianjiang Lanshi zupu*.

41. Given that the altar was not even established until the early Qing, when the integration of *she* altars with temples to local deities was well underway, it would not be unreasonable to expect that what the contract calls a *she* altar was actually nothing more than a village temple. In interviews in 1997, villagers gave me conflicting accounts of the deity worshiped at this altar, and I have not yet been able to resolve this issue satisfactorily. But it appears that at least in this part of Lianjiang, even into the Qing, some of the regulations on *she* altars continued to be strictly adhered to. The altar established by the contract no longer exists, but a similar one survives outside a nearby village. It consists of a stone platform surmounted by a small stone shrine, roofed but open on one side, with an upright stone in the position of honor in the shrine. A barely legible inscription, dated 1849, records the names of the ten *jia* households, each corresponding to a lineage from a village in the vicinity, and a set of prohibitions intended to maintain local order. ("Ji ertu shipai mingxing difang gongli guiyue," Inscription.) The content of the prohibitions suggests that the organization of the altar was probably also connected to the *baojia* and *xiangyue* collective security systems. Miki argues that late Ming provincial officials attempted to revive these systems in response to the failings of the *lijia* system. Miki, 77–99.

42. "Jiapu zonglin zhuan," in Ye Xianggao, 15:34a–37b.

43. Ibid., 15:35b–36a. The shrine is also described in "Yunshan sheci ji," in ibid., 11:32a–33a.

44. "Tiaoyue," in *Shimei Wushi zupu*. The late Qing genealogy of the Jintang Wang lineage of Fuzhou also explains that the deity is welcomed into the hall on the fourth day of the New Year. Incense is burned and rituals performed for the

deity. Then the hall caretaker assembles the men of the lineage for a feast. "Jintang Wangshi zhici guizhi," in *Jintang Wangshi zhipu*, 2:1b.

45. An almost identical version was gathered by Lin Yaohua during his fieldwork in Yixu in the early twentieth century. Lin Yaohua, 226–27.

46. Villagers in Luozhou currently use a similar term, Auxiliary Palace (*xinggong*) to describe their ancestral hall when the gods are present in it. As noted in Chapter 5, the Chen of Taiyu use a similar term to describe their ancestral hall during the festival of Chen Jinggu.

47. The contract goes on to specify the precise rights of each of the four lineages to place images in different parts of the temple. *Gantangbao suozhi*, 59a–b.

48. *Luozhou zhi*, 23b.

49. "Gexiang gongchang jingfen wanliang," in *Sanshan Yeshi sishi lu*, 4:18a–b.

50. "Jinqi zunwang benjing zongmiao tu," in *Langqi Dongshi pudie*.

51. "Chongjian zunwang dian shengmu gong chengxiang ci," Inscription.

52. Recall the discussion of shares (*guanding*) earlier, in n. 40. The names that appear here refer to founding ancestors of different settlements of the Lan.

53. "Hetong guiyue" (1836), in *Chongxiu Lianjiang Lanshi zupu*.

54. It is possible that these men were not even living at the time of the initial contract, and ownership of the share had always been endowed in the name of their respective estates and owned collectively by their descendants.

55. This is obviously a reference to the local *tudigong* and indicates clearly that the *tudigong* and the deity of the altar were distinct.

56. "Fenji tanshe guiyue" (1854), in *Chongxiu Lianjiang Lanshi zupu*.

57. Huang Yongnian, "Jiangjun miaozhi" (1866), in *Huqiu Yishan Huangshi shipu*, 1:25a–b.

58. Huang Fuji, "Shuilu zunwang miao zhi," in ibid., 1:23a–b.

59. *Houguanxian xiangtuzhi*, 1:29b–30a.

60. Temples to the Five Emperors, gods associated with epidemic diseases, were also commonly associated in Fuzhou with the adjudication of local disputes. According to Lin Zhichun of Linpu, "When the officials make decisions, [the people] do not believe and do not obey, but rather must call the Five Emperors as witnesses and only then submit. The documents and ceremonies of their Heavenly Immortal Palace are majestic, and upheld together with those of the officials." *Fujian tongzhi* (1871), 55:23a. On self-regulation, see Zheng Zhenman, *Ming-Qing Fujian jiazu zuzhi*, 242–57.

61. See the cases discussed in Dean, *Taoist Ritual*.

62. Two inscriptions, dated 1830 and 1831, explain the history of the deities and the benefits they offer to the villages surrounding the temple. The first begins by noting problems in the financing of the annual procession festival of the deities, in which they "look over the area, drive off evil spirits and bestow blessings." To deal with this problem, a land reclamation project was initiated, financed by a head tax on the local population. According to the second inscription, the right to rent the fields created was to be auctioned off each year, and the proceeds were to be used to support the festival of the deities. The participants in the project were ten villages in the vicinity of Qingpu, each described as a *lijia* household, showing that

this remained a significant marker of status even into the nineteenth century ("Wei Zhao er shuaigong tian bei," inscription; and Untitled Inscription, 1831.) The early history of the main cult of the temple has been studied by Davis. On such multivillage temples elsewhere in China, see Brim.

63. I have been unable to find the provenance of this local term or to learn why the more common term is not used. Villagers know the term *shenming hui*, indeed, my questions about *bashe* are often explained by saying that the *bashe* is just another word for the same thing. Each *bashe* sponsors a *tagu* in the temple procession festival. *Bashe* served in the past as investment vehicles. Informants in Yixu recall that the cost to join the last *bashe* founded in the town before 1949 was several hundred *yuan*. This money was pooled to purchase land. Responsibility for the collection of the rent on the land rotated through the membership annually. The chief responsibilities of the rota holder were to pay the costs of (1) involvement in the procession festival, (2) the offerings to the deities in the ancestral hall on the eighteenth day of the first month, and (3) the feast on the birthday of the deity in the eighth month. In this as in most *bashe*, the income was typically greater than the expenses that had to be met. The rota holder kept the difference, which in the better endowed associations was often enough to pay the costs of a wedding or a dowry. Land Reform records from Chengmen identify twenty-three plots of land, amounting to about two percent of total land under cultivation, as belonging to *bashe* associations (MHCA 89-1-5-10). In the past ten years, many former *bashe* have revived and new ones formed. These *bashe* now have mainly ritual functions. A typical example from Luozhou is the Orchid Southern Offering hall, founded in 1887 and organized around Supervisor Zheng, a subordinate of the Three Liu Kings. The activities of the club at present are centered on the parade festival: the members purchase, decorate, and then carry the *tagu* of Supervisor Zheng during the two stages of the parade; pay the expenses of hiring one of the musical troupes that entertain during the festival; and together make a large offering to the gods in the ancestral hall, after which the whole association holds a feast in the home of one of the members. Though the Orchid Southern Offering hall was formed on the basis of kinship by five brothers, *bashe* could also be based on geographic or economic links.

64. Chen, who had organized anti-Yuan forces in his native Xinghua, was captured and taken to Hangzhou, where he refused food and died. In 1997 a ninety-three-year-old male resident of Yangqi explained to me the origins of the temple:

> This story happened a long time ago. My ancestor was a farmer here. . . . One day, a corpse floated up by the riverbank. It was Chen Wenlong. [My ancestor] could tell because of the insignia on the clothing. The body didn't float away, even though the tide pushed and pulled it. He issued a challenge to the corpse: "If you are really numinous (*ling*), make this iron harrow float." Then he threw the harrow into the river, and sure enough it floated. So he decided to bury the corpse. He laid it on a plank, carried the plank as far as Houshan, and then the plank couldn't be carried any further, so he buried the corpse there. So he

decided to build a temple [at the current site of the temple]. All the lumber needed for the construction simply floated up to the bank.

65. Many of these worshipers have paid to portray criminals bound over to the god for judgment, in thanks for having received the deity's favor. See Katz, *Demon Hordes and Burning Boats*, 151–52. In the early 1990s, the worshipers accompanying the procession numbered several hundred.

66. Worshipers explain that the boat returns Chen Wenlong to his home in Xinghua; the following day, the incense burner of the temple is taken down to the river to receive him back again. Rituals involving the burning of boats and connected with the expulsion of pestilential influences have long been an important part of popular religious practice in Fuzhou and elsewhere in China. (See Szonyi, "Illusion of Standardizing the Gods"; and Katz, *Demon Hordes and Burning Boats*, 143–74.)

67. This was not the first time this problem had arisen. In 1797, the previous Head of the Boatmen had made similar demands, and the magistrate had issued an order to restrain him. (Untitled Inscription (1804).) The text has been included in the Appendix.

68. Since the Single Whip reforms, the service levy had been first monetized and then distributed as a surcharge on the land tax. Land taxes were thus expressed in terms of an assessment of the land tax itself, plus the service levy surcharge.

69. This is exactly the process that we saw in Chapter 2 undertaken by the Chen of Luozhou. As the inscription indicates, by the early nineteenth century, many of the households on whom the fishing tax had traditionally been levied no longer made their living exclusively from fishing. They were tenants on land reclaimed from the lower Min and its tributaries, paying rent to landlords who may or may not have registered the land with the authorities and harvesting the fish beds, land that had not yet been fully reclaimed, for shellfish. The question of whether the reclaimed land had been registered is actually extremely relevant to the dispute described in the tablet. If the land was registered, then the Dan tenants would have been paying the ordinary land tax in the form of a portion of their rent in addition to the levy on unregistered fishing households. In other words, they were being taxed twice.

70. Other examples can also be found of temples that served similar political roles for the Dan. On Langqi Island, for example, in 1848 Dan worshipers at the temple of Taishan organized themselves to resist the exactions of the local salt-tax authorities who were extorting a tax on the fishing boats as they returned from sea to their home ports. Untitled Inscription (1848).

71. Dean, "Transformations of the *She*," 71.

72. Faure, "Lineage as Cultural Invention," 29.

CHAPTER 7

1. See, for example, He Changling, ed, j.55 ff.

2. Chow, 80–88.

3. Rowe, "Ancestral Rites," 387–97. See also *Gongzhong dang Qianlong chao*

zouzhe, 5.163–64, for the original memorial, and discussion in Zuo Yunpeng, 107; and Lamley, 272.

4. Sun Yat-sen, 1:60–66; Strand, 329–38.

5. Lin Sen, "Shanggan Linshi zupu xu," in *Taojiang Linshi zupu*, 1:17a–b.

6. Mao, "Report of an Investigation," 45–49; and *Report from Xunwu*, 123–25, 131–32.

7. Potter and Potter, 56. For a sustained discussion, see C. K. Yang.

8. Duara, *Culture, Power, and the State*, 87.

9. James Watson, "Standardizing the Gods," 293. I use a different body of material to explore this same issue in "Illusion of Standardizing the Gods."

10. Wang Mingming, 56. For other examples, see Dean, "Transformations of the *She*," and the essays in Faure and Siu, eds.

APPENDIX

1. Presumably the same as the God of Supervising the Way referred to earlier. Villagers interviewed in the temple were not able to agree on the correct character.

Bibliography

The Bibliography is divided into two sections: Primary Sources in Chinese and Secondary and Western Language Sources. Primary Sources in Chinese is further subdivided into Archives, Gazetteers, Genealogies, Inscriptions, and Other Primary Sources in Chinese and Japanese. Location is indicated for rare works only.

The following abbreviations are used:

CLFZ   Changle County Gazetteer Compilation Office
CSJC   *Congshu jicheng* (Shanghai: Shangwu)
CT   Kristofer Schipper, *Concordance du Tao-Tsang: titres des ouvrages* (Paris: École française d'Extrême-Orient, 1975)
FHC   Family History Centre, Genealogical Society of Utah, Salt Lake City
FNU   Fujian Normal University Library
FPL   Special Collections, Fujian Provincial Library
LJA   Lianjiang County Archives, Lianjiang
MHCA   Minhou County Archives, Ganzhe, Minhou
P   Work in private hands
SBCK   *Sibu congkan* (Taibei: Shangwu)
SKQS   *Yingyin wenyuange siku quanshu* (Taibei: Shangwu)
SKZB   *Siku quanshu zhenben* (Taibei: Shangwu)
ZGFZ   *Zhongguo fangzhi congshu* (Taibei: Chengwen)

Primary Sources in Chinese

Archives (Minhou County Archives, Ganzhe, Minhou)

MHCA 89-1-3 Land Reform, Yixu district
MHCA 89-1-5 Land Reform, Zhongnan (Chengmen) district

Gazetteers

Bamin tongzhi. 1485. Reprint, Fujian difangzhi congkan. Fuzhou: Fujian renmin, 1990.
Changle xian Liuli zhi. [1964?]. Reprint, Fuzhou: Fujiansheng ditu, 1989.
Changle xianzhi. 1637. CLFZ.
Changle xianzhi. 1763. CLFZ.
Dayi xiangzhi. 1933. ms. Minhouxian wenhua guan, Ganzhe.
Fujian tongzhi. 1737. Reprint, Yangzhou: Jiangsu guangling guji, 1989.
Fujian tongzhi. 1871. Reprint, Taibei: Huawen, 1968.
Fujian tongzhi. 1938.
Funing fuzhi. 1762. Reprint, ZGFZ.
Fuqing xianzhi. 1547. Reprint, Tianyige Mingdai fangzhi xuankan xubian. Shanghai: Shanghai shudian, 1990.
Fuzhou fuzhi. 1520. ms. FPL.
Fuzhou fuzhi. 1596. ms. FPL.
Fuzhou fuzhi. 1613. Reprint, Xijian Zhongguo difangzhi huikan. Beijing: Zhongguo, 1992.
Fuzhou fuzhi. 1754. Reprint, ZGFZ.
Gantangbao suozhi. 1927. ms. FPL.
Gushan zhi. 1761.
Gutian xianzhi. 1606. Reprint, ZGFZ.
Haicheng xianzhi. 1632. Reprint, Xijian Zhongguo difangzhi huikan. Beijing: Zhongguo, 1992.
Haicheng xianzhi. 1762. Reprint, ZGFZ.
Hongtang xiaozhi. 1927. FPL.
Houguanxian xiangtuzhi. 1903. Reprint, ZGFZ.
Huangboshan zhi. 1842. Reprint, Taibei: Xin wenfeng, 1987.
Jianyang xianzhi. 1601. Reprint, Xijian Zhongguo difangzhi huikan. Beijing: Zhongguo, 1992.
Jinshan zhi. 1937. Reprint, Zhongguo difang zhi jicheng, xiangzhen zhi zhuan zhi, vol. 6. Shanghai: Jiangsu guji, 1992.
Lianjiang xianzhi. 1922. Reprint, ZGFZ.
Luozhou zhi. 1863. ms. FPL.
Min shu. 1629. Reprint, Fuzhou: Fujian renmin, 1994.
Minbu shu. 1586. Reprint, ZGFZ.
Mindu ji. 1612. Reprint, ZGFZ.
Minhou xianzhi. 1933. Reprint, ZGFZ.

Minqing xianzhi. 1921. Reprint, ZGFZ.
Minxian xiangtuzhi. 1906. Reprint, ZGFZ.
Pingtan xianzhi. 1921. Reprint, ZGFZ.
Sanshan zhi. 1182. Reprint, SKZB.
Shouning daizhi. 1637. Reprint, Xijian Zhongguo difangzhi huikan. Beijing: Zhongguo, 1992.
Tengshan zhi. 1948. FPL.
Wushishan zhi. 1842. Reprint, ZGFZ.
Xianyou xianzhi. 1770. FPL.
Xiapu xianzhi. 1925. Reprint, ZGFZ.
Xuefeng zhi. 1754. Reprint, Zhongguo fosi shizhi huikan. Taibei: Mingwen, 1980.
Zhangpu xianzhi. 1885. Reprint, ZGFZ.
Zhangzhou fuzhi. 1613. FPL.
Zhangzhou fuzhi. 1877. FPL.

Genealogies

Baxian Liushi Guizhifang zhipu. Liu Xiuyou, ed. 1881. FPL, FHC.
Changle Zhuti Linshi zupu. [late sixteenth century]. ms. FPL.
Chengshan Daicaotang Zhengshi zupu. Zheng Hengwang, ed. 1992 [includes photocopy of 1758 ms.]. P.
Chitoufang zupu. Chen Liyin, ed. 1988. P.
Chongxiu Lianjiang Lanshi zupu. Lan Jiankui, ed. 1874. ms. FPL.
Daicaotang Fengshan Zhengshi zupu. Zheng Li, ed. 1926. P.
Fenggang Zhongxian Liushi jiniantang zhi, Luojiang Jiangzhongcun shici. Liu Desai, ed. [1985?]. P.
Fuzhou Gongshi zhipu. FHC.
Fuzhou Guoshi zhipu. Guo Jiechang, ed. 1892. FPL, FHC.
Gongtou Duimen Linshi zupu. Lin Guangqian, ed. 1896. LJA.
Hongzhou Zhangshi shixi. Zhang Jing, ed. 1694. FNU, FHC.
Huangli hepu. Huang Liangbiao, ed. 1929. ms. CLFZ.
Huqiu Yishan Huangshi shipu. Huang Zunjie, ed. 1932. FPL, FHC.
Jin'an Dushi zupu. Du Fengshi, ed. 1936. FPL.
Jintang Wangshi zhipu. [late Qing]. FPL.
Junshan Renshi zupu. FPL.
Langqi Dongshi pudie. ms. FPL.
Langshan Yaqian Chenshi zongpu. Chen Nianhui, ed. 1713. P.
Lianjiang Linshi jiapu. Lin Zhichun, ed. 1746. FNU.
Luojiang Chenshi jiapu. Chen Baochen, ed. 1933. FPL, FHC.
Minyi Huyu Yangshi Tingqifang pudie. Yang Zhou, ed. 1830. ms. FPL.
Nanyang Chenshi zupu. Chen Yulin, ed. 1944. FPL, FHC.
Pingyang Chenshi zupu. Chen Xingjiong, ed. 1905. FPL, FHC.
Sanshan Yeshi sishi lu. Ye Dazhuo, ed. 1890. FPL, FHC.
Shimei Wushi zupu. Wu Fengyu, ed. 1680. ms. FPL.

Taojiang Linshi zupu. Lin Sen, ed. 1931. FPL, FHC.
Tongxian Gongshi zhipu. Gong Baochen, ed. 1883. FPL.
Wenshan Huangshi jiapu. Huang Shihe, ed. 1920. FHC.
Xiaojiang Qiushi zupu. Qiu Qingxie, ed. 1934. LJA.
Yingyang Sanxi Panshi zupu. 1730. ms. CLFZ.
Yuban Liushi zupu. Liu Chuili, ed. 1805. FHC.
Yuncheng Linshi jiacheng. Lin Maoji, ed. 1934. FHC.

Inscriptions

"Anlan huiguan beiji." 1805. Fuzhou Municipal Library.
"Chongjian houlou Linshi zongci zhujuan timing ji." 1990. Lin ancestral hall,
    Chengmen village, Fuzhou.
"Chongjian Yanshi zongci beiji." 1768. Fuzhou Municipal Library.
"Chongjian zunwang dian shengmu gong chengxiang ci." 1928. Zunwang temple,
    Linpu village, Fuzhou.
"Chongxiu shuilu sanwei zunwang miao." 1827. Huang Qingping. Sanwang
    temple, Yixu village, Fuzhou.
"Fuzhoufu sixue xinli xuetian ji." 1548. Zhang Jing. Fuzhou Municipal Library.
"Ji ertu shipai mingxing difang gongli guiyue." 1849. Near Kangyuan village,
    Lianjiang.
"Lin shangshu jiamiao ji." 1518. Fang Hao. Lin Han ancestral hall, Linpu village,
    Fuzhou.
"Nanhu Zhengshi jitian ji." 1827. Lin Zexu. Fuzhou Municipal Library.
"Shuilu zunwang miao ji." n.d. Sanwang temple, Yixu village, Fuzhou.
Untitled. 852. Near Linpu village, Fuzhou.
Untitled. 1458. Chen ancestral hall, Taiyu village, Fuzhou.
Untitled. 1804. Shangshu temple, Yangqi village, Fuzhou.
Untitled. 1831. Lingji temple, Qingpu village, Minhou county.
Untitled. 1850. Zhang Xieshun. Taishan temple, Langqi village, Minhou county.
Untitled. 1885. Lin ancestral hall, Chengmen village, Minhou county.
"Wei Zhao er shuaigong tian bei." 1830. Lingji temple, Qingpu village, Minhou
    county.

Other Primary Sources in Chinese and Japanese

Bai Yuchan. *Haiqiong Bai zhenren lu.* Xie Xiandao, ed. 1251. CT 1307.
Cai Xiang. *Cai Xiang ji.* Reprint, Shanghai: Shanghai guji. 1996.
Chen Chun. *Beixi daquan ji.* Reprint, SKZB.
Chen Guling. *Guling ji.* Reprint, SKZB.
Chen Shengshao. *Wensu lu.* 1842. Reprint, in *Licehuan chao, Wensu lu,* Beijing:
    Shumu wenxian, 1983.
Chen Shiyuan. *Jinshu chuanxi lu.* 1768. ms. Xiamen University Library.
Chunqiu zuoshi zhuan dushi zhijie. Reprint, Sibu beiyao, Taibei: Zhonghua, 1966.
Da Ming lü. 1397. Reprint, Yangzhou: Jiangsu guangling guji, 1990.

Da Qing huidian shili. 1899.

Dai Chengfen. *Rongcheng suishi ji.* [ca.1851–74]. ms. FNU.

Dong Hao. *Quan Tangwen.* 1814. Reprint, Beijing: Zhonghua, 1983.

Dong Yingju. *Chongxiang ji xuan lu.* Taibei: Taiwan yinhang, 1967.

Du Guangting. *Taishang huanglu zhai yi.* CT 507.

Fang Dacong. *Tie'anfang wenji.* Reprint, SKZB.

Fang Shuo. *Bozhai bian.* Reprint, Tangsong shiliao biji congkan, Taibei:
    Zhonghua, 1983.

Fujian shengli. 1873. Reprint, Taibei: Taiwan yinhang, 1964.

Gongzhong dang Qianlong chao zouzhe. Taibei: Guoli gugong bowuyuan. 1982.

Gu Yanwu. *Tianxia junguo libing shu.* 1811.

Haiwai sanren [pseud.]. *Rongcheng jiwen.* Reprint, *Qingshi ziliao*, vol.1, Beijing:
    Zhonghua, 1980.

Hayashi Shunsai. *Ka-I hentai.* Tokyo: Tōyō bunko, 1960.

He Changling, ed. *Huangchao jingshi wenbian.* Reprint, Taibei: Shijie, 1964.

Hong Mai. *Yijianzhi.* Reprint, Beijing: Zhonghua, 1981.

Huadong junzheng weiyuanhui tudi gaige weiyuanhui. *Fujian nongcun diaocha.*
    Fuzhou, 1951.

Huang Gan. *Mianzhai ji.* Reprint, SKQS.

Huang Zongxi. 1838. *Song Yuan xue'an.* Reprint, Taibei: Shijie, 1966.

Huaxu dafu. *Nanpu qiupo lu.* ms. FPL.

"Letter of thanks from the rescued Chinese ship." microfilm 108679, FHC.

Li Guangdi. *Rongcun quanshu.* Reprint, SKQS.

Lin Han. *Lin Wen' an gong wenji.* ms. FNU.

"Lin Lichang yishu." 1709. ms. FNU.

Lin Xiyi. *Zhuxi juanzhai shiyi gao xuji.* Reprint, SKQS.

Lin Yidong. *Shanggan xiangshi ji.* ms. P.

Liren Heqiu [pseud.]. *Mindu bieji.* [ca. 1851–74]. Reprint, Fuzhou: Fujian renmin,
    1987.

Liu Kezhuang. *Houcun daquan ji.* Reprint, SBCK.

Liu Xu. *Jiu Tangshu.* 945. Reprint, Beijing: Zhonghua, 1975.

Ming shilu. Nangang: Zhongyang yanjiuyuan lishi yuyan yanjiusuo, 1961–66.

Minshangshi xiguan diaocha baogaolu. 1943. Reprint, Taibei: Jinxue, 1969.

Ouyang Xiu and Song Qi. *Xin Tangshu.* 1060. Reprint, Beijing: Zhonghua, 1975.

Qin Huitian. *Wuli tongkao.* 1880 edition.

Rongyin xinjian. ms. FPL.

Sanjiao yuanliu soushen daquan. Reprint, in *Huitu sanjiao yuanliu soushenji,*
    Shanghai: Shanghai guji, 1990.

Shangshu li. 1994. P.

Shen Shixing, ed. *Da Ming huidian.* 1588. Reprint, Taibei: Dongnan, 1963.

Shi Hongbao. *Minzaji.* 1858. Reprint, in *Minxiaoji, Minzaji,* Fuzhou: Fujian
    renmin, 1985.

Sima Guang. *Zizhi tongjian.* Reprint, Beijing: Guji, 1956.

Sima Qian. *Shiji.* 91 B.C. Reprint, Beijing: Zhonghua, 1964.

Song Lian, ed. *Yuanshi*. 1370. Reprint, Beijing: Zhonghua, 1976.

Sun Yatsen. *Zongli quanji*. Taibei: Zhongyang wenwu, 1953.

Taishang dongxuan lingbao sanyuan pinjie gongde qingzhong jing. CT 456.

Wang Qi. *Xu wenxian tongkao*. 1586. Reprint, SKQS.

Wang Xiangzhi. *Yudi jisheng*. 1227. Reprint, Taibei: Wenhai, 1962.

Wu Hai. *Wenguozhai ji*. Reprint, CSJC.

Wu Zhenren. *Shiguo chunqiu*. Reprint, SKZB.

Xie Zhaozhe. *Wuzazu*. 1608. Reprint, Taibei: Xinxing, 1971.

Xu Fuyuan. *Jinghetang ji*, microfilm of Naikaku bunko edition.

Xu Shen. *Shuowen jiezi*. 100. Reprint, Taibei: Shijie, 1960.

Yao Cha and Yao Silian. *Chenshu*. 636. Reprint, Beijing: Zhonghua, 1972.

Ye Chunji. *Hui'an zhengshu*. 1573. Reprint, Fuzhou: Fujian renmin, 1987.

Ye Xianggao. *Cangxia cao*. Reprint, Yangzhou: Jiangsu guangling guji, 1994.

Yu Dazhu, ed. *Yurong guqu*. Fuzhou: Haixia wenyi, 1991.

Yu Ruji. *Libu zhigao*. Reprint, SKZB.

Yue Shi. *Taiping huanyu ji*. Reprint, Taibei: Wenhai, 1960.

Zhang Tingyu. *Mingshi*. 1739. Reprint, Beijing: Zhonghua, 1974.

Zhang Yining. *Cuiping ji*. Reprint, SKZB.

Zheng Guangce. *Minzheng lingyao*. 1757. ms. FPL.

Zheng Shanfu. *Zheng Shaogu ji*. Reprint, SKZB.

"Zhizuzhai shifang jiushu." 1864. ms. FPL.

Zhongguo minjian gushi jicheng; Fujian juan; Fuzhou shi Cangshan qu fenjuan. Fuzhou, 1990.

Zhou Lianggong. *Min xiaoji*. 1667. Reprint, in *Minxiaoji, Minzaji*, Fuzhou: Fujian renmin, 1985.

Zhou Zhikui. *Qicao ji*. Yangzhou: Jiangsu guling, 1997.

Zhu Zhe. *Tianma shan fangyigao*. Reprint, SKZB.

Secondary and Western Language Sources

Ahern, Emily. *The Cult of the Dead in a Chinese Village*. Stanford: Stanford University Press, 1973.

Ahern, Emily. "Segmentation in Chinese lineages: A view through written genealogies." *American Ethnologist*, 3.1 (1976): 1–16.

Anderson, Eugene. *Essays on South China's Boat People*. Taibei: Orient Cultural Service, 1972.

Aoyamo Sadao. "The Newly-Risen Bureaucrats in Fukien at the Five-Dynasty-Sung Period, with Special Reference to the Genealogies." *Memoirs of the Tōyō Bunko*, 21 (1962): 1–48.

Atwell, William. "International Bullion Flows and the Chinese Economy circa 1530–1650." *Past and Present*, 95 (1982): 68–90.

Atwell, William. "Notes on silver, foreign trade, and the late Ming economy." *Ch'ing-shih wen-t'i*, 3.8 (1977): 1–33.

Baker, Hugh. *Chinese Family and Kinship*. London: Macmillan, 1979.

Baker, Hugh. *A Chinese Lineage Village: Sheung Shui*. London: Cass, 1968.

Baptandier-Berthier, Brigitte. "The Kaiguan Ritual and the Construction of the Child's Identity." In *Minjian xinyang yu Zhongguo wenhua guoji yantaohui lunwenji*. Hanxue yanjiu congkan lunzhu lei 4. Nangang: Hanxue yanjiu zhongxin, 1994.

Beattie, Hilary. *Land and Lineage in China: A Study of T'ung-ch'eng County, Anhwei, in the Ming and Ch'ing Dynasties*. Cambridge: Cambridge University Press, 1979.

Bell, Catherine. *Ritual: Perspectives and Dimensions*. Oxford: Oxford University Press, 1997.

Berthier, Brigitte. *La Dame-du-bord-de-l'eau*. Nanterre and Paris: Societé Ethnologie, 1988.

Berthier, Brigitte. See also Baptandier-Berthier.

Bielenstein, Hans. "The Chinese Colonization of Fukien until the End of T'ang." In Søren Egerod and Else Glahn, eds. *Studia Serica Bernhard Karlgren Dedicata*. Copenhagen: Ejnar Munksgaard, 1959.

Blussé, Leonard. "The rise of Cheng Chih-lung alias Nicolas Iquan." In Eduard Vermeer, ed. *Development and Decline of Fukien Province in the 17th and 18th Centuries*. Leiden: E. J. Brill, 1990.

Bourdieu, Pierre. *The Logic of Practice*. trans. R. Nice. Stanford: Stanford University Press, 1990.

Bourdieu, Pierre. *Outline of a Theory of Practice*. trans. R. Nice. Cambridge: Cambridge University Press, 1977.

Brim, John. "Village Alliance Temples in Hong Kong." In Arthur Wolf, ed. *Religion and Ritual in Chinese Society*. Stanford: Stanford University Press, 1974.

Brook, Timothy. *The Confusions of Pleasure*. Berkeley: University of California Press, 1998.

Brook, Timothy. "Family Continuity and Cultural Hegemony: The Gentry of Ningbo, 1368–1911." In Joseph Esherick and Mary Rankin, eds. *Chinese Local Elites and Patterns of Dominance*. Berkeley: University of California Press, 1990.

Brook, Timothy. "Funerary Ritual and the Building of Lineages in Late Imperial China." *Harvard Journal of Asiatic Studies*, 49.2 (1989): 465–99.

Brook, Timothy. "Must Lineages Own Land?" *Bulletin of Concerned Asian Scholars*, 20.4 (1988): 72–79.

Brook, Timothy. *Praying for Power: Buddhism and the Formation of Gentry Society in Late-Ming China*. Cambridge, Mass.: Council on East Asian Studies, Harvard University, 1993.

Brook, Timothy. "The Spatial Structure of Ming Local Administration." *Late Imperial China*, 6.1 (1985): 1–55.

Chan Wing-hoi. "Ordination Names in Hakka Genealogies: A Religious Practice and Its Decline." In David Faure and Helen Siu, eds. *Down to Earth: The Territorial Bond in South China*. Stanford: Stanford University Press, 1995.

Chang Chung-li. *The Chinese Gentry: Studies on their Role in Nineteenth-Century China.* Seattle: University of Washington Press, 1955.

Chang Hengdao. "Shinsho no kaikinseisaku no kenkyū." In *Rekishi ni okeru minshū to bunka-Sakai Tadao sensei koki shukuga kinen ronshū.* Tokyo: Kokusho kankōkai, 1982.

Chen Cunxi, Lin Weiqi, Lin Weiwen. "Fujian Nanping Zhanghuban chongshe xisu de chubu kaocha." *Dongnan wenhua,* 79 (1990), 47–51.

Chen Jiancai, ed. *Bamin zhanggu daquan, Xingshi bian.* Fuzhou: Fujian jiaoyu, 1994.

Chen Jingsheng. *Fujian lidai renkou lunkao.* Fuzhou: Fujian renmin, 1991.

Chen Qi'nan. "Fang yu chuantong Zhongguo jiazu zhidu: Jianlun xifang renleixuejia de Zhongguo jiazu yanjiu." Originally published in *Hanxue yanjiu,* 3.1 (1985): 127–84. Reprint, in Chen Qi'nan. *Jiazu yu shehui: Taiwan he Zhongguo shehui yanjiu de jichu linian.* Taibei: Lianjing, 1990.

Chen Qingwu. *Fuzhou shiyi mingci daguan.* Fuzhou: Fujian renmin, 2000.

Chen Xujing. *Danmin de yanjiu.* Shanghai: Shanghai yinshua, 1946.

Chen Zhiping. *Fujian zupu.* Fuzhou: Fujian renmin, 1996.

Chen Zhiping. *Kejia yuanliu xinlun.* Nanning: Guangxi jiaoyu, 1997.

Chen Zhiping. "Qingdai Fuzhou jiaoqu de xiangcun jiehuo." In Ye Xian'en, ed. *Qingdai quyu shehui jingji yanjiu.* Beijing: Zhonghua, 1992.

Chikusa Masa'aki. *Chūgoku bukkyō shakaishi kenkyū.* Kyoto: Dōhōsha, 1982.

Chikusa Masa'aki. "Sōdai funji kō." *Tōyō Gakuhō,* 61 (1979): 35–66.

Chun, Allen. "The Lineage-village complex in southeastern China: a long footnote in the anthropology of kinship." *Current Anthropology,* 37.3 (1996): 429–450.

Chow, Kai-Wing. *The Rise of Confucian Ritualism in Late Imperial China.* Stanford: Stanford University Press, 1994.

Clark, Hugh. *Community, Trade, and Networks: Southern Fujian from the Third to the Thirteenth Century.* Cambridge: Cambridge University Press, 1991.

Clark, Hugh. "The Fu of Minnan: A Local Clan in the Late Tang and Song China." *Journal of the Economic and Social History of the Orient,* 38.1 (1995): 1–74.

Clark, Hugh. "Private Rituals and Public Priorities in Song Minnan: A Study of Fang Temples in Putian district." Paper presented at the Conference on Ritual and Community in East Asia, Montreal, 1996.

Cohen, Myron. "Agnatic Kinship in South China." *Ethnology,* 8.2 (1969): 167–82.

Cohen, Myron. *House United, House Divided: The Chinese Family in Taiwan.* New York: Columbia University Press, 1976.

Cohen, Myron. "Lineage Organization in North China." *Journal of Asian Studies,* 49.3 (1990): 509–34.

Crossley, Pamela. "Thinking About Ethnicity in Early Modern China." *Late Imperial China,* 11 (1990): 1–34.

Dardess, John. *A Ming Society: T'ai-ho County, Kiangsi, fourteenth to seventeenth centuries.* Berkeley: University of California Press, 1996.

Davis, Edward. "Arms and the Tao: Hero Cult and Empire in Traditional China." In *Sōdai no shakai to shūkyō*. Sōdaishi kenkyūkai kenkyū hokoku 2. Tokyo: 1983.

Dean, Kenneth. *Taoist Ritual and Popular Cults of Southeast China.* Princeton: Princeton University Press, 1993.

Dean, Kenneth. "Transformations of the *She* (Altars of the Soil) in Fujian." *Cahiers d'Extrême-Asie*, 10 (1998): 19–75.

Dean, Kenneth, [Ding Hesheng] and Zheng Zhenman, eds. *Fujian zongjiao beiming huibian, Xinghuafu fence.* Fuzhou: Fujian renmin, 1995.

Doolittle, Justus. *Social Life of the Chinese; With Some Account of Their Religious, Governmental, Educational and Business Customs and Opinions, with Special but Not Exclusive Reference to Fuhchau.* Two vols. New York: Harper and Brothers, 1865.

Doolittle, Justus, ed. *A Vocabulary and Hand-book of the Chinese Language.* Two vols. Fuzhou: Rozario, 1872.

Dreyer, Edward. "Military Origins of Ming China." In Denis Twitchett and Frederick W. Mote, eds. *Cambridge History of China*, vol. 7. Cambridge: Cambridge University Press, 1988.

Duara, Prasenjit. *Culture, Power, and the State, Rural North China, 1900–1942.* Stanford: Stanford University Press, 1988.

Duara, Prasenjit. *Rescuing History from the Nation.* Chicago: University of Chicago Press, 1995.

Dudbridge, Glen. *The Legend of Miaoshan.* London: Ithaca, 1978.

Eberhard, Wolfram. *China's Minorities: Yesterday and Today.* Belmont, Calif.: Wadsworth, 1982.

Eberhard, Wolfram. *Chinese Festivals.* New York: Henry Schumann, 1953.

Eberhard, Wolfram. *The Local Cultures of South and East China.* trans. Alide Eberhard. Leiden: E. J. Brill, 1968.

Eberhard, Wolfram. *Social Mobility in Traditional China.* Leiden: E. J. Brill, 1962.

Ebrey, Patricia. *Confucianism and Family Rituals in Imperial China, A Social History of Writing about Rites.* Princeton: Princeton University Press, 1991.

Ebrey, Patricia. "The Early Stages in the Development of Descent Group Organization." In Patricia Ebrey and James Watson, eds. *Kinship Organization in Late Imperial China, 1000–1940.* Berkeley: University of California Press, 1986.

Ebrey, Patricia. "Education Through Ritual: Efforts to Formulate Family Ritual during the Sung Dynasty." In William de Bary and John Chaffee, eds. *Neo-Confucian Education: The Formative Stage.* Berkeley: University of California Press, 1989.

Ebrey, Patricia. *The Inner Quarters: Marriage and the Lives of Chinese Women in the Sung Period.* Berkeley: University of California Press, 1993.

Ebrey, Patricia. trans. *Chu Hsi's Family Rituals: A Twelfth Century Manual for the Performance of Cappings, Weddings, Funerals, and Ancestral Rites.* Princeton: Princeton University Press, 1991.

Ebrey, Patricia, and James Watson. "Introduction." In Patricia Ebrey and James Watson, eds. *Kinship Organization in Late Imperial China, 1000–1940*. Berkeley: University of California Press, 1986.

Esherick, Joseph. "Cherishing Sources from Afar." *Modern China*, 24.2 (1998): 135–61.

Esherick, Joseph, and Mary Backus Rankin. "Introduction." In Joseph Esherick and Mary Backus Rankin, eds. *Chinese Local Elites and Patterns of Dominance*. Berkeley: University of California Press, 1990.

Farmer, Edward. *Zhu Yuanzhang and Early Ming Legislation: The Reordering of Chinese Society Following the Era of Mongol Rule*. Leiden: E. J. Brill, 1995.

Farmer, Edward. "Social Regulations of the First Ming Emperor: Orthodoxy as a Function of Authority." In Kwang-Ching Liu, ed. *Orthodoxy in Late Imperial China*. Honolulu: University of Hawai'i Press, 1990.

Faure, David. "The Lineage as a Cultural Invention: The Case of the Pearl River Delta." *Modern China*, 15.1 (1989): 4–36.

Faure, David. *The Structure of Chinese Rural Society: Lineage and Village in the Eastern New Territories, Hong Kong*. Cambridge: Cambridge University Press, 1986.

Faure, David. "The Tangs of Kam Tin—A hypothesis on the rise of a gentry family." In David Faure, James Hayes, and Alan Birch, eds. *From Village to City: Studies in the Traditional Roots of Hong Kong Society*. Hong Kong: Centre of Asian Studies, University of Hong Kong, 1984.

Faure, David, and Helen Siu, eds. *Down to Earth: The Territorial Bond in South China*. Stanford: Stanford University Press, 1995.

Feuchtwang, Stephan. *The Imperial Metaphor: Popular Religion in China*. London: Routledge, 1992.

Fisher, Carney T. *The chosen one: Succession and adoption in the court of Ming Shizong*. Sydney: Allen & Unwin, 1990.

Freedman, Maurice. *Chinese Lineage and Society: Fukien and Kwangtung*. London: Athlone, 1966.

Freedman, Maurice. *Lineage Organization in Southeastern China*. London: Athlone, 1958.

Fu Yiling. "Ming Wanli ershi'er nian Fuzhou de qiangmi fengchao." Originally published in *Nankai xuebao* (1982). Reprint, in *Fu Yiling zhishi wushi nian wenbian*. Xiamen: Xiamen daxue, 1989.

Fu Yiling. "Minqing minjian dianyue lingshi." In *Ming–Qing nongcun shehui jingji*. Beijing: Sanlian, 1961.

Fu Yiling. "Qingdai Fuzhou jiaoqu renkou de zhiye bianqian." In Ye Xian'en, ed. *Qingdai quyu shehui jingji yanjiu*. Beijing: Zhonghua, 1992.

Fu Yiling, and Yang Guozhen, eds. *Ming–Qing Fujian shehui yu xiangcun jingji*. Xiamen: Xiamen daxue, 1987.

Fuzhou diminglu. Fuzhou: 1985.

Fuzhou fangyan cidian. Fuzhou: Fujian renmin, 1995.

Gao Rong. "Guo Bocang." *Fuzhou lishi renwu* 4 (n.d.): 52–56.

Gardella, Robert. "The Min-pei Tea Trade during the late Ch'ien-Lung and Chia-ch'ing Eras: Foreign Commerce and the Mid-Ch'ing Fukien Highlands." In Eduard Vermeer, ed. *Development and Decline of Fukien Province in the 17th and 18th Centuries*. Leiden: E. J. Brill, 1990.

Gladney, Dru. *Ethnic Identity in China: The Making of a Muslim Minority Nationality*. Fort Worth, Texas: Harcourt Brace, 1998.

Goodrich, Carrington, and Caoying Fang, eds. *Dictionary of Ming Biography*. New York: Columbia University Press, 1976.

Gu Jiegang. *The Autobiography of a Chinese Historian*. trans. Arthur Hummel. 1931. Reprint, Taibei: Chengwen, 1966.

Hansen, Valerie. *Changing Gods in Medieval China, 1127–1276*. Princeton: Princeton University Press, 1990.

Hansson, Anders. *Chinese Outcasts: Discrimination and Emancipation in Late Imperial China*. Leiden: E. J. Brill, 1996.

Harrell, Stevan. "When a Ghost Becomes a God." In Arthur Wolf, ed. *Religion and Ritual in Chinese Society*. Stanford: Stanford University Press, 1974.

Hayashida Yoshio. *Kanan shakai bunkashi no kenkyū*. Kyoto: Dōhōsha, 1993.

Hayes, James. *The Hong Kong Region 1850–1911: Institutions and Leadership in Town and Countryside*. Hamden: Archon, 1977.

Hazelton, Keith. "Patrilines and the Development of Localized Lineages: The Wu of Hsiu-ning City, Hui-chou, to 1528." In Patricia Ebrey and James Watson, eds. *Kinship Organization in Late Imperial China, 1000–1940*. Berkeley: University of California Press, 1986.

Heijdra, Martin. "The Socio-economic Development of Rural China during the Ming." In Denis Twitchett and Frederick Mote, eds. *Cambridge History of China*, vol. 8. Cambridge: Cambridge University Press, 1998.

Hevia, James. *Cherishing Guests from Afar*. Durham: Duke University Press, 1995.

Ho Ping-ti. *The Ladder of Success in Imperial China: Aspects of Social Mobility, 1368–1911*. New York: Columbia University Press, 1962.

Hobsbawm, Eric. "Introduction: Inventing Traditions." In Eric Hobsbawm and Terence Ranger, eds. *The Invention of Tradition*. Cambridge: Cambridge University Press, 1983.

Hsiao Kung-Chuan. *Rural China: Imperial Control in the Nineteenth Century*. Seattle: University of Washington Press, 1960.

Huang Minzhi. "Fujianlu de sitian—yi Fuzhou wei zhongxin." *Si yu yan*, 16.4 (1978): 311–40.

Huang, Philip. *Civil Justice in China: Representation and Practice in the Qing*. Stanford: Stanford University Press, 1996.

Huang, Ray. *Taxation and Governmental Finance in Sixteenth-Century Ming China*. Cambridge: Cambridge University Press, 1974.

Hucker, Charles. *The Censorial System of Ming China*. Stanford: Stanford University Press, 1966.

Hucker, Charles. *A Dictionary of Official Titles in Imperial China*. Stanford: Stanford University Press, 1985.

Hymes, Robert. "Marriage, Descent Groups, and the Localist Strategy in Sung and Yuan Fuchou." In Patricia Ebrey and James Watson eds. *Kinship Organization in Late Imperial China, 1000–1940*. Berkeley: University of California Press, 1986.

Inoue Tōru. "Sōzoku no keisei to sono kōzō." *Shirin*, 72.5 (1989): 84–122.

Johnson, David. "Communication, Class and Consciousness in Late Imperial China." In David Johnson, Andrew Nathan, and Evelyn Rawski, eds. *Popular Culture in Late Imperial China*. Berkeley: University of California Press, 1985.

Kanai Noriyuki. "Nansō ni okeru shashokudan to shabyō ni tsuite—ki no shinkō o chūshin to shite." In Fukui Fumimasa, ed., *Taiwan no shūkyō to Chūgoku bunka*. Tokyo: Fūkyōsha, 1992.

Kanai Noriyuki. "Shajin to Dōkyō." In *Dōkyō* 2:*Dōkyō no tenkai*. Tokyo: Hirohawa shuppansha, 1983.

Kanai Noriyuki. "Sōdai Sekisei sonsha to dojin-Sōdai kyōson shaikai no shūkyō Kōzō." In *Sōdai no shakai to bunka*. Sōdaishi Kenkyūkai kenkyū hōkoku 1. Tokyo: 1983.

Kanai Noriyuki. "Sōdai no sonsha to shajin." *Tōyōshi kenkyū*, 38 (1979): 61–87.

Kanai Noriyuki. "Sōdai no sonsha to sōzoku." In *Rekishi ni okeru minshū to bunka—Sakai Tadao sensei koki shukuga kinen ronshū*. Tokyo: Kokusho kankōkai, 1982.

Kataoka Shibako. "Fukken no ichiden ryōshusei ni tsuite." *Rekishigaku kenkyū*, 294 (1964): 42–49.

Katayama Tsuyoshi. "Shindai Kantonshō Shukō deruta no hokōsei ni tsuite: Zeiryō, koseki, dōzoku." *Tōyō Gakuhō*, 63.3–4 (1982): 1–34.

Katayama Tsuyoshi. "Shinmatsu Kantonshō Shukō deruta no hokōhyō to sore o meguru shomondai: Zeiryō, koseki, dōzoku." *Shigaku Zasshi*, 91.4 (1982): 42–81.

Katz, Paul. *Demon Hordes and Burning Boats: The Cult of Marshal Wen in Late Imperial Chekiang*. Albany: State University of New York Press, 1995.

Katz, Paul. "Demons or Deities—The *Wangye* of Taiwan." *Asian Folklore Studies*, 46.2 (1987): 197–215.

Katz, Paul. "Temple Cults and the Creation of Hsin-chuang Local Society." In Tang Xiyong, ed., *Zhongguo haiyang fazhanshi lunwenji*, vol. 7. Taibei: Zhongyang yanjiuyuan Zhongshan renwen shehui kexue yanjiusuo, 1999.

Kojima Tsuyoshi. "Seishi to inshi: Fukken no chihōshi ni okeru kijutsu to rinri." *Tōyō Bunka Kenkyūjo kiyō*, 113 (1991): 87–213.

Kuribayashi Nobuo. *Rikōsei no kenkyū*. Tokyo: Bunri Shoin, 1971.

Kuribayashi Nobuo. "Shindai Fukushū chihō ni okeru shūraku to shizoku." *Risshō shigaku*, 39 (1975): 21–37.

Lagerwey, John [Lao Gewen] ed. *Kejia chuantong shehui congshu*. Hong Kong: International Hakka Studies Association; Overseas Chinese Archives; Ecole Française d'Extrême Orient, 1995–2001.

Lamley, Harry. "Lineage and Surname Feuds in Southern Fukien and Eastern Kwangtung under the Ch'ing." In Kwang-Ching Liu, ed. *Orthodoxy in Late Imperial China*. Honolulu: University of Hawai'i Press, 1990.

Legge, James. *The Chinese Classics*. Oxford: Oxford University Press, 1865–1895. Reprint, Hong Kong: Hong Kong University Press, 1960.

Leong Sow-theng. *Migration and Ethnicity in Chinese History: Hakkas, Pengmin, and Their Neighbors*, ed. Tim Wright. Stanford: Stanford University Press, 1997.

Li Yiyuan. "Ping Min shiba dong de minzuxue yanjiu." *Zhongyang yanjiuyuan minzuxue yanjiusuo jikan*, 76 (1994): 1–20.

Liang Gengyao. *NanSong de nongcun jingji*. Taibei: Lianjing, 1984.

Lin Meirong. "You jisiquan laikan Caodunzhen de difang zuzhi." *Zhongyang yanjiuyuan minzuxue yanjiusuo jikan*, 62 (1987): 53–114.

Lin Renchuan. *Fujian duiwai maoyi yu haiguan shi*. Xiamen: Lujiang, 1991.

Lin Renchuan. *Mingmo Qingchu siren haishang maoyi*. Shanghai: Huadong shifan daxue, 1987.

Lin Weigong. "Ji Minhouxian zhengui sizhong xiangzhen xiangtuzhi." *Fujian difangzhi tongxun*, 1985.4: 62–63.

Liu Yaohua. "Yixu zongzu de yanjiu." M.A. thesis, Yanjing University, 1935.

Liu, Hui-Chen Wang. *The Traditional Chinese Clan Rules*. Monographs of Association for Asian Studies, vol 7. New York: J. J. Austin, 1959.

Liu Shuxun, ed. *Minxue yuanliu*. Fuzhou: Fujian jiaoyu, 1993.

Liu Zhiwei. *Zai guojia yu shehui zhi jian: Ming–Qing Guangdong lijia fuyi zhidu yanjiu*. Guangzhou: Zhongshan daxue, 1997.

Luo Xianglin. *Baiyue yuanliu yu wenhua*. Taibei: Zhonghua congshu, 1955.

Makino Tatsumi. "Fukkenjin ni okeru Kanan shō Koshiken densetsu." In *Makino Tatsumi chosakushū*, vol. 5. Tokyo: Ochano mizushobō, 1985.

Makino Tatsumi. *Kinsei Chūgoku sōzoku kenkyū*. Tokyo: Nikkō Shoin, 1949.

Makino Tatsumi. "Sōshi to sono hattatsu." *Tōyō gakuhō*, 9 (1939): 173–250.

Mao Zedong. "Report of an Investigation into the Peasant Movement in Hunan." In *Selected Writings of Mao Tse-Tung*, vol. 1. Beijing: Foreign Languages, 1961.

Mao Zedong. *Report from Xunwu*. trans. Roger Thompson. Stanford: Stanford University Press, 1990.

Meskill, Johanna. "The Chinese Genealogy as a Research Source." In Maurice Freedman, ed. *Family and Kinship in Chinese Society*. Stanford: Stanford University Press, 1970.

Meskill, Johanna. *A Chinese Pioneer Family: The Lins of Wu-feng, Taiwan, 1729–1895*. Princeton: Princeton University Press, 1979.

Miki Satoshi, "Minmatsu no Fukken ni okeru hokōsei." *Tōyō gakuhō*, 61 (1979): 67–107.

Minhou diming lu. Fuzhou: 1986.

Mori Masao, "Weirao xiangzu wenti." *Zhongguo shehui jingji shi yanjiu*, 1986.2: 1–8.

Mote, Frederick. "The Rise of the Ming Dynasty, 1330–1367." In Denis Twitchett and Frederick W. Mote, eds. *Cambridge History of China*, vol 7. Cambridge: Cambridge University Press, 1988.

Murray, Stephen, and Keelung Hong, "American Anthropologists Looking Through Taiwanese Culture." *Dialectical Anthropology*, 16.3–4 (1991): 273–99.

Nakamura Takashi. *Chūgoku no nenchū gyōji*. Tokyo: Heibonsha, 1988.

Nakamura Takashi. *Chūgoku saishishi no kenkyū*. Kyoto: Hoyō shoten, 1993.

Naquin, Susan. "The Annual Festivals of Peking." In *Minjian xinyang yu zhongguo wenhua guoji yantaohui lunwenji*. Hanxue yanjiu congkan lunzhu lei, vol. 4. Nangang: Hanxue yanjiu zhongxin, 1994.

Naquin, Susan. "Two Descent Groups in North China: The Wangs of Yung-p'ing Prefecture, 1500–1800." In Patricia Ebrey and James Watson, eds. *Kinship Organization in Late Imperial China, 1000–1940*. Berkeley: University of California Press, 1986.

Ng Chin-keong. *Trade and Society: The Amoy Network on the China Coast, 1683–1735*. Singapore: Singapore University Press, 1983.

Nishijima Sadao. "The Formation of the Early Chinese Cotton Industry." In Linda Grove and Christian Daniels, eds. *State and Society in China: Japanese Perspectives on Ming–Qing Social and Economic History*. Tokyo: University of Tokyo Press, 1984.

Nogami Eiichi. *Fukushū kō*. Taibei: Fukushū toei gakkō, 1937.

Ortner, Sherry. "Theory in Anthropology since the Sixties." *Comparative Studies in Society and History*, 26.1 (1984): 126–65.

Overmyer, Daniel. "Attitudes Toward Popular Religion in Ritual Texts of the Chinese State: *The Collected Statutes of the Great Ming*." *Cahiers d'Extrême-Asie*, 5 (1989–1990): 191–221.

Overmyer, Daniel. "On the foundations of Chinese culture in late traditional times: Comments on Fang Xuejia, *Meizhou Heyuan diqu de cunluo wenhua*." Paper presented at the International Conference on Hakka Society, Hong Kong, 1998.

Pasternak, Burton. *Kinship and Community in Two Chinese Villages*. Stanford: Stanford University Press, 1972.

Pasternak, Burton. "On the Causes and Consequences of Uxorilocal Marriage in China." In Susan Hanley and Arthur Wolf, eds. *Family and Population in East Asian History*. Stanford: Stanford University Press, 1985.

Pasternak, Burton. "The Role of the Frontier in Chinese Lineage Development." *Journal of Asian Studies*, 28.3 (1969): 551–61.

Potter, Jack. "Land and Lineage in Traditional China." In Maurice Freedman, ed. *Family and Kinship in Chinese Society*. Stanford: Stanford University Press, 1970.

Potter, Jack, and Sulamith Heins Potter. *China's Peasants: The Anthropology of a Revolution*. Cambridge: Cambridge University Press, 1990.

Rawski, Evelyn. *Agricultural Change and the Peasant Economy of South China*. Cambridge, Mass.: Harvard University Press, 1972.

Rawski, Evelyn. "Economic and Social Foundations of Late Imperial Culture." In David Johnson, Andrew Nathan, and Evelyn Rawski, eds. *Popular Culture in Late Imperial China*. Berkeley: University of California Press, 1985.

Rowe, William. "Ancestral Rites and Political Authority in Late Imperial China." *Modern China*, 24.4 (1998): 378–407.

Rowe, William. "Approaches to Modern Chinese Social History." In Oliver Zunz, ed. *Reliving the Past: The Worlds of Social History*. Chapel Hill: University of North Carolina Press, 1985.

Rowe, William. "Success Stories: Lineage and Elite Status in Hanyang County, Hubei, ca. 1368–1949." In Joseph Esherick and Mary Rankin, eds. *Chinese Local Elites and Patterns of Dominance*. Berkeley: University of California Press, 1990.

Ruf, Gregory. *Cadres and Kin: Making a Socialist Village in West China, 1921–1991*. Stanford: Stanford University Press, 1998.

Ruskola, Teemu. "Conceptualizing corporations and kinship: Comparative law and development theory in a Chinese perspective." *Stanford Law Review*, 52.6 (2000): 1599–1729.

Sangren, Steven. *History and Magical Power in a Chinese Community*. Stanford: Stanford University Press, 1987.

Sangren, Steven. "Traditional Chinese Corporations: Beyond Kinship." *Journal of Asian Studies*, 43.3 (1984): 391–415.

Schafer, Edward. *The Empire of Min*. Rutland, Vermont: Charles Tuttle, 1954.

Schipper, Kristofer. "Neighbourhood Cult Associations in Traditional Taiwan." In William Skinner, ed. *The City in Late Imperial China*. Stanford: Stanford University Press, 1977.

Schwartz, Benjamin. *The World of Thought in Ancient China*. Cambridge, Mass.: Harvard University Press, 1985.

Shezu shehui lishi diaocha. Fuzhou: Fujian renmin, 1986.

Shiba Yoshinobu. *Commerce and Society in Sung China*. trans. Mark Elvin. Michigan Abstracts of Chinese and Japanese Works on Chinese History, vol. 2. Ann Arbor: University of Michigan Press, 1970.

Siu, Helen. "Recycling Rituals; Politics and Popular Culture in Contemporary Rural China." In Perry Link, Richard Madsen, Paul Pickowicz, eds. *Unofficial China: Popular Culture and Thought in the People's Republic*. Boulder: Westview, 1989.

Siu Helen, and Liu Zhiwei. "Lineage, Market, Pirate, and Dan: Ethnicity in the Pearl River Delta of South China." Paper presented at the Conference on Ethnicity and the China Frontier: Changing Discourse and Consciousness, Hanover, 1996.

Skinner, G. William. "Marketing and Social Structure in Rural China." *Journal of Asian Studies*, 24.1–3 (1964): 3–43, 195–228, 363–99.

Skinner, G. William. "Presidential Address: The Structure of Chinese History." *Journal of Asian Studies*, 44.2 (1985): 271–92.

So, Kwan-wai. *Japanese Piracy in Ming China during the Sixteenth Century*. East Lansing: Michigan State University Press, 1975.

Strand, David. "Community, Society, and History in Sun Yat-sen's *Sanmin zhuyi*." In Theodore Huters, R. Bin Wong, and Pauline Yu, eds. *Culture and State in*

Chinese History: Conventions, Accommodations, and Critiques. Stanford: Stanford University Press, 1977.

Strauch, Judith. "Community and Kinship in Southeastern China: The View from the Multilineage Villages of Hong Kong." *Journal of Asian Studies,* 43.1 (1983): 21–50.

Struve, Lynn. *The Southern Ming.* New Haven: Yale University Press, 1984.

Szonyi, Michael. "The Illusion of Standardizing the Gods: The Cult of the Five Emperors in Late Imperial China." *Journal of Asian Studies,* 56.1 (1997): 113–35.

Szonyi, Michael. "Local cult, *Lijia,* and Lineage: Religious and Social Organization in Ming and Qing Fujian." *Journal of Chinese Religions,* 28 (2000): 93–125.

Szonyi, Michael. "Village Rituals in Fuzhou in the late imperial and Republican periods" D.Phil thesis, University of Oxford, 1995.

Taga Akigorō. *Chūgoku sōfu no kenkyū.* Tokyo: Nihon gakujutsu shinkōkai, 1981.

Tang Wenji, ed. *Fujian gudai jingji shi.* Fuzhou: Fujian jiaoyu, 1995.

Taylor, Romeyn. "Official Altars, Temples and Shrines Mandated for all Counties in Ming and Qing." *T'oung Pao,* 83.1–3 (1997): 93–125.

Taylor, Romeyn. "Official and Popular Religion and the Political Organization of Chinese Society in the Ming." In Kwang-Ching Liu, ed. *Orthodoxy in Late Imperial China.* Honolulu: University of Hawai'i Press, 1990.

Teiser, Stephen. *The Ghost Festival in Medieval China.* Princeton: Princeton University Press, 1988.

ter Haar, Barend. "The Genesis and Spread of Temple Cults in Fukien." In Eduard Vermeer, ed. *Development and Decline of Fukien Province in the 17th and 18th Centuries.* Leiden: E. J. Brill, 1990.

ter Haar, Barend. "Local Society and the Organization of Cults in Early Modern China: A Preliminary Study." *Studies in Central and East Asian Religions.* 8 (1995): 1–43.

T'ien Ju-K'ang. "The Decadence of Buddhist Temples in Fu-chien in Late Ming and Early Ch'ing." In Eduard Vermeer, ed. *Development and Decline of Fukien Province in the 17th and 18th Centuries.* Leiden: E. J. Brill, 1990.

Twitchett, Denis. "The Fan Clan's Charitable Estate, 1050–1760." In David Nivison and Arthur Wright, eds. *Confucianism in Action.* Stanford: Stanford University Press, 1959.

Twitchett, Denis, and Frederick W. Mote, eds. *Cambridge History of China.* vol. 8. Cambridge: Cambridge University Press, 1988.

van der Loon, Piet. "Les origines rituelles du theatre chinois." *Journal Asiatique,* 265 (1977): 141–68.

van Gennep, Arnold. *The Rites of Passage.* trans. M. B. Vizedom and G.L. Cafee. London: Routledge and Kegan Paul, 1960.

Vermeer, Eduard. "The Decline of Hsing-hua Prefecture in the Early Ch'ing." In Eduard Vermeer, ed. *Development and Decline of Fukien Province in the 17th and 18th Centuries.* Leiden: E. J. Brill, 1990.

Wada Hironori. "Rikōsei to rishadan kyōreidan—Mindai no kyōson shihai to saishi." *Nishi to Higashi to—Maejima Shinji sensei tsuitō rombunshū.* Tokyo: Kyūko shoin, 1985.

Wakefield, David. *Fenjia: Household Division and Inheritance in Qing and Republican China.* Honolulu: University of Hawai'i Press, 1999.

Wakeman, Frederic. "Introduction: The Evolution of Local Control in Late Imperial China." In Frederic Wakeman and Carolyn Grant, eds. *Conflict and Control in Late Imperial China.* Berkeley: University of California Press, 1975.

Waltner, Ann. *Getting an Heir: Adoption and the Construction of Kinship in Late Imperial China.* Honolulu: University of Hawai'i Press, 1990.

Wang Mingming. "Place, Administration, and Territorial Cults in Late Imperial China: A Case Study from South Fujian." *Late Imperial China,* 16.1 (1998): 33–78.

Wang Yeh-Chien. "Food Supply in Eighteenth-Century Fukien." *Late Imperial China,* 7.2 (1986): 80–117.

Wang Zhenzhong. *Jin 600 nianlai ziran zaihai yu Fuzhou shehui.* Fuzhou: Fujian renmin, 1996.

Watson, James. "Agnates and Outsiders: Adoption in a Chinese Lineage." *Man,* 10.2 (1975): 293–306.

Watson, James. "Anthropological Overview: The Development of Chinese Descent Groups." In Patricia Ebrey and James Watson, eds. *Kinship Organization in Late Imperial China, 1000–1940.* Berkeley: University of California Press, 1986.

Watson, James. "Chinese Kinship Reconsidered: Anthropological Perspectives on Historical Research." *China Quarterly,* 92 (1982): 586–622.

Watson, James. "Standardizing the Gods: The Promotion of T'ien Hou ("Empress of Heaven") Along the South China Coast, 960–1960." In David Johnson, Andrew Nathan, and Evelyn Rawski, eds. *Popular Culture in Late Imperial China.* Berkeley: University of California Press, 1985.

Watson, James. "The Structure of Chinese Funerary Rites: Elementary Forms, Ritual Sequence, and the Primacy of Performance." In James Watson and Evelyn Rawski, eds. *Death Ritual in Late Imperial and Modern China.* Berkeley: University of California Press, 1988.

Watson, Rubie. "The Creation of a Chinese Lineage: The Teng of Ha Tsuen, 1669–1751." *Modern Asian Studies,* 16.1 (1982): 69–100.

Watson, Rubie. *Inequality Among Brothers: Class and Kinship in South China.* Cambridge: Cambridge University Press, 1985.

Wei Yingqi. *Fujian sanshen kao.* 1929. Reprint, Taibei: Dongfang, 1970.

Wiens, Herold. *China's March Toward the Tropics.* Hamden, Conn.: Shoe String, 1954.

Wolf, Arthur. "The Origins and Explanations of Variation in the Chinese Kinship System." In *Anthropological Studies of the Taiwan Area: Accomplishments and Prospects.* Taibei: National Taiwan University, 1989.

Wolf, Arthur, and Chieh-shan Huang. *Marriage and Adoption in China, 1845–1945.* Stanford: Stanford University Press, 1980.

Wolf, Margery. *Women and the Family in Rural Taiwan*. Stanford: Stanford University Press, 1972.

Wu Chunming, and Lin Guo. *MinYue guo ducheng kaogu yanjiu*. Xiamen: Xiamen daxue, 1998.

Xie Guozhen. "Qingchu dongnan yanhai qianjie kao." In *Ming–Qing zhiji dangshe yundong kao*. Taibei: Shangwu, 1967.

Xu Xiaowang. *Fujian minjian xinyang yuanliu*. Fuzhou: Fujian jiaoyu, 1993.

Xu Xiaowang. *Minguo shi*. Taibei: Wunan, 1997.

Xu Yangjie, "Song–Ming yilai de fengjian jiazu zhidu shulun." *Zhongguo shehui kexue*, 1980.4: 99–122.

Yang, C. K. *Chinese Communist Society: The Family and the Village*. Cambridge, Mass.: Technology Press, M.I.T., 1969.

Yang Guozhen. "Ming Qing Fujian tudi siren suoyouquan neizai jiegou de yanjiu." In Fu Yiling and Yang Guozhen, eds. *Ming Qing Fujian shehui yu xiangcun jingji*. Xiamen: Xiamen daxue, 1987.

Yang Guozhen. *Ming–Qing tudi qiyue wenshu yanjiu*. Beijing: Renmin, 1988.

Ye Mingsheng. *Lüshan jiao guangjitan keyiben*. Zhongguo chuantong keyi ben huibian. Taibei: Xin wenfeng, 1996.

Ye Mingsheng. *Minxi Shanghang Gaoqiang kuilei yu furen xi*. Minsu quyi congshu. Taibei: Shi Hezheng jijinhui, 1995.

Ye Xian'en, "Notes on the Territorial Connections of the Dan." In David Faure and Helen Siu, eds. *Down to Earth: The Territorial Bond in South China*. Stanford: Stanford University Press, 1995.

Yu Yingshi. *Zhongguo jinshi zongjiao lunli yu shangren jingshen*. Taibei: Lianjing, 1987.

Yu Zhijia, "Shilun zupu zhong suojian de Mingdai junhu." *Zhongyang yanjiuyuan lishi yuyan yanjiusuo jikan* 57.4 (1986): 635–668.

Zheng Lipeng. "Fuzhou chengshi fazhan shi yanjiu." Ph.D. thesis, Huanan ligong daxue, 1991.

Zheng Zhenman. *Ming–Qing Fujian jiazu zuzhi yu shehui bianqian*. Changsha: Hunan jiaoyu, 1992.

Zheng Zhenman."Ming–Qing Fujian yanhai shuili zhidu yu xiangzu zuzhi." *Zhongguo shehui jingji shi yanjiu*, 1987.4: 38–45.

Zheng Zhenman. "Putian pingyuan de zongjiao kongjian yu simiao tixi." In *Simiao yu minjian wenhua taolunhui lunwenji*. Nangang: Hanxue yanjiu zhongxin, 1995.

Zheng Zhenman. "Shenmiao jidian yu shequ fazhan moshi." *Shilin*, 37 (1995): 33–47.

Zhu Weigan. *Fujian shigao*. Fuzhou: Fujian jiaoyu, 1984.

Zhuang Jiazi. "Fuzhou de diandang, daidang, he zhanyizhuang." *Fuzhou wenshi ziliao xuanji*, 8 (1989): 35–45.

Zhuang Yingzhang. *Linyipu: yige Taiwan shizhen de shehui jingji fazhan shi*. Nangang: Zhongyang yanjiuyuan minzuxue yanjiusuo, 1977.

Zito, Angela. *Of Body and Brush: Grand Sacrifice as Text/Performance in Eighteenth-Century China*. Chicago: University of Chicago Press, 1997.

Zuo Yunpeng. "Citang, zuzhang, zuquan de xingcheng jiqi zuoyong shishuo." *Lishi yanjiu*, 5–6 (1964): 97–116.

Zurndorfer, Harriet. *Change and Continuity in Chinese Local History: The Development of Hui-Chou Prefecture, 800 to 1800*. Leiden: E. J. Brill, 1989.

Zurndorfer, Harriet. "Learning, Lineages, and Locality in Late Imperial China." *Journal of the Economic and Social History of the Orient*, 35.2–3 (1992), 109–44, 209–38.

Index